The Golden Thread

Other works by the author

The Wind and the Mill. Produced at West Wratting Mill in 1935 by the Festival Theatre Company, Cambridge. Directed by Joseph Macleod.

He was like a Continent. Produced at the Roosevelt Theatre, New York in 1938. Directed by Nicholas Grey. Published by Adam Press in 1947 in London, with a Foreword by Dame Sybil Thorndike.

The Brothers. Produced and directed by Peter Zadek at the Watergate Theatre, London, in 1951.

The Journey. Produced at the Round House, London, in 1976. Directed by John Baliol.

The Isle, the Sea and the Crown. An epic drama. Published by Poets & Patrons Press in 1981.

The Horses and the Charioteer. The second part of the autobiographical trilogy. Published by Charles Skilton in 1988, with Foreword by Lord Briggs of Lewes.

The Dance of the Opposites. The third part of the autobiographical trilogy. Published by Charles Skilton in 1989 with an Introduction by Colin Wilson.

The Great Heresy. An historical play, 1990.

THE GOLDEN THREAD

The first part of the
autobiographical trilogy

by PHILIPPA BURRELL

First published in 1979 by Skilton & Shaw.
(Fudge & Co. Ltd.)
Hardback ISBN 0 7050 0067 2.
Re-issued with amendments 1993 in Paperback ISBN 0 907302 01 7.
and Reprinted by
Thornton Printers,
Orange Street,
Alfreton,
Derbyshire DE55 7HY

Philippa Burrell
Los Angeles, 1917, aged 9.
(The original is a life-size oil-colour).

CONTENTS

The higher Self, with which every one of us is linked, is like a sphere of light, and gleams from It touch us through the intuition, flashes of inspiration which artists know, and revelations which open up to us, however faintly, the Nature of God. This link is our lifeline ... and it has meaning for the soul through the ages. For it takes us through all problems and trials *if* we take hold of the Golden Thread ...

We pray there may be more and more the world over who have found the Golden Thread, to lead mankind out of chaos to order, out of sickness towards that health which is of the soul itself, out of what seems endless strife to peace and reconciliation, out of ignorance towards that enlightenment which forever seeks to touch and lift him ...

Clare Cameron
Science of Thought Review

AUTHOR'S INTRODUCTIONS

1979

I realise that this book reads much like a novel or even a series of one-act plays — yet it is factual. Nothing has been added in the telling of the story.

The day has passed when rich material was automatically transposed into fiction and confined there. It would be easier and more comfortable to employ it in that way alone and hide inside it, but the human situation is too critical, too apocalyptic, the data of human experience and behaviour now too valuable for such limited treatment.

As science turns from the simple investigation of surrounding nature to the probing of the cosmos and of the brain and mind of man himself, man facing himself — and facing God — the writer uses the authentic, the lived material, directly as well as indirectly, to reflect these encounters.

Conscious evolution, the great adventure of our time, requires truth for its pursuit, every brand and size of truth, including lived and recollected personal stories.

1992

After this book was first published and then went out of print, I completed the trilogy and exhausted my writing powers but did not finish my task. I had to rescue my mother's work, assert her name and use her paintings, her genius, as prime agents in the regeneration of a town – before I was set free to go on.

With culture at a crisis, the planet raped and the world sinking to another turning point, art will redeem, restore sensitivity and show the Way through the coming violent changes to a new age of holistic thinking and raised consciousness.

Part I

1

The Dream

I WAS born during a thick fog in January 1908 in my grandmother's house in London. I was nearly born in the street.

When her doctor told her to climb a lot of stairs and laugh – to bring on labour, my mother walked down to the Coronet Theatre at Notting Hill Gate, with her mother and one of her sisters, to see a play which was advertised as being exceptionally witty and amusing.

Theatre galleries then were boisterous, uninhibited places, and being already in a foolish mood, they bought oranges and bottles of ginger pop and after climbing the interminable stone steps, settled themselves in the front row and looked round benignly and hopefully, determined to be amused by everything.

When the curtain went up they waited for the humour and hilarity but, after a slow start, the play and the players grew more and more boring. Desperate, my mother and her sister began sucking the oranges and swigging at the bottles. Then suddenly they laughed.

Their mother, whose life for years had been withdrawn and dull, was actually enjoying the play and at this point, leaning over the balcony and clasping her hands tragically, oranges and bottles tumbling onto the heads of the people below, she cried out 'No! No! Stop him! Stop him! Oh, don't let him do it!' The audience was electrified and the players responded. She went on participating passionately while my mother laughed and laughed and labour began. Then, jolting her out of her transports they dragged her away.

The atmosphere in the theatre was suspiciously smokey and when they opened the doors into the street, they walked out into thick, choking fog. Groping their way, holding onto railings, feeling along walls, bumping and stumbling and searching for landmarks, my mother often stopping altogether in pain, the short walk to the top of Campden Hill Square took them several hours. When they reached home, I came.

A few weeks later, the news arrived from South Africa that my father had died in the street in Durban from a heart attack while on his way to board the boat which was to bring him home.

It was a broken-down, dispirited family that my mother had returned to for my birth. So many had been driven by the same desire, had struggled or been pushed towards the same high purpose and made the same sacrifices. They longed to be great painters and believed passionately in their genius – the word itself obsessed them – but always the bright, bewitching talent withered, was stamped on or just thrown away, and all that came of their eagerness was disappointment.

Either the talent was not great enough, or the circumstances not favourable enough, the character not sound enough or the will and the light behind it not strong enough. But in each generation, as the faith was renewed, they tried and failed and tried again, tormenting each other as they came and went. Even my mother, with all her brilliance, integrity and strength and born with the same vision, died with her work scattered and her genius unacknowledged.

It may all have begun with my great grand-father, Tom King Margetts, who was a painter, a carver, a designer of stained glass, a collector of old furniture and an authority on prints. Every window of his house in Oxford was of stained glass and the walls and ceilings from the attic to the scullery were painted with elaborate designs upon which he worked for years.

Rare prints hung against these startling backgrounds and crowded into the rooms, like an antique shop were exquisite articles of furniture and bric-a-brac, most of which, long after his death, when the family declined – and England too – went piece by piece to America.

His elder child was disappointing. Epileptic from birth, he forced him (for his own good, of course) into work which he hated and in course of time the boy rebelled and took refuge, in his own way, from a dominating parent. He went mad. Later, when his father died and his mother came to live in London with her daughter, he came too, accompanied by a keeper.

Whenever he could elude this man, his favourite pastime was to slip out of the house with a piece of silver or porcelain, even a print or picture (my grandmother's home was now filled with the entire contents of the Oxford house) and stand on the pavement until someone came by. Then, with a rapturous smile and dignified bow he would present his gift to the astonished stranger.

Scattering treasures in this way, so happily avenging himself, he soon managed to get rid of much that his father had spent his whole life hoarding. One of these presentations was traced to the British Museum but the rest were never seen again and the family, at length, lost patience. He was sent away to an asylum.

Perhaps it was partly the hopeless disposition of his son which made my great-grandfather turn so vehemently towards his daughter, for at an early age he decided that she was a genius and he sent her to study under the leading art masters of the day. He not only admired her. He doted on her. She became the passion of his life.

Still-life painting was then the fashion and, together, father and daughter would travel up to London for the day to choose the objects for the next picture. Only at the great metropolitan fish-market at Billingsgate could a salmon or a lobster be found that was fine enough to be immortalised on her canvasses. And only at Covent Garden were the fruit and flowers sublime enough.

His faith and his efforts were soon justified. The Royal Academy began accepting her pictures and for the next few years she advanced from triumph to triumph. Again and again the jubilant pair set out for London to attend the Academy functions and frequent the studios of the fashionable artists. And everywhere the young prodigy was acclaimed, pursued and petted while her father listened and looked on intoxicated with love, pride and ambition. And then, the one thing that he had always dreaded, happened. She fell in love.

She was 18 when she met another young painter, tall and handsome with a golden beard who, like herself, had risen rapidly to the notice of the critics and the public and was now being delightfully battered by their praises and extravagant predictions.

William Luker came from a family of small country squires in Berkshire. United and agreeable, their lives were dedicated to music and they formed their own orchestra. But William broke away from this nest of music-makers to seek individual fame in London, as a landscape painter.

When my great-grandfather realised what was happening, he was frantic. He entreated his daughter to consider what she was doing, he implored her to turn back and to recover from her foolishness, reminding her of the high calling of the artist and of her duty to dedicate her life to a talent so rare and so glorious – beside which marriage and child-bearing were commonplace and contemptible. But his passionate appeals were of no avail. She married her dear William and with his dream dissolved her father very soon died.

And she never painted again. She had 12 children (of whom six survived), a large house and servants to manage and an adoring but egotistic husband who took his own genius extremely seriously but was totally oblivious of hers. And hers was always the greater.

William, being a countryman, had strong views about the right place in London to live. Chelsea, the artists' quarter, was naturally attractive but too close to the river, damp and unhealthy. Campden Hill, he decided, was the only possible locality in which to settle safely and the score or so of houses running along the top of the square he marked out as the most desirable. But as these were difficult to come by all at once he took a temporary house nearby and for five years waited patiently. Then No. 22 came into the market and he snapped it up and there the family lived for more than 50 years.

At first, everything went well. They adored each other, William was eminent and financially successful and his wife seemed content with the part that she had chosen. In spite of the ceaseless pregnancies, they were a sociable couple, doing the rounds every year of the exhibitions, varnishing days and receptions in the great studio-salons. Always, before the opening of the Academy summer exhibition, they gave their own reception and when the London season ended they joined the great holiday migration.

For the many years of his 'Scottish period', my grandfather regularly travelled up to the north to paint the Highland cattle. With a bonnet on his head and a heather-coloured plaid wrapped round him he sat out day after day painting the shaggy wide-horned animals against the misty backgrounds of their native moors and mountains.

So enamoured of Scotland was he at this time that he decided to transplant what he could of it to Campden Hill. He brought a bagful of thistle seed back with him one year which he scattered hopefully over the front garden of No. 22. In the hospitable London clay the seed did fantastically well and a fine crop of thistles sprang up at once. In time, there was a veritable forest, head-high and impenetrable so that from the pavement the entire ground floor of the house was obscured.

In the midst of the well kept, conventional gardens of Campden Hill the display must have looked most remarkable. At the end of every season, of course, the air became thick with thistledown, dropping gently and quietly into the neighbours' flower beds and travelling far and wide to propagate the parks and pleasances of Kensington. My grandfather was absolutely delighted; by the brilliance of the idea in the first place and then by its undreamed of success.

Always, when the great holiday pack-up was finished, a London passenger horse-drawn omnibus was hired and loaded with trunks, packing cases, bundles and baskets, children, servants, parents and animals, pulled off heavily for the station. There, the immense cargo was unloaded onto the train and reloaded at the other end onto farm wagons. After that, always in the dullest of dull places chosen solely for the quality and density of its bovine population, the family settled down to several months of boredom while, equipped with easel, canvasses, paint-box, umbrella, mosquito net and campstool my grandfather sat out contentedly all day with the cows.

There were many of these hopeful, happy years and then, something very curious and disquieting was noted. Fewer pictures were being bought and the galleries seemed less excited by the work of William Luker. And the critics and the public seemed almost a little weary of the portraits of cows and shaggy Highland cattle, while his innumerable representations of Burnham Beeches with every leaf and blade of grass so accurately observed seemed, all of a sudden, positively boring. And not just boring – but bad!

The canvasses piled up against the studio walls, William grew irritable, his wife looked worried, economies in the household expenditure had to be devised – and they filled the house with lodgers. And then the really deadly blow came. After an unbroken record of acceptance – he was rejected by the Royal Academy. Rejected – when he should have been elected an Academician!

After that, day after day, he sat huddled before his easel working over and over the same old subjects and cursing the world for its stupidity, wickedness and ingratitude. It was jealousy, it was favouritism, it was the cliques, he said, and the bad taste of the public. The causes of his downfall lay everywhere but in himself. The truth was that after the first fine dashiness of youth his art had not developed and so his work declined.

He stopped going out and refused to see his friends and, loyally, his wife did the same and they sank into a state of depression from which they never emerged. But they were not willing to suffer alone. Their children had to share their shame. The boys were taken away from their private schools and sent to the local Board School or into dead-end little office jobs, the younger girl was sent away to be brought up by the musical aunts and when the governess left, my mother was sent to a little nearby school where, locked in a room as a punishment, she drew caricatures in chalk of all the mistresses on all the walls – and was expelled. And that was the end of her education.

When the dream and the substance failed they behaved like ignorant or desperate working-class parents (of that time) with no resources behind them, heartlessly ignoring their children's desires, destroying their ambitions and exposing them to the most shabby influences, concerned only for the paltry wages they brought into the house. Only Willie, the eldest, was untouched. The other boys grew up with one idea – to acquire money – no matter how. For only money could extricate them from their mean jobs and depressing home.

Perhaps all the Victorians were prone to sacrifice their children, and my grandparents' behaviour, in their situation, was not unusual; yet they themselves were unusual. There was a helpless, irresponsible simplicity about them – attractive and at the same time maddening. They had no real awareness of the world. Their outlook was enclosed and misty for they were conscious only of themselves and of their role as artists, and when this failed them they were lost. The belief in their own genius and that of their eldest son then turned into something vain and cruel.

In the meantime, the children made the best of things in their own way, and practical joking became the boys' principal recreation. They were always thinking up new ways of annoying the neighbours and baiting the Police. A favourite pastime was to go down to the bottom of the square and where the trees overhung the pavement they tied an invisible cord to a branch and hiding in the bushes, then jerked it in such a way that the top hats of passing gentlemen were whisked off their heads.

Once, they padlocked the garden gates of the neighbours they disliked. In the morning important persons leaving for their offices had to climb over them to get out.

On another occasion Noel, the youngest boy, stole a barrel organ, blacked his face, dressed up as a nigger minstrel and then set off round the streets of Kensington. While he turned the handle he hopped about and sang. The people adored it and a crowd soon thronged after him. When he grew tired of the sport he made for home and pitching the organ outside his own house was about to give his final performance when the Police caught him up.

My mother had come out to see the fun, not knowing who it was and, dancing about, he lurched into her in the crowd and whispered, "open the stable door". He then took to his heels and raced along the top of the square and round the back into the mews with the Police pursuing from both sides. When he reached the stables of his own house the door slid open and he vanished. He hurried into the house, washed and changed and then sauntered out to enquire what all the commotion was about. Defeated again, the Police wheeled the barrel organ back to its owner.

If these pranks made the family notorious, the neighbours had still another reason for loathing them – their animals. The house was always full of them – dogs, cats, rats, mice, guinea pigs, pigeons and a monkey – and the monkey was as wild as the children. But the neighbours could be annoying, too. On one side lived a wealthy man who decided to instal a mechanical horse in the room next to my grandparents' bedroom. On this, early every morning, he rode energetically and the noise of the contraption reverberated through the party wall and its movements shook both houses. My grandparents complained politely but the nuisance continued.

Then, one day, he gave a garden party and although he detested the children and the animals and was barely on speaking terms with their parents, he sent word by one of his maids to ask if he might borrow the monkey for the afternoon – to entertain his guests. While the children peeped from the back windows it was handed over the garden wall. With a bound it leapt onto the host's head and chattering angrily, plucked out his hair in handfuls. No one dared to touch it and while the victim's cries rang up and down the gardens and he lurched about, a maid tore round for help and my mother went and rescued him. The guests were entertained – and the family avenged.

2

The Dream Abandoned

A RICH marriage was a way of escape and one of the boys married the daughter of Henry Moore, the sea painter. She had inherited her father's fortune and a house full of art treasures. He squandered the fortune and deserted her and shutting herself up in the big empty house with all the treasures sold, she took to drink and lingered on miserably for many years. When she died he bought a small clothing business in the East End with her money and selected from his employees a huge, grim, excruciatingly vulgar woman whom he took as his second wife.

Another son married a plain, mean, bad-tempered heiress to an Indian jute fortune. He longed for a home and children but discontented and restless, his wife could never settle anywhere. They spent their whole lives travelling and he was forever counting trunks, exchanging currencies and booking hotel rooms. For 40 years they circled and recircled the globe, aimlessly cruising from one continent to another until, hen-pecked, disappointed and travel-crazed, he died.

Noel, the youngest, became a libertine of exceptional scope and enterprise. He seduced nearly every woman he saw. He stopped them in the street, raped them on the tops of buses, leapt over high walls, climbed up drain pipes to high windows, hovered in dark areas at kitchen doors and was acquainted with nearly every house of ill-fame in London from one of which, he barely escaped with his life.

When the 1914 war came he joined the Navy, became captain of a minesweeper, was decorated for gallantry and came out of it a hero – but once more adrift. He then emigrated to New Zealand where life was hard until he met a dull, plain parson's daughter, was forced to marry her and then, with the aid of a saintly father-in-law, took Holy Orders himself. He made a great success of this and was soon widely respected for his piety and devotion, neither his parishioners nor fellow-clergy suspecting for one moment what ribald accounts of his ministry and hilarious paraphrases of his sermons he regularly sent off to my mother in England. He was attractive and talented and she was fond of him in an amused critical way.

But these amoral, foolish lives were not wholly the result of early treatment, for we are more than mere conditioning. My mother was also treated heartlessly while Willie the eldest – darling Willie who was doted on and pampered – was the worst of them all.

Willie was a genius so his parents maintained to the end. In the beginning there was some reason for this belief as he was a sensitive and beautiful child and, at a most precocious age, drew and painted divinely. He would be the greatest painter of his time, they said, and everything was done to help him.

But as he grew up, disquieting changes were observed. No longer the talented angelic boy, he grew coarse and cruel, stopped painting and prowled the house and neighbourhood seeking what he might destroy or hurt. At 17 he married the 'mother's help' and lived with her secretly in the house. When it was discovered, my grandmother fell screaming to the floor.

This was a catastrophe indeed! Even placing all the blame upon the woman did not obscure the fact that their 'darling' had deceived them and thrown himself away. Their hope, their joy, their bright genius who would succeed where his father had failed and soar beyond all rivals to the highest pinnacle of his art, had destroyed his own high destiny and the family's eternal dream. They felt despair, and for my grandmother this blow was far worse than that of her husband's failure which, most probably, did not surprise her. For in Willie, she herself lived and painted again.

When they recovered from the first shock, however, they had to admit that his marriage was not bound to impede the development of his talent (which had been in abeyance for some time and for which they were patiently awaiting a revival) and when the poor enticed boy left home to be kept by the wicked woman, they soon accepted it.

Maggie, in fact, was a staunch working-class girl, so affectionate and good that even my grandmother could not stay unreconciled for long. However much he made her suffer, she remained loyal to Willie and the family throughout her life. She bore him two children and loved and looked after him until, complaining that she did not earn enough, he left her and returned to his parents' house. She and the children suffered great poverty but he did nothing for them – and neither did the parents. They had their 'darling' home again and that was all they cared about.

My mother was still a child when he returned and immediately he began interfering with her. She repulsed him but it amused him to go about hinting that he made love to his little sister. She had always disliked him and now she loathed him.

For years he sat in an arm-chair by the dining-room fire waiting for the meals, and the in-between snacks and stimulants to follow each other, while at night he roamed the streets looking for servant girls. He did some mediocre work and when his mother had to sell the house, he found another woman and moved to another arm-chair beside another dining-room fire and waited for the meals to be served as before.

My mother's younger sister, Amy, was given a musical education by her aunts and, in due time, she went to a church school in Cornwall as a music teacher. Here, she fell in love with the headmistress and having a weak and malleable nature, at once became her shadow and her slave. Whereas all the other members of the family hardly touched my life and soon receded from it altogether, Amy's life indirectly determined mine and eventually converged with it.

* * *

From an early age my mother longed to paint. But no one in the family called her a genius. She had to wait for strangers to do that.

As soon as she was old enough she begged her parents to send her to an art school, but they pleaded poverty and would not listen, threatening instead to send her to work in the Post Office. Disregarding them, she enrolled at the South Kensington Art School but they soon took her away and sent her to the local high school as an art mistress. Then, hating the job and Willie and everything at home she sent her work to Hubert von Herkomer whose art school at Bushey was then famous. At once he offered her a three-year scholarship – but only for tuition. She had to support herself and her appeal to her parents was again useless. They were only hurt and resentful that she should want to give up her good job and the salary which they so badly needed.

The old man still sat hour after hour in his studio, growing more querulous all the time. My grandmother, her talent unused, seething and souring through 12 pregnancies, her husband's failure, and her son's and a life-time of heavy Victorian domesticity, had become a brooding, small-minded woman – jealous of her daughter.

Searching for a way of escape, my mother wrote to Amy's headmistress begging her to engage her as an art teacher until she could collect the money to pay for her first term's board and lodging at Bushey. A helpful reply came and she left for Cornwall.

She found the new life liberating and exciting. She taught in the school and was soon painting portraits of the local people. Miniatures were still a popular art form and, needing little paraphernalia, were easily carried about and it was here that she painted the first of the hundreds of little gems which, for the next 30 years, she scattered about the world. Quick, cheap and transfiguring, they were always sure money-makers everywhere.

It was here, too, that she began the friendship which was to have such consequences for me. Miss Morison, the headmistress, whom Amy so adored, was a strong personality with a magnetic charm which, to a lesser extent, also affected my mother. But she did not stay in Cornwall long for she soon had the money that she needed for Bushey.

Each year she won the 'Enamel', given to the most talented student and Herkomer predicted a great future for her.

One day before she left, there was a knock on the door of her lodgings and an old gentleman was shown into the room. He was very tall, with a proud, handsome face, wild white hair and a gorgeous strip of crimson taffeta flung carelessly round his neck which, he explained later, was a piece of his wife's petticoat that he had purloined and cut up for its colour. He had seen one of my mother's miniatures in the Academy that year and had come to be painted. He was Lord North.

He lodged in the village while she did the work and afterwards showed it to his friends. It was he who launched her as a painter of the Royal Family and aristocracy and in this exalted world she soon became well known.

They raved about her work and were not happy until they had been painted. She went to their great town houses and stayed with them in their country mansions, but just when she could have made a great career, a new rival passion arose. She longed for marriage and children. The pattern was repeated. But it was more than a Shavian marriage that called her, for she seemed to have a vision of one particular man who was preordained to be the father of her children and whom she knew she must now find. As he did not appear in England, she made a fantastic decision and, throwing away all that she had gained, went to Africa to search for him.

In Cape Town she began painting at once. I do not know how she got started then, but her methods were probably the same as those which, later, when we were together, she employed again and again in place after place, with invariable success.

On arrival, we would put up at the best hotel for a few days. There she would exhibit her portraits with a printed card beside them stating all the celebrities that she had painted. At the same time she would write to the town's leading citizen, begging to have the honour of painting him, and together we would deliver this letter with another sample of her work. The leading citizen – with only one exception that I can remember – was always enchanted and the same day, private secretaries, A.D.C.s and carriages would wait upon us. After that, all state business was set aside while, behind closed doors in an atmosphere of hushed expectancy, the great man sat for his portrait. When it was finished, and the court was called in to admire, and the great man beamed, and the affairs of state took a turn for the better, my mother was well in at the top.

In Cape Town, she rejected a wealthy banker and soon, while sitting on the stoep of the house of some English friends, the man whom she already knew, rode up on a horse. She did not fall in love with him, but admired and respected him – and within a month married him.

Philip Burrell came from a well-to-do family, living in Berkeley Square. One of his brothers commanded a county regiment, another was naval chaplain to King Edward, another tripped idly and elegantly about St James's, and his sister was married to a French aristocrat. They were all, without a doubt, very respectable, although his career was not conventional.

Injured by a cricket ball at school, a long sea voyage was recommended and he was put onto a cargo boat and sent round the world. But bored with being a passenger, he worked with the crew and afterwards, no longer interested in a formal university ending, he went to Mexico where he studied the architecture, the fauna and flora and the logging industry. He fought in the Boer War and then stayed on in Africa to make money, for he intended to stand for Parliament and for this, private means were needed.

When he met my mother, he was living in Johannesburg representing his brother's business, of which he was expecting to become a director. His brother, Alfred, had always wanted to be a sailor and when he was forced into the Church he compromised and became a naval chaplain. But he was never happy and on a cruise with the King he delivered his last sermon, damning everybody and everything, including God and the monarch himself. It was said that Edward enjoyed it, but at the end of the cruise Alfred resigned before they had time to sack him. Then, when he bought a small chemical business on the Thames, the family was even more shocked. But when it prospered they soon joined him, and before many years, with its works and its wharves ever expanding, it absorbed and enriched them all.

My mother enjoyed the gay colonial life in South Africa but when the first baby died at birth she nearly died, too, and as soon as she was pregnant again she left for England and my father, whose health had deteriorated, wound up his business intending to follow her. She returned to Campden Hill and when I was safely born, the news was cabled out to him — but a few weeks later he was dead. And she was very ill again.

3

Birth and Death

MY grandfather was dead and the two boys had married their rich wives, otherwise everything at home was the same.

When my mother first came back, with a well-to-do husband behind her, they treated her with great respect. But when he died, not leaving her much money, they changed at once. Willie tormented her and the others criticised and interfered. But she had neither the means nor the strength to leave.

The neighbour with the mechanical horse, whom the monkey had so punished, had long left and Mrs Llewellyn-Davies was now occupying the house next door – and J.M. Barrie was a regular caller.

My mother had made friends with the beautiful dying woman and her five boys, and when I was born, one of the younger ones was so curious to see what a new-born baby looked like, that I was held out of a bedroom window so that Peter could lean out of his nursery window to see me – the Peter of Barrie's *Peter Pan.*

One of the first to call after I was born was Miss Morison, the headmistress. She was now established in London in another church school and my mother had looked forward to showing her the baby. She was so sure it would delight her, especially as she was to be one of the godparents. But when she arrived she glanced at it perfunctorily and left as soon as she could.

Another caller was the Bishop of London, Dr Winnington-Ingram. He came to console the widow and to offer to christen the baby. And nothing could have pleased my mother more.

The other godparents all lived in the country and were unable to accept the invitation to the christening. But Miss Morison she was sure would come. The Bishop was her friend. It was he who had brought her to London and it was through her that my mother had met him. And she loved religious ceremonies. But she also declined.

When the day came, dressed in the beautiful embroidered robes which several generations of my family had worn before me, my mother, my nurse and I set out in a carriage for St James's, where the Bishops of London then lived when they came up to town from Fulham. As London House had no chapel, the Bishop himself decorated a little table with snowdrops and consecrated one of his tennis cups and at the moment of anointing, spontaneously added my second name – Joy.

Even if she felt deserted by her friends and the religious significance of the ceremony meant nothing to her, yet the Bishop's kindliness, the human side, the loving intimacy, made up for it and she told the story with all its secular and social details for years after.

Although it was settled at once that I was to go to her school as soon as I was old enough, yet during those first years of my life when we were in London and she was often seeing my mother, Miss Morison continued to ignore me when she could not avoid me altogether. My mother never understood the traumatic and far-reaching effect which my birth had upon her.

I was born with my feet curled up and when they did not straighten my mother consulted a doctor, who prescribed foot-irons. But not liking this advice she went to another — and then to another and after receiving the same advice, had some irons made. But when I cried day and night she threw them away and set off in search of someone more enlightened. And she found him. It was only the muscles, he told her, and he showed her how to massage and strengthen them. In a few weeks my feet were normal.

But for her instinctive knowing and determination, I would have grown up with club feet.

As soon as she was strong enough, she took up her work again. I am sure that she missed her husband but she did not grieve. It was his child that she married for and when he had given it to her and died – she let him go. And I grew up hardly aware of him. She wanted to get back to work and she had to earn at once. Old clients and new ones came crowding forward and she could soon afford a permanent nurse for, although she adored me, she never wanted to look after me all the time.

In that house two different worlds existed, two different sorts of lives were lived – my mother's and mine, and that of the family. My grandmother still brooding and jealous, Willie, still sitting about eating, fornicating and playing mean, mad tricks (leaving acid in the bath from his photographic work, before I was taken to be bathed), and Noel, still chasing women and filling the house with his flashy friends. This was the world of which my mother was conscious all the time and loathed, but of which I perceived nothing.

I remember the big dark Victorian dining-room looking out onto the square with a distant view of Notting Hill, the huge mahogany table and ponderous side-boards loaded with silver. I remember it all – but not Willie. I remember the little gardens in front of the houses and the old square sliding down the hill full of graceful trees waving and leaning all ways, with railings surrounding it. Trees and railings I thought so beautiful, so delicate and lacey, held and connected by such lovely patterns and reaching and pointing up so high. I remember all this but not the chorus girls and young men giggling and haw-hawing as they tore in and out of the house. I remember my little friends from respectable families who, with their smart uniformed nurses, walked every day to the park with me. To St Gover's Well and the Round Pond and the tiny fairies' house near the Serpentine and Kensington Palace where the young Victoria had been woken up in the middle of the night to be told that she was Queen. And I remember the fat old woman who sat at the gates at the bottom of the Broad Walk, from whom I bought a balloon every week on my way to my dancing class. I lived in Peter Pan's poetic, upper-class world of old Kensington and the world of my seedy, broken-down family I was never aware of.

When I grew up and met them again and heard all about them, I was ashamed of them and did my best to conceal and deny them. I did not know how much I was like them.

I have dreamed their dream of greatness and believed in my own genius, as they did, and followed the same irregular road, climbing and falling and losing my way, losing my conscience, going without pity and doing the same mad, shabby things. And when I changed and gave the world away for the dream, I lived rootless and floating, more demented than they, anchored to nothing but the purpose and power in myself.

Yes, I am one of them and, like the masters and monsters, all the ineffectual geniuses before me, I may fail in my turn. But through failure, we and our talents are trained in each life for the next.

They came with a gift which they lost or betrayed – but they loved. And meaning and merit are not in the fruits but large in the loving – in a life-time, or moment, of loving. I have loved as they loved, a force that can lift or destroy, misguide or serve as a Way.

When my mother could bear the house no longer, we moved into lodgings and she painted harder than ever. She never stopped, day after day and sitter after sitter. Royalties and grandees followed each other. Princess Marie-Louise of Schleswig-Holstein, Princess Alice, Prince Louis of Battenburg and Prince George all came to the dingy place. When Prince Louis called one day, not expected, he found no one at home. He walked in, and seeing the uncleared tea-table, stuck his visiting card in the butter where my mother found it later with mixed feelings of amusement and embarrassment.

She need not have worked like this. She could have gone to a cottage in the country and looked after me herself and lived on her income in a simple way. She could have gone to the continent and lived among artists and painted as she pleased. But if she ever thought of these alternatives they would not have appealed to her, for she had lived on the fringe of the fashionable world – and when she married, she belonged to it and she wanted me to grow up in it. And so, she had to paint and paint – the portraits she never wanted to do. And the strain began to tell. She had her first nerve attacks and when she was advised to go to a dry climate, she planned a six-month visit to a cousin in Canada.

On a dull grey autumn day in 1912, when I was four-years-old, we left England. Lifted up by my mother to the deck rail of the ship at Liverpool, I can remember waving and shouting to the sombre group of relatives and friends standing on the quay below. The whole family had come to see us off and Miss Morison, my godmother, as well.

My mother was so happy to be escaping again from everything; from the bitter sickness of the family, from the effort to keep up, to keep one's place and not sink into poverty and meanness, from the oppressiveness of England as she knew it. And my little nursemaid, Annie, was equally anxious to be off. She came from a poor London family, hoping to better her lot.

With the usual noise and commotion, the ship got under way and we waved our handkerchiefs energetically until, first the group on the quay, and then England, receded into the gloom.

Although he had the same name, Martin Burrell was not one of my father's family. He was distantly connected to the Lukers. He had emigrated to Canada as a young man and farmed for many years in the Middle West. When he was elected to Parliament he settled in Ottawa, and when we arrived he was Minister of Agriculture and Secretary of State in Sir Wilfred Laurier's government.

He lived in a small block of flats known as The Roxborough. This insignificant little building housed most of the governing talent of the Dominion. In small, compressed apartments, members of the Cabinet and shadow Cabinet were tightly packed together inside its walls. And soon we were packed in too, with Martin and his wife on one side and Mr Mackenzie King on the other. And we were soon the heroines of the capital.

The grand rough-diamond society took my mother to its heart instantly and embraced her with all the eagerness and power of a Rocky Mountain bear. People thought her so refined, so beautiful and so clever – and me so cute. They showered presents, flowers and candies upon us. Our apartment looked like a conservatory. Lumber kings and railroad kings, prairie kings and mining kings fell over each other, pursuing her. The adorable English widow and her dandy paintings convulsed the homes and industries and politics of Canada.

This was all most unexpected but, naturally, she loved it. And whether it was the climate or just happiness, she never had another attack although she worked as hard as ever. Her final triumph came when the Governor-General, the Duke of Connaught, smiled on us as well and commissioned portraits of himself and of his daughter, Princess Patricia, and parties at Rideau Hall then followed for us both. Although always more inhibited than the native royalty, the Duke threw off much of his English restraint and let himself go and was hearty and gay – and I was his pet.

As servants were unknown and the wives of the Augustans far too busy to cook, most of the inhabitants of The Roxborough repaired downstairs for the rather poor meals served in the dining-room. Like their counterparts in London high-society at that time, these wives spent their afternoons riding round in carriages or sleighs, leaving visiting cards in the doors of the little timber houses in which the rank and fashion lived. Modelling itself on London, Ottawa society indulged in a whole range of snobberies and conceits. Yet beneath it all was a refreshing simplicity and vigour.

Every day I was out tobogganing and skating. I never went to school, but my mother taught me to read and write, to sing and to recite poetry – and she kept up my dancing. Canadian mothers had never thought of doing things like this with their children, and my performances were everywhere in demand. I was looked upon as an infant prodigy.

Annie did not stay with us long. The egalitarian influences were far too strong. First, she stopped calling my mother 'madam', then she refused to wear her aprons and starched collars and cuffs, after that her striped gingham dresses and, finally her navy blue overcoat and hat. She grew surly and useless. Then, by mutual consent, she left. My mother sent to England for someone else, and in due time, Maud arrived. She was middle-aged and set firmly in the old traditions.

But this wasn't the last of Annie. After a few months she returned, begging to be taken back. She had been with several Canadian families but, although engaged as a nurse, she found that she was expected to do all the house-work, all the washing and mending, half the cooking and then, after that, look after the children. Her experiences had been a great shock. The right to call her mistress by her Christian name and to wear whatever garish clothes she fancied did not compensate for overwork. Poor Annie floundered between the old world and the new.

However, Maud was established. My mother offered Annie her passage home – but she did not want that either, so she found her what she hoped would be an easier place, and then we heard that she was married. Maud stayed with us and never faltered – but I liked Annie best.

The six months of our visit flew by but we showed no intention of leaving. And nobody wanted us to. We were still the darlings of the place. My mother rejected all her millionaire suitors, even her neighbour and future Prime Minister, Mr Mackenzie King (whom she disliked). She would neither marry again nor console herself with lovers for she was always afraid that if she had another child she might die and leave me an orphan. The fear of being orphaned was soon to get into the ground of my life.

Martin became my foster-father. We adopted each other at once. He was a sweet little man and something of a literary figure. He published books of essays and criticism and for years kept up a weekly literary column in the leading newspaper. He never grew rich like everyone else. Among all those dollar-spinning kings he remained the little poor man, living on his parliamentary salary and his weekly article and, in the end, on a pension. But they didn't despise this. There was something quixotic about his poorness which, in spite of themselves, they admired. And he was full of fun.

One day he took us to the House of Commons while it was in session. The Chamber is an exact replica of Westminster. We crept in behind the Speaker's chair, and giving me a gavel, he said, 'Go round to the big table in front of the man with the long wig and bang the hammer several times on the table as hard as you can and then shout as loud as you can – "Order! Order!"' I did exactly as I was told. There was a moment of silent astonishment and then a roar of laughter. I stood gazing round until the Speaker rose from the chair and came down to me and, smiling gravely, took me by the hand and escorted me out. Martin and my mother were peeping and laughing.

After nearly two years of this felicitous life, my mother grew bored and she was beginning to worry about my education. I was six-years-old and I had only had her lessons and, in her letters, Miss Morison was pressing her to return and let me start my proper schooling. When, finally, she decided to do so, Martin and his friends planned a trip round the world – the millionaires paying. For still nothing was too good for the lovely widow.

The jolliest party was formed and at the end of July 1914, without a fear in the world, we rolled serenely across the continent to the Pacific. When we arrived in Vancouver, war was declared. Leaving us there, the rest of the party jumped into the train again and went speeding back to Ottawa. 'Wait here till it's over!' they cried as they left. 'It won't be long. We'll soon be back. And we'll all carry on with our trip.'

We waited. After several weeks it seemed clear that we had a long, long time to wait.

4

The First World War

WE WERE stranded. If we had to wait until the war ended (and it would have been foolish, even if we had had the money, to travel on straight into it) then Vancouver, my mother decided, was not the place to stay. Victoria, she was told, was a small pleasant city where English people liked to settle and she made up her mind to try it. Maud found a job in Vancouver.

We put up at the best hotel and at once presented an introduction, sent by Martin, to the most important person in the place. Sir John had been governor of a colonial territory and, on retirement, had come to live in Victoria with his daughter.

We were invited to tea and, when we arrived, were shown into a stiff, cold, colourless room with the white blinds half-way down, to prevent the sun from spoiling the furniture. When Miss Mara at length entered, a tall, gaunt, colourless woman, she held out, with distaste, her cold bony fingers for us to shake. There was no doubt about her being an absolute English 'lady', and when she asked us to sit down, a grand English tea was served by a real English maid, with silver tea things on a silver tray and, in tiers one above the other on a silver stand, plates of finely cut almost invisible sandwiches and microscopic cakes.

She apologised for her father's inability to meet us. His life, she explained, was so crowded with important engagements. Then, after a few elegantly phrased general observations – the weather, of course, was an interesting topic there just as it is in England – she came straight to the point.

'My father, Sir John,' she began, 'has received your letter asking if you may paint his portrait but I regret to have to tell you that his position is far too high for him ever to consider anything like that. And as for anyone else,' she continued, 'I am afraid I cannot help you. Victoria society is very exclusive. In fact, I really must tell you that Victoria doesn't approve of art.'

Soon afterwards she rose to dismiss us, at the same time making it quite clear that the best thing we could do would be to leave Victoria at once. My mother was rather taken aback although not in the least upset and she laughed as we walked away down the long imposing English drive.

After that, she exhibited her work in the hotel and waited confidently. But nothing happened. She arranged another larger show in a shop window and waited again. There was no response. It was not the war for Victoria wasn't yet touched by it. Perhaps Miss Mara was right and Victoria 'did not approve of art'.

Things grew serious for our money was going and then, suddenly, we found ourselves in a large rambling house and my mother became a boarding-house keeper.

The garden was overrun by hens and reduced to a waste of foul black mud. Whenever I went out to play, my legs became red and live with fleas, and I climbed up a tree and sat on a branch knocking them back onto the ground.

In that frightening, filthy house anything could happen – and one night it did. We had a burglary although nothing of obvious value was stolen. Only my mother's desk was ransacked.

The Police came in the morning and over a nice cup of English tea, speculated wisely on how best to catch the odd intruder. Then, chancing to glance out of the window, they saw Andy emptying rubbish into the dust-bin. 'That's him,' they yelled and with a bound leapt out and fell upon him and my mother was hard put to it to get him released, explaining over and over again that he was her butler. Andy thought it was a great joke.

My mother was having a dispute with her employers and they had broken in to obtain some document to their advantage. The incident upset her and we left soon afterwards taking Ellen, the cook, and Andy with us. How the boarders survived when the manageress and staff walked out in a body, did not trouble us at all. We moved to a small timber house in a working-class road with a fine semi-basement, in which Ellen and Andy lived, and two spare rooms upstairs for lodgers.

Then, one day, soon after we got there, violent sounds came up from below and, in alarm, my mother went down but so many objects were flying about that she retreated quickly. At that moment Andy came in.

'What on earth is happening?' she cried.

'It's nothing,' he answered with a giggle. 'Only Ellen packing up.'

'Packing up?' my mother exclaimed.

'Yes,' he replied calmly and much amused. 'Packing up and smashing up. When she's finished she'll be going.'

'But she hasn't given me notice!' my mother answered indignantly. 'And how can you let her smash up all your things?'

Andy just giggled and then the uproar ceased as suddenly as it had begun. The next moment, from the window, we watched Ellen march furiously out of the house, turning again and again to shake her bundles in the air and scream her curses at Andy.

That day, for the first time in her life, my mother had to cook. A chicken was in the larder for the lodgers and when, oblivious of the fact that it needed drawing, she and Andy put it in the oven it somehow caught fire and flamed for a long time before they noticed it. But they scraped it and served it up and although a little charred, it was delicious. This was the beginning of a close relationship with Andy.

He was an Irishman. Law-hating and law-breaking, he lived a busy, imaginative life in a world of his own on the outskirts of society. He was immature and untameable but devotedly loyal to those whom, in his peculiar way, he was fond of. When the lodgers left and there were no others, for everyone was joining up, my mother could not pay him his wages. But he didn't care. And after that, night after night, he went thieving all over the town for us, returning at dawn with sacks of food and wood and other useful things. The basement became a veritable receiving den and my mother was so naive that for a long time she didn't realise how he got them.

For awhile, she was out every day looking for work of any kind and he became my nurse, and, teaching me to pick a lock, cut out a window pane and slip a catch, he took me on many of his nefarious expeditions. But whatever we did I was always safe in his hands.

One day, when I was riding pillion on his stolen motor bicycle, a troop of Mounted Police spotted him but instead of making a run for home and cover, he led them a chase all over the city – just for the fun of it. The traffic stopped, people shouted and shook their umbrellas at us and ran in all directions, as we dodged about and the horses came galloping after us. We reached home at last and slipped the bicycle into the basement. It was a hair-raising but exhilarating experience.

Soon another blow fell and our position became really serious. Our money from England stopped. The war, spreading its ravages wider and wider, now swept nearly all my mother's capital away. Even this remote quiescent corner of the world was feeling it now, was daily more involved, and as our own lives became ever more precarious a great fear got into me.

To get me better looked after, as she thought, my mother now sent me to a little dame's school and one day, we arranged to meet after school at a certain street corner.

I arrived there and waited. She didn't come. I went on waiting and she still didn't come. What if something had happened to her and she never came, I thought? What would I do? I would be an orphan and sent to an asylum and dressed in a uniform and have to live with hundreds of other poor little orphans. My fear and pity for myself grew to panic. I set off running to find her – then stopped and came back. An orphan! An orphan! Alone in the world without my sweet, my kind, my lovely mother. I set off again and ran further – then stopped and came back again, thinking of all the dreadful things that could have happened to her. I was so blinded by tears and alarm that when she came I didn't see her until she was beside me. I flung myself upon her and my love and dependence became even greater. She never really understood these scenes, for my fear of her death, I felt, was too delicate a thing to explain.

It was about this time that Pat came to us. I longed for a dog and persuaded the little children in my street that they all wanted dogs. We got pieces of string from our mothers and set off in a crowd – dog stealing. We were soon back with an entangled pack of variegated animals. My capture was a large black spaniel whom I took home and introduced to my mother. She was rather surprised – but the dog wasn't. He took to her at once and settled down contentedly. After a few days, when he showed no sign of leaving, she found out where he came from and his master took him away. 10 minutes later he was back. He was fetched again and tied up. He bit through the rope and returned. He was chained and locked into sheds but he always escaped and, at length, the man let him stay.

He was a well-known character in Victoria. He would go off into the forests for days, hunting, but when back in town he didn't exert himself. That is to say, he didn't walk if he could ride. He took street-cars everywhere – just to the end of the road or to their termini on the outskirts of the city where the forests lay. He knew where they all went to and waited at the proper stopping places to board them and the drivers and conductors all admired and served him.

My school-going ended very soon. The old dame used to take us to play on a vacant lot, all overgrown with beautiful weeds. Our game was to climb to the top of a high board fence and then see who could jump the farthest. I never wore shoes and one day I jumped on a broken bottle. The lot was a dump and I was crippled for weeks.

There were no lodgers, no portraits and no other work. The rent was unpaid, the creditors were clamouring and bailiffs began investing the house. Andy was away – perhaps he had to disappear for awhile – and so even food ran short. When my mother saw a poor looking woman in a butcher's shop buy an H-bone for a nickel she followed her out and asked her what she did with it. She said that she fed her family for a week on it and explained how she cooked it. My mother went back and bought one, too.

Then she was struck by a great idea! Near us a camp had been set up and beside it was an unused barn, and when the owner let her have it, she dug out the manure, white-washed the walls and put two chairs inside. Then she pinned

My grandfather and grandmother.

Unutterable boredom must have driven her out to the cows. She seems to have appropriated his easel and umbrella!

My mother — before her marriage

My father

John Gage

Models
Early miniature work

up a notice 'Quick portraits – 25 cents' and sat with her paints – waiting. After awhile, a shy young soldier appeared. She sketched him, he ran back to the camp with it and others came – more and more, until they were queueing outside.

I, too, took an interest in the camp. The soldiers fascinated me and I paid them a visit. I made some friends and went again and soon I was there every day. They taught me some drill and they talked about England and it was there, I think, in the soldiers' huts that my long love affair with England seriously began – so sweet a passion then.

Very soon, I asked my mother for a uniform and, in spite of our poverty, she found a tailor who, for a dollar or two, undertook to cut down a soldier's tunic to my size. She made the breeches herself and when it was all finished I put it on, winding the puttees round my legs and fitting the outsize cap on my head. I was nearly seven-years-old and my long hair hung loose round my shoulders. But I did not feel it incongruous and in wildest excitement I set off for the camp.

When I entered the hut the soldiers leapt from their beds with a roar. They crowded round me and lifted me up and one of them ran to the Quartermaster's stores and came back with a Sam Browne belt, and they put it on me and made me into an officer. Then, fixing a badge in my cap, they told me that I'd joined the regiment and that I'd be their mascot. I didn't know what that was but it sounded alright and I trusted my friends.

They taught me how to roll my puttees and how to polish buttons and badges and belts and boots. They taught me a lot more drill and about ranks and regiments and when I'd learnt all that there was to be learnt about soldiering, they ordered me out on parade.

Polished and groomed I reported for duty on Sunday. The regiment fell into line and then formed fours, the band took up its position and then they set me at their head and with one of my friends beside me and the band crashing and blaring behind me, we marched through the city to the Garrison Church. Along the route people waved and cheered and some fell in and marched beside us and I felt transported with joy and with pride.

The service was a rousing one and afterwards we lined up for the Colonel's inspection. He looked me solemnly up and down without any change of expression and I felt so confident when I led them back to camp. And every Sunday after that I paraded with the regiment.

In between, I went about with a recruiting sergeant. With rosettes in our caps we would take up a position at some busy corner, set up our props, a Union Jack and a large framed coloured photograph of a bull dog standing on another Union Jack, and with these splendid emblems to support us the sergeant, a rather fierce red-faced man with a wonderful moustache, waxed into two sharp points, would then harangue the crowd while I stood smartly to attention beside him.

In barking tones he appealed to all the healthy, patriotic young fellows standing in front of him to come and fight for King and Country, for the Mother Country – for England! When he had finished his speech, which was always word for word the same, and he had 'signed on' and given the 'King's Shilling' to all the healthy, patriotic young fellows who rushed forward to join the Colours, we would pack up our props and move on to the next point in the campaign.

For those few months I lived in a state of ecstasy, dreaming of battles and bravery, inspired by my new consciousness and pride in being English and overflowing with love for my soldier friends.

Then, one day, they told me that they were leaving – going at last to the war. I could hardly believe it. And I polished my buttons and badges, my belt and my boots for the last parade and loaded with packs and kit-bags we marched through the city to the docks. Union Jacks were fluttering everywhere, streamers waved over our heads and the whole population turned out. They waved and they cheered and they clung to the soldiers. The city went mad and, carried away, I felt certain that I was a soldier marching to war and to glory for England.

At the docks we broke ranks and the soldiers swarmed onto the troopship – and I with them. They massed along the decks and filled the life-boats and climbed up the funnels and the rigging. And I climbed up into the rigging, too, and they held me safe among them. And we looked down on the quay where thousands of people had gathered. And we cheered and they cheered. Then the band played hymns, the voices rose from the harbour and floated over sea and city and then we cheered again. I was sure I would be forgotten and that the ship would sail and when I was remembered it would be too late to turn and bring me back. Then 'God Save the King' was played and we all tried to stand to attention in the rigging and, being an officer, I had to salute. The ship's whistles blew and all the horns and hooters in the city answered and the soldiers lifted me down; patting me, kissing me and calling their good-byes, lifted me down – and down. My mother was waiting on the quay at the bottom of the gangway and I stood beside her, while the ship got under way, and cried and cried for my friends, my heroes, whose glory I would never share and for England, in her peril, whom I could not serve.

Very few of that shipload returned. I went on wearing my uniform, and nothing else until it became so small for me that I could hardly get into it and so ragged that it fell off me in the end.

When the soldiers left, my mother's main source of income went too, although she was now painting some civilians. She had even penetrated high society. Victoria was not so disapproving of art, after all – only rather slow in the uptake.

Mrs Shalcross, who was very high in high society, was delighted with her portrait and did my mother the honour of inviting her to dinner. My mother then returned the compliment and invited Mrs Shalcross to dinner – and she was pleased to accept.

My mother had become quite a good cook and she and Andy spent many hours preparing the menu. Of course, it had to be a typically English meal. I do not know whether Andy was able to come by a nice plump tender chicken and they risked setting it alight again or whether playing for safety all round, they decided on roast beef and Yorkshire pudding and they bought a sirloin from the butcher.

I feel sure that pastry followed for she was particularly proud of her light hand with the rolling pin. Anyway, by evening all was ready and perfect. Then, she suddenly recollected that she had forgotten to buy any flowers. Now flowers, as everyone knows, are as important at an English dinner party in high society as the beef.

'Andy,' she cried, 'I've forgotten the flowers! The shops are all closed but for heaven's sake find me some!'

Andy was gone in a flash, roaring away on his bike. He was soon back with an immense quantity of the most magnificent chrysanthemums. They made the table look gorgeous and gave the whole house, poor common little box that it was, an air of grandeur.

The guests arrived. Andy, dressed up in his butler's clothes, served each course with expertise and élan and Mrs Shalcross was impressed. The dinner, she whispered (for it is improper to pass remarks upon the food in high society), was superb and as for the chrysanthemums (and here it was permissible to speak as loudly as she liked), they were marvellous – even better than her own and hers were all prize-winners and reputed the finest in Canada. My mother promised to let her know afterwards where her butler had bought them.

The guests left at last, enchanted with everything and the doors of Victoria's high society were flung wide open to the charming English artist and her delightful paintings. When they were gone my mother hurried out to the kitchen where Andy was tucking in.

'Andy,' she said, 'where did you get those wonderful flowers? They just *made* the party.' With his mouth stuffed full Andy giggled.

'From Mrs Shalcross's conservatory.'

The next day, on the strength of his triumph, he proposed. He told my mother that he had been wanting to ask her for a long time for he was sure that they ought to marry. It would be the best thing for both of them, he said. And she was furious with him. But he didn't care. He giggled as usual and skipped merrily away on his business – his business of small-town thief.

It was now that Miss Morison first wrote to me on my baptismal day; an affectionate letter telling me that this was the most important day of the year for me, the day when I was first received into the religion of Christ and she said how glad she was to be my godmother and how much she was looking forward to having me at her school.

I was surprised and pleased by this letter for my mother was always telling me what a wonderful person she was. But replying to it properly was a great effort, and although it was splendid to have such a godmother and to receive such a letter yet it was a relief to know that she wouldn't write to me again for a whole year.

This was the opening up of our relationship. When I was born she was so jealous that the very sight of me was unbearable but, as time passed and she recovered from the first shock and could think about me calmly, she must have changed and begun wanting to approach me, waiting then until she judged I was old enough.

My mother had made friends with a roving Scots family who owned a large cruising motor boat and when summer came and we were still waiting for the war to be over, she gave up the house and sold the furniture and with enough money to support us for several months, joined up with them and their friends.

Early one morning, with Pat and our bundles, we set off in the boat and cruised all day among the virgin forest-covered islands looking for a good camping place. At night we dropped anchor and at dawn sailed on again. Then Jack, our skipper, bellowed to us all as he steered for a small sandy bay and we rowed ashore in the dinghy to survey the place. There was fresh water and a clearing and soon we were rowing backwards and forwards unloading the baggage and before long a fine camp arose with the big living tent in the middle and a ring of small ones pitched among the trees all round.

I was now seven and Donny, Jack's boy, was 10. We bathed in the sharp cold sea and set out at dawn to fish the great salmon that lie in those waters. We explored our own island and all the others within rowing distance, running the dinghy up into a cove, breaking through the dense undergrowths to follow the streams to their sources, climbing the great rock clusters and crawling into caves. We became like young savages, barefoot and half naked, alive to every sound in the forest, to every sign and track and movement and to the tides and currents and sudden tricks and dangers of the sea.

We grew skilled with our oars, skimming the water soundlessly, and with our fish lines. We could play a fish as big as ourselves, bring it alongside the boat and, still fighting, lift it and land it. And we knew how to kill with precision.

One day, we had been out exploring as usual and were on our way back to camp with one more rocky point to get round, when a squall caught us sharply. The wind rushed on us, the sea boiled up and the rain came down like a tank being emptied and our little boat was flung about like a chipping of wood. Each time we plunged from a crest to a trough we came nearer the rocks, appearing and disappearing as the sea embraced them and left them, then struck them again. When the boat filled, Donny took my oar and I baled. Keeping the bows turned into the waves we rowed and we rowed and rounded the point and the squall very soon died out.

About once a month Jack returned to the city for fresh supplies and war news. Even in this Arcadia we could not shut out the war altogether. It lay like a driven-down pain in every mind.

He always brought new people back with him and, one day, he arrived with a little fat woman and another small tent was pitched among the trees for her.

That night, after I had gone to bed, an angel voice came down from heaven and floated through the forest. I sat up and listened and then crept out of bed and followed it through the trees to the big tent and peeped through a slit in the canvas. And there she was, the little fat woman, sitting on a log by the stove – singing to them all. And she sang and she sang, old English folk songs, and I sank onto the ground, bewitched.

When she stopped at last I went back to bed and my mother soon came. She was surprised to find me awake and I told her that I'd been listening to the beautiful singing. And that set us talking, as things so often did, and we lay in the dark with the forest breathing and sighing around us, and talked of the stars and of the heavens and of God, or whatever it was that had created them and, finally, of Earth and of ourselves. I adored these conversations in the night.

I changed my allegiance from Donny to the little singing woman. I took to following her about. And she knew why I did it and often and often she sang for me alone, for she not only had an angel voice but she was an angel herself and walking with her beneath the monarch trees beside the grey-green waters of the northern Pacific, every song she sang, however simple and ordinary, sounded to me like a beautiful aria.

One day, we went in a party on a long expedition to one of the big islands

– and *she* came too. We spent the day exploring and it was dark when we rowed back to camp. The night was still and starry and the sea thick with phosphorus, every little ruffle igniting it, stirring it into white glittering flames. Jack was rowing, hardly making any sound, just a soft soft plash as the oars dipped into the silver fire and pushed us along. I was wedged in the bow, leaning over and trailing my fingers in the water to make it dance. And she was in the stern singing with all her heart. Her bell-like voice hung in the air around us and then floated away over the water to enter and sink and die in the forest.

She did not stay with us long. The night before she left I was allowed to stay up late and I sprawled on the ground in the big tent while she sang to us for the last time. And as I stared at her, devoured her, I became aware of something inside myself – an alluring, disturbing and unrelinquishable burden.

In the morning Jack took her away – and the camp was never the same. The singing of the trees and the winds and the waters could never compare with the singing of the little fat woman from town. At the end of the summer, when the nights grew cold, we packed up and left.

Back in the city my mother took two empty rooms at the top of an office building. It was not a proper flat. We had to use the public lavatory and wash-place on the landing and cook on a methylated spirit stove in a corner of the sitting-room – or studio, as she was pleased to call it. She chose it because it was central and easy for her sitters to come to. But no sitters ever came.

That winter was the worst that Victoria had ever known. Blizzard after blizzard swept over the city and the whole population was continually engaged in digging channels through the streets and organising food supplies. For months we lived under siege conditions and how my mother got us through it, I do not know.

When spring came at last, we moved to a great shack of a house standing by itself, over-looking a beautiful bay. We rented it for next to nothing and only lived in two rooms and we only possessed two beds, two chairs and a table and the floors were uncovered and the windows uncurtained. But we loved it.

At once, I longed for a boat and with some boys who lived near in a tumble-down shack, I went off to the forest and we chopped down some trees and dragged them back and cut them to size and nailed them together. We erected a mast and fixed up a sail and for the rest of the summer we sailed and paddled about.

It was while we were in this house that I was overcome by the last of my panic fears and I very much disgraced myself. My mother had just painted a little boy, the child of the father's second marriage. Thè girl, of his first marriage, was about my age and I was invited to go and play with these children. They had an English governess.

My mother left me at the house and soon we all sat down to tea. I hated the governess at once. She was a grim sour-looking woman. The little boy chattered away and looked happy but the girl looked miserable. She never spoke and the governess corrected everything she did. I sat silently eating and watching – and pitying her. Then, suddenly, I knew that this could happen to me. My mother could die and I could be adopted by people who did not love me and this thought was so terrible that I could not bear to stay a moment longer in the house. I jumped down from the table and ran into the hall and seized the telephone but the governess ran after me and stopped me, so I grabbed my coat and made for the door but she caught me and bolted it, high up out of reach. I felt imprisoned then and when the step-mother came, drawn by the noise, and the two of them held me and told me how silly and naughty I was – I fought and screamed until my mother came.

For a week or two I went to a little school but I found it too boring to stay. When I was not out on my raft, however, I began to develop an intense intellectual life of a military character.

I read the newspapers for the war news and the maps and I found some books on war and tried to understand them, for my passion was greater than ever and I still grieved for my soldier friends. But soon, all this enlightenment seemed dry and useless; it was getting me no nearer to France and a front-line trench – into action. Then I thought of a wonderful way.

There was a large empty room at the top of the house and now, after days of hard labour digging up the garden and carrying up buckets of earth, I managed to spread the entire floor with six inches of mud. Then, from the maps and photographs in the newspapers, I modelled and constructed a section of the Western Front.

With wood and cardboard I created the semi-ruined town of Ypres and around it famous war-torn villages. I brought in branches and planted trees but where the fighting was heavy, only leafless twigs. I raised up hills and traced out rivers, I brought in sand from the beach and built roads and then, when Belgium was finished, began work on the net-work of trenches around the salient. Front-line, support-line, communication trenches and dug-outs, cut deep into the mud, squiggled about from one end of the room to the other. And when everything was ready, in went the troops.

For a long time I had been collecting lead soldiers. With joy now, I placed them in their positions, fighting, relieved and resting and when I read of the mud of Flanders I saw to it that my mud was equally terrible and I poured jugs of water over it regularly. Imaginary battles took place daily and my happiness was profound for at last I was in it – at last I was fighting for England.

For two years we had been waiting in Victoria for the war to end and my mother grew bored and restless. We saved up and sold up and then boarded a ship for Los Angeles.

We left Pat with Andy. They would share the same bed and drink out of the same cup and lead their own especial predatory lives and meet when they felt like it and, however much he may have missed my mother, we believed that his life there would still be a good one. But, eventually, we heard that he had died.

5

Hollywood and Los Angeles

WHEN WE arrived in Hollywood we went straight to one of the big hotels and while my mother was signing the register I stood beside her staring about. I was now eight-years-old.

The desk was at the end of a large lounge which was arranged in a most extraordinary way. Innumerable deep settees were placed arm to arm in about half a dozen parallel rows. Seen from behind they looked like a series of hurdles with people sunk in the ditches between them talking, napping or just sitting. They were irresistible. I took a run from the desk and jumped over them all.

My mother watched this feat with admiration – and then waited for the storm. But nothing happened. A few of the sunken guests looked up dreamily but most went on talking and napping and sitting and the clerks at the desk and the porters looked utterly blank and indifferent, as if jumping the sofas was a regular practice. My mother was delighted for we had certainly come to the right country.

Within a few days, the same jumped-over guests were eagerly waiting their turns to be painted and soon my mother was out at the film studios painting the stars of the moment. And I always went with her.

One day, after watching a film being shot in a cardboard reconstruction of an English village, we were asked to step into the office to meet someone of importance. The great man was sitting with his feet on the table and a cigar in his mouth but he pulled himself up when we entered.

'I sure am pleased to meet you folks,' he began genially, holding out a huge fat hand. We all sat down smiling.

'I gotta swell proposition for you, Ma'am.' My mother was sure that he was going to commission a life-size portrait of himself. 'I wanna make this cute little kiddie of yours into a film star. I gotta contract right here an' all you gotta do is sign it. Why, Momma, this kid'll be making you millions before you can turn round.'

My mother was astonished but she did not hesitate a moment.

'Your offer is very kind,' she replied rather primly, 'but I don't really want her to do this – and we shall soon be returning to England.'

'Come, come now, Ma'am,' he went on in a humouring, confident tone.

'Maybe you won't never wanna go back to England when this kid's scoopin' up all that dough. Maybe you'll settle down right here.' My mother got up. 'You jes go right home, Ma'am, an' do some reel hard thinking an' then come back,' he said as he squeezed her hand and patted me on the head. We walked away thoughtfully through all the cardboard shrines of Europe.

She was already disillusioned with Hollywood. She disliked the stars, the bosses and the whole meretricious place. It was bad enough prostituting her own art, but not for all the money in the world would she risk the corruption of my character. We moved to Los Angeles. And she never regretted.

She was now serious about sending me to school, to one of the public, or state, schools which she heard were so good but when she asked which were the best (meaning, of course, in a class sense) she was told that there were no 'best', that they were all equally good and, misinterpreting this, she cheerfully took a furnished apartment in a building surrounded by empty lots, brown, treeless and dusty. While she was unpacking I went out to look for some children.

I stood for awhile listening and when I heard some cries and yells, headed in their direction and when I came within view stopped, and sat down and watched, conscious that I too, was being observed. They were playing baseball and after awhile I moved a little nearer.

A mighty swipe and loud report sent the ball flying in my direction and I leapt up and sped after it and hurled it smartly back to them, thus demonstrating my prowess and friendly intentions. After that, I advanced again, acting as unofficial out-fielder and then, creeping still closer, for a few tense moments I was among them – in the game. Then they stopped and the gang came crowding round me.

'What'chu doin' here?' one of them asked.

'I've come to live in the apartment house in Manning Street.' I sensed hostility at once. My voice gave me away.

'Where you come from?' asked another.

'I'm English.'

'English! England's a bum country!'

I'd never heard that word before but I guessed it was an insult.

'England's a fine country,' I answered.

'We beat the English in the War of Independence.' They were all shouting now. 'We threw the tea into Boston Harbour. King George III was an' old bum.'

I was thunderstruck by all this. I knew nothing about Anglo-American history and I didn't know what to answer. And the unfriendliness and rudeness hurt me.

'England's the greatest country in the world!' was all I could think to retort.

'England's a dirty stinking country.'

'It isn't.'

'It is.'

One of them had been drawing nearer and nearer and at this moment he flung himself upon me. I had never fought before, never been in such a hateful and inexplicable situation. We clutched and twisted and threw each other about; we coiled our legs round each other's legs, we tripped each other up and bent each other over backwards and rolled together in the dust. Neither could get the better of the other and we only stopped when we were both exhausted. I arrived back in the new apartment covered with dust, my clothes torn – and weeping.

The United States had not yet come into the war and the Hearst chain of German-inspired newspapers were doing their best to keep her out, drenching the country with anti-British propaganda.

My mother knew nothing about the War of Independence either, so we went to a library the next day and studied some history books. Then, armed with all the counter-arguments, elaborated to improve and colour my case, I went back to re-engage the enemy.

'What you said about England was wrong,' I shouted as I tore into the middle of their game. 'You didn't beat the English. It was only mercenaries you beat, hired soldiers from some inferior country. And England didn't want America any more, anyway. She was sick and tired of such a troublesome lot and so silly and wasteful, too, throwing all that good tea into the sea.'

I waited to see the effect, expecting another fight. But they were not even listening. I could hear the smack of the ball dropping into their gloves as they lobbed it lazily from one to the other. They had lost all interest.

'Gee, kid, when you gonna quit talkin'?' drawled my enemy at last with a bored expression as, good naturedly, he pushed his bat into my hands. 'C'mon, yer can bat'. And the next moment we were far away from Boston Harbour and all that, completely absorbed in the game.

This was my first *real* fight for England and afterwards, I entered these contests filled with valour and fought, according to my mood as one of the Knights of the Round Table or as a British officer leading my men over the top. And I became invincible.

The gang soon initiated me into another much more violent game. We lined up along the edge of our lot while across the unpaved road a rival gang faced us, each with a pile of stones – and then the battle began. We would fling and dodge until our piles were gone and a truce was called and we scoured the ground for the stones which had fallen round us.

It may have been a feud, or it may have begun simply as a harsh, self-testing game and then developed into war. The gangs really hated each other and as I watched the line of boys across the road day after day, their faces set and hard, viciously hurling their stones and, dodging, saw and felt them whizzing past me, I too, began to hate them.

So many American games were of a violent nature. It was not just the exceptional vigour of the children. There seemed to be a masochistic need to match their courage with danger, to put themselves through extravagant tests, to submit to constant ordeals.

I don't think I was affected by this games ethos for I never courted danger for its own sake, simply for the satisfaction derived from facing it. Often I turned back if I thought it prudent. I only faced it when I enjoyed it or when it stood between me and something that I wanted – some purpose. Much later, I began consciously seeking out experience for the knowledge to be gained from it and not for pure satisfaction (generally there was only pain). And later still, I sought experience for the experience itself without desiring fruits of any kind. These are three different springs of action.

The local school was rough, grim and depressing but my mother was soon aware that we had settled in the wrong quarter and among the 'worst' schools and so we moved and kept on moving (and nearly everywhere there was a fight) until we arrived in one of the 'best' residential districts and I entered one of the 'best' schools.

We travelled with a large Saratoga trunk full of cushions, lampshades, pictures, books, ornaments and cutlery (we couldn't eat, even when camping, unless we had silver forks and spoons and ivory-handled knives) and when we arrived in a new place, while I was reconnoitring the neighbourhood, she arranged the rooms. She could do everything herself except hang the pictures. 'Oh there you are at last!' she would cry gaily when I reappeared. 'Now let's do the pictures.' And while she climbed on a chair with the hammer and nails, I took up my position on the opposite side of the room and concentrating hard, indicated the centres of walls, levels, and distances apart. During the seven years that we lived abroad we went through this process of home-making again and again, always with the same enjoyment and satisfaction.

My mother could make homes anywhere; in sordid lodgings and boarding houses, in ugly bungalows and apartment houses, in tumble-down shacks and even tents, out came these touches of England and herself and our home always seemed beautiful and stylish and superior to everybody else's. And when her paints were unpacked she sat down to work.

West Adams Street, where we were now settled in a bright little apartment house, was the western arm of a broad main road running across the city and ending at the coast. All along it stood large houses in tropical gardens occupied by wealthy businessmen and in the roads leading off it, were smaller houses in which mostly professional families lived. Not far from our apartment house was Orchard Street and it was there, as one of the 'Orchard Street Kids', that I now entered upon another rapturous period of living.

My mother was soon painting some of the Orchard Street families and by one of these I was formally introduced to the 'kids' and I joined in their games at once and, for a few days, believed that I'd been accepted. Then a big girl picked a quarrel and out came an insult to England. These children would not have been infected with propaganda by their parents but they picked it up at their schools.

I retorted with my stock defensive arguments and the next minute we were fighting. The contest was between nimbleness and bulk. My strategy was to get her off her balance and trip her up, hers to crush me with her weight. Often she picked me up bodily and then I coiled round her like an octopus; sometimes, locked together, we rolled each other over and over on the ground but when she seemed to be pinning me down, I always wriggled out and clambered over her again. We unclenched, only to spring at each other afresh and then, suddenly, I tripped her and flung her to the ground and stood looking down at her, believing I had won. But with one accord the kids cried out, 'you've gotta *keep* her down! you've gotta *keep* her down!' and she sprang up and the whole thing started again.

My mind was like a fist of iron now and when I threw her once more, like a demon I jumped on her. 'Sit on her head! Pin her arms down over her head!' they cried helpfully. And brutally I forced her arms above her head and pressed down on them with my whole weight until tortured, she gave in. And the kids looked down on us and approved. I was accepted.

My new school was unique in having a children's orchestra, of which it was very proud. Every morning, the four musicians played us to our class-rooms with great verve and they were able to make such a stupendous noise that we could hear it far away on the edge of the playground where we lined up on arrival. After the band of the regiment I thought it ludicrous but I felt that they were working hard and aspiring in the right direction and I swung up the stairs gaily to the thumping of the piano, the tinkling of the triangle, the squeaking of the fiddle and the blast of the fourth instrument whose precise contribution to the ensemble I fail to remember.

It was at this school, because it was so musical, no doubt, that I learnt to sing the 'Stars and Stripes' so well. The classes were enormous but I did not feel lost. I was very happy there. The playground was full of swings and slides and I thought a lot of my teacher, Miss Kelly, even when I decided that her moral code was not the same as mine. I was always catching her out in fibs and I knew she was not to be trusted. But she was young and pretty and gay.

But very soon my mother learnt from her wealthy sitters that private and most exclusive schools also existed in this egalitarian country and soon I found myself in the most ultra exclusive of them all. It was also in West Adams Street; a fine white neo-colonial house in a beautiful garden with a bamboo grove at the end.

My teacher, Mrs Lennox, was English and she made a great thing of her genteel voice but, sad to say, I disliked her at once. And she disliked me. She was elderly, with a girlish bounciness which greatly irritated me and when I got to know her, I thought her snobbish and vindictive.

Soon after I arrived, she took us to a gymnastic class in a room which had the appearance of a salon. Crystal chandeliers hung from the ceilings, gilt framed mirrors were on the walls and fine satin curtains adorned the high windows. She stayed watching, sitting on a Louis Seize chair.

We were told to take our shoes off. I hesitated, for my socks had two large holes in them and when, at last, I did I felt all the snobbish, exclusive eyes focused upon my heels – especially those of Mrs Lennox.

The children were so smartly dressed, so loaded with possessions and large automobiles, driven by uniformed chauffeurs, brought and fetched them every day. All these marks of wealth fascinated me although the children themselves, I found very dull. They never wanted to play and just sat round the garden talking.

I was always being punished for something but, one day, Mrs Lennox over-reached herself. She accused me of leaning to one side so that the girl behind could overlook my work and she moved me to a baby desk at the far end of the room where I had to sit alone. I waited a few days and when it became clear that the punishment was to be perpetual, I decided suddenly that I'd had enough – and enough of Mrs Lennox and the whole school.

The morning break came and we all went into the garden and while she chattered and giggled and the children vied with each other to hold her hand and sit beside her, I vanished into the bamboo grove. I couldn't wait until the afternoon. I couldn't endure her a moment longer. And, of course, the pleasure of imagining her consternation when I didn't come in and the fuss she would make and the frenzy she would get into, added savour to the dramatic departure.

When they were gone, I came out of the grove and made my way through the bushes to the high front fence. I climbed it and dropped down into West Adams Street. I still had to pass the house which was close to the road with a low hedge in front of it and two wide in-and-out gateways. I shot across the first of these and crept along below the level of the hedge. When I stopped a moment to peep I could see, through the open windows, the senior children and teachers in the big front rooms and hear the lessons going on. Once past the house I never stopped running until I reached home.

In absconding as I did, with no intention of returning, I was never for one moment afraid of my mother's displeasure, never afraid that she would force me to go back. I was only afraid of her disappointment, her regret that I was not remaining at such a fine school. I knew what a lot of money it cost her, what a lot she thought of it and to leave like this, seemed ungrateful and a reflection on her judgment. I was sure she would be very hurt and dejected.

She was certainly very surprised to see me and while she listened I watched her face but I could see no sudden change. She remained quite cheerful and when I had finished my account, her reply absolutely astounded me.

'I've always thought Mrs Lennox looked a silly old thing and if *you* don't like her and you don't think much of the school then there's no point in you staying there.'

I was so relieved, so delighted; not only because I hadn't had to disappoint her, but because my judgment was proved right. I so often judged wrongly. But this time, in this big important matter, I was not mistaken. This success, of course, strengthened my predilection for making my own decisions.

Before I left, a curious thing happened. During the rainy season the deeply sunk gutters, running along the high flood pavements, became like raging rivers. Plank bridges, tied to lamp-posts, were flung over them for pedestrians and it was customary for motor cars to stop and give lifts over the impassable places.

One morning, I had reached the big cross-roads – West Adams and Figuroa Streets – enjoying the fun of it, but there the torrent was tremendous and I could get no further. I went to a place where I could be picked up and a car soon stopped. A particularly unpleasant type of man opened the door and told me to get in. This was not the custom and I had been warned never to get into any car, for the kidnapping of children was a common crime. Rich children for the ransoms and little girls for the brothels. They were whisked over the Mexican border and never heard of again. My mother lived in fear of this.

I told him that I would stand on the running-board, that everybody crossed like that. But he wouldn't hear of it. I would not be safe, he said, and he didn't want me to get drowned. And why couldn't I get in and sit beside him? Where was the harm, he asked? He made me feel so foolish and ungrateful and only some deep residue of my mother's warnings and my own distrust of the man, enabled me to withstand him. I stayed where I was, keeping well out of his reach.

'If you don't get in I won't take you,' he then shouted angrily and I came out of his spell at once. My will was my own again.

'I'll stay here. I shan't fall off,' I repeated – firmly now.

'I'm not taking you! Get off!' he yelled, slamming the door and driving on. I was so upset and so afraid of all other cars that I turned and went home, missing school that day.

If the man was just an over-careful and well-intentioned person then the incident is trivial and of no significance. It is because the experience was one of such strongly sensed evil and fear which I feel even now that, although unprovable, I recount it.

After leaving the millionaires' school I stayed at home for awhile. But I had plenty of interests and my life with the Orchard Street kids was enthralling. Every afternoon, when they came home from school I tore across the road to join them.

Sammy was our leader. He was 12-years-old, short and broad and tough with a broken front tooth, freckled face, small light, enigmatic eyes and an aloof taciturn nature. I never thought much of his looks nor his charms but as a leader he was splendid; wild as wild and brave as brave. I was then nine.

He was constantly in trouble with the Police and often locked up, his father bailing him out in the evening. Once he was left all night in a cell in the hope of cooling him down. But it did no good. Gaols didn't scare him.

One day, he stole a motor car parked at the school gates, drove it back to Orchard Street, piled all the kids into it and took them on a joy-ride to the coast. The open car was literally stuffed with children; sitting up on the folded hood, crammed together in the back, spilling over the sides and hanging over the windscreen – with Sammy at the wheel. As I stood watching, they cried out to me to squeeze in quick and come too. But my mother's injunction never to go far from home and my own inner prudence restrained me.

He stepped on the clutch, let in the gear, the car shot violently forward, then gathered speed quickly and whirled into the traffic of West Adams Street. Conscious of their contempt I went home. There was no one left to play with. The Pied Piper of Orchard Street had lured all the children away.

They returned safely, even more joyously than they set forth, having had a wonderful time. Sammy, of course, was in trouble again. But what did he care? He had had his fun. He just laughed.

The time came when he decided to put himself and all of us on trial. It was not a struggle for supremacy for he was already our acknowledged leader, but just a testing of the gang, a marathon obstacle race up one side of Orchard Street and down the other. We scrambled over high fences, shinned up trees, dropped onto garage roofs, clambered over sheds and galloped through people's gardens.

The next day he made the course stiffer, runners fell out at once and we strained to keep up with him. Only four of us were left when he led us to a three-storey house. Like a monkey he ran up a drainpipe and then crawled up the roof to the ridge and disappeared. I followed but when I reached the roof and saw how steep and slippery it was, I climbed down again. The others made no attempt at all. The next moment, Sammy appeared, having descended on the other side. He had passed the test and the kids had all failed.

But this was not the end. The next day, we gathered once more for the final trial – for the conquest of the Kingdom itself. At the end of another elimination course he ran up to the bole of the Great Tree.

Standing in the middle of Orchard Street, like a lone giant, was an immense tropical tree. At its base it must have been at least six feet in diameter and it grew erect and tapering into the sky. Secretly we worshipped it. It was our totem-pole.

No one had ever climbed it. It was believed to be unclimbable and my mother had forbidden me ever to try. We stood at its base and looked up through the thick dark maze of its branches – and I was appalled. The kids gathered round to watch. We took off our shoes.

Choosing a part of the tree's body where the bark was deeply scored, Sammy dug his fingers and toes into the dry fibrous casing and lifted himself off the ground. He climbed a few feet, then lost his grip and dropped and started again. This time, he worked his way up to within reach of the lowest branch – and then fell again ... The third time, climbing steadily and strongly, he again drew level with the branch and flung himself at it, kicking out at the trunk with his feet for leverage – and he dragged himself over it. Silent and serious he straddled it and watched us struggling below.

Again and again I started, each time scaling the rough ribbed wall a little higher, my fingers and toes getting the feel and the measure of it. I knew I could do it if I kept at it long enough and when I reached that first forbidding bough, with a violent effort I pulled myself over it. Two others followed. We were four who had conquered the base and set out to conquer the tree.

We looked up and studied the way, then Sammy moved. At first the branches were thick and widely spaced and our progress was slow – and I was the last. Through the dark lower reaches we climbed silently, withdrawn from the world into a shaft of powerful and mysterious beauty whose living steps led up and up into a blissful light and moving tenuous reality which drew us on, but still we could not see. About a third of the way we could feel the tree's movement and the breeze sift through the outer wall of leaves and hear the branches scraping and ringing. Sammy climbed faster now and I pressed for a moment and passed one of the others.

Halfway, the tree was swaying and light was reaching through to us and vignettes of the outer world kept appearing, sliding, changing, vanishing and reappearing as the thick sprays and heavy clusters moved in the wind, opening and closing, rising and falling as in a dance. I looked down but the ground had gone, we seemed to have left the earth and to be swinging free in the sky like a bird in a cage held by an invisible chain let down from the heavens above. The one below I could no longer see and the one above me was climbing more slowly and I passed him – and now Sammy and I were climbing together.

Three quarters of the way the tree swayed frighteningly and I waited, held by the rocking and my sudden alarm. Sammy went on. The others had stopped and when I moved again, Sammy and I were climbing alone.

With each wide swing it felt as if the tree would fall or as if I would be shaken off. I didn't dare look up or down or out but kept my eyes fixed on the soft brown trunk, clinging to the branches almost in despair, pulling and pressing so that one by one I reached and passed them, not knowing how or why. Then suddenly, just when it seemed as if there was no end to this, Sammy spoke and I looked up – and there we were, at the green and waving pinnacle.

The tree was swinging violently now, the houses looked like little boxes, the kids staring up at us like dolls and the other trees like bushes and I remembered that my mother had forbidden me ever to climb it. And she was always right, always right about everything and so would she be right about this, I wondered in wildest panic? Would I ever get down, had I climbed the tree, climbed to the top – and climbed to my end? I sat gripping the tree – gripped by my terror.

But after awhile, sitting together in the sparkling crown with the leaves and branches humming in the wind, I got used to the rocking of the strong safe cradle and we began to talk. We looked down upon the great untidy city spreading in all directions, upon the desert beyond it stretching golden brown until the mountains rose and stopped it. We looked for buildings that we knew and for palm groves sheltering the old Spanish Mission Houses and, in the west, we could see the blue Pacific. Searching for things that we had heard of, we found things that we knew nothing of. In the swaying crest of the Great Tree we discovered an eagle's speering world which we kept to ourselves, were never able to describe – and never wanted to.

A few days later, when he came home from business, Sammy's father walked up to him and with a wink and a grin, hooked his foot round his ankle and with a jerk sent him sprawling. He thought he was looking too cocky – and the kids all laughed. But I hated seeing him tossed like that before us all. He was so brave and brilliant. It was a mean thing to do, I thought.

We were now rather close but I had no inkling of anything like love until, one day, the kids announced our wedding. There were no more games for they were all too busy constructing our honeymoon house and we were forbidden to approach and left alone to amuse each other. We soon found our life together most boring and were thankful when the kids had finished their work.

They built a framework of wood on top of a flat-roofed garage and then stretched material over it so that it looked like an elevated bedouin tent. When the day came, I wore a voluminous wedding veil and after the ceremony we were conducted, arm-in-arm, to the base of our house. We climbed up and then stood for a moment on the parapet, acknowledging the homage of the kids.

Inside, were two wooden grocer's boxes and between them on the floor, two large ice-cream cones melting onto a piece of newspaper, a bag of popcorn, two cigarettes and some matches. We sat down on the boxes and fell to. Outside, sprawling on the ground, the kids waited and listened.

We didn't speak and when the nuptial feast was ended we sat and looked at each other; just sat and looked and grinned, with the kids waiting and listening. Then, we jumped up and rushed out and the kids sprang up as we sprang down. I tore off my veil as I ran and with whoops and yells we stampeded away to hurl ourselves into some game.

It was a great life in Orchard Street. We must have been the scourge of the neighbourhood yet there was no hostility between the householders and the children, no unpleasantness at all. I only remember one poor woman protesting when her garden was trampled over – and she was very mild. This was, indeed, the country of the children.

As well as this exciting outer life, I was now developing a lively inner one. All sorts of problems were beginning to interest and disturb me and, although I chattered to my mother about everything else, I said nothing about these.

I discovered first what seemed to be my dual nature; my two sides which I called 'soft' and 'hard', noting how I changed from one to the other in a matter of seconds.

My soft side I revealed only to my mother. But in the past a love mood, 'let's have a love', had always been involuntary. I never knew when to expect it. Now, I found that just by consciously thinking, or willing it, I could command it – switch it on and off, as it were, and I practised doing this.

My hard side was the one which I showed to the world and it, too, I found I could command. I was quite baffled. I was not one person as I had always believed – but two, and doomed for the rest of my life to be always on the move, shuttling backwards and forwards, in and out of my two selves.

Another anxiety and aspect of my multiple nature, was the poorness of my judgement. I so often had to make decisions, whether to do this or do that, stay here or go there, and nearly always I chose wrong – or so it seemed to me. I thought I must be very stupid, mentally 'wanting' perhaps.

I think the cause of my confusion was that I could not distinguish between reason and intuition. In a rational environment I grew up distrusting my intuitive faculties, so often refusing to listen to the powerful voices which seemed to speak out of my whole body. Instead, I struggled to reach decisions by means of my intellect and when it failed me or when the answers clashed with those of my body, I went wrong. When education and an even more pressurised environment developed my intellect, the intuition was suppressed still more.

I was years finding out that there were four ways of knowing, four disparate bodies, and until I did I floundered between them, listening to their divorced and incompatible voices, never knowing which to obey and which to stifle.

These were not my only problems. I had others of a higher order. All my American schools had most thoroughly succeeded in teaching me about George Washington and the cherry tree – and his little axe, of course. I was most impressed by this story but at the same time desperately downhearted because I knew that I could never equal him in moral perfection. In fact, I knew that I had no moral courage at all. I was so often chopping down a cherry tree and so seldom was I brave enough to own up. I felt very humiliated to be cutting such a poor figure beside him and worried too, for without a doubt, there was a flaw in my character – and I didn't know how to repair it.

Fitted somewhere among all these new anxieties – and interests, for they were absorbing as well as painful – I passed through a long period of agonising over the crucified Christ. Although I knew that it all happened 2,000 years ago, yet He seemed to suffer still and I wept whenever I thought of Him stretched on the Cross. And I was terrified of pain and knew that I was not only a moral coward but a physical one, too.

Although my new inner life was so shattering yet, thanks to some saving mechanism, my confidence in myself and joy in living were in no way affected. Then something momentous happened. I had a vision – at least, that is what I called it.

I was playing alone one day when everything round me suddenly vanished, I left my present self and leapt forward into the future where I could see myself raised up and looking down upon the world. And the figure that I saw was a military hero, a very valiant English soldier, a colonel, riding on a horse and leading a great column of men while below in the vacant lots were my friends, grown no bigger, still grovelling in the dust playing the same childish games and as I passed I looked down on them, proudly and pityingly. And riding on, I seemed to grow and grow in strength until I was filled with a marvellous power and I knew there was nothing that I could not do; that I could lift, I could lead, I could rescue the world. And I wrote my first poem.

What ho my lads what ho my boys
Still playing your little games
Me on my hors trotting along
Leading my men
Alas the carnel is dead
Down to the ground he falls
But we still remember him to this day
As brave old carnel South.

Perhaps the 'carnel's' pride and downfall predict my ambition and achievements — and ultimate worldly failure.

When the vision faded I contracted to my normal size but I lived in a state of exaltation for a long time. On that day, I believe, the pattern was repeated and another family genius was launched. Of course, my mother had been certain from the moment I was born that I was a genius and she constantly talked of the remarkable, still unrevealed, talents that I possessed and although I would have liked to believe her, yet I could never take her praises and predictions seriously. Such assumptions, I felt, were extravagant and just the fantasies of an adoring mother. For how could she know? What had I done? What proof had she?

On the other hand, I had to admit that I myself had for a long time believed in my special destiny – and without any proof. I was sure that I had some great work to do and the feeling of obligation and uncertainty always made me uneasy. But now I had proof that this vague irrational belief in myself was valid and that my life was a dedicated one. The ending of the uncertainty was a relief, the proven knowledge of my future frightening but exhilarating. I spent the next 15 years looking for the road which my vision had marked out for me.

The war and my days with the soldiers in Victoria first aroused my love for military heroes and putting on a uniform myself first transformed me into a man and inspired me with a desire for martial glory. But this continuing transposition into the masculine sex I believe had other, more complex reasons.

I had become very conscious of the inferiority of my sex. I was always noticing that boys were thought more of than girls and, in all the books that I read and stories I was told, the heroes were all men, the great deeds were performed by men – never by women. This put me in a very difficult position. I was going to perform great deeds myself but according to all the records and prevailing evidence this was physiologically impossible.

From this dilemma I could see no way out. The inescapable fact of my inferiority and incapacity often shook my belief in myself, yet in spite of the evidence and appearances, my confidence always revived and the power of my vision now made it unassailable. But still the dilemma remained. And so, to do what I was going to do I felt, in an obscure way, that I would somehow have to change my sex and that is why, in the vision, I saw myself not just as a military hero – but as a man, to whom achievements were permitted.

6

Money, Motor Cars and Gangsters

THIS YEAR, Miss Morison's baptismal-day letter was very effusive – and with it came a cheque. With this money, she wrote, I was to buy myself a gold wrist-watch and have the words 'From your loving Godmother' inscribed on the back.

I ought to have been very pleased with this wonderful letter and generous gift but, somehow, I wasn't. I didn't want a gold watch. I was very fond of my big, black-faced dollar twenty five Ingersoll and the thank-you letter I knew would be very difficult to write.

However, I had to do everything she asked me. I was so lucky to have her as my godmother and I was looking forward to going to her school some day. My mother and I set off down-town to choose it and have it inscribed and, when it was done, we brought it home and put it carefully away and I sat down to describe its beauty and tell her how grateful I was.

I got as far as 'My dear Godmother' (she had asked me to call her that) and then I stopped. I could not bear that name – on paper or at the back of the watch. I read her letter again. She seemed to love me so. But I didn't love her. I didn't know her. But I could not write coldly back as I felt. That would hurt her. And how *could* she love me as much as she did and expect me to love her, too? For she seemed to expect it. I didn't know how to answer. And I couldn't confide in my mother. I was too inarticulate and I knew how much she loved Miss Morison herself. It would hurt her, too, if she knew that I didn't.

In the end, overpowered by thinking, I decided to write in the same tone that she wrote to me. I would have to *pretend* to love her until I met her and *really* did. And so, it was a loving, grateful, humbug letter that I sent.

I am sure Miss Morison believed that it was purely a godmother's love that she felt for me. Perhaps this very godmother position had been instrumental in developing and then confusing one love with another. She adored me now, not with the cool touch of a mother-in-God but with the bosomy warmth of a flesh-and-blood mother – and this bitter maternal passion grew.

As well as my own entrancing lives in Los Angeles, I led yet another most interesting one with my mother and her friends. By this time, she was moving busily and gaily in and out of two quite different worlds – the millionaires' world and the Bohemians' – and in between, belonging to no distinct group at all, there were many other quaint or exotic people.

On a slight rise to the west of the city was a row of mansions and one of them, red brick pseudo-Georgian, we came to know very well. The best feature of the whole palatial property, so far as I was concerned, was the enormous tiled swimming pool below the wide imposing terrace.

Inside, were countless awe-inspiring rooms, each a replica of a different period and country. The dining room, which I knew best, was unmistakeably English in style and restraint. One of the drawing-rooms was a veritable paradise of gilt, glitter, sparkle and sheen; of golden chairs and tables, canopies of chandeliers and weightless cabinets filled with clouds of translucent china; of satins and fine brocades and silken ropes and monstrous tassels and hangings like high ceremonial vestments and carpets as soft and rare as the ground of heaven itself. Another room was a thick rich riot of rococo and baroque while the bedrooms were so gorgeous, the beds so exquisite that one would never have dared to sleep in them, and as for the bathrooms – they took one's breath away!

The creators of all this sumptuousness and tumult were my mother's patrons and friends, Virginia and Russell Taylor. Although still quite young, Russell had made a fortune in the east and retired to a dream life of perpetual idleness and pleasure – with which he appeared perfectly satisfied. He was always smiling and relaxed. Nothing upset him and everything pleased him.

Virginia, on the other hand, was nothing like so content with a life which was, and still is, the envy of mankind. She was always nervous and on edge and for hours together, she regaled my mother with stories of Russell's shortcomings. But nothing, it seemed, could be done about them and so she filled her life with distraction and he was happy to assist.

It appeared as if their lives were composed entirely of picnics and bathing parties – the agreeable entertainments to which we were regularly invited. But I suppose they were only the climatic counterparts of high-life everywhere.

A fleet of cadillacs would take us either to the foothills of the mountains where, in exotic valleys we spread ourselves beside warm lakes, or to exclusive country clubs. And, in between these excursions, were the parties round the pool when the most delectable dishes and amazing drinks never stopped flowing out of the house, onto the terrace and then round among the guests, who sat about under coloured umbrellas and jumped in and out of the water. It was a life of active indolence beneath the cheerful and seductive Californian sun.

The magnetic centre of Bohemia was a lively, gregarious little man called

William Rust. He lived and worked and entertained in a long, low, one-roomed shack built on the edge of a ravine, shaded from the sun by eucalytpus and pepper trees. Here, once a week, people gathered, bringing their food and pooling it on arrival. He had no money. He was a writer.

In the long room and out on the veranda the guests split into small groups and passionate talk about art and life went on half the night with the happy host moving among them. From time to time the groups broke up, flowed for awhile and then reformed and always, sooner or later, there was music. Sometimes, the evenings were entirely musical. Professionals would come and play informally. And over the house the leaves of the trees glistened and their scent was heavy. I adored these nights.

When the hot months came and our friends had all left for cooler places and we wilted in Los Angeles, having no money to go away – one of the Bohemians invited us out to his shack on the coast.

William Swift Daniell was the most terrible painter but the kindest of men. He daubed from morning to night and his output, naturally, was enormous. He was never satisfied with less than three finished pictures a day and the canvasses piled up until they stood in stacks round the walls of the shack. But he knew what he was doing. There was demand for his work and he had to supply it. He gave one-man shows in a big department store in the city and his products sold as fast as automobiles and ice-boxes.

When we arrived, he announced that he would like to paint a picture of my mother reclining on the sands in a bathing suit. She fell in with this charming idea and the next morning we three set forth to carry it out. Mr Daniell set up his easel and umbrella, my mother posed and work began. But very soon she realised that she was being burnt alive – and so was I, racing about the beach. Abruptly the work stopped and with flaming flesh we returned to the shack. Soon, we were in such pain that we had to take to our beds where, for several days, we lay in burning misery. We were new to that cruel sun and the bathing-beauty picture was never finished.

The Pacific rollers were gigantic – or so it seemed to me then. They came in fast and each in turn rose up and opened like the terrifying mouth of a leviathan and then closed again, crashing on the beach with a roar. One had to dive into a towering mouth before it snapped and caught one, and swim through the deep blue throat, up and out beyond them. To get back, one rode in on the head of a monster and landed, if one timed it right, clear of the next one. I loved this game.

It was a lonely barren part of the coast and we always kept to the beach for the scrub was full of rattle-snakes and the hinterland was cactus-covered desert.

It was walking up the wide beach that my mother stepped into a quicksand and was sinking fast as we all ran up to her. We circled round as near as we dared, something was improvised and thrown to her and, already buried to her waist, she was pulled out.

People thought nothing of such experiences in a country where there were so many natural and man-made hazards to life. When the heat was over we returned to Los Angeles.

I had not been to school for a long time and as my private pursuits were losing some of their flavour and the idea once again became attractive, my mother searched for somewhere else to send me and discovered the ideal establishment. Ideal, at any rate, for me.

It was in a plain, unpretentious house, also on West Adams Street, and run by an elderly spinster and her mother. Except for a *real* mademoiselle who attended twice a week, these two comprised the entire staff. Miss Fulmer had a gentle voice and gentle, kind, unhurried ways. It was a happy little school with no sharp correcting and no punishments and the first in which I really learnt something. I was excited by everything they taught me. Yet, in this sympathetic atmosphere, I am sorry to say, I committed a most serious moral crime.

America had come into the war and, being patriotic, we all had war gardens. I was passionately interested in mine. I dug up the seeds every other day to see how they were doing and watered them so abundantly that it was a wonder they were not all washed away. And when they actually appeared out of the earth, watching and measuring their progress, my enthusiasm growing as they grew – I deluged them.

Then, one unfortunate day, looking about and making comparisons between my plants and others, I noticed that one of the plots was dust dry and apparently forgotten. I should, of course, have made sure that the owner was not on his way to attend to it. Instead, without taking thought at all, and rather pleased at the chance of some extra watering, I filled a succession of cans and effectively swamped it. I had no sooner finished than a hullabaloo arose. 'Somebody's watered my garden,' screamed the owner all over the school and everyone hurried to the scene. In an instant, a harmless if not strictly correct action, had become a serious crime.

'Did *you* water Tommy's garden?' Miss Fulmer asked me.

'No,' I blurted out.

She believed me and strolled away leaving me paralysed with shock and shame. For as soon as I had denied it I recovered from my bewilderment and could easily have owned up. But now it was too late. I had committed a second and far worse sin. I had lied. I was quite stunned by the terrible situation I had got myself into. If I had not liked Miss Fulmer so, perhaps I would not have minded so much, but to sink so low in her eyes, to have her confidence in me shaken – was agony. And more and more agonies were disclosed, vanity and pride; I piled them one upon the other until my soul was in a desperate state. And soon, I became convinced that I must, in some way, be transparent and my guilt visible to everyone. All day long I wrestled with myself and when, at last, I was ready to confess and I looked round expecting all eyes to be fixed upon me, watching and waiting for the awful moment of repentance – no one so much as glanced my way and Miss Fulmer was just the same, showing no signs of disappointment in me whatsoever. No one cared any longer who watered the garden and the whole incident had blown over – like the War of Independence. It had never meant anything to anyone – except me.

Jimmy North and his wife had first come for their health and then stayed on in California. They lived near us and we were in and out of their house daily. He was something of a philosopher and would hold forth for hours on end, his wife and my mother joining in occasionally and I stretched on the floor listening.

'Los Angeles is a city of the quick or the dead!' he would exclaim and then travel away through all the countries and continents of the globe and on and out through all the systems and beliefs to the boundaries of the universe and knowledge itself and then return abruptly to 'this hell-bent, crazy country of money, motor cars and gangsters!' They lived old-fashioned English lives with books, needle-work and a few like-minded friends. We loved them. They were like grandparents.

Charles Lummis was a poet and historian and one of the leading authorities on the indigenous races of North and South America. He had lived for years among the Indians, recording their folk tales and songs and for his work in restoring old Spanish Mission Houses, he had been decorated by the King of Spain.

Wrenching the rock out of the desert he had built his own house and continually added to it – designless, growing out in all directions with a tower-like room rising up in the centre. It was covered by thick, tangled, richly flowering creepers and did not look like a house at all, but like a huge tropical plant, half tree, half bush, pushing out of the sand and scrub and cactus, reaching out further every year with its roots, spreading and growing until its ragged, bulbous form dominated the plain.

I remember two of the rooms; the tower, reached by a winding stone staircase, with windows on all sides from which, as he worked, Mr Lummis kept watch on the surrounding expanses – and the dining-room or refectory, thrusting out like an arm from the centre with a cloister on one side.

The interior was a mingling of Indian and Spanish styles. Woven rugs and covers, basket, bead-work and pottery combined naturally with monastic-type furniture, tall candle-holders and huge finely chased brass and silver platters and ampullas. It was civilised and patrician in its orderliness and still, purposed beauty – while the outside was tribal. Indian women, shy and withdrawn, darted about the kitchen quarters, peeping or staring, while dark babies crawled and tumbled about the court-yard among the hens and goats – everything untidy and untouched with a moving, variegated beauty.

My mother went to this desert outpost to paint Mr Lummis. She was taken up to the tower room by a servant where she waited until, suddenly and silently, he came. He had strong features, a proud, grave expression – and the mark of a bullet in his cheek.

'Can you work in this room?' he asked her, in a withdrawn slightly absent tone.

'Yes. The light on the north side is splendid – if I may draw the curtains where the sun comes in.'

He went from window to window swinging the curtains together while she placed a chair in position.

'Shall we try this?' she said, and he sat down and remained motionless and silent while she walked about, testing the light and gazing at the different angles of his face.

'I want to do you three-quarter view,' she said at last.

'Be sure to do the side with the bullet hole,' and he smiled then.

She was using oils as a medium now whenever she could, for the larger work paid better and was less of a strain. While she was preparing her things he recounted the wild story of how he was shot. When she was ready she looked him critically up and down again.

'What clothes would you like me to paint you in?' she asked him.

'What I've got on will do.'

'Underclothes?' He looked vaguely down at himself in vest and pants. 'They're so ugly. I don't want to paint them,' she said.

'Alright, I'll go and put something more on.' And he left the room as silently as he came, in his soft mocassin shoes.

After a few minutes he returned, looking most remarkable. He had flung on a home-spun shirt which reached to his bare knees, an old leather jacket and, round his neck, the decoration given him by the King of Spain.

'Will this do?' he said as he sat down again.

'Yes, that's lovely – most paintable.'

She went several times and when the picture was finished he hung it among the treasures and relics of American history and his own adventurous and creative life, in that high desert watch-room in which it was painted. After that, whenever she returned, she took me.

Charles Lantz, the humble little Jewish lawyer, lived alone in a large tasteless house on Figuroa Street and as soon as he met my mother he became her adoring and selfless slave, expecting nothing, never showing his feelings, hardly ever speaking – content just to be in her presence.

For years now, ever since my birth, my mother had never for long stopped painting. Every day, for many hours, she sat bent over her drawing board often with an exacting sitter in front of her, turning out, like a machine, delicate sensitive little portraits – often two a day. They were still miniatures although they were done on paper (she had given up ivory long ago) and she never knew their value. She charged so little. She was always afraid of over-charging and so she found it hard to save. She could seldom do more than just keep us going and she daren't stop. The strain was enormous and when our second summer came her 'giddy attacks' came on again.

Mr Lantz understood all this and every evening, until she had saved enough to take us away, he drove us out into the country rent-collecting. It was cooler outside the city as, with the windscreen down, we circled and crossed the arid, dusty plain, cut and disfigured by straight rough roads and hideous houses. And whenever he stopped at one of these squalid little boxes we waited outside in the car. They all had an impermanent look as if pitched there by some abominable nomads who threw tin cans and severed parts of automobiles about and then moved on when the ground became too foul to tread on.

Mr Lantz had a pale, sombre face and he wore rimless glasses. To the tenants he must have seemed an incongruous, sinister figure in his black lawyer's clothes with receipt book and pen in his hand. He would walk briskly up to each house and rap on the door. Sometimes it opened promptly but often it didn't and then he would rap again, louder, and listen for sounds inside. If it still didn't open he would disappear round the back, peeping through the windows as he passed. But whether his reception was good or bad he always returned to the car silent and expressionless.

One evening, instead of driving out to the country, he took us back to his house. Although it was a hot night there was a roaring fire in the grate. We thought it was for us, in our honour, the English love for their open hearths being well known.

Another guest was already there, a tall gaunt distinguished-looking man with sunken, burning eyes in a skull-like head and an expression of suffering and resentment. He was an Englishman. He looked at me with hatred as we all sat down, my mother and Mr Lantz in rocking chairs.

The conversation was immediately interesting for the strange man talked well and I grew excited, listening and watching. Then, suddenly, he stopped, his face contorted, a spasm of coughing convulsed him and, pulling a special cardboard cup out of his pocket, he bent over and spat into it. Afterwards, the conversation continued as if nothing had happened. But I could not listen any longer and when he coughed again and this time shot the loathesome gobs across the room into the fire, I jumped up and whispered to my mother that I wanted to go – and we left the room.

'Darling, we can't leave yet,' she said. 'The poor man is dying of consumption and it would hurt his feelings. You must try to put up with it and I promise you that I won't bring you here again.'

We went back. The dying man shot an angry glance at us as we resettled ourselves. Soon, my mother was rocking again in time with Mr Lantz while I sat grim and motionless, waiting for the next horrible interruption and trying not to show how I felt. I did not look at him. I kept my eyes on the floor and when he coughed again I wanted to stop my ears.

It was the first time that I had seen someone who was dying and in such an ugly, shocking way – too vile, I thought, to parade and impose upon everyone else. Such sounds and sights were indecent. I felt no sympathy – only outrage.

But my mother and Mr Lantz seemed to accept his gruesome afflictions and not to mind in the least. Or did they mind as much as I did but were more compassionate, more ready to share the victim's pain? And did the victim go about unconscious of the effect of his malady – or did he enjoy inflicting something of his anguish on everyone he met? It was all beyond my understanding.

Before we went away, my mother became involved in a sensational court case and Mr Lantz acted as her prosecuting attorney, underwriting all the costs.

Mr Rust died suddenly and his son, from whom he had been estranged for many years, descended upon the shack and emptied it of everything, including my mother's large oil-colour portrait of his father which for several months had hung in the long room, admired by everyone. And he refused to give it up. She had to prove that Mr Rust had neither bought it nor been given it, that it had only been lent to him and was still her property. She was very upset for she did not want to lose this picture and no one knew how the case would go.

Then Mr Lantz did a very smart thing. From the defendant's solicitors he managed to obtain possession of it for a few days and, concealing it carefully, rushed it after dark to my mother who copied it and then substituted the copy for the original. After that, the affair became a joke.

The case of the dead man's portrait was given a lot of publicity and on the day of the hearing the court was packed, not only with old Mr Rust's friends and admirers, but with the general public as well.

My mother went into the witness-box and was questioned by her own counsel. Then, Counsel for the Defence rose to examine her.

'When did you paint this picture of the deceased?' he asked her.

'Last year,' she replied.

'Why did you paint this picture?'

'Because he was a paintable subject.'

'I suggest that he asked you to paint him?'

'No, he didn't. I asked to paint him. I admired him and wanted to take the picture to England as a memory of my life in California.'

'How much did he pay you for it?'

'He paid me nothing. He was too poor to order and pay for portraits.'

'I suggest he paid you for it but you prefer to deny it.'

'He did *not* pay me for it,' my mother answered hotly.

He stopped and, turning round, picked up a large leather-bound book which had been lying on the table behind him and walked across to the witness-box. Holding it up in front of her, he asked menacingly,

'Do you recognize this book?'

'Yes,' said my mother smiling, 'It is Mr Rust's "Visitors Book".'

'Exactly,' answered counsel sarcastically, 'the book in which his friends recorded their names, their addresses and other items of information when they went to visit him. I am mighty pleased that you remember it. And now, do you remember ever entering your *own* name in this book?'

'Yes. I must have written my name in the book many times.'

'Ah ha! I am mighty pleased that you have not forgotten that.'

'Why should I?' questioned my mother in reply.

'Why should you?' answered counsel. 'Because there might be something in this book, I suggest, something that *you* have written in this book that you might prefer to forget, that you might wish I had never discovered when I was looking through it.'

'The book is full of nonsense.'

'Ah ha! Full of nonsense! Is that what you are going to say? Now do you remember attending a party given by the deceased on February 14 of this year?'

'I can't remember dates. I may have been at that party. There were many parties.'

'A very large party. I have counted over 100 entries on that date.'

'I was probably there.'

'Since you have forgotten whether you were at this party, since, I suggest, you *prefer* to forget I shall now help you to remember. I shall show you that you surely *were* among the guests on that date, that you were the 28th entry and I shall read out to you what you wrote. On February 14 you wrote your name in the first column and beside it your address ... maybe you're beginning to remember now?' And here he swept his eyes round the court-house and paused for effect, 'and the address which you wrote ... wrote down in this book was ... the Red Light District!'

There was a moment of astonished silence, then a ripple of laughter ran round the court-house. The jurors leant forward in their seats, the public gallery became charged with expectancy and the reporters smiled knowingly at each other. Even the judge seemed more attentive.

This book was one of the jokes of Mr Rust's house. All his guests wrote their names in it and such flattering, witty or talented phrases and drawings as they could invent on the spur of the moment or think up beforehand. And as they struggled ever more eagerly to display their brilliance its pages grew more and more extravagant. In it they wrote poems, proper and improper, they drew pigs with their eyes shut and everything else they could think of with their eyes open – and my mother competed to the best of her ability.

Throughout the turbulent proceedings the portrait of Mr Rust, freshly copied, stood propped upon a table beneath the judge's bench staring out upon the wranglers.

When other entries in the book had been cited for their obscenity, all the witnesses had been called and my mother denounced as a common prostitute, Counsel for the Defence waved the book dramatically at the judge and at the jury and brought his case to a lurid and noisy climax.

'Your Honour!' he shouted. 'Members of the Jury!' he yelled. 'This book has proved to you the kind of people, the low shameless folk, who visited the house of the deceased,' (It did not trouble him that the picture for which they were contending was of the deceased, and his client's father) 'the kind of parties that were held in that lonely shack hidden among the trees with no neighbours to watch out and see what went on there. Members of the Jury, just imagine for yourselves what *did* go on in that long room where the electricity was not fixed and only a dim oil lamp illuminated the horrible proceedings. Just imagine the people, who they were, what they did for a living and where they came from – painters and poets and musicians they called themselves, Bohemia they called the place. Members of the Jury! *my* name for it, *your* name for it, every clean, honest, decent citizen's name for it is Hell, Hell, Hell and again Hell!' He paused for a few moments to regain his

Mrs Miller
An early commission

The author
Miniature

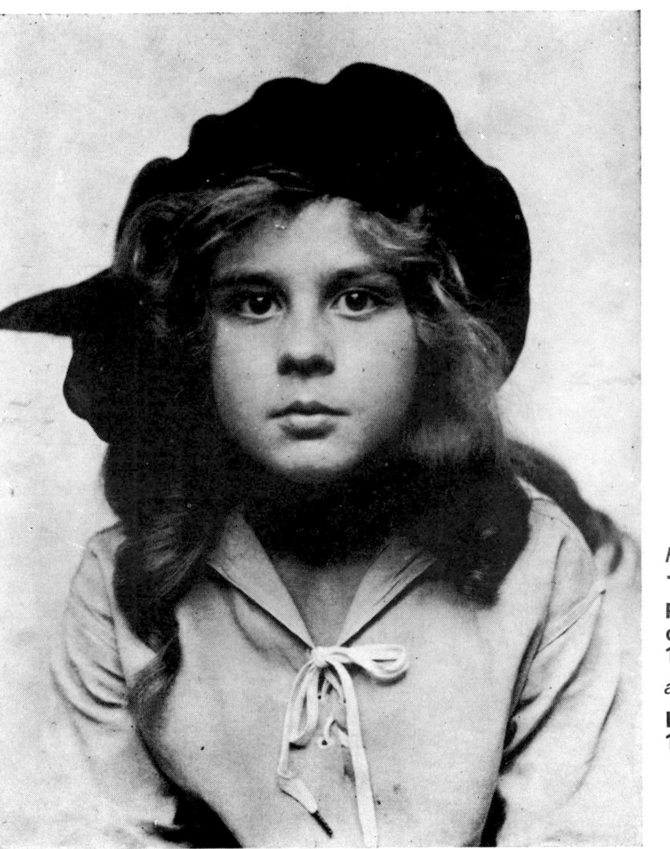

Far left:

The Author.
Recruiting campaign, Victoria, 1915, aged 7.

and right:

Los Angeles, 1917, aged 9.

Charles Lummis
Los Angeles, 1918.

Augustine Birrell
Water colour studies. Much reduced.

breath and mop the sweat running down his face.

'And now, Members of the Jury, I come to the concluding portion of my case, this shocking and painful case, yes, shocking and painful – to me, to you and to the millions who will be reading about it in the newspapers. Not so long ago the plaintiff stood there in the witness-box and claimed that the picture of Mr William Rust, deceased, was her property, claimed that he had never bought and paid her for it. And then later, under my cross-examination, she admitted that on February 14 of this year she wrote her name in this book and beside it, gave as her address, as her *only* address, mind you, boldly, brazenly and impudently – the Red Light District.

'Members of the Jury! I think I can take it that there is not one person in the whole court-house who doesn't understand what that means, who doesn't know where that place is – even if, as I am quite sure, not one of you has ever been there. Of course, the plaintiff made a joke of it. But what else could she do? When she wrote it in the advertising column of this book she never thought the book was going to find its way into my hands and from my hands into this court-house. She had to pretend it was a joke. And if she was driven to pretend that, perhaps she has been driven to pretend something else? I suggest that a woman who comes from the Red Light District is not particular about what she says and is not the kind who does anything for nothing. Members of the Jury, I suggest she painted the deceased and rendered other services and was paid – was paid for them, I say.'

At this point Prosecuting Counsel rose to protest but was shouted down by Counsel for the Defence who never paused in his tirade.

'And now, with the eyes of the world upon her, and the glaring lights of publicity searching out the truth and the voice of American democracy, *your* voice, Members of the Jury, demanding justice; with all these decent honest folk and social forces catching her up – what can she do but pretend and pretend and pretend that she was never paid for that picture?

'Members of the Jury, I ask you, I appeal to your consciences, would it be right to take this picture away from the man who is its rightful owner, the son of the deceased, who long ago broke with his father and his way of living and chose, instead, the life of an honest American business-man with a clean, pure woman, a decent American wife beside him and little innocent kiddies around him? Would it be right, I ask you, to take it away from him and hand it over to this woman here, this loose, light, self-confessed harlot who is not even an American citizen, who comes from England and declares she is soon returning there? And would it be right, I ask you again, to cause shock and pain to simple, virtuous folk everywhere and to give advantage and satisfaction to that small, very small I sure am glad to say, filthy bunch of libertines – those poets, painters and musicians – calling themselves Bohemians?

'Members of the Jury, I implore you, I entreat you, in the name of Liberty, Fraternity and Equality, in the name of American decency, honesty and purity, to give this picture to the man who owns it – and deserves it.' He swung abruptly round towards the judge. 'Your Honour, my case is now concluded.'

In spite of this great performance the judge, in his summing-up, directed the jury not to take the evidence of the 'Visitors Book' too seriously and he remarked decisively that he did not have the impression that the plaintiff was at all the type of woman the defence sought to prove her. When the jury returned, their verdict was in my mother's favour.

Although they mourned their old friend more than ever, there were celebrations in Bohemia that night. And when, as his reward, Mr Lantz was given the copy which, in fact, was as good as the original picture, for an instant he showed his feelings – his delight.

7

A Melting Pot of Children

WHEN THE case was over we went away. My mother had planned this holiday months before and chosen the most beautiful and exclusive resort on the Pacific coast – Carmel. It was not a long journey and we travelled northwards through the dry desert plain between the coast range and the mountains of Nevada, excited to be on the move again.

After a few hours the train stopped in the middle of a wilderness, and in the windless, scorching heat we waited. Pestered for information, the train attendants knew no more than we did and soon there was near panic. The ice-water containers were empty, the children were crying and people were continually jumping out and climbing back again for the heat outside was even worse than the oven-heat within.

The hold-up continued and the sun was going down behind the mountains before some officials at last appeared. They told us that a tunnel had collapsed on the train that was in front of us, that our train would now go back to a junction and then proceed by another route and we should all have to change at different places according to our destinations. We had to get off at a place in the Mojave Desert.

At once the wailing and clamouring stopped and our sufferings were forgotten or endured in silence as, shocked and subdued, we talked to each other and pictured in our minds the fate of the travellers before us, the fate that could have been ours.

Our train rumbled slowly over the new track stopping continually at small settlements, at junctions with only a house or two and often at nothing at all and it was left to the passengers to find out for themselves where they were. There were no name-boards and so, at every stop they yelled to the people outside. This worked well enough until it grew late and there was no one to shout to. Then, scenes of dismay and confusion followed. Families would tumble out into the dark with all their baggage, grope about, discover they were wrong and then come stampeding back to the train, shouting, screaming and clambering on again, often when it was already moving.

My mother grew very nervous. As no one else in our carriage was getting out where we were she paced the whole train, shouting the name of the place and asking if anyone else was changing there. At last she found someone who knew it and in the early morning, when it stopped again, we were told to get out. We jumped down onto the ground, our luggage was thrown out after us and the train went on, leaving us standing beside the track with nothingness all round.

We settled down where we were to wait for the dawn. We were comfortably arranged, propped up against our suitcases discussing our situation when, our eyes growing accustomed to the dark, we saw a speck of light. My mother jumped up at once.

'It must be a house,' she said, gathering up our things. 'Come along. Whatever it is, it will be better than this.' She had grown very nervous of that wild rough country, of the things that could happen to unprotected people.

We stumbled along, keeping our eyes on the small faint beacon and as we came nearer we could see the outline of a house. We walked up to the open door of a room in which, propped up in bed with a tiny oil lamp beside him, was an old man suffering from asthma. I could see how thankful my mother was as she stood in the doorway explaining who we were and all that had happened.

'Come right in,' said the old man kindly. 'There's a chair for you, ma'am, and the kiddie can sleep on the floor.'

We settled ourselves in the room and I lay in a dark corner and for a long time watched the old man sitting up in his brass bed in the lamplight with a patch-work quilt drawn over him, breathing with such difficulty and every now and again choking and gasping. And I thought of the dying man at Mr Lantz's and the same feeling of horror swept through me. But as I went on watching him I marvelled at his serenity, at his acceptance of his lonely suffering and I pitied him, at the same time loathing his infirmities. Decay of the body I detested more and more, worshipping vigour and faultlessness of the flesh. But now I knew that this was wrong, that one ought to be tolerant of the body's failings however revolting, and not only tolerant, but positively sympathetic. And because I wasn't I felt guilty.

I went to sleep at last, shutting out the noise of the old man's afflictions and listening instead to the howling of a coyote far away across the desert, a wild seductive sound that moved and drew me.

We were woken early by banging doors and a woman's loud voice coming through the partitions of the flimsy house. The old man was still awake, still propped up against the pillows and the bed-head, gasping and wheezing, still calm and kind, just as when we found him. We thanked him for his hospitality and walked out into the dawn.

There were only three things to be seen. The house, which was a typical frontier hotel, the railroad track and the desert. We entered the saloon where a big fat woman (with the loud voice that had waked us) was working. After explaining once more what had happened, we asked for breakfast and sat down at a table covered with oil-cloth pitted with cigarette burns beneath a festoon of sticky, corpse-cluttered fly-papers, with spitoons all round us on the floor.

Soon life came to the place as ranchers and cattle-men came riding in. They tethered their horses outside and ran their cars up close to the track and then gathered in the saloon, talking and drinking. They had come for their mail off the train.

When the time came, we said good-bye to the old man and the fat woman and made our way to the track, the men carrying our luggage. When the train arrived we climbed onto it, not knowing where it was going. My mother would have gone anywhere just to get away from where we were. Cowboys and spitoons did not appeal to her, she saw no romance in this desert outpost – only squalor and potential kidnappers. The men waved and shouted friendly good-byes and I was sorry to be leaving such an interesting place so soon.

Eventually, after many more halts and changes, we arrived in Carmel and tumbled straight into a furnished two-room shack set among the pine trees, above the sea. The next day, with a load of pictures, we went to the hotel.

They were soon arranged in a prominent place with the well-used card, the list of royalties, propped beside them. As always, enquiries came at once and in the front room of our shack, my mother started work. Even here, she could not stop – and she daren't waste any time. Our margin of money was so small. The better climate, the beautiful place, new, interesting people and picnics and bathing in the afternoons were her refreshment – as much of a holiday as she could take.

Her clients were people from the east, New Yorkers and Bostonians and she was very excited by them.

'I do like Mrs so-and-so,' she would burst out when the sitting was over and I was back from the beach. 'You would hardly know she was American, she has no accent at all. How different these people are – so much more cultured. If the war goes on much longer we'll save up and go and live in New York. I would get plenty of work there. I might even put my prices up – and we'd be half-way to England.'

By this time she was thoroughly tired of waiting and wandering. She was longing for England, for a settled home and the security of her own country and time and distance made even the family seem less unendurable. And although my life was so happy, I was always conscious of its impermanence and unreality and the longer we stayed away the more vivid became the dream of returning.

Carmel was a beautiful place, outlined by low cliffs edged with dark twisted trees blown into fantastic shapes by the wind, with blue blue water below. Painters flocked there as well as the stylish New Yorkers.

Next to us lived an artist – kind, quaint and very poor. She owned her one-room shack and lived there all the year round, muddling along happily in a most uncomfortable way. Bats lived in the eaves and a skunk lived under the floor-boards and the shack had fallen into such a state of disrepair that whenever it rained the water poured in everywhere, each time in a new place so that she was always hurrying out to the hardware store to buy another bucket.

I loved visiting her during a heavy shower with the water dripping, or cascading, into the buckets while in the middle, quite unconcerned, she stood before her easel with a large umbrella over her, hung from a beam by a piece of string, and another one over the canvas. The bats swirled round and round colliding now and again with the umbrellas and a powerful stench came up from below.

'Hullo there, kid!' she would call out through the roar. 'Sit down and make yourself at home.' And I would look for a chair that wasn't broken and place it carefully between the waterfalls and stay and talk, or rather shout, to her. I was very fond of her.

She wasn't sure if she really liked the smell of the skunk and several times I crawled under the house to try to drive it away. But I never succeeded; and when I climbed up a ladder to dislodge the bats, instead of flying away they flew inside and circled round her head and clung to the beams more persistently than before. And she was fond of them. She would have missed them if I *had* driven them away – even the skunk.

When we returned to Los Angeles, one of my mother's wealthy friends lent us her chauffeur's bungalow which stood in a corner of her garden, facing onto the road at the back. Jean turned out some furniture from her big rooms and together they made it very attractive. It was a long time since we had lived with good things.

The view over her garden from our windows was beautiful but behind, where the rough poor district flowed up against the rich, it was squalid. Ugly little bungalows lined the road with vacant lots between them, worn bare and dusty by the children, garbage and tin cans were dumped round the edges and away on one side, were some shops.

I had no difficulty in finding the local gang. The empty lots were swarming with children of all nationalities. I was 10-years-old now and very tough.

Boldly I crossed the road. I was at once surrounded.

'Hullo, you come ter live there?' one of them shouted, jerking a thumb towards our bungalow. 'Where's yer pa? What's his job?'

'He's dead. I live with my mother,' I replied.

'Whatta you? Where you come from?' several cried out at once. My voice had betrayed me again and I knew that I was in for trouble.

'I'm English,' I replied challengingly, sizing them all up.

'England ain't no good!' one shouted then, speaking for them all.

America was in the war now with England as her ally – but it made no difference. I didn't wait for any more. It was I who was the fighter now.

'How dare you say that about England!' I yelled as I flung myself upon him. He was my own size but he didn't stand a chance. I had him on the ground at once and made him 'take back' his insult to England and then I rose, letting him go, and stood looking at them all, conscious that I had mastered them.

In this very mixed community, many of the children were neutral in this perennial quarrel. Only honest-to-God Americans, of Anglo-Saxon stock, boiled up at the sound of my voice and fought King George III all over again. And it must have been very provoking, for my mother and I had taken no end of trouble to preserve its obnoxious tone and verbal purity.

'That's an ugly American word,' she would say. And I never said it again. And I kept a check on her, too.

'You said that with an American voice,' and she would repeat the phrase and we would both repeat it, over and over, until we had purged it of its displeasing tone and it rang pure again.

Often she would say, 'you must not arrive at Miss Morison's school with an American accent.' And I would think of that wonderful school, the 'girls' Eton' they called it, and visualise myself entering the front door and startling my godmother, that wonderful person, with a strong nasal voice. How terrible I would feel. And I watched myself harder than ever. The deeper we got into American life the more English we became.

But for me, this Englishness was no longer just the agreeable and satisfying sensation that it had once been. There was a new disturbing aspect to it.

With so many other countries littering the globe, all so inferior and undesirable, the fact that I had been born English, born onto that tiny spot of land (always coloured red on the maps), that remarkable empire-owning island, unmatched anywhere in achievements and splendour, seemed utterly amazing to me, seemed like luck raised to a degree of importance that was terrifying. Life was founded on good or bad fortune, it appeared, and the world was a chancy affair.

These thoughts greatly agitated me and although, on a deeper level, I felt sure that the world could not possibly be run on such a meaningless principle, yet still I wobbled between doubt and confidence in the ordering of the universe.

I returned to Miss Fulmer's school but although I loved it, my home interests still conflicted with my education (the more so as I had a garden of my own again) and I generally attended alternate months. The fees were paid by the month and when I had an important project in hand (a tree-house or network of trenches) my mother always encouraged me to keep it going for the full period.

Baseball and marbles were the games in our back street. No girls took any part for the play was rough and uninhibited. The boys boasted and swore and urinated openly. But their behaviour did not concern me and I soon developed a gambler's passion for marbles. Every day, with an intensity which was painful, I played match after match. To risk and lose the bright treasures was agony and to win them was glorious – or was it? There was a catch somewhere, a feeling of guilt and the marbles I won I was ashamed to use. But I went on, day after day, crouching in the dust, throwing and thumbing, seizing and surrendering.

Near us lived a German family, a woman and her three sons. They were very poor and their house was a slum. They had one bed, a table and some broken chairs and the mother, who was fat and blowsy, seemed to possess only one garment, a thin, black, shapeless dirty cotton dress beneath which one could see her huge pendulous breasts resting on her stomach when they were not swinging about. But she was good-natured and the boys were gentle and chivalrous and for this family I soon had the highest regard.

Karl, the eldest, became my special friend. He was a master of marbles and, one day, taking me as his partner, we won match after match, scooping them up until there were no more to win. And he gave them all to me.

For the moment this seemed good, but when I got home, with my pockets bulging, and I laid them out and looked at their beautiful colours and knew to whom each had belonged, I felt mean. I felt as if I had stolen them – and I never played again. I was cured of the passion.

It was about this time that I became conscious of my relationship with my mother, and I marvelled at it. I observed the clever way she handled me; and her reading of my mind, her sensing of my desires and understanding of my problems seemed to me, quite uncanny. I compared her with other mothers. I listened to the silly things they said to their children and watched the frustration which they caused and I knew that their relationships were not like mine. Mine was a great friendship. And I wrote her a letter. (See page 84).

I also noted how she behaved to other children, how quick she was to go to the help of a child in trouble, how readily she involved herself with difficult parents. And I noted, finally, the way other grown-ups behaved to me, how foolishly they addressed me and what inane things they said – and I scowled my contempt.

My mother told me stories of her own childhood, of the succession of stupid nurses and governesses who had thwarted and punished her and who frequently drove her into a state of irritation and fury which always ended in a paroxysm of screaming and breaking things. On one occasion she hurled the contents of a box of coal at one of them.

'They called me a difficult child. But I wasn't difficult at all. It was just that I wasn't allowed to paint and I was always being made to do things that I hated doing – while Willie painted and had everything he wanted.' And she once added bitterly: 'I am sure those frenzies ruined my nerves for life.'

I was very disturbed by these stories, not only because I was so sorry for her but also, because I knew that I would be just the same were I managed by anyone less understanding and loving than she was.

'Children are intelligent and reasonable,' she was always saying. 'If their reason is appealed to they will respond.' And so she gave me my freedom (of course, in the circumstances, she had to) and I grew headstrong and undisciplined – yet still sensitive to her warnings and advice. And I resolved that when I had children of my own I would try to bring them up as she had brought me.

I even planned to write a book on the right and wrong way of bringing up children – for the instruction of all mothers and as a reminder for myself. I was so afraid of forgetting. But like most of my literary projects of this time, it was never written. I lived too hard. Existence itself was too intoxicating, the environment too vigorous and magnetic, the climate too good. To stop, even for an instant, and turn to the stillness of intellectual pursuits was impossible. Or was the impossibility only in myself?

Although my love for my mother was more vehement than ever and I valued her more and was conscious all the time of what her loss would mean to me, yet I no longer suffered those panic fears of losing her. Of course I was older and stronger, but I also think that our environment, although lawless and crude, was more reassuring – less mean and lonely than Victoria. For Los Angeles was a warm-hearted generous place.

But even if the spirit of Victoria was frightening, I was happy in that 'little England' on the other side of the world; neat and clean, law-abiding and respectable, small and safe, where a five cent tram ride carried one out of the city to the most beautiful forests and beaches.

Los Angeles was huge and hard to escape from with vulgarity and violence on every side. We moved from one hideous house to another and I played with tough uncultured children in dusty sordid vacant lots – and I had to fight before I could play. And I was happier still. Not just happy – ecstatic! My happiness grew as I grew and I now believed myself to be the most fortunate child in the world – and I went about singing.

All this ecstasy must have been very gratifying to my mother. She must have felt that it proved the rightness of the ingredients she had used in my making – love, liberty and reason.

About this period, too, I discovered another remarkable thing about her. From the time that I first became conscious of the inferiority of my sex I had feared that, for all her great love for me, she must be sorry that I was a girl and not a boy. I was sure that she could not help being imbued with the prevailing preference even if she managed to hide it better than most other people did. One day, I tackled her directly on the subject.

'When you were waiting for me to be born – did you hope all the time that I would be a boy? Were you very disappointed that I wasn't?'

'Of course not!' she burst out, 'I didn't care which I was going to have. All I wanted was a baby and I adored you as soon as I saw you. All babies are lovely and girls are just as lovely as boys – and women are just as fine as men.'

I believed her implicitly. I knew now that she was not pretending and that she loved me without one grain of regret.

This testimony of hers I thought remarkable. Against all the world's evidence she had shown me that another deeper truth existed which, suddenly, I realised I had always known but never been able to see. It seemed now as if we shared a great secret, as if only she and I knew that women were as valuable as men. I did not need to change my sex.

We had not been long in the bungalow when the Armistice was signed. For us, the news was overwhelming. England, the beloved country, had survived and was again victorious! Misty, green and beautiful, England – our England, was still there for us to come to. Noble, brave and righteous, sweet exquisite island anchored in a crystal sea, wrapped in clouds of poetry and pageantry, like no other place on earth. The long long wait was over.

Three pictures of England were always in my mind and I gazed upon them, each in turn. One was the England of the newspapers and letters, of casualty lists, zeppelins, food shortages and heroism and it was very real and sad but inspiring; the second was of my loving godmother, the splendid school and the curious remnants of my family and this was rather dark and hazy and, through the haze, slightly alarming; the third, which I loved best of all, was derived from books and my own imagination.

My mother brought a small stock of children's classics away with her and these were read over and over again to me in Ottawa until I knew them all by heart. *Peter Pan, Alice in Wonderland, King Arthur and the Knights of the Round Table*, Beatrix Potter, Kate Greenaway, *The Pied Piper of Hamelin* and *The Story of a Round Loaf*, are some that I remember. In the third picture, all these books merged together to create a fairy-like unfading landscape of such innocence and delicacy and beauty that I looked on it with rapture and longed to walk through the sweet green meadows and climb the little stiles and meet all those lovely graceful children, those almost-human animals, and feel all about me the presence of those stately kings and queens and goodly knights.

The war was over but we could not travel at once. Mines were still drifting in the Atlantic and ships were still sinking – and we had to save up. So, when the first excitement was over, we went on as before – but not as before. The world had changed. We could plan and look forward.

For fashion's sake, Jean kept two dogs. She ignored them altogether and left them to the mercy of the negro maid who kicked them and bawled at them by day and shut them in the cellar at night where they slept on the coke-strewn concrete floor.

I made friends with them and Yen, the little yellow cross-bred chow, decided at once to change homes. She came over to the bungalow and attached herself to us, even following me to school and waiting there all day. My mother was reluctant to adopt her but, like Pat in Victoria, she adopted us. And I loved her. I adored her.

Like the weather in England, the perennial topic of conversation in Los Angeles – at least among the rich – was burglaries. Everyone was being burgled regularly and the dinner parties were kept going with the latest stories while the bedrooms upstairs, very likely, were being rifled as they talked.

My mother often spent the evening with Jean and one night, coming home in the dark and passing the garage, she heard a noise inside. The next day it was discovered that a burglar had also spent the evening in her house, sorting his spoil afterwards in the garage.

On another occasion, in broad daylight, there were shots in our street and a car full of masked men drove by. They had killed a young boy as he sat on his porch – because he knew too much. All this made my mother more and more nervous for what she always feared, were the kidnappers. There were times, when she was desperate to leave.

The Japanese children never joined in our games. They hovered on the edge in a mute, trance-like way with inward-looking eyes. One of them, a little girl with long sleek black hair, attracted my interest. It was her hair that fascinated me. I stared and stared at it and then went up to her and touched it and after that, I was seized by an irresistible desire to chop it all off.

I invited her into my garden and sat her down under a tree, then ran into the house for some scissors.

'I am going to bob your hair,' I said gently when I came back, trying not to frighten her. 'Everybody has bobbed hair' (except myself). 'It will look much nicer.' She didn't speak or change her expression or move. She was the perfect victim.

I picked up a handful of the lank black stuff – and chopped. The sensation was marvellous. A square chunk slid down her arm onto the ground. I picked up the next section and chopped again. Then, my passion reaching its climax, I clutched the top of her head with my left hand to keep it steady and ran the scissors all the way round, hearing and feeling the silky crunch as they sliced it away and seeing the chopped ends falling about. It didn't take long.

'There!' I exclaimed when I'd finished, looking at my work with satisfaction and thinking how exceptionally well I had done it. Then, to reassure her I added, 'You look lovely. Much better than before. You've got bobbed hair like everybody else.'

She got up slowly, still without speaking, and together we walked away. I rejoined the other children. She went straight home.

That evening, there was a gentle knock on our front door. I knew who it was and let my mother go to open it. Outside the fly-screen stood the father and child. Only then did I see that her hair was all jags.

He was not angry – only grieved. And anxious, after the event, because I might have poked the scissors in her eye. He just came to make a formal complaint and to parade the damaged object of my barbarism. He was a very civilised man. He owned the local greengrocer's shop.

My mother gave him some money to have the child's hair trimmed and the episode ended in smiles.

Another of my friends was a little Mexican girl, a most talented child who danced and sang like a professional. Her gaiety and liveliness attracted me and we became very intimate. She lived in a poor-looking house beside the shops and I soon discovered that when she was not singing and dancing about the streets – she was thieving. This made her even more interesting. My mother wsa sure that her family were all thieves.

Before long, she asked me if I would join her in a raid which she was planning on her school. Not since my days with Andy had I done anything like this and although, in theory, I disapproved, nevertheless, the chance of an experience so unusual and interesting was not to be missed and I agreed at once to go with her.

When the day came, we waited until it was dark and then slipped into a narrow passage which led to the back of the building and climbed through a window. She led the way up to a class-room, prised open the locked door of the stationery cupboard and cleared the shelves in a business-like way, dropping the note-books and pencils into the bags she had brought. When they were full we heaved them onto our shoulders and set off downstairs again.

The place seemed very eerie now and the sound of out footsteps was terrible. The whole building seemed alive with criminals and I expected someone to jump out of the dark and grab us. When we got out I lugged the heavy load back to Tina's house, relieved that the interesting and unusual experience was over. But if I had done more of this, I am sure that I would soon have felt the fascination of it and gained plenty of confidence and I would have taken up burglary with the same enthusiasm that I took up everything else.

My mother let a room to an old woman and Tina soon told me that I was missing a great opportunity in not stealing from her. I didn't act on her advice but when, before long, I discovered that she herself was climbing in the window and taking her money, I was just as culpable, for I didn't protest. The old woman, of course, thought it was me and began to dislike me, as well she might, for when I sold my possessions before we left, I accepted Tina's money, knowing well where it came from, with scarcely a qualm.

My mother was working so hard now, earning the money to take us home, that she couldn't listen so well to my daily prattle and I didn't confide in her so much – and with George Washington away, I led my own rich, shadowy unguided life.

On a large lot a big tent went suddenly up and we all watched and waited to see what was coming. When the bills were pasted up announcing that Billy Sunday would be holding a revivalist meeting, the kids lost interest and drifted away – but I decided to go to it.

When the night arrived, I slipped out of the house, sneaked across the lot and crawled under the canvas behind the platform. It was pitch dark there for the platform had a high back to it on which were draped the 'Stars and Stripes' and a lot of texts – and that side was brilliantly lit. The people were pouring in and when all the benches were overflowing, the gangways filled and they stood six deep round the sides, the meeting began. I lay peeping behind.

I never took in what Billy was saying but his fervour and the emotion which he aroused in the crowd amazed me and I watched the scene for a long time. Then, a diabolical idea came to me and I slipped out of the tent and scoured the ground outside for pebbles. Looping up my skirt, I used it as a bag and when it was full I crawled back. Calculating then where Billy was standing,

I quickly lobbed handful after handful over the back of the platform onto his head.

He stopped speaking and for a moment the only sound was the rattle of my pebbles as they bounced off him onto the planks. Then there was pandemonium. The supporters on the platform jumped down, the audience rose and surged forward and then all of them stormed round the back – as I slipped once more under the canvas and ran home.

Virginia, Jean and my mother went off to a fortune-teller together. A celebrated clairvoyant was visiting Los Angeles and her powers were exciting the smart set.

My mother returned very thrilled for she had been told that, although her own talent would never be fully realised and acknowledged, yet her child, seen standing under a dazzling star, would one day make a name. She was completely convinced of the woman's psychic powers for this was just what she had always believed herself. And so had I – yet I was sceptical and her excitement I discounted altogether.

And now, she was suddenly quite sure that I was going to be a great singer. She could see me standing on platforms, looking ravishingly beautiful, thrilling the world with my divine voice. And I toyed with this prospect for a short time wondering if, by chance, she was right and this was the road that I was looking for. But I had something more important to do than just sing – and I dismissed the idea with contempt.

And why a singer? What made her think of that? What proof had she? Although my intuition was my strongest perceiving faculty yet I never supposed that anyone else could possess the same means of knowing. I was still not properly conscious of it and I still demanded material proofs. But my carolling about the garden was not proof of great vocal talent. I had no illusions about that.

I loved being praised and having my deep, disturbing certainties about myself confirmed, yet, the more my mother did this, with or without the help of fortune-tellers, the less I believed her. In the strong family current of desires and premonitions I swam confusedly.

It was 1919. The savings in the bank were mounting and my mother reckoned that by the autumn we could travel and the seas then would be safe. She had no money to spare for a holiday that year but an opportunity arose of getting away.

On West Adams Street lived a wealthy family with a lurid history. The only child was born blind but she grew up unusually attractive and intelligent and the father adored her. The mother, blaming him for the affliction, grew more and more jealous and resentful until, one day, she was caught creeping up to the child with a knife in her hand. After that, she was sent away to be brought up by relatives, occasionally returning to visit her parents.

Now, in her early twenties, she was spending a few weeks at home and my mother was commissioned to paint her – and the portrait was a great success. Everybody raved about it and then the mother decided that she, too, would be done and a delightful plan was devised.

Mr and Mrs Crindlewood owned a summer residence at Coronado and they invited us to visit them. The idea was that my mother would paint the portrait and then take a rest and, in the company of her grateful hosts, enjoy the attractions of the place and the felicities of its smart society.

My mother was very pleased about this. It would be a free holiday by the sea and she looked forward to being waited on by servants in a comfortable house. She needed a rest. The only flaw in the scheme was that we couldn't take Yen. She was not invited. When Jean's husband came back from France, they shut up the big house and went to their ranch in the mountains, leaving Yen with us. And so, we had to put her in some kennels.

Overflowing with warmth and charm, Mr and Mrs Crindlewood met us with their limousine and drove us to their villa on the west side, the smart side, overlooking the sea. But I was disappointed. A motorway and promenade ran between the house and the crowded beach – it was a built-up popular resort.

We were given the most sumptuous rooms and for the few days that were allowed to my mother to recover from the journey, we were taken for bracing drives and strengthened with gorgeous food. Never for a moment were we free from the tonic attentions of someone. Comfort, consideration and esteem were piled and poured upon us and the air was thick with waves of desire and expectation.

At last the longed-for day arrived and the painter and the subject shut themselves up in a room together. The house grew silent, everyone waiting – everyone sure of success.

My mother knew nothing about the family and it was only later, when we were back in Los Angeles, that her friends told her all about them. But Mrs Crindlewood was animated and easy to paint and by the end of the morning the picture was finished and she jumped up excitedly, and came round behind my mother to look at it. There was a gasp, followed by silence. My mother turned and looked up at her. The woman's face was contorted with rage.

'I don't like it. I don't look like that,' she stuttered at last and she was trembling all over. 'I won't have it,' and burying her face in her hands, sobbing and groaning, she rushed out of the room.

My mother jumped up and stood back from the sketch to see what was wrong with it. In a flash she knew. She had painted a devil!

She hurried after her but she was locked in her bedroom and the whole house was in a state of alarm. Then, finding the agitated husband, she expressed her regret and undertook to do another.

Mrs Crindlewood did not appear for lunch and so strung-up were we all that the marvellous meal was hardly tasted. Mr Crindlewood tried his best to be reassuring, making all kinds of excuses for the behaviour of his wife. In the afternoon, my mother and I went out for a bathe, thankful to be among the despised crowds on the beach and away from that charged and oppressive house. When we returned, Mrs Crindlewood was recovered enough to rejoin us, it being understood that another portrait would be started the next day.

She did not appear for breakfast but, in spite of a bad night, she presented herself later and this time, she was dressed in a low-cut, royal blue velvet gown. Rubies and diamonds circled her neck and hung in bunches from her ears and her face was a mask of make-up. With her black hair and white skin and sharp searching eyes, in a certain vulgar way, she looked very impressive. Once again they withdrew.

She sat down on the same chair, stiff, unmoving, like a wax-work figure and never spoke. My mother walked up and down and round her, studying her face and searching for a new angle. When she had finally posed her she talked, the fabulous figure relaxed and she strove to see and paint the face that was wanted.

The work went slowly and when the sitting was over she would not let her see it and the loaded, flaunting figure withdrew to her room to disrobe. Left alone, she scrutinised the portrait and, with dismay, realised that the same expression was in it. And the more she touched it up the worse it became. Exhausted, she gave it up. The only thing to do was to start again and when she went into lunch she told them that the dress and jewels were taking her longer and she would need another sitting before she could show it. They were disappointed but the day passed off amiably.

The next morning, the struggle began again. Mrs Crindlewood chatted away and my mother made up her mind to produce a chocolate-box picture, all velvet and jewels and a prettified face, even if it scarcely resembled her at all. After an hour or so, she begged Mrs Crindlewood to leave her to finish it alone, assuring her that it was almost done. Obediently she retired and my mother went on working. Then she gazed at it hard. She was blind to it by this time – but it seemed alright. It was pretty and gaudy and grand. All she cared about now was to please, to be paid and to go.

She picked it up and went to the drawing-room where the husband and wife were sitting. They jumped up and followed her across the room where she propped it on a table in the best possible light. Then they stared at it in silence. But when Mr Crindlewood began muttering something pleasant he was cut short.

'It's just the same,' screamed his wife and, rushing at the picture, she snatched it up and threw it on the floor and stamped on it.

'I don't look like that!' she shrieked. 'I won't have it! I won't let anybody see it!' then she turned to my mother. 'You're doing it on purpose! You want everyone to know! I hate you! Get out of my house!' We almost ran from the room. We flew upstairs, flung our things together and fled out of the house.

We walked to the shopping centre and enquired about lodgings. We had no money for a hotel. Then, above a shop on Main Street, we engaged a cheap, shabby room and when the slatternly woman gave us the key – we could have hugged her.

There was a gas ring in the passage and while I dashed down into the street to buy some food, my mother borrowed a kettle from the woman and when I came back we sat down to what seemed like the loveliest meal we had ever eaten. We felt as if we had escaped from a padded cell and from the alternate blandishments and frenzies of a maniac.

Although we hated Coronado, we decided to stay. The heat was intense for it was close to the Mexican border – but the sea was there to bathe in. And the first thing we did was to send for Yen. A few days later, she arrived in a box on a railway truck and when she saw us, she sprang about and cried with joy – and I tore at the box to open it.

For a few lazy, lovely days we roamed about the noisy, crowded, horrible place, rejoicing and Yen and I gambolled together. When my mother began to worry, we went with some pictures to the big hotel and commissions followed.

Our room was too sordid to use as a studio and the sun poured into it all day, and so she worked in the hotel or in the clients' houses. And soon, she was so busy that I was left to myself. But I was used to it – and I had Yen. We set out to explore the place.

Before long, we fell in with a gang of kids straying about all day like us. But they had lots of money and were constantly dropping into drug stores to quench their thirst and get cool, whereas Yen and I had none and were accustomed to dropping into the sea. While they sat on the high stools sucking up their sodas through straws and licking up their sundaes, we watched or waited outside. And soon I was corrupted. I, too, acquired a longing for these delicacies and I began asking my mother for money and she would give me a dime, or even 15 cents.

Then, everything went wrong again. Early one morning I woke, hearing the sound that I always dreaded, the sound of her illness. For a few moments I lay on in bed, stiff with shock and apprehension and then I forced myself up and went over to her. The attack was more violent than ever before, but when I tried to help her she pushed me away. 'Go back to sleep,' she said. I hovered round her for awhile, loathing it – the pain, the odour and ugliness of it all. Then I crawled back into bed. The retching went on.

At length, I dressed myself, again tried to help her and then just hung about, waiting for each terrible spasm. She had been so well and gay the night before and now she was half dead, her face drawn and old and wet with perspiration, her hair matted.

'There's nothing you can do. I'll soon be alright. Go out and play, my love,' she whispered whenever I came near her.

After several hours, when she realised that I was still there, she repeated the words and guiltily I walked to the door and opened it and looked back at her for a moment and then, with Yen beside me, went out.

In the street, the holiday people were talking and laughing and moving along – but my life had stopped. Every sound and everything I looked at seemed unreal. There was nothing in front of me and I felt as if I couldn't move, as if I was standing still within a small closed ring of pain and fear, cut off from everything.

Drifting about with Yen I felt a little better, but when I climbed the stairs again the same feeling came back. She was even weaker although the retching was less violent. I stayed with her then – doing nothing, afraid to leave her.

The curtains were drawn but the sun beat through them and the noise was fearful. The tram cars clattered past with their bells jangling, automobiles hooted and the paper-boys were bawling out the news.

All the afternoon I sat watching and listening and she didn't even know that I was there. Then, in the evening, for a few appalling moments, I thought she was dead.

I bent over her and fumbled for her heart to feel if it was beating. I woke her and she said again, 'Go out and play, my love, I'll soon be alright'. I crept into bed and in the end went to sleep.

When I woke, early the next morning, and saw that the attack was really over and she was still alive, I leapt out of bed and ran to her and then dressed and waited impatiently for the shops to open. When they did, I fetched the recuperative things she always needed and gave them to her joyfully. Then I went to the hotel to tell them that she was ill and, after that, when once again she said to me, 'go out and play now. I'll soon be well' – I went.

For days I ran crazily about, joining different gangs of boys. Occasionally I returned to see what she needed but for most of the time I neglected her, staying out for hours on end, often late into the night, roaming the streets and promenades trying to obliterate the fear, the pain and the guilt.

And then it all went wrong again. A crowd of us were drifting along when, passing a drug store, one of them cried out as always, 'C'mon, kids, let's stop fera soda,' and they all trooped in, jingling the money in their pockets. When I did not follow, one of them turned to me.

'Aint' yer comin', kid?'

'I don't want one,' I replied.

'Aw, shucks, kid, s'pose yer aint got'n'y dough?' he answered, half sympathetic, half taunting.

'I'll get some,' I shouted. 'Wait for me.' And I shot off back to our room.

My mother was not asleep. She knew when I came in and I could easily have asked her and she would not have refused me. But I didn't. I went to her purse and out of it I took a dollar – a whole dollar! A little fortune to us. I don't remember what I did with it. I could not possibly have eaten a dollar's worth of sodas and sundaes. I suppose I treated the whole gang. I only know that I spent the lot and never told her.

That night, I wanted to confess to her but, unlike George Washington, I didn't have the courage. To steal from someone lying ill and helpless, from the person one so loved, was the meanest most miserable thing that one could do. And I didn't understand how I could have done it, and what made me take so much? I never meant to take all that. I couldn't think what had happened to me and my returning joy was shattered by new, most frightening doubts about my character, my despicable character. For weeks I was depressed and ever afterwards I thought of it with shame and sadness.

When she recovered we returned to Los Angeles – not to the bungalow but to the big house which Jean and her husband lent us. And now, my mother was determined to get home. She borrowed money, the amount she still needed, from Virginia and booked us passages from Quebec to Liverpool. Then, to help still more, in a delicate way, Virginia took me down-town to one of the big department stores and set me up with a trousseau of American clothes, most of them incongruous and useless in the world to which I went.

The time passed quickly. We went about saying good-bye to all our friends and farewell parties were given for us and then, for me, came the really tragic parting. A few days before we left, Jean and her husband motored in from their ranch to say good-bye and to take Yen away.

When the moment came, I hugged her and I kissed her and I lifted her into the car and watched her sitting on the seat trustfully, believing that I was coming too. Then, as the car moved slowly away, I saw the look of anxiety come into her eyes and I saw her jump at the window and gaze back at me, frightened and appealing. And then she was gone. Such sorrow I had never known. And I knew that her pain was like mine. For months, for years I grieved for her.

If we had been rich, my mother told me, we would have taken her with us. We did to Yen just what we did to Pat.

We spent the last evening with the Norths, the dearest of all our Californian friends, and because we could not sleep that night for excitement, we got up very early, before it was light, and walked back to their house. But we did not wake them. We just sat on their porch for awhile and then slipped finally away and took a taxi to the station.

While we were there, watching our last golden sunrise, a man darted out from behind some trees on the other side of the road and padded rapidly along the side-walk in rubber shoes clutching something that bulged inside his coat. Instinctively, we both shrank down behind the balustrade, for those who knew too much – or saw too much – were so easily shot. When he had gone, my mother said passionately: 'Thank God that we are leaving'.

We reached Quebec and boarded the boat. The hawsers were cast off, the horns and whistles blew, the tugs hooted and pulled and churned the water at their sterns and the liner moved slowly out into midstream and then down with the current towards the open sea.

We came away for six months – we stayed away for seven years. After so much wandering and working and growing up in other countries we were going home, going home to England, at last.

Footnote to page 72

Whenever we went into town, I always availed myself of the writing facilities in banks and other public places. Notepaper heading and letter.

The Roma
Los Angeles

I adore you so much you are a little love. We live together with five cents in our pocket and we are just companions.

Whenever I want anything no matter how much money you have you get it me. With all the love my heart and soul and body have I give it you.

Part II

1

London

AS THE train ran slowly in beside the platform, my mother hung out of the window scanning all the waiting people. When it stopped we walked with the crowd to the barrier and stood, looking about in all directions, feeling sure that something had gone wrong, that at least her sister should be there to meet us.

The Campden Hill house had been sold and we didn't know where we were staying – where to go. Then, we saw her – saw Amy gliding forward slowly and delicately, a dreamy expression on her face, quite oblivious of where she was and, it almost seemed, of what she had come for.

'Hullo, Amy,' my mother called out, thankful to see her at last.

'Dearest Louie,' she replied in an affected tone as if she had rehearsed the greeting beforehand, 'how wonderful it is to have you both back.'

She bent over my mother and then over me and pressed on our shoulders for a second with the tips of her fingers while her face swayed into our faces and away again without touching. She didn't seem to know how to kiss and embrace, but she had charm, she treated me with great deference and although I thought her rather peculiar, I liked her.

'What happened, Amy? We've been waiting ages,' said my mother.

'Dearest, I thought I had plenty of time.' And then she turned to me. 'P. dear,' (that was already Miss Morison's name for me) 'Godmother sends you her love and says she is longing to see you. It is going to be splendid having you at school.' Then she turned to my mother again. 'The only sad thing is that Arm' (those were Miss Morison's initials and Amy's name for her) 'will not be here next term when P. starts. You know that we are going to the Holy Land' (here she dropped her voice and a pious note came into it) 'and Miss Kiddle will be acting-headmistress. Arm is *so* disappointed. She *did* hope that you would wait until we returned.' Miss Morison had written asking us to do this.

'We couldn't change our plans at the last moment,' my mother replied, 'and Philippa will be alright. Miss Kiddle is a dear old thing. Now let's get a taxi. Our heavy luggage will come later. What lodgings have you found for us?'

'Dearest, I haven't found you any. Arm told me not to. She said she would take P. at the boarding house and you could go to the hotel where mother is.' I was horrified by this idea and so was my mother.

'But Amy, we don't want to be separated like that. Now I shall have to start hunting myself. And where shall we go tonight? We can't waste money on a hotel. Why didn't you do as *I* asked you?'

'Dearest ...,' she began, then stopped, her mouth pursed, her big, empty uncertain eyes searching my mother's face nervously.

'I know what I'll do,' my mother went on in a determined tone, 'I'll ring up Arthur and see if we can stay with him.'

'But dearest, Arm is expecting Philippa ...' her voice died away as my mother marched off to a telephone and I followed her.

Arthur was an old Campden Hill neighbour who had once been in love with her. Unfortunately, he was away and his niece answered the telephone and was not at all hospitable. But pressed by my mother, she gave way and agreed to receive us. After that, parting rather coolly, Amy took one taxi back to the school and we took another to the flat.

The niece was very unfriendly, treating us as intruders of the lowest kind. We had a roof over our heads but it was a chilly uncomfortable one. Our homecoming was painful.

It was the end of October and when I woke at my usual time the next morning, it was dark. It seemed extraordinary to be getting out of bed and dressing while it was still night. When daylight came at last I went to the window and looked out upon London.

The flat was high up and I could see over the roof-tops a forest of chimney pots, thousands and thousands of them, all shapes and sizes, short ones and tall ones, straight ones and crooked ones, friendly ones and menacing ones, all emitting their own little trail of smoke like a host of weird, dark, frightening people – frightening little dwarfs. And as I watched them they seemed to be watching me and I waited for the sun to rise and drive away the gloom and throw its golden cheerful light on all their dismal smoking heads. But no sun ever came and soon the roofs grew darker still as drops of rain fell, turning quickly to a fine cloudy drizzle which obscured all but the nearest pots and left me staring out upon a grey depressing blindman's world of shadows and leering phantoms. I could have cried with misery.

My mother was soon at the telephone speaking to her friends. Miss Morison was very pleased, of course, that we had arrived although she seemed a little annoyed that we were both in Arthur's flat.

Then Amy came. The vexations of the day before were all forgotten and she wafted in like a diffident breeze, quivering with affection and delight. She was fair like my mother but tall, thin and arid whereas my mother was short, vital and beautiful. Although Amy had the same features one was only aware of her faded blue, prying eyes and her thin mouth fixed in a weak smile, ingratiating at one moment and patronising the next, according to the person she was with. She dressed well in a dull way and looked quite distinguished as she sailed about with a purposeful vagueness, with a grand inconsequential air and could often have been taken for someone extremely aristocratic – especially when she had recently been in aristocratic company. Like a sensitised film, she always bore the impression of the last person she had been with. She altered as she went about, taking on the opinions and mannerisms of everyone she met – met and admired, that is. She really had no identity of her own and only by attaching herself to Miss Morison and absorbing and reflecting something of her nature had she been able to acquire any stability of character at all.

Arthur's niece admired her and the atmosphere improved when she came. After lunch, we took a taxi (Amy never travelled any other way) to the hotel in which my grandmother had been living since the house was sold. When my mother was paying the taxi Amy took the opportunity while her purse was open, of asking for a small loan – only until tomorrow, she said.

Leaving the Square, after 50 years there, had been a great shock to my grandmother and she longed for her own home again. There was talk at once of us sharing a house with her which would have suited us all, but my mother knew that she would have Willie in and out all the time and so she could not do it.

While they talked I stared round the room and my attention was at once caught by the enormous number of medicine bottles which were ranged along the marble top of her washhand-stand. She had always been immensely strong and well but she had a weakness for doctors and now, and until she died, she went every few months (as soon as she was bored with her current malady) to a new specialist, invariably coming home with the disease in which he specialised. This pastime filled her life with ever-changing interest and enriched a multitude of doctors and chemists. She painted occasionally; the view from the window, flowers, little objects of still life and her work was still strong and fine, even after 50 years of damming up her talent.

Arthur returned the next day and greeted my mother warmly. When she explained why we invaded his flat, he laughed.

'I'm so glad you did, Louie,' he said. 'When I wrote to you telling you that I'd come through the war unscathed, I remember saying that if I could ever help you in any way I would.'

Then my mother laughed. 'It was that letter that made me do it.'

The next thing was the visit to Miss Morison. All the waiting years abroad, the years of growing up, all our thoughts and plans and preparations, the journey home and even these forlorn bewildering days of nearness and suspense in London – all seemed to be directed to this meeting. It was arranged when I was born, one could almost say, and was implicit in everything that followed. It was the culminating moment of my childhood when my life was taken up into new and powerful hands and poured into a mould which was waiting for it, which had been prepared by those hands and which, it was believed, would hold it. I looked forward to it and I dreaded it.

We took a bus to Westminster and after passing through several well-appointed streets, turned into a narrow, drab, depressing terrace. When we came in sight of the school I had a shock. The grey, smoke-grimed building, with a public-house opposite and dingy little working-class cottages all round, looked to me more like a work-house than the fashionable school – the 'girls' Eton'.

It was just as grim at close quarters although the polished mahogany door and brass plate, engraved with the school's name, gave it a certain tone.

A grey-faced seedy-looking porter opened the door and left us standing in the hall while he went to inform Miss Morison's secretary. And soon a tense little woman with a twisted lip and enigmatic expression appeared and led us up the stone staircase to the first floor, through an ante-room and then to some ladder-like steps which we ascended one after the other. Looking up, I saw Miss Morison standing at the top to greet us.

She was short and plump and dressed in black. Her hair was black, too, parted in the middle, looped and held by combs each side, then coiled into a pancake at the back. Her face was grey-white and her grey eyes were set wide apart. Her mouth seemed wide, too, and a small blue mark was in the middle of her lower lip. Several fringed pieces hung down the front of her dress and another long loose panel hung down her back. Later, when I went to school this wide black band flying out behind, was always the last thing seen of her as she swept through doors and disappeared round corners. On her large bosom was a small black button from which hung her pince-nez which she pulled out and in.

She and my mother shook hands warmly, her secretary picked up some papers from the desk and disappeared and then, as I advanced from the top of the steps, she rushed at me, lifted me off my feet and, hugging me tightly to her so that my face was pressed into her bosom, whirled me round and round, at least three times, before coming to a stop and letting me go. I landed back on the floor quite breathless.

'P. darling,' she then burst out, bending forward and staring into my face, 'to think that you are here at last! I can't believe it!' And she clapped her hands together and seemed to dance up and down.

I was astounded by all this emotion. I didn't know what to say or do, so I just smiled. Then, still staring hard into my face, she seized my hand and dragged me to a sofa.

'Come and sit beside me, darling. I want to hear all about your life in California and I want to tell you all about my school. You are going to be so happy here. You don't know how lucky you are.' And here she squeezed my hand so hard that it hurt. 'And I've been thinking of all the wonderful things we are going to do together. Your old godmother still has a lot of life in her.' And she laughed in a strained humourless way.

I wriggled away from her but I could not free my hand which she went on clutching. I hated this demonstration of godmotherly affection. Eventually, she calmed down and talked normally to my mother.

She had decided everything. I was to start school at once while she was still there. Although the term was half gone, the circumstances were exceptional and she waived away all difficulties.

I was appalled. I wasn't used to such high-pressure methods. I wanted to drift about with my mother for awhile as I always did, getting used to London and a new life. I was in no hurry to start school. In fact, now that I had seen the place and met Miss Morison I didn't want to start at all.

As the flat was so far from the school she suggested again that I should come to her as a boarder. But my mother would still not agree to this. Instead, it was arranged that we would leave the flat and join my grandmother at the hotel and that I would go as a day-boarder, returning to the hotel every evening.

This plan was such a shock to me and listening to them working it all out so upset me that I almost forgot the important thing I had to do, the first obligation I was under. Just in time before we left, I remembered. Freeing myself from her grasp, I pulled up my sleeve and showed her the gold wrist-watch. Then I took it off and showed her the inscription on the back. As she read the words 'from your loving Godmother' she caught her breath and her eyes seemed to glitter as they pierced into the gold.

I said how beautiful it was and how much I liked it. And my words were false. But again I felt that I must respond to all this love, that I must play up to her. Meeting her didn't change things. I was still a humbug. Right from the start I was a humbug.

As we rose to leave, she talked again about her journey to Palestine and we stood for a few minutes longer, listening.

'To visit the Holy Land, to follow in Our Lord's footsteps has been the great ambition of my life and now, at last, I am to realise it. We shall spend

Holy Week in Jerusalem.' She turned to me. 'P. darling, what a lot I shall have to tell you when I return.'

We said good-bye and left. In the street I burst out.

'Why must I start school at once? What does it matter if she's here or not?'

'The reason why I fell in with her plan,' my mother replied, 'was because I shall be house-hunting all day long and I couldn't drag you round with me. You would get so bored and tired.'

'I wouldn't. I would like to come with you. I always came before and it never took long. I could help you. I'd love it. I don't *want* to start school yet.'

'But house-hunting is harder here, my love. Everything is harder and takes longer. I know it's horrid starting but you'll soon make friends with the children and like it. And the mistresses are all so kind. They know that you are new to everything here and they'll help you all they can.' I saw how keen she was for me to go and so I submitted. Two days later we moved to the hotel.

It was 1919 and the place was crammed. After all the upheavals and separations of war, millions of people, mostly returning soldiers, were still pouring back into London, passing through and meeting again there, and every sort of accommodation was in demand.

The hotel lounges were all dormitories, even the bathrooms were being slept in and because building work was going on, one of the walls of our room was a tarpaulin. At meals, we sat with my grandmother in a cold draughty corridor and as for my mother's house-hunting task, it seemed hopeless. The agents laughed at her. And so, she just tramped the streets looking for anything that might be turned into a home. She could never be daunted.

As soon as we arrived at the hotel she took me back to the school and left me. I was taken to an empty class-room and soon Miss Kiddle came in with some long sheets of paper in her hand. I liked her, but when she told me that I now had to do the entrance examination, I nearly fainted with fright. Although I was nearly 12-years-old I had never done an examination and I knew how ignorant I was.

I sat down at a desk and while she was spreading the papers out in front of me, she chatted in a friendly humourous way. But I couldn't appreciate her humour. I just stared at the huge sheet covered with questions and at the pile of blank ones on which they had to be answered – and froze. I wanted to jump up and run out of the room, run out of the building and run right away as I had always run away from grown-up encounters that I did not like. But now, for the first time, I couldn't. I was committed to all these people and to this dreadful building. I could no longer make my own decisions and do things, for things were now being done to me all the time. I didn't belong to myself any more. I wasn't free. I sat there without moving, staring at those horrible papers, not knowing what to do or what would become of me. Then, the door opened and Miss Morison came in.

She walked straight up to my desk and gathered up the papers.

'There's no need for Philippa to do the entrance,' she said to Miss Kiddle. 'She can go straight into your form. She's the right age for it and you can look after her.' And at that moment I loved her. I felt drawn to her by a strong magnetic force. The next day, I started school in the lower third.

When I arrived I was given a peg and boot-locker and then taken up to my class-room. But the moment I got there a gong sounded, followed by chimes, there was a scramble for prayer books, a rush for the door and in single file, Miss Kiddle calling out, 'one at a time, don't push', we all set off downstairs again for morning prayers.

About halfway down the staircase, suddenly, my head was jerked violently back as someone behind seized my hair in a forcible attempt to change places. I twisted round and looked into an unfriendly mischievous face and grabbed the pig-tail behind it. Clutching each other's hair we descended to the big hall. Later, I made friends with this girl, and later still I had reason to be grateful for her loyalty. But now I hated her and hated this beginning.

In the hall we waited in silence. Soon there was the sound of a footstep, Miss Morison walked rapidly in and we all stood up as she passed between us and then mounted the platform. She went to the lectern and pulled out her pince-nez and fixed them on her nose and the service began. On one side there was an organ, played by one of the older girls with a small attentive child pumping.

I stared at Miss Morison. She stood in a characteristic attitude with her heels together and her toes pointed outwards. She was certainly the Head. Her power could be felt as soon as she entered and from the platform, she dominated everyone.

I went on staring at her even when I was kneeling and supposed to be praying. The child next to me shared her prayer book and I pretended to follow the service. I had to pretend for I knew nothing about religion and even when the places were found for me in the book, it was bewildering. And I wanted to go on staring at my godmother.

When the service was over she inclined her head towards the girl at the organ, the small child began to pump energetically, a dreary march boomed out and we paraded solemnly from the hall. When we reached our class-room we dropped onto our knees again for more prayers.

Miss Kiddle had no teaching qualifications but in her two subjects, Prayer Book and English Grammar, I am sure she was very competent. And from her beautiful handwriting she derived considerable prestige, for her notices could be seen pinned up all over the school. It was like the Mediaeval monkish script in old church psalters. And she looked like a monk herself. She was thin and pigeon-breasted and she had flat feet. Her long brown sack-like dresses reached to her ankles, her eyes and her hair were brown and her bony, knobbly hands, large as a man's, were always red with chilblains.

She also adored Miss Morison. But whereas Amy maintained a certain hollow dignity in her enslavement, Miss Kiddle grovelled before the object of her love. She had also come with Miss Morison from Cornwall and her passion had been so steadfast. Alternately encouraged and scorned, every smile followed by some cruelty, every moment uncertain, joy and suffering ran confusedly together until the spirit was exhausted and all that was left was a broken abject creature.

Because of their special relationships with Miss Morison, she and Amy lived at the school. They occupied austere, impersonal rooms, one above the other, in the corner of the building where Miss Morison's office was situated. Their lives were entirely bounded by the school.

The first few days were very bewildering. Bells were ringing all the time, along the stone passages there was the sound of scuffling feet and upstairs and downstairs we trailed. I felt all wrong in Virginia's clothes – and not even my hair was my own any more. I was told to put it into plaits. When I sat at my desk in the lower third, I spent most of the time gazing out of a window, paying no attention to anyone.

The lower ones were all of frosted glass. Only the upper ones were plain and through one of these I could see a small grey patch of sky and when a cloud moved across it or a bird flashed by, I nearly cried. I thought of the sun and the sea and the trees and the wild rough games – my freedom, my absolute freedom, and I felt like a prisoner sentenced for life.

My first essay opened with the sentence 'England is a prison and this school is a prison within a prison.' I couldn't laugh or even smile and I didn't make friends with the children. In a numbed trance-like way I went through the programme and in the afternoon, walked in the crocodile to the boarding-house.

On Sundays, at Miss Morison's special request, I went with her and the boarders to morning service. Except for the military parades in Victoria, I had never been to Church. I watched the other children, even the smallest of them, open their prayer books with a masterful air and repeat the Creed and bow their heads at the right moment and turn towards the east and give the responses and sing the psalms and canticles as if they had been doing it all their lives which, of course, they had.

Day after day my mother trudged about the streets of Westminster and when our money ran short and we could not afford to stay on at the hotel, another crisis arose.

Miss Morison still wanted me to live at the boarding-house, but now this idea frightened me even more than before and my mother still would not agree. Finally, she offered us a terrace cottage belonging to the school and attached to the main building, occupied from time to time by a junior mistress.

Because of the war it had not been modernised or decorated. A tap on the landing, from which the maid filled the bedroom jug, was the only water supply and gas mantles fizzing in the middle of each room lit up the dingy yellow walls and flaking chocolate paint. Because of the coal shortage we sat before a tiny ineffectual fire and lived in our overcoats.

Outside, every night, demobilised soldiers shouted and fought, vomited and urinated, as they rolled in and out of the public-house and by day, thin white-faced children with sharply pointed chins and black decaying teeth played hop-scotch in the pavement squares or hung listlessly about the door-steps.

We were living free of charge now and it should have been a rest; but it was on the charity of Miss Morison and we were conscious all the time of the obligation we were under. And now she asked me if I would like to take riding lessons.

I had always wanted to ride a horse but now I only wanted to be with my mother on Saturdays. I saw so little of her. But Miss Morison was so keen. It was so good of her and we were living in her cottage, so I couldn't refuse.

The school at Richmond was run by an ex-cavalry sergeant. Grooms mounted us on our horses, we walked them into the building and then lined up in single file round the walls. The sergeant came in, holding a circus whip, and stood in the middle.

He shouted some orders, cracked the whip and the horses moved at a walk. A few minutes later he cracked it again, they broke into a trot and I bumped up and down. When the whip cracked once more they were off at a canter. I hung onto the reins and clutched the saddle and each time we rounded a corner I was almost swept off. Then, flicking them with the tip of the whip he stung them into a gallop.

The line broke, they bunched together and when some couldn't turn at the corners, they literally ran up the walls. The children slid down their backs and dropped under their tails, dropped under their hooves, as they scrambled round. I was soon slipping. Still clutching the reins, I went down and down until I was under the horse's belly and then I let go and dropped under its feet and the horses behind galloped over me. Then the man with the whip stopped the ride.

We picked ourselves up and mounted again. The whip cracked and the lesson was repeated. Every time we were saved by the marvellous sensitivity of the horses.

For three weeks I endured these ordeals and then Miss Morison invited me to ride with her in Richmond Park. I accepted gratefully – *anything* to get away from the riding school.

I waited for her outside the underground station and I was astounded by the figure that approached me. She wore a bowler hat and a black old-fashioned riding habit with voluminous side-saddle skirt and she carried a hunting crop. She was very excited.

The horses were waiting at one of the gates of the park. She didn't look at them, she might have been mounting a bicycle. She swung herself clumsily into the saddle and hooked her leg round the horn, the groom adjusted the stirrup, she arranged her skirt and then looked triumphantly down at me.

When I was mounted, too, we moved off. After a few paces she cried out, 'let's have a gallop' and striking her horse with the crop it plunged ahead and mine followed. She went on beating it until we were tearing along as if we were trying to win a race. We jumped over ditches and bushes and banks, we swerved round trees and ducked under branches and clattered across the intersecting roads. Up hill and down dale we galloped without pause and when her horse slackened she beat it again. I tried to slow up but I couldn't. And she wouldn't have heard if I'd called. She was too far ahead. And I wouldn't have called. I would not have admitted how unhappy I was. Every moment I thought I was going to fall off.

We galloped right round the park and back, we were galloping still when we got to the gate. The horses were covered with lather and trembling and I felt half dead. But she noticed nothing. As we walked to the bus her eyes were glittering. That night I was ill and the doctor said I was not to ride any more.

Soon after that, the first letter came from Los Angeles. It was from the Norths. Not long after we left, they wrote, Yen had arrived at their house – hungry and exhausted.

She must have left the ranch as soon as she got there and travelled down through the mountains, across the desert and then round the great sprawling city. She must have been on her way while we were still in the big house. She must have gone there first to look for us. They had tried to comfort her, but she spent her days sitting on the porch looking up and down West Adams Street – waiting for us. When she had recovered they would find her a good home, they said, where, in time, she would forget and be happy.

I was utterly shattered by this news and by all that had befallen me. Again, I wanted to run away, run back to my darling Yen. But I was trapped, trapped before I was born, by an old and dismal world that seemed to possess me, that had seized me as soon as I came and was holding me tight in a grasp that was sweet and yet cruel, holding me down in a dark disciplined place, taking all my joy and my freedom away.

They said she'd forget and be happy. But I knew better. I knew she could never forget me, could never be happy again. And I knew I could never be either.

The term ended and the same evening we went to say good-bye to Miss Morison and Amy. They were leaving early the next morning. We sat down in Miss Morison's sitting-room and she came and sat beside me, but she was excited and restless and kept jumping up. Amy floated about the room smiling nervously – ready to run errands.

Miss Morison had some fine expensive Christmas gifts for us which we received with exclamations of surprise and gratitude. When we got up to leave, after promising to write regularly, my mother walked out of the room with Amy and then Miss Morison hugged me and kissed me ardently. I was thankful that they were going.

My mother's determination had now been rewarded. She had discovered a small Georgian house in Eaton Terrace which, because it was so dilapidated and depressing, had been over-looked by everyone else. It had been used as a brothel all through the war.

She had £500 of capital left. She paid a premium to the Westminster Estate for a short lease and the rest went to the builders for doing it up.

We spent Christmas Day with my grandmother. After that, we were very busy supervising the work and choosing carpets and curtains for the lodgers, for my mother intended to live on the house.

When 22 Campden Hill Square was sold, the contents were divided by lot among the six children and now my mother arranged for the delivery of her share and at the end of January 1920, on my twelfth birthday, we moved into our smart new English home.

2

A Depressing Year

MY mother wanted the new house to be gay and tasteful. A rich flowery wallpaper made the hall and staircase very lively and a sheeny white one with a faint classical design made the drawing-room very grand and, as always, we were both very satisfied – at least, I tried to be.

But not much of all this gaiety and grandeur was going to be ours, for the two fine rooms on the top floor were designated for one lodger and the two equally desirable ones on the ground floor were for the other. We had to squeeze into the floor between them, into the grand drawing-room and the small bedroom behind it.

My mother was now quite sure that our worst trials were over. I don't think she felt that they had ever been very serious. Her efforts and anxieties had often been much worse abroad, when we were so alone. She felt very secure and confident, now that she was home and among friends. She admired Miss Morison even more than before and she thought the school was wonderful, full of aristocratic little children and she was sure that I would settle down and like it. I think she looked back on the past as being of no importance at all, as a hard and irksome period of enforced waiting for the moment when my real life would begin. From now on, she was certain, that I would progress from one success to another as I forged a brilliant place for myself in the society of opportunity and consequence to which I belonged.

In Los Angeles, I subscribed whole-heartedly to this grandiose, ever-ascending life plan but now, suddenly, it had crashed and I was thoroughly confused. With my reason I still partially believed in it, but with my intuition I didn't, and I still could not distinguish between them. I still listened to my mother imparting her dream, but at the same time some speechless force inside me was rejecting it. I no longer lived. I just existed in a stony suspended state.

All this doubt and disillusionment, however, in no way affected my faith in my genius which was as strong as ever, but only the road for which I was always looking. In the meantime, I submitted to my fate. I was too shocked and saddened to do anything else.

As soon as we were settled my mother engaged a cook and house-parlour-maid and shortly afterwards two well-to-do gentlemen were installed in the house. They each paid three guineas a week for two rooms with full board, and coal fires were provided in their sitting-rooms – at an extra shilling a scuttle.

Miss Morison's long ecstatic letters describing first the wonders of Egypt and then, all her ineffable experiences as she moved from place to place in the land of the Bible, arrived regularly. It was the stamps on the envelopes that I liked. When I replied, I told her how well I was getting on at school and not only my own reports upon myself, but everybody else's were most satisfactory. All the mistresses had taken to me. I was obedient and subdued and kept all the rules. I never laughed, I very seldom smiled. I was a paragon of a child and Miss Morison's letters grew more and more expectant.

Before the term ended, however, the excitement over the boat race momentarily stirred me out of my apathy. All the children were personally and passionately involved in the contest. Their fathers had been up at Oxford or Cambridge in their time (some had rowed in the race) and their brothers were there now. They professed a kind of fixed family allegiance to one or the other.

I felt very much out of all this. I didn't know which crew to support. And support was not enough. The whole vulgar world was doing that. It was imperative to belong to, to *be*, so to speak, one of the sides oneself. I questioned my mother about my father's family. I knew how uneducated and disreputable all her relations were, but I was sure that his people were of a different quality. Unfortunately, she knew nothing about them in this respect and I was compelled to make my own choice according to my fancy. I chose Cambridge and sported a light blue rosette, but I did so without conviction, feeling that it was only a senseless and dishonest posture.

However, so great was the excitement the day before the race that I was quite carried away, and when a crowd of us were in the dressing-room, I jumped on a table and shouted to them all to divide into factions – Cambridge on one side and Oxford on the other – and then I yelled to the two sides to charge and fight each other. When I was satisfied that they were properly embroiled, I leapt into the middle of the swaying mass just as a whistle blew and several irate mistresses rushed upon the scene.

The fighting stopped and there was a moment of awful silence. Then the instigator of this disgraceful behaviour was ordered to own up. I put up my hand. It was a great shock to them to discover that I, the little paragon, was the culprit.

The crime was reported at once to Miss Kiddle. But she was not a punisher and I was let off on the grounds that I was still new and did not understand public-school ways. When the race was over I sank back into my usual state of quiesence and my popularity with the staff was soon restored.

After Easter the travellers returned, Miss Morison loaded with gifts. Scarabs and leather-work from Egypt and religious trophies from Palestine and, best of all, sets and sets of most wonderful stamps.

Our reunion was ecstatic. With her life's ambition fulfilled and exalted by her experiences and confident of her powers, Miss Morison looked forward excitedly to the future. Miss Kiddle stood down from her high post and, once again, the assertive black figure with canonical band flying out behind swept rapidly down the aisle and up onto the platform to take morning prayers.

Although all was well and the school had not foundered, Miss Kiddle relinquished her burden under a hail of criticism followed by pinpricks which went on hurting for months. Miss Morison resumed her weekly New Testament lessons, inspired now by her recent pilgrimage, but I found them as boring as before she went away.

I had had so little education, yet catching up had not been very difficult. The only really baffling subject was religion. I knew quite a lot about Jesus but little or nothing about God. In the world that I had lived in He no longer existed. But here He still did. If, like all the other children, I had encountered Him early in life and grown up with Him, enjoying years of familiarity with Him, I am sure I would have accepted Him, as they did, in a dull incurious way. But I would have missed all the excitement of a surprise meeting. For the sudden bombardment of His personality in lessons and daily services, relatively late in life, had a portentous effect upon me.

The discovery of God was like coming face to face with a new monstrous character in the world and a close relative at that – a father – and I tried my hardest to accept and understand Him. Yet, although His appearance, disposition, occupation, habitat and commandments were all minutely described to me, I could never make out exactly who and what and where He was. He seemed so real yet at the same time so nebulous; so very much here but at the same time nowhere. I was sure that this bafflement was due to my own ignorance and stupidity and that everyone else understood Him perfectly and I was afraid to give myself away and for a long time, pretended that I did, too. Then, when my curiosity became more than I could bear, I plucked up the courage to ask the awful question.

'Who *is* God?' I burst out to Miss Morison, soon after she came back.

'God is Love,' she replied instantly and went on with the lesson.

This made it even harder and I wanted to ask then: 'What is Love? How can Love be a man?' But I daren't. Instead, I thought about my love for my mother and for Yen and wondered how the angry old man of the Old Testament, the more reasonable one of the New, and the father-benefactor of our daily prayers could be one and the same as that. How could a man be equated with a feeling? However much I tried to personify Love, I couldn't manage it and in the end I gave it up and God became for me, also, the vague shelved paradox that He was for everybody else.

Miss Morison soon made a habit of inviting me to go out with her on Saturdays. Sometimes she took me shopping and I returned with some new clothes or an expensive present, and sometimes she arranged a special treat. She played up to me, flattered me and I felt strained and uncomfortable and obliged to go to Church with her the next day. I felt her magnetic power but I so seldom had an excuse for refusing, I always had to do what she asked – and *I* played up to her.

My mother now felt settled enough to think of painting again and she wrote to all her old clients. But her painting world had changed, too. Many had died and never answered; many had moved and her letters came back; many had grown too poor to pay for pictures and many were too broken. The only ones who responded came with photographs of the dead.

Their faces set and tragic, they brought these relics, some already fading, and laid them out before her and described the colouring and qualities of men in the prime of their capabilities and of boys, sensitive and beautiful, scarcely more than children. They talked and then they left her to the work of preserving, as finely as she could, the memory of the slaughtered generation.

During that first summer term, I still did everything that was expected of me. I hated swimming in the public baths; the insipid water, the shut-inness, the slippery concrete, the smell of chlorine and the echoing amplified noise. But I walked there twice a week in the crocodile. And then, one day, I saw my name up on the notice board and the games mistress told me that I had been chosen to swim in a match. She spoke as if it was a great honour and as if I ought to be very pleased. But I wasn't in the least interested.

Miss Glenday was an Oxford graduate combining literature and games. She had a yellow greasy complexion, large red-brown, muddy brown, ogling eyes and greasy black hair strained back into a bun with a band of velvet ribbon circling the top of her head. Her body was fat, coarse and aggressive but she had suppressed the voice that went with it and cultivated instead a small, breathless, modulated one which, when she spoke to Miss Morison, rolling her eyes all the time, came out in little nervous gasps. Like them all, she adored her.

The mistresses were all basically the same and they reminded me of Mrs Lennox. They were frumpish, solemn and joyless or artificially frisky; sad, freakish shades of the vast dark underworld of European history. Although I accepted them because I had to, I always felt as if I was associating with people from another planet. And soon, when I caught the virus of social snobbery, I looked down on them as well.

On the day of the match when my first race came and the starting signal was given, I dived in and shot ahead and reached the opposite end half a length before anyone else. Miss Glenday was beside herself with joy for I had won the race for the school.

The next time, I raced easily ahead as before and then slowed up and was ambling lazily along when, suddenly, I became conscious that all the people along the sides were screaming and waving at me. I could not think what was the matter. Then I realised that I was supposed to go on racing. I put on a spurt and reached the end still well in advance and as I touched the rail, another swimmer hurled herself in. Then I learnt that I was swimming in a relay race.

In spite of my bungling the start, the school won the race and the match and we returned in triumph. Now, I was not only a perfect pupil and the apple of my godmother's eye – but a useful one as well. I could be counted on to win all the swimming matches for the school.

However indifferent to competitive games these women really were, they had to subscribe to the cult of organised sport and Miss Morison, with an eye always on Eton, followed all the sporting events of the school year with tremendous interest and excitement. The climax came in the summer term with the two big sports days – the athletic events on the Richmond playing-fields and the swimming competitions in the Westminster Baths.

The athletics programme went up on the notice board first and, quite indifferent, I put my name down for the high-jump and the 100-yards race. I simply did what everyone was doing.

When I arrived at Richmond I was surprised to see a large crowd of distinguished-looking people, the parents, and as I watched the mistresses fluttering about with flags and tapes in their hands and the children darting here and there and talking in animated groups, I half rose to the excitement and half recoiled from it.

A big crowd gathered in a circle to watch the high jump. When we cleared the rope there was clapping and cries of 'well jumped'. When somebody failed and fell out, there were groans and sympathetic calls of 'bad luck'. At length, only two of us were left and then the excitement ran high.

I did not know the girl that I was jumping with. She was not in my form and she was bigger than me. But I liked her. Cynthia was a shy, sweet child and I was pleased each time she cleared the rope. I never thought about winning. I didn't know that we were competing for a prize and I smiled at her when I jumped and didn't jump against her, but against the rope and when, at last, she won – I didn't care a bit. Then the crowd cheered and clapped and pressed round us, thumping us both on our backs. And Miss Morison was there. She had been watching all the time without my knowing.

For the race, I lined up with the others and with a crowd on each side clapping and egging us on, we ran for the distant tape. I made no real effort to win and again came in second. And Miss Morison was there.

When I entered for these sports I thought that we were going to jump and run with each other just for the fun of it. I could never have imagined that the natural and joyful actions of children could be transformed into anxious, straining competitions marked by so much pride and pain and into something so important that hundreds of busy, eminent grown-ups would travel to Richmond and spend the afternoon clapping and cheering and getting so excited. The winner of each contest was immediately made into a heroine and the meeting itself had the standing of almost a national event. I hated it. But by the worked-up glamour of it all I was already infected.

After the race, I had nothing more to bother about and I strolled round with the crowds. But I wasn't interested in the athletics – it was the parents that I watched. This was the first time that I had seen them and they fascinated me – especially the fathers. They wore such lovely clothes, so beautifully shaped, so subdued and yet so striking. Some, of course, were tall and handsome but many were not, yet that didn't seem to matter for they all possessed the same subtle, indefineable qualities, a cool, unconscious poise, a casual fastidiousness, a nonchalance that paired with a look of gravity and authority. I knew that I was seeing and studying the English gentleman. My mother's brothers were all bounders whom we were trying our hardest not to meet. But my father had been a gentleman. I was quite sure of that and I wondered now if he had looked like all these splendid men. And I wished he had not died. I wished that I, too, had a father whom I could walk beside.

Towards the end of the afternoon, a table was set out in front of the pavilion and chairs were arranged each side and when Miss Glenday was seen laying out the cups and prizes, the excitement became intense. I watched these preparations for the crowning ceremony with still more surprise and as the parents began filling the chairs, I joined the group of prize-winners.

Presently, Miss Morison, accompanied by a tall good-looking father with a military moustache, walked to the table followed by Miss Glenday, holding the list in her hand. Miss Morison and the father sat down together behind the table while Miss Glenday sat slightly apart. Then Miss Morison stood up again to speak.

'My Lords, Ladies and Gentlemen,' she began. I was very taken aback by this. It had never occurred to me that some of the fathers whom I had been examining so closely and admiring so much were lords. 'Once again,' she went on, 'I have had the great pleasure of attending, as headmistress, this important event – our annual school sports day. As I walked about the field this afternoon watching the many exciting contests, it seemed to me that the athletic standard of the school was higher than it has ever been,' (applause and 'hear hear' from the rows of parents on each side) 'and that the sporting spirit was finer and more evident than ever before.' (Still louder applause) 'As you all know only too well, my Lords, Ladies and Gentlemen, it is the school's policy to concentrate, not only upon academic studies, but on the equally important educational activity of sport. For while the one develops the mind, the other develops character and some would say that character is the more important of the two. But however that may be, I think we can all congratulate ourselves upon what has taken place today. On occasions such as this I make no attempt to conceal my pride in the school.' (Applause) 'And now, my Lords, Ladies and Gentlemen, I am going to call upon that old and loyal friend of the school, Major General Sir Horace Dawson, to give away the prizes. Nothing makes us more happy than when he is among us.' (Loud applause) During these last remarks she kept turning graciously towards Sir Horace who now rose as she sat down.

'Miss Morison, my Lords, Ladies and Gentlemen.' He addressed himself primarily to Miss Morison at first. 'You have described me as an old friend of the school, and that is very proper for I began attending its functions when my children first entered as kindergarden pupils before the war and I have attended them ever since, even during the darkest days of the long struggle when the school carried on so valiantly and I was able to escape for a pleasant hour or two from my duties on the General Staff.' (Loud applause) 'And so, knowing the school so well, I can certainly agree with everything Miss Morison has just said. The athletic achievements which I have watched today with so much delight are ... quite remarkable' (applause) '... for girls ... *most* remarkable' (more applause) 'and the sporting spirit everywhere is also ... quite remarkable. With such a spirit running so strongly through the school ... nothing can ever go wrong and before presenting the awards for so much brilliant effort, I feel I must congratulate Miss Morison who, without any doubt, is responsible for these wonderful achievements and for the wonderful spirit which distinguishes the school.' (Loud applause) He turned towards her again. 'On behalf of the parents may I thank you most warmly, Miss Morison, for the great example which you set, for the confidence which you inspire and for the brightly shining results which we see springing out from this great trust.' (Loud applause) 'And now, I am to have the pleasure of giving away all these fine cups and prizes to the winners and the runners-up who so well deserve them.' (Prolonged applause.)

Then Miss Morison stood up again and at a signal from her, Miss Glenday began reading out the names and the children walked up one by one to receive their prizes from the genial hands of Sir Horace. When the high-jump results came, Cynthia went forward and I went after her. It was a new experience to walk through a crowd of such fine, important people – generals and lords, ladies and gentlemen – all applauding me.

The most exciting moment of the whole afternoon came at the very end with the presentation of the Victor Ludorum to the child who had won the most events. This cup was coveted by everyone and the winner was the heroine of the hour and of the year.

My two second prizes increased my prestige and that evening Amy dropped in to congratulate me and to bring a message from Miss Morison. She sent word to say how proud she was of me and to ask me to go out with her the next day, which was a Saturday. When we met she was ecstatic about my successes and she flattered me more than ever before.

I still could not understand how so much fuss could be made over such trivial little feats of running and jumping. I pondered over the two speeches and although I could understand the bits about character and its importance (I had so often worried about my own character), I could not see the connection with sport. If I participated in the school sports once a year and swam in a few matches, how would my character be improved in any way? And what was the sporting spirit? I only felt, obscurely, that something simple and joyous had been turned into an elaborate ritual of winners and losers, the chosen and the rejected, with a high priestess officiating, assisted by an adoring band of believers and a large mixed chorus.

At the same time, I was now very much aware of the society in which the school played an important part. Suddenly, I had a clear vision of the high privileged world to which it was linked, the world that my mother had talked about and coveted for me and I had dreamed of, my father's world of kings and queens and pageantry, of ancient offices and ruling orders, the fabulous world of empire and tradition, the England of heroic poetry and history. And for the sake of all this I found myself accepting the school. It appeared to me now, like a long unpleasant avenue through which one had to pass in order to arrive at the fine, fantastic world beyond. And the trees in the avenue were generals and lords, gentlemen and ladies egging one on and applauding, as one walked miserably but hopefully between them.

At the swimming sports a few weeks later, the parents filled the gallery all round the bath and I won my races to the accompaniment of shouting and applause which, bouncing off the tiled walls and trapped by the glass roof, echoed until it sounded like the roar of lions. I was now established in the world of sport. I had become a pillar of the structure which I so disliked.

With a wary, suppressed kind of excitement, the school broke up for the summer holidays and I came home with my report for the year. On the work side, my marks were average and I was moved up into the next form, but the character side was anything but average. The square reserved for the headmistress's remarks was filled with quite incredible reading matter. Miss Morison must have been hard put to it to find words adequate to describe all my perfections – the excellence of my disposition, my noteably good influence, my blameless record and the splendid public-school spirit which was so evident in all my actions. I was surprised to learn that I actually possessed this spirit without even knowing it.

Miss Morison and Amy went to Italy together to visit churches and my mother and I set off in the opposite direction with a less pious purpose. We had some Scottish cousins who lived in a small country house in East Lothian and my mother had written to them to ask if we could come and camp on their land for the holidays. 'Yes,' they had replied, 'but not in tents – you can have the empty coachman's cottage.' And they white-washed the walls and filled it with essential furniture.

A few weeks before we left London, there was an interesting development to this plan. My mother had never lost touch with her friend, Florence Leach (whom she had once painted) and now they met again, exchanging all the news of the separated and eventful years.

Florence was one of the 'new women' whose war service finally won the franchise for women. Having a powerful personality she had risen rapidly when the opportunity came and was appointed Commandant of the Women's Auxiliary Army Corps. When I first met her she was still in uniform, looking beautiful and formidable. I still adored soldiers and uniforms and I was still beset by my own feminist problem. The discovery that there had actually been women soldiers serving beside men (at least behind the lines) had a great effect upon me. And when I heard that Florence was to come and camp with us in the coachman's house, I was very excited.

She was very tired and depressed at this time for she was resigning from the service after six strenuous years and divorcing her husband. All she wanted now was to disappear from the world.

We went on ahead and settled into the cottage. It was built into the middle of a row of old vine-covered stables, with a cobbled court, a pond and beautiful wood in front and the tennis court and fields behind. When we entered the kitchen with its flagstone floor and ancient fire-place – I loved it all. Here, at last, was a piece of England – no, Scotland – which I could admire. And when I met my cousin, wearing a kilt, and saw his father dress for dinner every night in Highland regalia a new, romantic world was revealed and I fell in love with Highlanders and clans and with Bonnie Prince Charlie.

An old kilt was given me to wear and when I was not racing about the woods and fields I was reading books about the Jacobites and striving to discover that my name, after all, was Scottish and not English. But the deeper my researches took me, the more disappointing were the findings. Instead of following the Young Pretender, defending him with their claymores and singing their laments when he was driven over the ocean; instead of living in gloomy impregnable castles rising out of the dark waters of desolate lochs; instead of fighting the Redcoats and feuding with other clans and raiding the Sassenach cattle in between, I found that my family had been established on the border by William the Conqueror for the prime purpose of holding it against my Highland heroes and their turbulent ways.

At first, I felt forced to accept my ancestry and to reconcile myself to it, but soon, pushing away the disagreeable knowledge, I somehow managed to adopt this family as my own and, for awhile, I became spiritually Scottish, looking south across the border at all the things I hated so. At the ugly smoking cities, at the poverty and squalor, at the claustrophobic meanness of my school, at the love and the cruelty, at the whole oppressive spectacle of England.

Although I turned against the country which I had once loved so passionately and tried to escape from it by changing my nationality, this did not mean that I had ceased to admire the world of the parents – the Court of St James's, St Stephen's and Carlton House Terrace. They were as fine as ever but so out of reach and far away and unconnected with so much that I had seen. I could not understand all the contradictions – and my own situation.

We often motored to the coast and bathed in the Firth of Forth and picnicked on the long lonely beach. There were tennis parties and big family dinners – and then she came! The great Dame Florence, fabulous woman soldier and portent of the new age!

I was disappointed that she was no longer wearing her uniform but I had to admit that she looked even more stunning in civilian clothes. She was tall, with auburn hair and a white flawless complexion, and the voluminous travelling veil covering her head and framing her face made her look very romantic. She seemed very pleased with the cottage and I ran round her like a batman.

She was charming and magnetic. It would have been easy to fall in love with her, to be dominated by her because, in contrast to Miss Morison, her personality was refreshing and she used her power over people in an acceptable way although she, too, could be very alarming.

Every night, she spent a long time creaming her face and wrapping it up in cotton wool. Then, in the morning, she spent even longer unwrapping it and anointing it with one lotion after the other. When she finally appeared for lunch she looked so elegant, so rare and so unrelated to her surroundings.

Abroad, my mother's friends had all been so simple and easy to know. But here, people were complicated and hard to understand and they made one nervous – and Florence was not a comfortable person. She was too uneasy herself and critical. I always felt that she, too, was putting me through tests, sizing up my character and judging me according to some high martial standard.

After a week or so, she took to coming down to breakfast and then going back to bed again. This was to save my mother carrying trays upstairs. Thanks to our cousins, we lived so stylishly that we actually had a toast rack and one morning, as I reached for it to hand it across the table to her, she called out 'fingers!' in a commanding way. I took no notice and picked it up and then, as if she was giving an order to a company of W.A.A.Cs, 'fingers!' she cracked out again. Instantly I reasoned with myself. Should I obey her, which I was reluctant to do, or should I stubbornly go my own way? I decided to obey because I felt that behind the order there was something friendly and advancing. She was trying to break down my conventional manners and my stiffness and make our relationship more intimate. And if that was the only way that she could do it, well, what did it matter? I selected the choicest piece of toast and handed it to her in my fingers and she gave me an approving powerful look.

She had had no children herself which was a great sorrow to her and I did not know until many years later that my mother had left instructions in her will that, in the event of her death while I was still a child, I was to be adopted and brought up, *not* by Miss Morison, my godmother, but by Florence Leach.

I never thought now of going to look for village children. The class rules were so rigid – and I had changed myself. But as I played alone, I realised suddenly, one day, that the paralysing blanket of depression had been lifted away. I felt different. I would not have said that I was happy again for I knew what happiness was, absolute happiness, but for even this limited feeling of lightness I was thankful. And perhaps this *was* happiness – *here*? the most one could ever expect? Perhaps I had altered completely and was now really English?

With this change, my zest for living came back and however much I disliked my situation, I was ready to adapt myself to it and live it through, whatever it did to me, as fully as I could.

Our holiday in the coachman's house restored us all. When we travelled back to London, Florence was so revived in body and mind that she took good care to let it be known that she would be passing through Edinburgh on a certain day, at a certain time. She also made sure that we should be burdened with all the camping luggage. She travelled neatly looking what she was, an elegant important person – while we looked like tramps.

When we walked onto the platform of the London train, weighted down with bags, baskets and parcels and with a porter and loaded trolley beside us, we caught sight of a platoon of W.A.A.Cs. We slipped quickly away and watched from a distance while the Officer-in-Command advanced and saluted and then accompanied her up and down the ranks as she inspected her Guard of Honour. I thought of the times when I had lined up with the soldiers in Victoria to be inspected by the Colonel. And now I wished that I could have served through the war as a real woman soldier – and served under Dame Florence Leach.

We reached London without any more embarrassments and parted most affectionately. A few days later I went back to school.

3

Prison Within a Prison

IT WAS my new clothes which made the return to school bearable. Miss Morison had given me a smart navy blue gym tunic with a square velvet yoke and some beautiful white viyella blouses. For a year I had worn Virginia's dresses and loathed them and so my new school uniform gave me great satisfaction. Now I looked like everybody else and it helped me to feel like them as well.

Although so many of the children came from grand fine families, one of the first things that I noticed was their semi-soiled, untidy appearance. Their white blouses were always grey, their gym tunics stained and crushed, the box pleats seldom boxed, their shoes knocked about and their hair was so often unwashed. Abroad they were all so neat and clean.

I soon learnt that it was not just the smoke of London but that dinginess was one of the hall-marks of aristocracy, for Eton was the same. When I was first taken there – not for one of the great social events but on an ordinary school day – I noticed how dirty the boys were. In their top hats and swallow-tail coats and Eton jackets – stained, frayed and battered – they looked more like a crowd of Dickensian waifs and seedy characters than the gilded sons of the aristocracy and *haute-bourgeoisie.*

However, I soon imbibed this upper-class attitude to appearance, this cult of carelessness about one's looks, and when an extremely wealthy child arrived in my form, without a word being spoken, I intuitively joined in the general contempt which was felt for her.

It was not her wealth in itself that we scorned, for the right sort of wealth we honoured. Hers came from beer and stout and vulgar advertisements. But even worse than her wrong sort of wealth – was her neatness and cleanness. She arrived in a Rolls Royce and wore a clean white blouse every day and when she took off her coat in the cloakroom, she slipped on a pair of navy blue alpaca false sleeves!

My contempt, I believe, went deeper than the prevailing one, for my own position in the school was peculiar and also very vulnerable. I was conscious all the time that I had no family, no position and no money and that I had entered only because of my relationship with the headmistress. I felt myself classed, not with the children whose grandeur I now admired so, but with the staff whom we all despised. I did not want it to be known that Miss Morison was my godmother and Amy, my aunt. And now, when I made friends and brought them home to tea, I was always afraid they would discover that the house was full of lodgers. Although I had won a position for myself in sport, it never seemed enough – for I did not really belong.

Therefore, when that child was condemned and politely ostracised by the whole form I was pleased to join with her detractors, not just because I thought her silly and too rich and too clean, but because it gave me a chance to align myself with the children. It turned any imagined criticism away from me and gave me the horrible satisfaction of persecuting someone who, in essence, was the same as myself – someone who did not belong. And we drove her away. At the end of term she left.

Our new form mistress was another 'dear old thing'. I did not realise until later how lucky I was to have my first two years with these good, kind archaic old creatures whom we so often laughed at – Miss Kiddle and Miss Skinner. Miss Skinner also adored Miss Morison, but not so desperately and hopelessly. She did not grovel and she was not quite so monkish. Her long blue dresses, with the waist line where her bosom should have been, were even slightly fanciful.

Now, recovered from my paralysis, I lived with intensity once more. If there was no real happiness, there were moments of enjoyment snatched from the forbidding environment. I can still feel and see the oppressive blight which lay over everything, ran through and hung behind everything; a half-seen, half-lived world in which there was no growing, no seeking, no leaping and loving – where all was stopped and bent.

I was attracted, naturally, to all the most spirited and unruly children and we drew together and tried to push through the blight and get outside it. The most we did was to forget it occasionally.

Few of the children were really brainy. Although much lip-service was paid to scholarship, it was rare for a girl to go on to a university – perhaps because so few wanted to. My friends, with one exception, were the most brainless of them all and I cared less and less about my work.

The exception was the girl who pulled my hair on my first day. Intellectually, she was very advanced and later went up to Oxford, but emotionally she was slow to develop and she behaved in a mischievous irresponsible way. At home, on the other hand, in the presence of her parents, she often took the lead in the many high-brow conversations and then I admired the clever talk, the Medici prints on the walls, the books and all the interests and activities of the family. But it was Ione's school self, the clowning, anti-social side of her which most attracted me and for which, as time went on, I was more and more grateful.

Another friend was a boisterous girl who lived alone with her aunt, a grim strict woman. As an orphan I pitied her, but she seemed happy enough for she had a jolly irrepressible nature. I often went to her house and tore noisily all over it but always, sooner or later, the aunt came panting upstairs and the expression on her face was so weary and glum that I put on my coat and went home.

Betty was in very bad odour at school. The mistresses, one and all, disliked her. They thought her flamboyant and rowdy, sexually precocious and, worst of all, 'common'. I thought her one of the most affectionate and generous-hearted children that I had ever known and if she liked to dress up and become a woman at week-ends and flirt with boys – I did not care.

I rushed into a lively friendship with Rachel and was soon intimate with her aunts and uncles and cousins, all living in Chelsea and calling themselves the 'new poor'.

They were a distinguished family, connected to the aristocracy and descended from poets and scholars. Although Rachel's own people were neither talented nor in any way impressive and their house was a tasteless barn, some of the others were very interesting – especially Augustine Birrell, whom my mother soon painted.

Rachel, herself, was an empty-headed child but high-spirited and gay and she was always running round to her great-uncle to borrow books. One day, to assist her school work, she borrowed Macaulay's *History of England* in four volumes and a few days later, landed with a bound at the bottom of the basement stairs, burst through the sound-proof doors and bounced into the old man's library.

'Hullo, Uncle Austin,' she cried gaily, 'I've finished them. Shall I put them back?' And she began shoving the books into the first gap that caught her eye.

'No. No. Not there! Not there!' he said irritably. 'Bring them to me. I'll put them away.' And then he smiled. 'You've read them all ... right through from beginning to end?'

'Yes. Yes. It didn't take me long.'

'You are certainly a wonderful reader,' he went on with amusement. 'Even I couldn't do that.' But she wasn't listening.

'I must go now. I've got something terribly important to do. Thanks for the books.' And she was gone as flightily as she came.

When I first went to tea with her I stared at everything and listened to the family talk but as soon as I looked out from a back window and saw some waste land – a vacant lot – everything else vanished from my mind as I gazed upon this paradise. Then, shouting with joy, I rushed downstairs, out of the back door and over the garden wall with Rachel following me.

It was a large tract of land overgrown with grass and weeds and bushes which covered some old ruined cellars. We explored these and roamed all over the mounds and valleys, doing no harm to anything and then, we heard an angry shout and saw a red-faced man in shirt-sleeves approaching us quickly.

'Wot chu kids doin' in 'ere? This is private property an' I'm in charge. If you don' git out quick I'll call the Police,' he yelled at us.

'Alright, call the Police!' I shouted back as I darted to the top of a mound and laughed and he came running after me. Then I led him a splendid chase all over that wonderful waste of weeds, old iron and rubble. When I had had enough I slipped back into the house and, peeping from a window, watched him puffing and panting and staring angrily about.

I was, in fact, already known to the Police for the many entertaining games which I could play at home by myself.

One dark foggy night, wrapped in a sheet, I wandered moaning plaintively up and down the street, gliding up to people suddenly and frightening them. Before long, the Police appeared and although I vanished quickly into the house, they were not deterred. They knocked and rang the bell peremptorily and my mother had to go to the door and receive the complaint and give an undertaking that the prank would not be repeated.

I loved the ancient town game of throwing water out of the window onto passers-by, especially water-bombs which exploded on peoples' heads so marvellously. They were made with tissue paper filled with water, screwed up at the top like a balloon and then projected quickly onto the target before they leaked. But this delightful pastime ended as swiftly as the others when a cantankerous woman, unable to appreciate how clever and amusing these missiles were, threatened to sue my mother for a new fur coat – and a policeman was at the door again.

However, I kept on devising new entertainments and it was a long time before the combined forces of the London public, the Police and the school suppressed me altogether.

At school, my altered behaviour was noted at once and with the gravest concern. No one could have imagined that the change was in myself and that what they saw now was the real me – or something of it. Miss Bullen, the Latin mistress, stopped me in a corridor.

'I want to speak to you,' she snapped. 'You have always been admired for your dignity and seriousness. But this term you have changed. You are always smiling. You are smiling now. Why? There is nothing to smile about. In future, I shall expect you to stop smiling.'

She walked on. I did not know that I went about smiling, and if I did – why shouldn't I? After that, whenever I saw her coming I switched quickly to a glum expression.

Then, one day, Miss Kiddle asked me to stay behind when school was over. I was fond of her and not frightened and I wondered why she couldn't have said what she had to say, straight away. At four o'clock I knocked on the staff room door and she came out and took me to an empty class-room. Then she spoke.

'All through your first year at school you were serious and quiet but now you race along the corridors and run up the stairs, breaking the rules, and your whole bearing has become frivolous and undignified. We are very concerned about you and we feel sure that the reason for this change is that you have come under a bad influence. Among your friends, there is one girl that you have made a great mistake in getting to know so well – Betty – and for your good, you must have nothing more to do with her.'

I was so shocked I could not speak. She spoke so sweetly and yet what she said was so terrible. I could never have believed that Miss Kiddle could be so cruel and I was sure that the others had made her do this.

I went home dazed, not knowing what I was going to do. I was growing more and more of a snob myself, already I had a fine sense for all the nuances of class and I weighed up everyone I met and 'placed' them in my mind exactly where they belonged – just as we all did and as my mother had always done. But this snobbism was still no more than an intellectual exercise for it would never have occurred to me, on my own, to apply it to my personal life. I forgot that, in consort with my form, I had applied it to the rich girl and was applying it every day to the mistresses. I didn't see how muddled and inconsistent I was getting.

I was still shocked by the bald idea of choosing or rejecting a friend according to her class, for I knew that it was Betty's class that they were down on. If she had been a peer's daughter they would have tolerated her impulsiveness, her flirting and our friendship.

I didn't tell my mother. I kept all baffling things to myself now and thought about them secretly. If she had known about this she would have protested to Miss Morison at once. And it is a pity that she didn't.

When I recovered from the shock, I dismissed the whole episode from my conscious mind as if it had been only a bad dream and I carried on exactly as before, rollicking about with my friends, and with Betty, too. And nothing more was said.

The term before, I went out with Miss Morison nearly every Saturday. I had to, because I never had an excuse for refusing. But now, I had lots of engagements and it was easy for me to decline her invitations. When I had refused for several weeks on end, my mother would get rather worried.

'I really think you ought to go out with her next Saturday,' she would say, or 'you don't go often now, just put up with it for once and go to Church with her tomorrow. She is so fond of you, she is doing so much for us and it is rather rude and ungrateful to refuse her all the time.'

Sometimes Miss Morison herself, would get impatient and resentful and grumble over the telephone to my mother. 'Philippa is always out with her friends at week-ends. I never see her.' Or Amy would report how sad and disappointed Arm was feeling, seeing so little of me.

Then, I went out with her again. And she had changed, too. At school she was more autocratic; sharper, ruder and more impatient. But never with me. Whenever we met now she was soft, humble, sometimes abject. Sometimes, I felt her power and loved her, too. Often she seemed to magnetise and repel me at one and the same moment.

It was never difficult to make conversation. She listened avidly to everything I said and, treating me like an adult now, she talked about herself; about her ambitions, achievements and disappointments – even about her health, confiding to me the secrets of her body.

My mother was still unable to get much portrait work and the lodging-house business was not going at all well. She could never get a good enough cook and the lodgers kept complaining of the food and leaving. The house was like a hotel now with people moving in and out; often, with no cook at all, my mother struggling in the kitchen herself with a tweeny, a little 14-year-old orphan, to carry up the trays and make the beds. We were so poor that it was painful to have to ask her for the fare to Richmond (where we played games on Saturday mornings) and I was often thankful when the weather was so bad that we could not go. And she was often desperate.

One day, I picked up a pound note in a public place and was going to hand it in.

'No, keep it!' she hissed as she snatched it. 'The world has done us down so much, we need to get our own back sometimes.'

For the first year she had paid my school fees, but now Miss Morison was paying them, and for my books, my dinners, the extras which I took – and for my clothes. And all the time I was trying my hardest to avoid her and when I couldn't, pretending that I liked her. At least I had stopped pretending that I loved her.

Lacrosse was our winter game. In spite of all the fuss that was made about sport, we practised little, the coaching was poor and our standard low. Only a handful of children played. Most of them preferred to spend their week-ends participating in their parents' vivid social life, or migrating to country houses.

It was hardly surprising, therefore, that I was soon picked for the First 11 and I played in a match, experiencing the power and speed of a first-class team. Running up and down the field battling frantically to save the game, I felt so small and ineffectual beside those monstrous brilliant girls, so responsible for the outcome and so despondent as the goals mounted against us.

Later, I did not take our matches so seriously and when the good teams trampled over us, often quite literally, to their annual victories, I did not wear myself out fighting and then I was criticised for my lack of courage. At the same time, it was easy to see that some of these schools were not 'like us' and then our defeats were ascribed simply to class, to an aristocratic refinement in us which made us incapable of anything but feeble performances. Yet Eton knew how to play hard and win. It was all very perplexing. There was no consistency anywhere.

Before the war, Miss Morison's Shakespeare productions had been big events and now she revived them. A few weeks before Christmas she told me that I was to be one of the fairies in A Midsummer Night's Dream and rehearsals began at once.

After tea, every day, we waited in the big hall. When she arrived, she was always in a touchy state and soon she was shouting angrily at everyone – everyone except me. I was sure that the way she singled me out from criticism must be noticeable and that our relationship would be guessed at. And I hated listening to her castigating everyone else. I would rather have been shouted at than treated as her favourite.

On the first night, she was more wrought up than ever and she came into the dressing-room before the performance, hissing furiously at everyone – except me.

The big hall was noisy with talk and laughter and scraping chairs. When I peeped from behind the wings, I could see row upon row of starched and bejewelled persons. Half the nobility of England had come to watch us, plus the Cabinet, the General Staff, at least one primate, the whole bench of bishops and countless lesser divines from the sees of York and Canterbury.

I had never seen people in such fine evening dress. My mother could never look like that although she was just as beautiful as any of them, I thought, and just as distinguished-looking. And I had no idea that when men dressed up at night, they wore black suits with long satiny collars and white cardboard shirts. I had seen our cousin dress up in a kilt, but that was different, they were different, that was only fancy dress. And the jewels that flashed on the women's necks, the simplicity yet regality of their dresses and their wonderful hair styles and the way that they took their seats, the way the men bent and bowed and looked after them, lifted off their fur coats so deferentially, the way they all arranged themselves and sat talking and smiling and acknowledging their friends (they all seemed to know each other) and the expressions on their faces – all so easy and so self-assured, so secure they all looked. I admired them more than ever.

After 'God Save the King' the curtain went up. Miss Morison sat in the front row and she was dressed up too, in a dull dowdy way. I could see her across the footlights staring at the actors with an intensity which was mesmeric and whenever I went onto the stage I kept catching her eye, she seemed to be looking at me all the time. There was tremendous applause after every scene and at the end, the ovation was deafening.

Speeches followed and everyone was praised and congratulated, especially the brilliant producer, 'that great and splendid lover of Shakespeare who,' we were all reminded, 'had worked selflessly so many times that our girls might live inside and love the noble lines and varied characters of the great dramatist and carry away with them for life, not only the memory of these performances, but something of the sublime spirit of the Bard himself.'

When it was all over, still in a state of elation, I walked home with my mother. She was not so impressed by Miss Morison's brilliance nor uplifted by the sublimity of Shakespeare. She thought the children were just puppets, over-strained and nervous, and she didn't like Miss Morison losing her temper beforehand. She did not know how she had behaved at rehearsals. I never told her. But as we walked along she calmed down and began making excuses for her. She was so fond of her.

'She works so hard and gets so over-strained herself that I suppose she can't help venting it on the children sometimes. It's a pity. She's such a wonderful person. I hope her holiday will do her good.'

We could not go away for the Christmas holidays for we had no money and my mother could not leave the house. She spent her days preparing meals for the lodgers and her evenings – writing. In later years, she enjoyed telling her friends that, when we were on the verge of losing our home and everything in it, she bought a beautiful walnut bureau in which to keep her unpaid bills and at which to sit and write the letters which kept her creditors at bay. Unfortunately, the bureau often failed her and the bailiff became a regular caller.

Occasionally, she received a commission for a portrait but instead of getting better, the times grew worse. There were strikes and lockouts everywhere. Revolutionary communist ideas had been carried across Europe by the returning soldiers and in the whirling post-war world of sorrow, poverty and despair they took hold and the country was heaving with unrest. It was no time for art.

On Christmas Eve two servants arrived at our door, literally loaded with presents from Miss Morison. When I opened mine the next day I was astounded. They were all the things I had always wanted; marvellous things, expensive things, better than anything that the millionaires abroad had ever given me. I was beside myself with joy. And there were presents for my mother, too; lovely things, expensive things, things that she had always needed. And with *her* presents came a letter, written a few days earlier.

> Dearest Louie,
>
> I send these few things with my love hoping that they will make Christmas a little happier for you both. I am so sorry for you. I only wish I could help more to relieve your terrible situation. There is only one thing that I can think to do, one offer that I can make which will perhaps lighten your mind and lessen the weight of your worries. If the worst comes to the worst and you have to leave your home, I will take Philippa into the boarding-house and pay for her and care for her for as long as your position is difficult. At least you need never worry about her future which, out of my great friendship for you and love for her, I will *always* ensure. I sincerely hope, dear Louie, that this solemn promise to you will make Christmas, the festival of the birth of Our Dear Lord, a more joyful occasion for you both.
>
> Ever your loving friend,
>
> Arm.
>
> PS. Amy and I leave for Bournemouth this afternoon. I am utterly exhausted.

My mother was very quiet after she read this, not as joyful as she was expected to be. And a few days later, I sat down to the ever more difficult task of composing my thank-you letter. The presents were not quite so wonderful as they had seemed when we opened them.

4

The Crisis

WHEN WE all met again on the first day of the new term, Betty was missing and when she didn't appear the next day, or the next, and we asked the reason why – we were told that she had left.

I sensed at once that it had something to do with me and when I got home I told my mother all about her and how they had told me that I must stop being her friend. She was incredulous but quite certain that Miss Morison had had nothing to do with that – or with her leaving.

She saw her a few days later and when she learnt that it was she who had disapproved of the friendship, who had told Miss Kiddle to speak to me and, after that, asked the aunt to remove her, my mother protested strongly. But resenting criticism, Miss Morison turned upon her at once, reminding her of all that was being done for me, rebuking her for not being grateful for the protection which she was giving me.

I wanted to go and see Betty, but the next thing I heard was that she had been sent away to a boarding school and by the time the holidays came, my own life was so troubled and engulfing that I never went – never went to assure her of my loyalty.

Miss Morison's invitations were renewed and now there was no refusing her for those wonderful presents had to be paid for.

My mother never opened the front door now without peeping from a window first and every time the bailiff caught her with his superior wile and pushed his writ of summons into her hand, it was as if he had struck her and depression settled on us both. Even *she* lost some of her optimism now for she didn't know how to pay her debts and how to live without incurring more, unless she sold the lease of the house. Then, very reluctantly, for she clung to her possessions just as her parents once did, she began selling things. Her sixth share of the property was considerable and on the heels of the bailiffs, came the dealers.

Chairs and cabinets were lifted out, the mirrors came down from the walls, the porcelain disappeared from the mantelpiece, the room gradually emptied until all the colour and richness and old fine beauty were gone – my great-grandfather's treasures.

After each sale we both felt wonderfully relaxed. She paid up the summonses, bought a few essential things, I could ask her for the fare to Richmond and then it would all begin again.

This selling spree had unexpected repercussions. Amy began selling too. She had no financial worries. She earned enough pocket money for her needs from her music teaching and she was kept by the school and, in the holidays, by Miss Morison. She always liked to be doing what someone else was doing, to imitate, but the real reason for selling her share of the family goods lay deeper, beyond her understanding altogether.

Miss Morison was already using her things and now, watching keenly all that was going on, she suddenly woke up to their value. She could not have feared that they would ever fall into our hands for she had settled the terms of Amy's will in her own favour, years before. (In her naive way, Amy told us this.) But she wanted to make sure that she would not have to support her in her old age and so she jumped at the opportunity of turning her possessions into capital.

When the orgy was over, Amy was very pleased with herself. She had never had so much money in her whole life and she wafted about with a smirk on her face which was positively regal. And selling things had become a new game, something clever that she had learnt to do and she now carried her trading adventures even further.

She had observed my mother regularly taking our old clothes to a second-hand shop in Pimlico and one morning, she arrived in a taxi, jumped out and rang the bell and when the latest little orphan opened the door, dashed upstairs.

'Dearest Louie,' she cried, 'I've got a taxi full of old clothes. Do come and help me sell them.'

Very reluctantly, my mother put on her hat and coat and followed her out and they jumped in on top of an enormous bundle of deadly-looking garments spilling all over the seat and floor.

'I've collected all mother's old things and all my own. I'm sure they're worth an awful lot,' she burst out.

They drove to Pimlico but found the shop closed that day, then on to another in Chelsea which was open but with only a girl in charge who was empowered to sell but not to buy. 'If yer comes back in an 'our the lidy wot buys will be 'ere,' she told them. But obviously, they wouldn't do anything so ridiculous as that. Their valuable cargo would be disposed of long before and they jumped back into the taxi. But as their knowledge of second-hand shops was now exhausted they consulted the driver and, after some thought, he drove on to World's End.

Neither of them had ever heard of it, that sad desolate point, world's end indeed (it was then), full of monstrous public-houses and tiny overcrowded cottages where the Chelsea of the artists and intellectuals petered out into the slums of Fulham. And now their hopes rose, for he stopped in front of an important-looking establishment with a table outside on which was a heap of mangled clothes and a row of soiled and seedy things hanging from a wire stretched above it. Sunning herself in the doorway, was a blowsy creature.

They jumped out once again and together dragged the bundle across the pavement and into the shop. The creature heaved herself out of her chair and, stooping over the pile, picked it over slowly while the taxi meter ticked away outside and the driver enjoyed a restful, carefree smoke before dropping off to sleep in the spring sunshine. Then, after much thought, she spoke.

'They ain't the kinda things wot sells, dearie,' she began. 'I couldn't sell any of this stuff, honestly I couldn't. My customers just wouldn't fancy it ...' Here Amy burst out with an injured air.

'But they're beautiful things. All of the very finest quality, all from Marshall and Snelgrove's. Some of them are quite new, never worn at all.'

'That's just it, dearie, they're *too* beautiful, *too* posh. My customers don't want quality stuff like this. They want somethin' strong and serviceable.'

'I can't understand it,' said Amy pathetically, almost in tears now. 'I'm sure you're mistaken. I'm sure the people here would love to wear such clothes.'

'Come on, Amy, let's go,' said my mother exasperated and she began bundling up the clothes. At this moment the woman shifted a little and a wary look flashed over her face.

'Well, m'dears,' she said quickly, 'although the stuff ain't no good ter me, although I can't do nothin' wiv it, I don't want ter disappoint yer, especially seein' as yer've got a taxi waitin' and yer won't want ter spend any more money cartin' the stuff 'ome, so I'll make yer an offer even tho it'll be a dead loss ter me – I'll give yer seven bob the lot.'

'But that's ridiculous!' Amy answered with all the hauteur of which she was capable. 'These clothes are worth pounds – pounds and pounds! I wouldn't think of giving them away to you for seven shillings.' And she stepped elegantly out of the shop with her head in the air leaving my mother to carry out the clothes.

'I'll make it seven-and-sixpence,' the woman called out, but Amy got into the taxi without answering and my mother shoved the bundle in after her.

'What an outrageous woman!' she exclaimed when they were both inside. Then she called through the window to the driver who had just woken up.

'Driver! How could you bring us to such a dreadful place. Please take us at once to a really high-class shop.'

'Amy, this is idiotic,' my mother burst out. 'The taxi fare is already more than you'll ever get for the clothes. Why don't you take them home and give them to the poor?'

'Oh, but dearest,' she replied, 'I know I shall get a lot of money for them if I once find the right shop.'

'You won't,' said my mother brutally.

Amy did not answer. Suddenly, she seemed far away, quite unconscious that her legs were deep in coats and combinations, blouses and bloomers, that she had just been haggling with a frowsy woman at World's End and was on her way to haggle with another. She sat gazing out of the window in a grand, abstracted way, looking as if she was driving to a reception behind a chauffeur in a limousine. Then, glancing at her watch, she jumped forward.

'Dearest,' she cried, 'I didn't know it was so late. I am meeting Arm at the top of Sloane Street at twelve o'clock. I'll *have* to leave you. Driver! Driver!' she called through the window again, 'Stop at once!' The taxi drew into the curb and stopped abruptly and she leapt out.

'Dearest,' she called back, 'please take all these things back to the school and leave them at the side door and I'll sell them another day. Let me know what the cab comes to and I'll give it you tomorrow.' And she was gone.

My mother was aghast. Although she had suffered this sort of thing from Amy all her life yet each new incident seemed to take her by surprise. She looked again at the meter. The fare had mounted to nearly a pound – and she knew she would never get it back from Amy.

'Please go back to the shop at World's End,' she called to the driver.

Fortunately, it was still open and the woman was still sitting in the doorway. She lugged the things across the pavement once again and dropped them in the same spot.

'Here you are,' she said. 'I'll take seven-and-sixpence for them.'

'Oh, dearie me,' answered the woman staring incredulously at her. 'I never did expect yer back. Them nice lidies'll give up an' go 'ome, I sez ter meself. Its reely upsettin' me ter see yer.'

'What do you mean?' said my mother. 'Please give me seven-and-sixpence quickly so that I can let the cab go.'

'But dearie, I can't, I reely can't. I made a big mistake when I offered yer all that jes now. 'enrietta, I sez ter meself when yer was gone, 'enrietta, yer never should 'ave done that, yer was too generous, yer was carried away by them two nice lidies, yer was goin' ter rob yerself yer was, yer reely must be more careful in future.'

My mother was dumbfounded. 'But ... but ... do you mean to say that you are going back on your offer ... going back on your word ...?'

'Dearie, they're jes not worth it. I tell yer, I made a big mistake jes now. But I want ter 'elp yer all the same. I can see the spot she's left yer in. She's that sweet ter look at, aint she. Yer dont want ter 'ave ter pick all that stuff up again. Yer must be sick an' tired of it. I'll take it off yer for five-an'-sixpence an' give it away ter some of them poor women wot can't afford ter buy nothin'.'

By this time my mother was in a state of utter exasperation.

'Alright, give me five-and-six,' she said, 'and do be quick about it.' The woman waddled across the shop to her hiding place and then returned with the money.

'A pity yer didn't leave the stuff the first time,' the man said as she paid him. It was a wonder she had enough. Then he twisted round and looked into the back of the cab.

'Yer've left somethin' be'ind, Ma'am!' he called out as she was walking away. On the seat was a pair of new woollen bloomers.

'Thank you,' she said as she seized them. Then she turned and waved them at the woman before stuffing them into her pocket.

'I'm keeping these. They're not included in the deal!' she shouted as she walked away from World's End – back to the world's fine centre.

She went on engaging cooks but most of them were incompetent, dirty and dishonest. Occasionally, a good type strayed into the house, but as soon as she realised her mistake, realised that she had been lured into a common lodging house by a charming 'lady' who wasn't a 'lady' after all, she left at once.

My mother was always missing things and again and again, on the suspect's afternoon out, she would send the tweeny off on some errand and post me on the staircase to keep watch and then, in a nervous fury, descend to the slum bedroom and ransack her stinking drawers and luggage.

Sometimes she found her things, more often she didn't, but nearly always these descents into hell ended in a row the next morning and a month's notice.

I loathed these property searches and for the first time in my life, inwardly criticised my mother. It seemed to me odious to invade the private quarters of these dreadful women and I wished she would let them have the things and go in peace. And often, I was sure that the things had only been mislaid. But it wasn't long before I was the same.

While the awful month was passing, the cooking became more vile than ever and hatred filled the air. When, at last, the woman left we sighed with relief and my mother ran downstairs to clean up the squalor and start cooking again herself.

Some of the orphans were fine little girls. One stuck it out through several of these storms, but most were unhappy and appealed to their Homes to recall them. My mother was good to them but the house below stairs and above was too chaotic for any motherless child, however tough, to thrive in.

My mother would cook for awhile and then try again; engage another well-spoken horror. And then, one day, the pattern changed. A friend passed on to us a most superior little woman; an excellent servant, she said, with only one eccentricity, and that very harmless – an adoration for the Queen. She was parting with her because she did not get on with the other servants and because of a vague feeling of unease which she could not explain.

Batten arrived, accompanied by a huge, black, castrated cat called Tippoo, and they both settled down in the basement. She wanted no other servants, not even a weekly charwoman, and she didn't mind the lodgers. She was scrupulously neat and clean. Every meal was divine, the house soon gleamed, the lodgers were delighted and life at home became peaceful and altogether more respectable.

Every day, she bought two expensive bunches of flowers and gave one of them to my mother. She implored her not to waste her money, but she went on doing it – for she adored her. We didn't know what she did with the other bunch.

Not long after her arrival, my mother's morning interview chanced to be a little later than usual. They were talking together in the kitchen when the distant sound of the Guards' band came floating through the house. A detachment marched down Eaton Terrace at the same time every day. Batten started and listened, her expression changed, and as the music came nearer she walked out of the kitchen and up the stairs. As she didn't return, my mother followed her and saw her at the open door, drawn up to her full height, straight and proud, her head thrown back, standing to attention, waiting for the soldiers to arrive.

'The Queen has sent them,' she murmured to herself. 'Wherever I am she sends her Guards to protect me. She never forgets me.'

When they passed, with drums resounding and fifes ringing out between the houses, she stood there on the door-step, like a queen herself, taking the salute.

When they were gone and the music died away she turned and came down to the kitchen again. But now all the pride and elation were gone out of her, she seemed shrunk and humble and ordinary, just a little servant woman talking about the dinner and her household duties to her mistress.

But to us, she was never ordinary again. My mother recognised the royal eyes and features – the Battenburg face. She had once painted both Prince Louis and Prince George. Now we understood why she spoke coarse cockney English but with a cultured voice, why she did her hair and wore clothes like Queen Mary and now we knew that she walked every afternoon to Buckingham Palace to give that other bunch of flowers to her relative, the Sovereign. We treated her now like the noble personage she was; a bastard, perhaps, but all the same a princess of the House of Battenburg. And every day, when the Guards passed, she stood at the front door taking the salute.

We were very comfortable now and the lodgers were satisfied and settled but still we could not live. They did not pay enough, my mother was not earning and the bailiffs went on calling and there was nothing more to sell. It seemed inevitable that we should have to sell the lease and find some other way of living and I was sure that, for me, that meant the boarding house.

Then, just as years before in Victoria when, at her wits' end, she had set up her studio in the cowshed beside the soldiers' camp so now, she was inspired again with what, in those days, was a novel idea.

She decided to sack the lodgers and the royal paragon, to divide the house into two, move upstairs and let the lower half as an unfurnished flat. And she went ahead. The project was so simple. She just emptied the ground floor and basement and advertised for a tenant. The bathroom fell to the lower flat. We did without and were not bothered in the least.

Applicants came queuing to the door and she chose an elderly White Russian doctor who willingly paid twice as much for his empty flat as she had ever received from the lodgers. She gave Batten her notice in the most delicate and deferential way.

'I have always felt that this post is not really good enough for you,' she told her, 'and now that we are moving upstairs I shall not have room for you and Tippoo and I must ask you to look for another place. I shall be very sad to lose you. But you need not hurry away. Until you find a house that suits you – and suits Tippoo – in which you can feel honoured and happy, you can stay here and occupy the nice room behind the drawing-room, the one my daughter and I are in now. We shall be moving up to the big room on the top floor.' And Batten appeared to take all this quite serenely.

My mother made only two alterations to the house. She had a sink put into the back bedroom on the top floor and turned it into a kitchen and she had the wall broken through and an arch made between the drawing-room and the room behind. She had always admired the L-shaped drawing-rooms in all the grand houses that she knew and now she decided to have the same herself. When the work was finished, the new arch was temporarily boarded up for Batten and Tippoo. This arrangement was quite satisfactory except for the fact that the temporary structure was not sound-proof. But no one minded and life went on as smoothly as before.

She stopped the daily bunch of flowers now and, in the circumstances, we thought this sensible and my mother was thankful. Sometimes she seemed more withdrawn than usual and now and again we were surprised by a hard, furtive look on her face. But we thought nothing of these trivial changes, ascribing them to worry over her own future. She was out every day interviewing prospective mistresses and she had not yet selected a suitable suppliant.

Then, one morning, while she was downstairs scrubbing the front door-step, my mother went into the kitchen to wash something in the sink. She was swishing it about and the running tap was making a lot of noise when, suddenly, she felt uncomfortable and she straightened herself and then saw, reflected in a small mirror which was hanging over the sink, the figure of Batten standing behind her – and the expression on her face was fiendish!

Instantly, my mother swung round but keeping her arms in the sink, for if Batten had come any nearer she meant to fling the lump of washing in her face.

Drawn up in the same proud way as when she was taking the Guards' salute, she stared fixedly at my mother – but irresolutely, and during those few trembling seconds, straining to deflect her mind, my mother laughed and chattered inanities until that awful face gave way, the figure slumped and once again the little servant woman stood humbly before her.

My mother was very upset by this incident. She thought of going to the Police but the evidence was hardly enough to have her committed to an asylum ... yet supposing it was and they came and took her ... and took Tippoo away from her ...? And going over the scene again and again in her mind she even wondered if, being in a highly nervous state herself, she had exaggerated the whole thing, felt threatened when there was nothing more to it than Batten's annoyance at finding her mistress in her kitchen.

But as the day wore on she became more anxious. She had been waiting week by week for Batten to decide on a new place and for her prospective mistress to telephone her for a reference and now she wondered what she would say when the enquiry came. If she told her all that she knew and guessed and now felt, the woman would cancel the engagement and Batten would be left on our hands in a frame of mind that was terrifying to think about. On the other hand, she could not let her go to new people without a warning of some sort. And the only alternative was the Police ...

We always knew that she talked to Tippoo but now we could hear her, through the partition, crooning and talking incessantly to the old cat. We got used to it and hardly noticed it but that evening, after I had gone to bed, my mother was sitting quietly writing her usual letters when, suddenly, she was electrified by the words coming through the wall.

'Yes, Tippoo darling, that's what I'll do. Yes, that's what I'll do, my darling. I'll lift my 'and to 'er, I'll lift my 'and to 'er, an' it'll 'ave an 'ammer in it, yes, an 'ammer in it, an' I'll give 'er such a crack on the 'ead, such a crack on the 'ead, my beautiful boy. Oh, Tippoo, my beautiful boy ...'

For a few moments my mother sat there frozen. Her problem was solved and she knew what to do. But she couldn't telephone at once with Batten listening and she daren't go out, leaving me alone with her. It never occurred to her to appeal for help to the old doctor. He was so foreign and remote from us. She decided to wait until the morning.

She crept out of the room, past Batten's door and upstairs to our room and barricaded us in. For most of the night, then, she lay awake listening, ready to scream from the window at the first sound of assault. But nothing happened and not a single suspicious noise disturbed the stillness of the house. In the morning she waited for Batten to come up to the kitchen, but even this she didn't hear. But then she might not, for she was always very quiet. When I woke, she told me what had happened and when we were dressed we moved the barricade and emerged cautiously onto the landing. Our plan was to leave the house together, my mother going to the police station and I, to school.

The kitchen door was half open. We were certain that Batten was behind it with a hammer in her hand. We darted past and down the stairs. Her bedroom door was half open, too – very unusual, for Tippoo might escape. It must be there, behind that door, that she was waiting to spring. We rushed past it and into the drawing-room, quickly closing the door and wedging it with a chair. Then we listened, with our ears pressed against the partition. But there wasn't a sound. The stillness in the house was quite uncanny. We opened the door a crack and peeped and when we came out and stood on the landing and listened again – we knew that Batten had gone.

She had packed and fled in the night. And that was the end of our royal maid – so mad, so murderous and so pitiful.

We were by ourselves now and living rent free and it all seemed so good, but unless my mother earned, we still didn't have enough to live on. And then she was inspired again.

Beauchamp Place, once a very ordinary little street, had recently been invaded by all sorts of intrepid people, many of them 'the new poor' trying out new ways of surviving. Shop after shop changed hands and the new traders soon transformed the street into a fashionable and fascinating shopping centre.

Attracted herself, my mother wandered up and down it, gazing into the rich, sophisticated windows and wondering if she, too, could not participate in this revival. Finally, she stopped before the smart little door of 'The Merchant Adventurers'. They were interior decorators; the 'new poor' teaching the 'new rich' how to look as if they were the 'old rich'.

She went in, showed them a picture and made them a startling proposal. She asked if she could sit in their window and paint quick portraits. The idea certainly surprised them but true to their name, they grasped its publicity value and agreed to let her try.

The next day, the old list of royalties, a card with her fee, five guineas, a sample sketch and two chairs were all placed in the window. One of the shop women was glad to start things going and they both sat down and my mother began. A crowd collected outside, a queue formed and at the head of it was Mrs Stanley Baldwin. And soon, with a waiting list, she settled down to a regime of two a day. The shop took no commission, content with the publicity and pleased at her success.

Suddenly she was earning £50 a week! Relief and joy flooded into our lives, everything seemed to lighten and expand, England seemed less of a dreary prison and even my school, less of a 'prison within a prison'.

Miss Morison watched all these developments and professed to be overjoyed at the improvement in our affairs. The school itself was now in trouble and she was exceedingly worried. A new Act of Parliament had made it encumbent upon all private schools to conform to certain minimum standards, failing which they were liable to be taken over by the State.

Government inspectors came and a multitude of errors and omissions were uncovered. For awhile its very foundations tottered. Miss Morison could see herself and most of her staff deprived of their jobs and with desperate energy she now fought to save the school's rarified position and her own entrenched eminence.

The salary increases for higher qualified teachers could be met by raising the school fees but to construct a playground, which was now obligatory, and to bring some of the old buildings up-to-date she needed £20,000 – a large sum in those days.

The School Council met again and again and parents' meetings were called. At one of these, when the big hall was packed to the doors, there was a really shocking incident.

After Miss Morison had made a long passionate speech extolling the advantages of the school's private status and appealing for money and effort to save it, a man stood up at the back and, in a quiet firm voice, remarked, 'I don't think the school is worth saving.'

Miss Morison turned deathly white, my mother said afterwards, and a storm followed, everybody protesting at once. Then, a resolution calling for the saving of the school was passed with cheers, an appeal fund was launched and the meeting ended with a vote of confidence in Miss Morison and a quite delirious ovation. The revolutionary voice was just what she needed to secure her victory. Flushed with triumph, more confident than ever of her power over people and events, she then turned back to my mother to make quick use of the friendship which bound us so closely to her.

'Can I come to tea with you, Louie?' she said when they met, and my mother was glad to be able to support her at this critical moment in her career.

'Wasn't that man awful!' she burst out as they left the school together.

'Who was he?' my mother asked curiously. In a secret, paradoxical way she rather admired him.

'He's of no importance. He's only Mr so-and-so. He carries no weight at all, as you could see. I hope he takes his child away at once.'

They walked on, talking about it all until they reached our house where, settled comfortably with a cup of tea, she gradually relaxed.

'Louie,' she then said suddenly. 'Will you help me? There is a way in which you *can* help me.'

'Of course,' replied my mother, willing but apprehensive. She knew from experience that helping Miss Morison was always an exacting business.

'I have thought it all out – and this is my plan,' she went on. 'You have plenty of money now, you are earning £50 a week. I want you to start the Building Fund off with a donation of £100 but *not* in your own name. I want you to send it to the Archbishop of Canterbury with a letter, which I will write, saying how splendid you think the school is, how dreadful the threat to its existence and that you would like to donate this money through him. Don't you see, by doing that I can drag the Archbishop into the campaign. I can make him seem to head the list of subscribers.'

My mother was rather mystified by all this but she was quite ready to give £100 to the school. It would be some repayment for all that Miss Morison had done for us and if it pleased her even more to get it through the Archbishop, that was all to the good.

The next day, an elegantly worded, somewhat oily, letter was dropped through our door and in the evening my mother copied it and posted it to Lambeth with a cheque. It was acknowledged by return, the Archbishop only regretting that she had not sent it direct to Miss Morison as a greater mark of encouragement and high appreciation of what she was doing.

'£100 – per Archbishop of Canterbury' headed the Building Fund subscription list. And now Miss Morison worked like a fury and drove everyone else. Money-raising projects followed each other in rapid succession – bazaars, concerts and displays (we were always rehearsing or working for something). Appeals went out far and wide, the parents were squeezed and squeezed again, *Debrett's Peerage* and other special directories were culled for likely names, there was scarcely anyone in England above a certain rank and of the Anglican persuasion who was not badgered. And she did it! Within a year she had the money! Within a year the school was saved!

And when she saved the school she saved herself. Miss Morison grew up in the poorest of circumstances, climbing out by means of scholarships and force of character, using anyone of influence who came into her path. When her father died of drink, she brought her mother to London and hid her away in a flat. She was a rough, harsh old thing, my mother told me long afterwards.

'Alice never lets me com ter th'schoal,' she grumbled in her thick brogue. But Alice spoke the King's English, Alice was now a 'lady', an important headmistress and a power in the land and she wasn't going to be given away by her old Scots mother.

When the school's future as a private establishment was secured, her prestige and power, within that world in which she worked and lived, could hardly have been greater. Had she failed, her whole career would have collapsed for she had climbed to the top but with nothing of substance beneath her. She had no degrees. She was a most ignorant woman with no intellect at all, but clever enough to know it and to hide it. Her powerful personality was like a suit of armour, her determination and adroitness like offensive and defensive weapons and the hollowness and all the fears and passions that swirled inside were never seen or known. She was too old to start again and talents such as these were no longer so easily employed.

I do not know when she first took up religion. Her mother was not pious. I think she must have encountered it when she first came to England, grasped its many possibilities and attractions, both consciously and unconsciously, and then used it in several ways. As a vehicle in which she could travel more easily and comfortably than by any other method, as a means of enhancing her prestige (she was always admired for her devoutness) and as an emotional practice, near to an art, which satisfied a temperament, so largely that of an actress.

Sometimes, when I watched her, I felt that she was floating, that her feet were not touching the ground and, looking up, that she could see God and they were talking to each other.

On Sundays, she attended every service, contriving to reach the church door, not late – heavens no! but just a little later than everyone else. I think she must have timed her entrances to the five-minute bell when the church was full, the audience waiting motionless and expectant, when the organ was playing and the stage was empty and the spotlight was ready to catch and hold her moving figure in its beam.

Always dressed in black, (she once told my mother mysteriously and tragically that she wore permanent mourning, not only for her mother but for a wondrous person who had loved her but being too good to live, had died and left her forever grieving) she marched up the centre aisle to the front, with eyes cast up, and there she would stop, cross herself, bow slowly and solemnly to the altar, step into the pew and drop to her knees in prayer. These splendid entrances were watched by the whole congregation and, Sunday after Sunday, they must have felt that a saint was in their midst.

5

Godmother's Triumph

THE BIG event of the spring term every year was Prize-Giving Day. This year, Princess Mary came to honour the school and a large dais was built for her in the big hall, tiers of benches were constructed above the platform for us and extra chairs were hired for the great concourse of parents and friends. For weeks beforehand we practised songs and anthems with Mr Bates, our singing master.

When the day came, we climbed up onto our benches which mounted to the very ceiling and looked down on the crowd below. All in white, with our hair combed out, stacked together, floating in God's firmament, we must have looked like a massed choir of angels – or like a bank of monstrous tropical flowers. The purple-bordered ecclesiastical programmes fluttered in the parents' hands and the roar of their talk came up to us.

Suddenly, there was silence and the next moment the Princess entered with a train of grandees; lords and ladies-in-waiting, bishops, generals and admirals, and among them all, walking beside her – Miss Morison.

As the Princess passed between the parents along the red carpet, they curtsied and bowed, she nodded graciously to right and left and then, the moment she put one foot upon the dais, Mr Bates waved his baton and we led the great assembly in 'God Save the King'.

To sing the anthem of England at the top of one's voice to a princess standing there in the flesh below, to hear the grand martial tune swell as the parents, especially the fathers, took it up, fill the great hall and then float out through the windows – was wonderful!

Then, one after the other, the personages on the dais got up to speak – all men they were – Miss Morison was the only woman to compete. Although their speeches were all the same, they were received as if each was an original piece of oratory. They praised the school and quoted its motto 'That our daughters may be as the polished corners of the temple', expanding it, repeating it, getting quite lyrical about it and quite stuck in it and each ended with a heartfelt tribute to the headmistress.

I knew all these speeches by heart but I still admired the men who made them – their expressionless but handsome faces and their arrogant upper-class voices.

Colonel Wigram was always to the fore on these occasions. He was one of the King's equerries and a member of the School Council. With his swallow-tail morning coat he always wore a black silk stock and a diamond pin. Short and square-looking, he was particularly pompous. But he covered it over in a clever sort of way, with a genial fatherly manner which I found irresistible and coming through it all, through the pomposity, geniality and fatherliness, emanating from him, as it were, was that same ruling, authoritative 'something' which intrigued and attracted me so.

Then the Princess gave away the prizes. Throughout, her role was entirely passive and she looked rather surly and unattractive. But I admired her. As the prize-winners mounted the dais to receive their books, she smiled in an automatic way and the parents clapped. I was sorry that I had not won a prize for more and more I liked to be one of the elect.

At intervals, we stood up on our cloud and sang and the whole fine affair was brought to a close with Blake's 'Jerusalem'. How I loved that song. I could have gone on singing it to the Princess, to the fathers, to that grand glittering world and to myself forever and forever. I could no longer hear that the walls mocked the words that we sang.

Then the head girl called for three cheers for Her Royal Highness, we shouted our hurrahs, the luminous party stepped down and made their way slowly between the same waving rows of bobbing, bowing people and after that, the golden crowd dissolved and another splendid show was over.

When the school sports came round again, with the summer term, I entered for everything. I did everything now. Cynthia had gone with her parents to America for a year and I had no rival anywhere. And now I wanted to win. I strained to win. And I did. I won everything. When the prizes were given away, I walked back and back again to that silver-loaded table until my arms were full of cups and the parents were applauding and applauding me. And I walked back finally, to receive from the hands of the smiling father, that cup of all cups – the Victor Ludorum. And now I was truly a leader in the school.

When Miss Morison took me out to celebrate my triumph, she asked me if I would spend part of the holidays with her, in some beautiful place that I had never been to – abroad perhaps. But I told her that my mother had already arranged our holiday and that I couldn't leave her. And it was true. Having plenty of money now, she *had* planned something nice for us.

The school year was drawing to an end and I thought I had got through it well. I had been admonished for minor misdemeanours and for curious things like my smile and my friendship with Betty, but nothing serious had happened and I felt successful and rather pleased with myself.

Then, one day, racing upstairs, I was caught again and, the next morning, ordered to present myself before Miss Morison at four o'clock. I went cheerfully to her office and knocked on the door.

'Come in,' she called. She was busy writing at her desk. Removing her pince-nez she turned and looked at me for a second and then put them on again and went on writing. 'I'll attend to you in a minute,' she said coldly, 'Sit there.' And she pointed to a chair. I sat down and waited – and soon began to fidget. I wanted to get home. At last she put her pen down, took off her pince-nez again and let them spring back to her bosom – and turned to me.

'I have something very serious to say to you, Philippa. You are now 13-years-old, you have been nearly two years here, quite long enough to have learnt all the rules and the high code of behaviour, to have discovered and made part of yourself the spirit of the school. You have distinguished yourself in sport, you have become a leader that everyone looks up to, and for this I am proud of you, as you know. But a leader must set an example in *every* way. Success in sport is not enough. The right spirit must go with it and this, I am sorry to say, you do not have.

'It has been reported to me that you were seen by a prefect yesterday, running up the main staircase two steps at a time. As you know perfectly well, the rule is *one* step at a time – and it is an important rule – and this is not the first time that you have broken it. I have called you here to tell you that, in future, I shall expect you to observe this rule and to alter the spirit inside you which governs your behaviour. It makes me sad to have to say these things to *you*.'

She got up and I thought the interview was over and I murmured something about being sorry. But instead of dismissing me, she moved two chairs into the middle of the room.

'Sit there,' she said pointing to one of them and when I did, she sat down on the other, facing me, and so close that our knees were almost touching. Then, for a long time, she just stared into my face. And I stared back into hers. Then she spoke again. But now her voice was different. The note was low and there were hardly any pauses, she talked on and on in a monotonous, repetitive way, gazing into my eyes all the time.

'You run up the stairs two steps at a time breaking an important rule letting the school down ... why do you hurt me so ... you don't appreciate this splendid school my school your godmother's school ... you go running up the stairs two steps at a time letting me down ... why do you hurt me so I had such hopes of you hopes that you would love my school love the spirit that pervades my school but you are failing me running up the stairs two steps at a time letting the school down letting me down ... you do not understand the spirit of my school you refuse the gift which I am trying so hard to give you and you will grow up without it and grow into a useless and unhappy woman ... you are failing me failing yourself you break the rules you run up the stairs two steps at a time ...'

I stared into that white face, into those wide-apart grey eyes, I could see the swollen lips moving and the blue mark on the lower one seemed twice as large, and I could not understand why such a trivial little thing like running up the stairs was such a dreadful sin, why it hurt her so and why I was such a failure. And then, as the monologue continued, the same phrases repeated over and over again, I felt something happening to me, I was getting weak, I was nearly crying and I couldn't think why, for I didn't feel sorry or sad. I hardly heard her words any longer, just the sound of her voice and a sentence occasionally and then – a question ...

'Why don't you speak? Why don't you say something?'

But I couldn't speak. If I had I would have cried. She was closer to me now, bending forward, her face getting nearer and nearer to mine and although I strained to hold myself together, I was trembling and tears were running down my cheeks. And a strange look was coming into her eyes, a glittering, wild, triumphant look which frightened me.

'... running up the stairs two steps at a time breaking the most important rule letting the school down letting me down why do you hurt me so ... why don't you speak ... why don't you say something ...?'

And then I broke. I dropped my face into my hands and wept uncontrollably and at the same moment she flung herself upon me and clasped me in her arms, crying out again and again, 'my darling, my darling, oh my darling'. Then she lifted me onto my feet and wiped my face with her handkerchief, smiling at me – and then she kissed me, bent down and kissed me all over my face and on my lips. I stopped crying but now I was stiff all over, hating this even more than the other and I stood, pressed against her bosom, hard and resistant. But it didn't discourage her and she went on kissing and clasping me and calling me endearing names until, at last, she drew me to the other side of the room and opened the door which led onto the back staircase.

'Go and wash your face before anybody sees you, darling, and then go straight home,' she said as she released me. I stumbled down the steps to the half-landing and went into the wash-place. It was on this staircase that Miss Kiddle and Amy lived.

I stayed in there a long time trying to recover. When I came out her door was shut and I went down to the cloakroom. There was no one about and I put on my hat and coat and slipped out of the front door.

I was longing to tell my mother all that happened to me, but by the time I reached home I knew that I couldn't. I still felt stunned and ashamed of my own weakness and I didn't know what to tell her, how to describe it. I could make no sense of it myself, so how could I make sense of it to her? She wouldn't know what I was talking about. She would just think that her dear friend had been reprimanding me for some little thing and then consoling me afterwards with her godmother's love. And it wasn't just that. But what it was I didn't know and so I said nothing. I just told her that I had had a row at school and she didn't even ask what it was about.

No. It wasn't just that. Not a godmother's love and not a jealous maternal love any more. It was an illicit – almost incestuous love.

When the term ended, my mother was quite worn out. Painting in that window was a great strain and she had had to give the whole thing up. For three months we had been rich, but now the game was over. But she didn't worry. She had found her way into a new, influential world and given her address to all her sitters and she was quite sure that there would be a steady flow of work which she could carry out in her own home. Nor was she nervous about her health. Two months of sea bathing she was certain would restore her and so we packed up happily and went away together to enjoy a summer's respite from it all.

6

Sir Vincent Caillard

IT WAS in Southwold and Walberswick, on the Suffolk coast, that for so many summers my grandfather had sat out on the marshes beside the River Blythe, painting the cows. It was in Southwold that my mother rented a cottage and now, as I ran about, the commons and the beaches and the marshes seemed beautiful. All seemed as good as it was abroad – yet was it? Where was the wildness, the grandeur and exhilaration of those other places? It was civilised and organised and tame. Even the sea was less gigantic and exciting and old Sam May was always sitting in his boat beside the bathing raft, leaning over the oars puffing his pipe, ready to rescue us if we got into trouble. And when the sea was a little rough, a red flag was flown and we were forbidden to go in at all.

Yes. It was fun but it was tame. Yet I no longer noticed for I had changed and was forgetting. I had grown tame myself. Or, had my old wild nature only been suppressed?

I took up golf and sat out sketching with my mother – not cows, she hated them (at least in pictures), but churches and old streets and the lighthouse and I felt free and happy – according to my new standards.

As soon as we were back Miss Morison invited me out and as I chattered about everything, she listened with great intentness and seemed delighted that we had had such a good time. Then, a few weeks later, without telling anyone, she set off for Southwold herself for a long week-end and, while she was there, bought a little house in the same street as the one that we had stayed in. She came back very excited and astounded us with the news.

I was now in the lower fourth, with Miss Bullen as my form mistress and I might have had to worry a lot about my smile, now that I was constantly in her company. But it had disappeared and was no longer a cause of anxiety. However, I soon clashed with her over something else and when she kept me behind to reprimand me, she ended with yet another condemnation of my character.

'It is a great pity,' she snapped, 'that you never understand the spirit that underlies the rules and institutions of the school so that whenever your character is put to the test, it always fails you. I shall only give you a warning now, but if I have to speak to you again it will be much more serious for you.'

When I was abroad, I so often worried about my character yet now, when it was being constantly impugned, I didn't care a bit. I cared about the rows. I hated and feared them. But I never took to heart anything that was said to me. And before, I had always liked to be liked. Now, I noticed that I could survive quite well without being liked and admired by the whole world. I no longer cared how people regarded me – for I no longer had regard for people.

But I was shocked when I observed a much worse change in myself – that whenever I saw someone in trouble, I was pleased. When I thought about this hard I found that I never wished ill to anyone I liked, but from this I went on to discover how many I disliked and how many of the children I envied. For all my deep contentment I did envy their belonging. I still felt like an outsider and I had suffered so many shocks and hurts myself that now it was not only a consolation but often a cruel satisfaction when I heard that one of 'them' was experiencing some misfortune.

However, even if I could not like the people and the life I had to live, I was participating passionately and I was no longer a spiritual Scot. I was English again, fully sharing my mother's vision of the world and once more confident of the validity of her ambitions and predictions for me. The school was still something that I had to endure, but beyond it lay the marvellous world of the parents in which, after all, I would find my task and fulfil my genius. And not only would they be revealed and acclaimed in the quickest possible time but, again according to her, happiness would be my lot in life as well. Two dazzling awards lay before me, bliss and renown, waiting to be seized and known and worked into the pattern of my destiny.

No books or journals came into our house. The *Daily Mail* was delivered and I propped it up in front of the milk jug at breakfast every morning and read it with great earnestness. It was the political news, the state of the nation, which was now of the utmost personal concern to me and I began to wonder if politics was my road and if, as a Member of Parliament and the first woman Prime Minister, my task would be accomplished.

The world was still stormy and the *Daily Mail* was running the 'Red menace' hard and, more and more, I felt certain that my mission was to restore peace and harmony. When I read about some rough and bloody scene, I saw myself plunging into the middle of a furious mob, climbing onto a window ledge and, lifting my arms for silence, preach to the angry men my message of love and beauty and a better world. I was a Conservative, anti-Red, anti-revolution, firmly on the side of the 'establishment' – yet my sympathies were always with the rioters.

The school was an integral part of that establishment – Church and Court and the Tory Party. Even without politics in my home, politics surrounded me and when my mother's new Beauchamp Place sitters began coming to the house, the influence grew still stronger.

Among them were many well-known political families and Mrs Stanley Baldwin (as she then was) became a patron and good friend to my mother and later, for a short time, an important person in my own life.

One day, when she was sitting for her portrait, hoping to interest her in me, my mother told her of my new ambition and later, she called me into the room.

'I hear you are interested in politics, my dear,' she began at once. 'Of course you read the debates in *The Times* every day?'

Although I had never heard about the debates, I did know that *The Times* was the right paper to take, for in my friends' homes it was always lying about. But we couldn't afford it and, anyway, my mother would never have had the time or patience to read it. As I did not want to disgrace her by letting on that she took the wrong newspaper, or give away my own ignorance, I murmured something vague by way of reply.

'You should also read *Hansard* and go to as many political meetings as you can. You will soon be able to join the Young Conservatives.'

These were important tips, important lines of advance towards the premiership and I asked my mother for the money to buy some copies of *The Times*. I was very disappointed. I found the debates unutterably boring and when I dipped into *Hansard* at the public library, I was even more shattered. These speeches and questions were not my idea of politics. Mine was messianic, although I did not know it, violently revolutionary, an appeal for nothing less than the building of Utopia and the brotherhood of Man. It was a relief to go back to the passion of the *Daily Mail*.

But the struggle which lay ahead, my new insights into the difficulties of adult life and the problems which would beset my genius now frightened me so much that I lost faith in the happiness half of my mother's vision – and soon, even while hating my childhood, I lived in dread of its ending. The present was filled with nightmare scenes and the future with imagined tortures and ordeals and there was nowhere else to go, no other viable division of Time. Only my mother and my home made life bearable at all.

It was not long after that interview with Miss Bullen that I received another summons to Miss Morison's office. The crime was different, but it was equally petty and move by move and almost word for word the pattern was repeated and although I was prepared this time and I tried with all my strength, yet I could not withstand that horrible power. I did not recognise it as horrible then, it was just incomprehensible. It was all so sweet and yet so deadly. It was not her strength which impressed me so much as my own weakness. Again, I said nothing to my mother and from that time onwards I prayed, in my own irreverent way, for the strength to stand up to her.

All through that autumn my mother was painting hard, extending her reputation among the Beauchamp Place people and getting known in the school as well – for the two worlds were the same. Rachel's family was one of the first to be interested and she was asked to paint Augustine Birrell – their favourite uncle.

He had been Chief Secretary for Ireland in Mr Asquith's government and, as one of the last of the nineteenth century scholar-politicians, was well known as a poet and man-of-letters.

When my mother arrived by appointment and was shown into the library, the large untidy figure crouching in a big arm-chair behind a table on which was a pile of books and papers, did not move. A green-shaded reading lamp lighted the room for the windows, looking out onto the garden, were below ground level and some book-shelves in front of them blotted out what light there was. She advanced towards the scowling white-haired lion.

'How do you do,' she said, 'I'm afraid I'm interrupting your work?' There was a grunt as the lion rose for an instant to shake hands and then sank down again.

'May I look round the room to see where the light is best?' She walked about and then unpacked her paints and went back to him.

'I hate disturbing you,' she said, 'but the only place that I shall be able to see you will be near the window, behind the bookcase.' At that he shrank still deeper into his chair.

'I'm very busy. I don't want to be painted. It's all my niece's idea, not mine,' he growled suddenly.

'Oh, I am sorry,' said my mother sympathetically. 'I didn't know that. Well, look here, you needn't move at all. Go on with your work and let me sketch you just as you are, hunched up in your chair, lit by the lamp, with your books and your work all round you. You needn't keep still, you needn't take any notice of me, you'll hardly know I'm here. And I shall enjoy it much more.' And she gazed at the corner in which he was sitting; the bookshelves, the old prints on the wall above the fire-place, the shaft of dull light from the window behind, the rays falling from the lamp onto the table and, in the middle, the splendid old man with the shaggy white head and fine (still scowling) face.

Not another sound came from him and she went to the kitchen to get her water jar filled. When she came back she fetched a chair from the corner of the room.

He went on watching as she took command, not in the least mollified by these painless arrangements, if anything, even more resentful at being caught so completely in her toils.

Everything was ready and she sat down. As she did so her legs flew into the air, she turned a backward somersault and crashed onto the floor. At that, he leapt from his chair and plunged to her rescue.

'Are you hurt? I hope you're not hurt?' he asked with alarm.

'What happened?' she gasped, half laughing, from the floor.

'That chair only has three legs,' he replied as he helped her up. 'I *am* so sorry. I do hope you're not hurt.'

'No. I'm alright,' she said and they both laughed. He roared with mirth as he carried two sound chairs over to the window and then came back to help her with her paints. He talked all the time then and quite enjoyed the sitting.

Although my mother was working steadily now and not over-exerting herself yet, even so, she was finding the small water colour sketches more and more trying. She was tired of them and she, herself, was tiring and Mrs Baldwin was always urging her to do bigger work and charge more. So, she took the pictures of Charles Lummis and William Rust to an art shop and they put them in the window. Very soon a most interesting enquirer came.

Sir Vincent Caillard was one of the great industrial leaders of the day. He was in his seventies then, tall and exceedingly good-looking, but not the bland, well-tailored handsomeness that I saw and admired in so many of the parents. His face was intelligent and sensitive and the just perceptible Jewishness gave it subtlety and depth.

He ordered a life-size oil-colour portrait of himself and as he had no time for sittings during the week, it was arranged that the work would be done at his country house, at week-ends. I had to be left behind at the boarding-house.

Everything went forward rapidly and my mother was soon worrying over her wardrobe for the grand visit. She was much more nervous of being a sartorial failure than of failing with the picture and she rushed round the shops in search of country house necessities and sat night after night sewing and washing and pressing.

They arranged to travel together one Friday afternoon, meeting at the station. Although it was all for his convenience (and he was only paying £50 for the picture), she had not asked for her expenses and she bought herself a 3rd Class ticket and waited with her canvas and her cases. Five minutes before the train left he strolled onto the platform looking like the magnate that he was, his private secretary beside him and his valet behind. He ushered her gracefully into his reserved compartment and when the train started, the secretary remained behind and the valet withdrew to another carriage.

He talked politely for awhile and then, keeping *The Times* for himself, handed my mother a selection of other quality papers. Soon, however, he opened what looked like a Cabinet despatch-box and for the rest of the journey, applied himself to his work – while my mother read *Punch* and mused comfortably in her 1st Class corner.

Then unfortunately, the ticket collector appeared and she handed him her ticket. For a moment, he looked baffled. Then, recovering himself, he addressed her politely.

'Are you aware, Madam, that you are travelling in a 1st Class compartment with a 3rd Class ticket?'

There was a long embarrassing silence. Whether she did not have enough money in her purse to pay the difference or whether 1st Class travel was something so exotic, outside her whole life's experience and the price of it outraged her, touched some nerve made sensitive by habitual poverty, I do not know. I only know that there *was* a limit to her money senselessness for she looked meaningfully at Sir Vincent – and said nothing. Annoyed, he pulled out his wallet.

A limousine was waiting in the station yard and during the long drive, he talked. He was happy now for he loved that house that he was going to, the long low Elizabethan mansion. They drove into the park, then through the extensive gardens and then, with a crunching of gravel, the car swept up to the great porch where a butler and footman were waiting.

My mother was conducted to her room and there handed over to her personal maid. When, a few minutes later, she hurried out into the passage the footman, who had been waiting there discreetly, escorted her to the drawing-room where Lady Caillard and the house party were gathered, waiting for the new arrivals and the glories of afternoon tea.

When the introductions were over she sank into a gorgeous chair. One behind the other, in splendid procession, the servants carried in the heavy silver tea-pots, jugs and muffin-dishes on heavy silver trays – a variety of sumptuous confections on richly patterned plates were already spread over the lace-covered table and mounted one above the other in the many-tiered cake-stands – and the sort of visit she adored, gracious, other-worldly, now began.

When, later, she returned to her room she found her clothes unpacked and put away, but confident that all the mending and darning of the last week had surmounted this first hazard, she relaxed in the restfulness and security of the house. Yet she could never really rest, never lose her aloneness and the nerve-wrack of those everlasting portraits.

The sittings began the next morning. The work went easily and the visit was very successful. Old Lady Caillard was so kind and when she learnt that my mother had left a child at home, she pressed her to bring me with her the following week-end. My week-end was disturbing and depressing.

I had already paid several visits to the boarding-house and hated the suffocating atmosphere and Miss Morison creeping restlessly about, listening, hovering, and then bursting suddenly, for no apparent reason, into the crowded room where we were working or playing.

Always before, I had slept in one of the dormitories but this time, I was told, they were full and I would have to sleep in the attic where, all by herself, Miss Morison had her bedroom. I did not like this prospect. But I liked my little room when I saw it. I had never had a room of my own before.

Mrs Just came from the school every evening to cook the boarders' supper. There were some 30 children in residence and Miss Morison was a good organiser. The boarding-house was her private business.

There was no one about on the top floor when I shut the door of my room and got into bed, but I had scarcely done so when it opened again and Miss Morison came in. She had that strained, tense look, the hard glitter in her eyes that I knew so well. She came up to my bed and looked down on me for a moment and then she bent over and put her hands on my shoulders and kissed me. 'Good night, my darling. Sleep well, my darling,' she murmured as she stayed leaning over me. I lay stiff and silent. After the rows, I hated her kisses even more than before. I longed for her to go, but when at last, she did I was sorry for my coldness. She meant well, I thought, she was only trying to take my mother's place, saying good-night to me as she thought my mother would. But I felt uneasy, all the same, until I fell asleep.

I woke and saw a rectangle of light shrink quickly as the door closed quietly. It must have been one of the servants, I thought, coming in by mistake. I listened and waited and then slept again.

There were the usual games at Richmond in the morning and in the afternoon Miss Morison took me out. She came into my room again, that night, and sat down on the bed and stayed for a long time, talking. Tender, godmotherly things she said to me and although my body was as taut as before, I responded with some grateful affectionate words, trying my hardest to feel what I was saying. Then, again, she bent forward and kissed me, calling me her darling, her beloved child. Slowly and reluctantly she rose and left me.

When she had gone, I got out of bed and went to the window and pulled back the curtains and opened it wider. The room was too dark and I felt suffocated. Several hours later, I woke – and there she was standing over me, gazing down at me, looking like a ghost in the night glow of London. When I cried out 'What is it?' she flung herself down on the bed.

'Don't make a noise, my darling,' she whispered. 'It's alright. You were talking in your sleep, that's all. You called out for me. Go to sleep again, my beloved, and don't worry. Nothing can happen to you for your godmother is next door, always ready to look after you.' She kissed me and then glided away.

I lay with my mind in a turmoil. I had never talked in my sleep before. If I had my mother would have told me. And if I did, why did I call for *her* – and not my mother? She was in her nightgown with her long black hair hanging down her back. I groped under the pillow and drew out my luminous watch. It was half past three! I wondered if I could lock my door and I crept across the room to see. But there was no key in it and even if there had been, I would not have dared to turn it. I was afraid to go to sleep again, afraid that if I did I might call out for her again and bring her back into my room. I slept in the end, but very soon the getting-up bell went clanging through the house.

It was Sunday. The church bells rang noisily and commandingly in the distance and close at hand the day was like all other Sundays; silent, unnatural, a half-stopped, half-alive oppressive day of sitting about, waiting about, looking about and walking to Church. Miss Morison and the girls who had been confirmed, went to Holy Communion before breakfast. The rest of us waited for the eleven o'clock service. In the afternoon, we went again and in the evening Miss Morison sallied forth once more with a handful of exceptionally pious children, those who had been drawn into her magnetic circle, were caught in the grip of a passion and, trying to please and play up to her, had caught religion, too.

For Miss Morison and her chosen few, Sundays were veritable orgies, days lived on another plane filled with ineffable experience; passionate days when they offered themselves to God, receiving grace and joy and an abundance of His love. It is no wonder that, after every service the waves of power that habitually streamed out of her seemed stronger than ever.

For me, the only living, loving, truly joyful thing in the whole day was the roast beef dinner cooked hotly and splendidly by old Mrs Just in the kitchen below.

Through all those years I lived so near to God. I had only to open my eyes and I could have seen Him, reach out my hand and I could have touched Him, I had a godmother to guide me and a church school enclosing and encouraging me – yet I remained a blind resistant clod.

That night, I waited for her with dread. She sat down on the edge of the bed again and laid a hand on my hard braced body and talked to me about Jesus Christ. 'Soon,' she said, 'you will be able to come to the Communion Service with me. We shall receive the blessed Sacrament together, partaking of His Body and His Blood.'

When she kissed me and went away she was not so excited as before but I was sure that she would come back and I lay watching the door for what seemed like half the night. And now, in a queer, uncertain way, I wanted her to. Small pleasing waves of love were passing through me. But she didn't. In the morning I was cold once more and perplexed by that turn of fever in the night.

When my mother returned and I went home I heard that next time, I was to go too. When she had finished telling me all about the visit, I asked her if I ever talked in my sleep and I told her how Miss Morison had come into my room because she said I had called out for her.

My mother looked surprised and said she had never known me do that. But I said no more. Feelings were so difficult to describe and make sense of and, even if I had tried, she would not have understood for she did not see Miss Morison as I did.

As my position, a point between two points, grew more difficult, so it grew harder to tell her things. She had chosen Miss Morison as my godmother and brought me back to England to go to her school. She had planned or helped to plan, the whole grand pattern of my childhood and struggled and suffered so much to realise it and if I failed with both my godmother and the school, she would be so disappointed, for the first outline of her whole beautiful vision would be spoiled. That is what, with my reason, I believed and I knew that I had somehow to get through it and whatever happened on the way, she must never know. And so, I told her less and less until – I told her nothing.

I scrambled through the week at school not caring about anything – for the visit was before me.

7

Love and Sir Vincent

I WAS given a lovely chintzy room and I ran round it looking at everything and trying everything. On the beautiful desk was a box filled with thick embossed notepaper and I wanted to sit down and write to everyone I knew. But I couldn't. I had to wash my hands and brush my hair and go to meet my hostess.

Lady Caillard was alone in her private sitting-room. The other visitors were scattered about the house and countryside amusing themselves and some had not arrived. At first, I thought how ugly and expressionless she was, but as she talked her heavy face lightened a little.

When tea-time came we went to the drawing-room where logs were burning in the great Tudor fire-place and heavy brocade curtains were drawn over the high mullioned windows.

People were coming in all the time. Interesting looking men, down for the week-end and an assortment of attractive wives, a married daughter carrying her embroidery, a hobbledehoy sort of woman wearing riding clothes and a comic one, who made everybody laugh and whom everybody loved, and then, and then my host – Sir Vincent himself! A moment before I had thought the others very fine, but now they all seemed commonplace – for he looked like a king!

There was a chorus of greetings, his daughter jumped up and kissed him, the men moved towards him, he put his hand on his son's shoulder, shook hands with my mother and me, gave his wife, sitting behind the tea-table, a peck and sat down.

How tall, how commanding he was and yet, at the same time, how sensitive. He could have been a priest, no, not just a priest – a pope! A poet! He was, in fact, a musician. After a single cup of tea he rose and, muttering something about his work, left us for the lonely mountain top.

When he was gone, there were jokes and laughter and we went on eating. There was so much to eat and all so unutterably delicious that I didn't know where to start and where to stop. I wanted to work my way through everything. But I didn't. I was on my best behaviour.

The talk was not very interesting, but just watching them kept me entranced and feeling all the time that I was there, not looking at them from outside, but inside, right in the middle of them, one of them – belonging!

My best party dress was not one of Miss Morison's purchases (she had not advanced so far) but a cheap affair of orange coloured imitation silk which my mother had made herself. Orange was her favourite colour then. I didn't like it but she assured me that I looked beautiful in it and so, although I didn't much care what I looked like then, I took her word for it and wore it peacefully.

It was this dress that I put on that night. It was the first time that I had ever dressed for dinner and when the gong sounded at half-past eight (the time I was usually in bed) and we all trooped into the dining-room and Lady Caillard told me where to sit, I was naturally very awe-struck and excited. And my mother was right, everyone told her afterwards how beautiful I looked. But such remarks I thought rather foolish and I still didn't like that dress. In that house it was garish and vulgar, I thought.

Another hazard of high-life is, of course, one's table knowledge and behaviour. During that first week-end my agility and cunning were put severely to the test. The quantity and variety of knives, forks and spoons which were set before me and the mass of mysterious silver cannisters and cruets, sifters and pots, cut glass bottles and gold-lined boxes which were banked directly in front of me, together presented me with a prodigious problem.

If it was just a matter of starting on the outside and working inwards, or vice versa, it would be no problem at all. But it isn't simple like that. Sometimes, an odd fork or knife has to be used for some quite unrelated work on the wings and the top of the design has to be taken into account right from the start, a tool set perversely up there can throw the whole procedure out.

Butlers must vary in temperament and talent like everyone else. Some will, no doubt, lay their lords' tables with more subtlety and complexity than others. They must not pile and place beyond the bounds of understanding altogether for if they did, the meal would degenerate into a feast of absurdity. But even when they base their plan upon tradition, they still have scope for the exercise of considerable imagination and innovation. And it is this artistic uncertainty which always makes dining in high-society difficult but so interesting.

And so, when the first course was served to me, I did not move. Just as when I was shamefully picking up religion in a hurry and I had to watch what my neighbours were doing and shoot furtive glances from side to side at their prayer books and bibles – so now I did the same.

It sounds so easy just to take a quick look at the implements which the person next to one has taken up, but in practice it isn't. It is very difficult. For it is little things like *this* that house-parties like *that* have eagle eyes for, a sixth sense for. Planted up to the waist deeply and securely round the table they know, without even looking at you, when you *don't* know, when you are slyly squinting right and left.

However, I did fairly well at my first grand dinner and the Caillard family, although keen-eyed and aware, were not cruel like some.

The next morning, Sir Vincent and my mother closeted themselves together, the other guests disappeared to their pleasures, Lady Caillard was busy and I was left to myself. I walked about the garden but it was cold and dull and I soon came back. I did not want to read any of the books in my room but I had seen one that I liked – in the lavatory!

The lavatories were just as splendid as all the other rooms. They were very large, the polished mahogany seats stretched from wall to wall and, with the lids down, were very comfortable to sit or lie on. There were heavy pile carpets, rich damask curtains, period wall-papers and, in every one – a small library. Ideal places for serious study.

Ours was particularly well stocked and I went straight there and chose my book. But I didn't remove it. I believed those books were put there for a purpose, to while away the time of constipated visitors and that under no circumstances should they ever be removed. And so, it was there that I spent most of my time on that first visit to Wingfield House.

I put on my orange dress again for dinner and without waiting for my mother, strolled out of my room, along the gallery and down the main staircase towards the dining-room. When I reached the angle of the stairs and turned, I saw Sir Vincent at the bottom. He was looking up at me and smiling. Then, to my amazement, he held out his arms and stood as if waiting to embrace me.

I stopped. I was instantly filled with emotion. 'A father! a father!' was my one thought, 'more wonderful than any of them!' I wanted to leap into his arms and cry for joy. But I was afraid of giving myself away, the great longing that was in me. For I wasn't sure if he meant it. He had children and grandchildren, he was surrounded by people, he had wealth and high position, he had everything – so how *could* he want me, have room for me as well? And so soon? I walked down and when I reached the bottom he took me in his arms and kissed me on my forehead.

There were sounds of people approaching and he let me go. The next moment, talking and laughing, the house-party streamed towards the dining-room door and we all went in. Several times, during dinner, I caught his eye and I knew that it was not just by chance – and I marvelled at what had happened to me.

The next morning, he and my mother were shut away again and I did not see him until lunch-time and then, not alone. But I knew that he had not forgotten me. Afterwards, we left for the station. He was going to Washington very soon and, although the portrait was nearly finished, the last touches had to wait for his return. The whole house-party crowded to the door to see us off.

'The portrait is going splendidly,' Sir Vincent said as he shook hands with my mother, and Lady Caillard effused as well. 'We are all looking forward to your next visit. And be sure to bring Philippa with you,' he called out as we got into the car.

During the drive to the station I talked all the time, but I said very little about Sir Vincent. This desire for a father, I felt, was a reflection upon my mother, as if her great love for me was not enough, all her sacrifices insufficient, as if I was greedy for a father as well.

The next day I was back at school. But everything was different for I had a father like everyone else. I half imagined that I had a family too, and position and security. I was one of 'them' now. I belonged.

Soon after this, we heard from Florence that her sister had died, leaving five children and she asked my mother to help the family in any way she could. The father, 'poor darling', was said to be rather overwhelmed by his problems.

My mother went to Lewisham and reported an ugly suburban villa and a harum scarum crowd of children all muddling along quite happily under the guidance of the eldest girl. We were surprised that Florence, who was so well connected, should have these seedy relatives hidden away in what to us, was such an awful place.

When a housekeeper was found to look after them, until such time as they could be adopted or otherwise disposed of, my mother stopped going and then, every evening when he left the Ministry, the broken-hearted father spent an hour or two at our house, being petted up with drinks and food and sympathy.

I did not like him. From the very beginning I distrusted him. He was good-looking, with iron grey hair and a military moustache. And his monocle and double-breasted waistcoats and neat grey spats gave him quite an air. Yet there was a flaw somewhere, something wrong about this stylish pseudo-gentleman.

He went out of his way to be nice to me, but it did not make me like him and I was jealous of the amount of my mother's time that he took up. But I got used to him and during the last weeks of the term I was too busy to bother about him.

We were rehearsing The Tempest and this year, I had an important part. I was Ariel, the part I wanted. And my mother was painting the scenery. The back-cloth took one's breath away – the 'yellow sands' and tropical sea, the palm trees and the foliage of that fabulous island.

The dress rehearsal was chaotic. As Miss Morison saw it, idiocy marked every moment and the air vibrated with hysteria. She stood in the middle of the hall storming and raging – the tempest on the stage was like a gentle summer gust compared to the tempest that roared round her. The mistresses fluttered hither and thither like bits of blown paper and the actors huddled together like cattle with their backs to the blast. She was wise enough to keep away from the dressing-room the next night and it was my mother, doing the making-up again, who gave courage to all the frightened players.

The thunder rolled and crashed as the curtain rose upon the storm. As the stricken vessel reeled and tossed, I leapt from the wings onto a broken spar and then into the rigging. With a torch in my hand, I darted like a fire-fly, from the yards to the gunwale, from the bows to the stern and when the lightning revealed me I laughed and I laughed. I was wild as the waves and happy as the wind.

After that, I skipped and danced through my scenes until there came that lovely freedom song 'Merrily, merrily shall I live now, under the blossom that hangs on the bough'. First high in a bough I sang it, then, spinning round that sylvan glade and when I dropped onto a bank, into a circle of wild flowers, I sang it for the last time – and the play came to an end.

That was my part alright. I didn't have to act. The pity was that I could not go on playing it, that only on a stage could I regain my freedom and live merrily like that.

After the last performance, the most triumphant of them all, the actors were called back and back, Miss Morison went up onto the stage and the honours, it was said, were evenly divided between the brilliant producer and the wild spirit, Ariel.

In the dressing-room afterwards, when the parents came crowding in excitedly to collect their children, Colonel Wigram – (Sir Clive he had become) and his wife came up to me. He looked so courtly, so magnificently pompous – and she so languid.

'Bravo, bravo, well done, my little Ariel!' he shouted above the din, his fat square face quite florid with emotion.

'Congratulations!' he called out to my mother rather patronisingly. 'Philippa put up a splendid performance! A credit to the school! You must be proud!' Then, as an afterthought 'and your scenery! Wonderful ... wonderful ... made me feel I was back in India. Congratulations!'

Still smiling fatly he then turned, his wife turned too, and their child went with them.

Two days later, when the school broke up, we left London with Miss Morison to spend the Christmas holidays in her new cottage in Southwold.

8

Success and Disappointment

SHE HAD had a bathroom built and other improvements made and some furniture sent from the school – and she was proud of her new property. As soon as we arrived, she took us all over it and we went on admiring it for the rest of the day, as we were expected to do. After unpacking in our rooms, shouting gaily to each other through the open doors, we went downstairs to the jolliest of teas.

She was at her very best, vibrating with fondness for us both, a forced sort of humour and a heavy sort of charm. And how attractive she could be. There were times now when I was powerfully magnetised, when love for her swept through me and I responded to her jokes, her flattery and her arch antics. But it was never for long, always I recoiled again and the seeds of infatuation which had sprouted for an instant in my heart, died when the cold came back. And then I had to keep up the charade.

Our holiday, as with everything else, had to be paid for. We knew that we were going to help her do a little painting, but we didn't know that we were expected to decorate the whole house.

The next day, we set off for the shops to buy the paint and brushes. Miss Morison knew nothing about such things, she had never handled a paint brush in her life. Nor could she cook and my mother had to do that, too.

On Christmas Eve she went to the midnight service and, early the next morning, to Holy Communion. She came back solemn and intense, very tired for she hadn't slept much but, as it was Our Lord's birthday, she had to feel happy – and she soon recovered.

At breakfast we exchanged presents. Hers, of course, were marvellous and we opened them with cries of delight and gratitude. We, on our part, had made a great effort to give her something that would please her and the meal was eaten in a strained yet happy glow of mutual love and thankfulness for God's goodness and the miraculous event which we were celebrating together.

I went with her to Morning Service. My mother made no attempt to accompany us, she never did, and Miss Morison had long ago accepted that she was a hopeless unbeliever. But with me it was different. I was her godchild, she had captured me in time, my mother's light and empty influence was heavily outweighed and I would never follow in her sad and barren path. She would see that I chose the right road, her road, the Church's road. Of all this she was absolutely certain as we set off together on that Christmas morning, stiff and strained but intimate, we two sharing something that my mother could not reach, becoming close without her, following the good people of Southwold and the bells.

Unaware of all this, my mother stayed cheerfully in the cottage cooking the Christmas dinner.

In the afternoon, we two went for a walk together. My mother hated aimless country walks, as I did. She only walked if she could sit down at the other end of it and sketch. As Miss Morison was new to Southwold, she asked me to show her everything and I marched her all over the town, up and down the beach, across the common and over the marshes. And all the time she talked, telling me more and more about herself – and about myself, flattering me, telling me how clever I was and how promising my future, so long as I would trust her and always let her guide me. And, of course, she talked about Our Lord (how I loathed that archaic emotional way of speaking about Christ) whom we praised and adored. After tea, we went to Evensong and when the edifying day was over, we had never seemed so close.

The next day, we all put on overalls and began scraping the wood-work, but after a few minutes, Miss Morison made an excuse and disappeared. When we were ready to open the paint pots she returned, very excited. She loved the idea of painting her own house. It was so easy, such fun, and it was the fashion now to do basic things like that. She could boast about it afterwards to the parents.

Ignoring my mother's instruction, she plunged the brush up to the hilt in the paint and then slopped it onto one of the doors. Most of it ran down the handle and oozed through her fingers and the rest dropped onto the floor and in no time she had painted herself from head to foot. In a fury, she flung down the brush and vanished.

During the fortnight of our visit, we decorated the whole house and the chocolate paint and dark cream walls made the pretty little cottage look as ugly and as much like an institution as the school.

When Christmas was over, Mrs Just arrived. Now that she had the cottage, Miss Morison was anxious to give holidays to all her friends and servants. And poor Mrs Just was so in need of a rest. She worked so hard, she had a ne'er-do-well drunkard of a husband and two children and lived in the deep dark school basement and never got away. Now was her chance, Miss Morison said, to give her a real treat and to show how grateful she was for all the years of her devoted work.

After cooking 100 school lunches and 30 boarding-house suppers every day, cooking just for us would be nothing to her, Miss Morison said. She would be able to rest the whole time, go to bed early and get up late, put her feet up all day and feel absolutely carefree.

Mrs Just was a large heavy woman and stone floors had given her flat feet. And she was deaf. She could lip-read enough to understand simple things, but most of the time she lived in a quiet closed world, communicating only with her sympathetic eyes and sweet smile. She adored Miss Morison and was steadily wearing herself out in her service.

She cooked the supper when she arrived and the next day, rose at her usual time and brought us early morning tea in bed.

'*Dear* Mrs Just,' cried Miss Morison from her pillows, 'you shouldn't be doing this. I told you to stay in bed late. But it *is* sweet of you. You know how much I love it.' And the early cups continued.

After breakfast she put on her hat and coat and with a basket over her arm, came to ask Miss Morison for the shopping list.

'Here it is,' she said, handing her a carefully prepared document. 'And while you are in the town, please buy me some stamps at the Post Office and then, it won't take you a minute, do drop into the draper's and get me a reel of blue cotton and some pins. I want to begin sewing the curtains. Oh, and just one more little thing, it won't take you much out of your way, do call at the plumber's and tell them that one of the bathroom taps is dripping. That's all, that's really all, *dear* Mrs Just, and when you get back you must put your feet up and have a good rest.' With a grateful smile Mrs Just set off. When she returned, laden with groceries, there was a conference in the kitchen.

'Where will you put all these things, Mrs Just? In these cupboards?' asked Miss Morison as she crossed the room and opened some doors. 'Oh dear, how dirty they are! Before you go to rest, it won't take you a moment, do give them a scrub out and, at the same time, you might just do the floor, too. Then the kitchen will be fit to use.' She turned to go, then stopped. 'I've just remembered something very important. Before you do the kitchen, *dear* Mrs Just, could you help me unpack that case of china? If we do it together it won't take long. You'll have the whole afternoon to rest. There won't be a thing more to do. I can manage by myself. I'll even get the tea.' With the same gentle smile, Mrs Just followed her out of the room and very soon she was unpacking the crate alone (Miss Morison having skilfully removed herself) and, on her tired feet, going to and fro carrying the china to the kitchen.

Mrs Just was kept toiling from morning till night. The sea air and the change may have done her good and living in such intimacy with the mistress she adored may have warmed and satisfied her heart, but so far as physical rest went, she would have done better at home.

Although we were very sorry for her, my mother and I could not help seeing the comic side of these demands, the endlessly repeated phrase, '*dear* Mrs Just, before you go to rest, it won't take you a minute, will you just ...?' We mimicked these words when we were alone and when we heard them again, looked at each other and almost laughed aloud.

One of the first things to come into the house with the groceries was a bottle of whisky which was put into the dining-room cupboard. A week later, when we were turning out the room to paint it, we found the bottle nearly empty.

'Good heavens! Who has been at that?' exclaimed my mother. 'It couldn't be Mrs Just. She wouldn't do a thing like that – and her husband has given her a horror of it.' And she rushed away with it to Miss Morison.

'It must be the plumber,' she said, glancing casually at the bottle. 'Anyway, I wouldn't worry about it, Louie. I'll hide it to stop it happening again.'

She was very interested in my visit to Wingfield House and I told her all about it and when I mentioned the orange dress, she reacted at once.

'When term starts, darling, we will go shopping and I will buy you a really beautiful dress so that you need never wear that dreadful orange one again.'

Immediately I felt uncomfortable, criticising what my mother had made for me and liked and planning with Miss Morison, to replace it.

'Oh, it's alright. I don't really mind it,' I replied airily, contradicting everything I had been saying. She just smiled in a strong confident way.

When the novelty had worn off and I grew bored with painting I used to stop and, encouraged by my mother, go to the golf course. I loved the game now – and I loved the course. The soft green fairways, the rolling gorse-grown common and the scent of the sea and beyond the dunes, from a knoll or the top of a dyke, the sight of the sea and on windy days the roar of the waves pounding the shingle beach. Yes, I loved it, whether striding out with a partner or playing a round by myself.

Then, one day at breakfast, Miss Morison announced that she was going to take up golf herself. And she asked me to teach her.

The same day, we set off for the common. I could see at once that she would never make a golfer. However many times I corrected the position of her hands, her fingers, her arms and her body, she could never get her stance right.

The next day, she joined the club and we drove off from the first tee (she would not be dissuaded) with people watching. After a dozen violent swings she managed to dribble the ball a few yards and, desperately ashamed, I picked it up and made her follow me to where we could make fools of ourselves without being watched and obstructing other players. Then, hacking up the ground and occasionally chopping the ball, we crawled about after it, forever searching the gorze.

And we did this every day. But I didn't show what I felt. I counted the days to the end of our visit, determined not to spoil it and upset the friendship.

When we left, Miss Morison felt nearer to me than ever before and she was sure now that bribery and perseverance would soon bring me even nearer, detach me from my mother and draw me onto the path which would lead ultimately to life with her.

When we reached London, the bereaved friend called the same evening – to help us unpack and get settled, he said. He was almost one of the family now, coming and going in an easy intimate way. To have a man thinking about her, waiting on her, needing less and less sympathy as his spirits rose and their relationship changed to one of mutual interest and companionship, must have given my mother great pleasure and a feeling of protection after all the lonely struggling years.

Although she was so sorry for the children and so good to them, she did not like them all. And she thought the baby, whom she made such a fuss of, a noisy, dirty, grabbing, greedy little horror!

These contradictions were so confusing then. It seemed to me that her heart was in conflict with itself. She could love Miss Morison, criticise her shrewdly and bitterly sometimes – yet go on loving her. She was full of love; loving widely, even when disappointed, and only at the very end did its radius contract and focus upon one point, one person – upon me. Her optimism never changed.

I also grew up loving, in a fine uncritical way and I went on loving the human race even when I came to dislike and criticise so many of its members. Now I have learnt that I must try to stop this incessant judging and see the oneness – love the divinity in everyone.

It was the awful baby who was adopted first, another was taken by an aristocratic relative of her mother's and the eldest went off on her own. Two were left and they came to us every Sunday. But I could not take to them – and I still didn't like the father. The whole situation troubled me.

Sir Vincent was now back from Washington and we went to Wingfield House again. Although we were greeted warmly by everyone, he did not kiss me as fathers always do when they have not seen their daughters for a long time. But I thought nothing of this for, after all, we had only just discovered our relationship.

As for my mother, never had I seen her so gay, so carefree and looking so attractive. The portrait was practically finished and she could abandon herself completely to the pleasures of the visit, enjoy the praises which were given to the picture and the esteem which was accorded her. And there was something else as well, giving her new confidence and poise – the bereaved friend in London, the handsome widower.

That evening I put on my new dress. It was the most expensive one in the children's department at Marshall and Snellgrove's and I loved it the moment I saw it. It was made of soft brown velvet, classical in design, with the Greek key pattern embroidered in dull gold round the yoke, the sleeves and the hem. It was so dignified, I thought – and not conventional. And my mother liked it, too.

Now, I was conscious of being looked at and I wanted Sir Vincent to admire me. And he did. I could see his eyes light up when we met at the dining-room door and he put his hand on my shoulder as we went in. And Lady Caillard noticed my dress and said how beautiful it was. I felt just right now and very fine and confident. And my birthday had been the week before. I was 14-years-old.

After dinner, we went to the music room to be entertained by Sir Vincent at the organ. He was passionately fond of the instrument. Sitting up on the bench, the hooded light shining down on the keyboards and the stops, he swayed from side to side. Even his back was splendid and for a whole hour, I watched him without moving. Then he stopped and turned round to us.

'That's enough. I'll do some practising now and join you later.'

There were murmurs of appreciation. Lady Caillard rose first, slowly and stiffly. As I followed her to the door, I smiled at him. I wanted him to know how much I admired his performance. He responded with a quick inviting gesture.

'Do you want to come and look at the organ. Philippa?' he said, and the next moment I was standing at the bench behind him. When the others had gone and their voices had receded into the distance, he put his arm round my shoulder and began explaining how it worked. Then he stopped, suddenly losing interest, and twisted round towards me.

'What a lovely child you are,' he said, staring into my eyes. 'You make me want to kiss you whenever I see you.' And with both arms he drew me to him, holding me tight against his body and then, bending down, he kissed me on the mouth, so hard that his teeth hurt my lips and he didn't stop until, recovering from my surprise, I pulled away. Instantly he let me go.

'Now run away quick, darling, and catch up the others,' he said.

As I hurried upstairs, I could still feel the devouring pressure on my mouth, his unpleasant breath was still in my nostrils, his body still hard against my body. I felt stupefied and when I reached the drawing-room, I had something to hide now and I felt ashamed. I sat down near my mother, unhearing and unseeing, absorbed in the thing that had just happened to me. Very soon, thinking I must be tired, she told me to go to bed and after awhile she followed me.

'What is the matter with you tonight, my love?' she said as she stood looking down at me in bed.

'When I stayed behind in the music-room to look at the organ, he kissed me,' I replied. My mother smiled as if very amused.

'But why should that upset you so?'

'Because he kissed me so hard, it hurt my lips, and for so long and I didn't like it.'

'I shouldn't worry about that, darling. He's such a lovely man, even if he is rather old, and a kiss or two won't hurt you.'

She thought me so beautiful herself and she was pleased that Sir Vincent thought so too. She was beginning to be interested now in my growing up and the delicate attentions of so fine a man she thought quite harmless, in fact, quite good for me. She believed that young girls should learn gradually about life from honourable men. Growing up in a large family, in such a different environment, she had been wise to things much earlier than I was. Then, she kissed me herself and went back to the drawing-room.

I couldn't get to sleep. I still admired him, yet there seemed to be a flaw in him, something unpleasant which I now knew about. He was not the god I had believed him to be, not the perfect man and benign large-hearted father, feeling protective towards me and adopting me as another daughter. He was something that I didn't understand and didn't like – an old-man lover. I wept with disappointment.

I did not see him in the morning until, returning from a walk, I went to the drawing-room where the portrait was on view with everyone admiring it, all insisting that my mother send it to the Royal Academy.

I felt shy of him, then. But he soon put me at my ease, talking to me in a serious respectful way, as if nothing had happened between us. But something had – not only to me, but to him. He was looking at me all the time now, I was always catching his eye whether I wanted to or not and his eager expression half flattered and pleased me and half frightened me. When I smiled at him now, I did so in a careful closed-up way. I was already on the defensive but at the same time preparing myself for new adventure.

Beneath my new attitude to him and behaviour, there were several lines of conscious and unconscious thought. If I had lost him, or never had him as a father I didn't want to be deprived of an interesting and powerful friend as well and I knew already that if I rebuffed him, he would lose interest in me at once and dismiss me from his mind as a silly child, not worth noticing and talking to. To keep his friendship I knew that I must suffer him.

On a deeper level, there was something else leading me on, of which I was not yet conscious – an inability to turn back. I could never refuse any experience. I always *had* to go forward, no matter where the going took me and, as time went on, and I recognised this inner law I obeyed it ever more recklessly.

I had no idea what Sir Vincent really wanted from me, but I had to go on and find out, however awkwardly and cautiously – for I was cautious still. If I had stopped and stayed as I was and wanted to be, a simple unworried child, I would have despised myself. As I waited, wondering what he would do next, I knew that I was back in my old position, outside, struggling to keep a door open and a place inside that delectable mansion which chance and patronage, not right, had brought me into.

After lunch, when Lady Caillard had gone to her room and the others were dispersing, Sir Vincent said casually to me, 'Would you like to see the library where I work? You can choose yourself some books.'

I walked beside him down the corridor without talking and into a beautiful room with French windows leading out onto the lawn, the walls lined with books and chairs in comfortable reading positions.

'What a lovely room,' I said, rushing forward to the books.

'I thought you'd like it. And now, while you are choosing, I'll do some work.' And he walked over to his desk.

For a long time I rummaged about, reading indices, introductions and passages. I had been into Augustine Birrell's library but I had never been able to look at the books and, in those days, the books in the public libraries were not kept out in open shelves. One had to choose from a catalogue and this, for me, was very difficult. Now that I could see and dip into them all, advance from shelf to shelf, a whole new world rose up before me.

'How are you getting on?' he asked after awhile.

'I want to read them all. But I think I've chosen two.'

'What are they?' I carried the two thick volumes over to him.

'They should keep you occupied for some time. You can bring them back on your next visit and choose some more. And now, stay and talk to me for a moment.'

'I would like to. There are so many questions that I want to ask you.'

'Are there? What are they?' he replied curiously.

'Last night, at dinner, you said you thought the government ought to bring in protection to stop the dumping of cheap goods. But if they did, wouldn't the other countries retaliate and, surely, a free market is the only way to carry on world trade?' All my political opinions and anxieties came from the *Daily Mail*. He gave me a long and careful explanation of his views. His arm was round my waist.

'What else do you want to ask me, sweetheart?'

'I would like to know what you think of the political situation generally? I think it very serious.'

'Darling, you *are* a little political animal, aren't you!' he said smiling. 'I'm sure you are right. I also think it very serious. But that is such a large question. It would take so long to answer it. Let me tell you tomorrow. Let's talk about something else now – about you. Wouldn't you like to know what I think about *you*? I think that's a much more interesting question.' And he jerked his chair back and drew me close to him. I changed immediately.

'Shall I tell you?' I didn't answer. 'I think you're the most fascinating little creature that I've ever known. Doesn't that please you? Won't you give me a kiss for telling you something nice like that?' And he put his arms round me and kissed me in the same fierce, painful way. And again I pulled away.

'Why are you so frightened, darling? There's nothing to be afraid of. You like me, don't you? You trust me, don't you? Just give me one more and then I must go on with my work. But this time, don't jump away. Kiss me, too. Learn to kiss me as I kiss you.'

I endured it longer, but in the end I couldn't bear it and again I drew away. Annoyed, he let me go, almost pushed me from him and I turned and picked up the books. I thought that was the end and I walked to the door. As I opened it I looked back. He was gazing at me hard. He was still interested in me. If only I could talk to him, I thought, and not have to kiss him. If *only* he were my father and not my lover.

I saw him alone once again. I was coming in from the garden before lunch the next day when he was walking up the main staircase. When he saw me he turned and came down again and, looking quickly up and down the corridor, beckoned me into a small ante-room. He closed the door carefully, and without a word, without any preliminaries, caught me up in his arms quite violently and kissed me for a long time. I was so pinioned that I couldn't move. Again his teeth ground against my lips, his breath was horrid and, this time, I could feel his tongue probing my mouth. I hated it. But I didn't struggle. I had seen how impatient he could be and I didn't want to lose him. If I didn't like his kisses, more and more I liked being with him. He released me hurriedly.

'Darling, you must come again in the spring when we can walk in the garden together and then you must learn to kiss me properly.'

He opened the door a crack and listened. Then he stepped out into the hall and again looked up and down, then beckoned me to follow and when I did, he disappeared one way and I went the other. I was now engaged in a clandestine affair.

We left after lunch, taking the portrait back to London for framing. My mother had had a lovely week-end, restful and sufficing and a long intimate talk with Lady Caillard. In the train, in strictest secrecy, she told me all about her.

'I seem to have everything in the world,' she had said. 'Yet it all means nothing to me, for my heart is still breaking.'

She was old and stout and plain and her face was blotchy. Sir Vincent had always been capricious, the irresistible conqueror of beautiful women everywhere and now he was so bored and cold that he could scarcely bring himself to speak to her. They lived in the same house, sat at each end of the same long dining-table – they might as well have been living in different continents.

We had already sensed this tragedy for the coolness in the house, the distance that divided them, was plain for everyone to see.

'These tragedies are inevitable,' said my mother, 'for how could such a fascinating man stick all his life to one dull, doting woman?'

9

Re-marriage

HOWEVER much I disliked my school life, I could not call it dull. There was always something good or bad happening, in fact, it seemed to consist of a succession of small dramas – although they did not seem small at the time – and the tensions were continually increasing. Soon after our return from Wingfield House, in a Latin lesson with Miss Bullen, there was a disturbance.

'If you don't behave I'll send you all to Miss Morison,' she shouted.

'I wouldn't mind going to her,' I answered back cheekily, despising her for having to use that threat because she couldn't keep order herself. It was bravado – for I minded very much.

The next day – I went. This time, it lasted longer and was more cruel – and more loving. The pattern was the same. The two chairs facing each other, the white strained face and the slowly turning torture which went on and on until I broke and then the wild embrace, the kisses and the ecstasy.

There was one development. When we struggled up from the two chairs I weak and blind with tears, she dragged me out of her office and into Miss Kiddle's bedroom next door and pressed me against the edge of the bed until I fell backwards and she fell on top of me.

The only thing that I now fully understood about these scenes was that, with one exception, the mistresses and prefects were all her spies, reporting everything that happened. And nothing was ever forgotten. Incidents, going back for years, were played back to me by the perverted and tormenting instrument which held them and I craved for the strength to withstand it.

The one exception, the only one of them all who was never corrupted, whose soul remained her own, whose behaviour was invariably splendid, was the French mistress, Mlle Bonneau.

She was far above all the pettiness and morbid, torturing concern for our characters. She was only interested in the language and literature of her country and this passion made her gloriously tempestuous and gay. She would come rushing into the class-room, smiling and vibrant, mount the rostrum and looking at us without seeing us, as if on a stage with the footlights between us, instantly begin declaiming one of the great classical dramas.

Carried away by each role in turn, she would roar with god-like rage at one moment and whisper brokenly the next, wave her arms about, fling herself about, tear her hair, weep, laugh, groan, hiss and then shock us even more with a long, agonising silence. She tore up and down the whole scale of the emotions and lived and played through such transports and such tragedies that when the lesson ended not only she herself, but all of us, were in a state of near-collapse.

It never occurred to her to wonder how much of it we understood. I am sure she felt that such magnificent words were self-penetrating and if she had ever guessed that most of us were sitting there nodding, smiling, grimacing at the right moments without grasping so much as a word of it, she would not only have been incredulous – but furious.

If anyone made a noise she picked up a ruler, an ink-pot or anything that she could blindly seize and, without a pause, hurled it at the insensitive fool below. She was wasting her life. She should have been on the stage of the Comédie Francaise.

This was confirmation year for my form. At the beginning of Lent Miss Morison made the announcement and told us to obtain our parents' consent and then come to her for instruction.

I had been waiting for this. But the injunction to obtain our parents' consent seemed to me quite unnecessary. I might tell my mother what I meant to do, but it was years since I had asked her consent for anything. And to ask her about something like this seemed utterly senseless for, beyond believing in her usual optimistic way in an after-life that was going to be wonderful – that is to say, a life in which she would be able to paint as she pleased, not have to paint portraits, not even a portrait of God Himself – she had no views about religion at all. She had no patience with the Church, but if she had thought for a moment that being confirmed would in any way improve my chances of success in life, she would have been enthusiastic about it. But as this was not very apparent she would have left the decision to me, anyway, had I bothered to ask her. I can imagine her saying something like this.

'If all the others are being confirmed and you don't want to be out of it, then you'd better join Miss Morison's classes even if they are a bit of a nuisance and give you more work. But you do as you like, my love.'

I neither asked her consent nor volunteered because I did not want to eat that wafer and drink that wine every Sunday, for I did not believe in it and also, because I knew so well that Miss Morison had set her heart on it for me; that to her, initiation into the Christian mystery was an essential experience, that after baptism, it was the next evangelical duty that a godmother must discharge and the first spiritual fruit to be gathered after long years of watching, tending and praying. Just because it meant so much to her – it meant nothing to me.

I never believed that I would get out of it. But I wasn't going to please her by meekly coming forward. If she wanted it she must ask me, force me. And I was sure that she would.

The classes began a week or two later but not a word was said to me. All the others gathered round her piously for the esoteric instruction. I, alone, was absent. I was amazed but apprehensive.

Soon afterwards, on my christening day, I received a present from her as usual, but this time it was a most *unusual* one. It was inspired. Amy was sent to Harrods to procure it and having chosen it at random, having no natural eye or sense for such a mission, she arrived in a taxi holding it gingerly, as far away from her as she could. It was a little brown dog on a lead.

I always longed for Yen and thinking about her was still as painful as ever. But so much time had passed that I could wish now for something to take her place and I loved the little dog as soon as I saw it. With it came a message from Miss Morison asking me to bring it round to the boarding-house in the evening for her to see.

When I took it up to her sitting-room she danced round it in a pleased and lively way and I thanked her with more real gratitude than I had ever done before. As we sat together, watching the dog playing about the room, I loved her. It was one of those days when she seemed so kind and generous, when her love seemed purged and undemanding. I felt ashamed of all my hard resentful thoughts and my stubborn stand against her. I wondered if it was too late to volunteer for her confirmation class.

She had decided that the dog should be called 'Mars'. Those were her initials, she said, rearranged; and Mars, she went on, proudly airing her classical learning, was the god of War. The initials linking him with her I understood, but what he had to do with war I could not imagine and the ominous note in the naming, neither of us heard.

Mars was a Welsh Border terrier, affectionate, intelligent and gay. I adored him. I played with him all the evening and by the time I was ready for bed I had resolved to join the confirmation class. The next morning at school, however, I wasn't quite so keen and I postponed my decision. I rushed home in the afternoon to take him for a walk and by the evening, once again, I was ready to submit. The day after, I changed my mind once more and I wobbled painfully like this for nearly a week until the grateful impulse finally died. It was too late now to be forced or to offer myself and the contest was put off for another year. Mixed with the shame of my ingratitude went the pleasant sensation that, for the first time, I had won.

I now acquired another friend. She was a new girl, a little younger than I and in a lower form and she lived in a ponderous house in Eaton Square cradled in prestige and wealth and surrounded by protectors. She was Neville Chamberlain's daughter.

Just as I had once looked up to some of the older girls and wished I could make friends with them, so Dorothy looked up to me. It was her father that I looked up to. But I didn't meet him when I first went to tea, or even her mother. I met the governess, the butler, the footman and caught sight of maids galore but of *him*, not so much as a glimpse. I was very disappointed.

However, the tea-party in Dorothy's sitting-room went well for I liked the governess – and she liked me, which was all-important, for it was her job to inspect me and make sure that I was a suitable friend for Dorothy. I chattered away to them both, unaware that I was undergoing an examination and when, somehow, I passed it, opportunities of consorting with, and giving advice to cabinet ministers, at once opened up before me. I was clearly on the road to Downing Street now.

Very soon, I went again and this time I met Mrs Chamberlain and we all had tea together. Her clothes, her glazed, white, unweathered skin, her dark hair brushed obliquely up from her face so that it turned into a sweep and coiled into a splendid mound on the top of her head, her aloofness and fine surroundings made her seem mysterious and turned quite an ordinary woman into something like a queen.

She sat there in her drawing-room on one side of the marble fire-place with the usual mass of silver on the lace-covered table in front of her, gilt frames and mirrors on the walls above her, velvet and brocade surrounding her and the tall windows facing out onto the square behind her, and I thought her the most beautiful woman that I had ever seen.

She said very little and seemed only to ask questions and although I was very awe-inspired, I talked to her easily. Her slow charming smile and sudden bursts of laughter always surprised me, but what intrigued me most was her strange detachment, a quality which I had never met in anyone before. She was with us and yet not with us, as if she was living two lives at once, one with us and another secret one somewhere else. And because of this she didn't seem properly alive.

Afterwards, I was told how tired she was, quite worn out by her social life and the exacting duties that went with her husband's position – he was Minister of Health then. Whether this wholly explained her lethargy or not, the information came as another surprise for it had never occurred to me that high-life could be rigorous and exhausting. Without having given this aspect of it much thought, I had always supposed that it was one long invigorating progress or else a carnival of ever wheeling power and pleasure.

After tea, the governess went to her own quarters and Dorothy and I returned to the sitting-room. I had now been twice judged as a fit companion and we were left alone together.

The revolutionary wave had receded and the country was steadier, but exports were falling and unemployment was rising and art was again suffering.

If my mother had still been painting the small water-colour portraits, cheap and fascinating, a field in which she had no competitors, I am sure that she would not have been affected by the slump that followed the war boom. But the burst of mass-production work in the shop and afterwards was the end of them, and now, with no commissions for the large oil-colours ahead, she was worrying about money once more.

But her new friend was not aware of this. We looked so prosperous now on the surface and he believed that we were comfortably off, whether she worked or not. And she had her reasons for wanting him to think this.

Even the oils were an effort. Although we did not know it, as she cast about for fresh avenues along which to push her work – she was worn out.

Now, her mind went back to the compassionate old man who, 14 years before, had arranged snow-drops round an improvised font and christened me with specially consecrated water out of a tennis cup – the Bishop of London, Dr Winnington-Ingram.

Using the old approach, she wrote, reminding him of the past and asking if she might paint him and afterwards present it to him. He responded at once and a few days later, she set out for Fulham Palace.

He received her as lovingly as before and, while he sat, asked all about our lives and was not satisfied until he had pieced the saga together. He did not ask why we had been so long in England and only just come to see him, nor if the child he had baptised was now a good Christian. He was tactful and forbearing.

She was working in water-colours, for convenience, but doing a large head which was finished the same morning. She told him that she would do the figure at home and then bring it back for him to see.

'You must both come to tea,' he said. 'I want to meet Philippa again. I'll come and fetch you next Tuesday afternoon at half past three.'

We were ready waiting at the door and when the car drew up we dashed out onto the pavement. But he didn't like that.

'We won't go yet. I want to see your house first,' he cried, jumping out of the car and running nimbly upstairs. He insisted on seeing the whole flat and only then was he ready to leave.

During the long ride to Fulham I sat between him and my mother, looking round as often as I felt was polite at the pink-faced, cosy old man and listening to his chatter. Although I had seen him before at school and plenty of other bishops, I had never seen one at such close range, never sat beside one and I enjoyed the experience.

When I was not looking him in the face my eyes were travelling up and down him, from his gaiters to his comic hat. I saw exactly how the brim was attached by flying cords to the crown, I counted the buttons on his gaiters and the pieces of braid on his fine fancy cuffs, I wanted to stroke his black coat for the cloth was so smooth and I wondered whether his lovely purple bib was tied by a tape round his neck.

When we arrived at the Palace, a long low Tudor building, we were taken into a large room, a bachelor's room, with windows looking out onto a great expanse of lawn running down to the Thames. Tea was brought in and we sat intimately together round the fire.

He was dismayed when he heard that my mother had torn the picture up. For she had. As soon as she got it home she knew that it wasn't good work and now she asked if he would sit again. He agreed at once. He would have agreed to anything, he was so obliging. He felt pity for the young widow 14 years ago, perhaps he understood why she had suddenly asked to paint him – and felt pity for her now.

She went back and tried again and showed it him, and he liked it. But she wouldn't give it him. She said it was weak and not good enough to be exhibited and then hung up on his walls. She could have made a third attempt in oils. He would have sat again, done anything to help her, but she was too tired to make any further effort. The forlorn attempt to gain publicity by exploiting the old bishop had failed and soon afterwards she told me that she was going to marry John.

He loved her, she said, and had asked her several times but she had always refused, because of me. She was afraid I would not like it. But now she felt she must. She did not explain why she must and I thought it was because she loved him, too. I said I would not mind. I said I was pleased. But I did mind. I hated it.

'He will give up the house in Lewisham and come to live here,' she went on. 'The girls will go to a boarding school and we shall only see them in the holidays. It won't make any difference to you and me, darling, our love will be just the same. We need someone to take care of us and he is very fond of you.'

I left the room and sat on the staircase for awhile with my arms round Mars and then I ran out of the house with him and round the quiet opulent streets, feeling jealous and miserable.

And now, my mother heard from the Royal Academy that the portrait of Sir Vincent had been accepted and was to be hung 'on the line'. He was delighted and we were invited down to Wingfield House at once. But we could not go for she and John were being married very soon.

Not long before the wedding, we heard that John had been posted to Manchester and so would not be coming back to live in the flat after the honeymoon. I was glad that the day of his entry and ownership of my mother was put off for awhile.

Neither of them ever went to Church – but they were married in one. Miss Morison and Amy came to the service, but not Florence. She was busy with marriage manoeuvres of her own now and all her actions became suddenly very circumspect. But she was pleased about John and my mother.

'I'm so glad, Louie,' she said again and again. 'I know you'll make him happy. The poor darling has had such a bad time.'

When the day came, my mother and I arrived very early at the church, just as if we had been catching a train – and with us went Mars. I settled myself in a pew and tucked him away underneath. He knew exactly what was happening and never moved or made a sound.

When Miss Morison and Amy arrived they joined me in the same pew. They both fell to their knees in prayer and then sat back and waited. Miss Morison was in a good mood for she was also pleased about this marriage. Then, deciding suddenly that her umbrella was in her way, she bent forward and pushed it under the pew. At that moment she caught sight of Mars. She exploded with horror.

'How could you do such a thing, Philippa? You know that dogs are not allowed in Church. It's sacrilege! You must take him out at once. And you'll have to stay outside with him. You can't come back.' And with a lot of scuffling and commotion, Mars and I squeezed past them out of the pew and walked down the aisle and out of the big door. When John arrived and the ceremony began, I opened the door a crack and peeped. And that was how I attended my mother's wedding.

Immediately afterwards, the bride and bridegroom drove off in a taxi to the station and Amy and Mars and I followed in another. When we got there, John was walking down the platform carrying cups of tea and I could see him properly now. He wore a new brown suit with a loud stripe running through the tweed and his bow tie was a spotted green. In his button-hole was a carnation, his hair had been cut too short and, as always, that awful monocle kept falling out of his eye. He looked so different from Sir Vincent and all the other fathers. He looked such a bounder.

I kissed my mother and the train moved away – moved away without me. And I thought of all the journeys that we had made together, all the adventures at the end of them. Now we would not travel or be together any more. For 14 years I had had her for my own, we had roamed about the world without any sure home, without a real family and with few or lasting friends. We were not just mother and child, we were all things to each other – family, friends and fate. And out of this experience had grown an understanding and a love and a physical position which seemed to me unshareable and unchangeable. Yet now it had to change and now I had to share her.

Miss Morison had expected me to spend the fortnight of the honeymoon at the boarding-house. She had told me that I could have the same little room and bring Mars with me. But I didn't go there, for one of my friends invited us to stay with her and, in my sadness, I was glad to be with her and her family.

When my mother returned, she didn't seem quite so happy, but I supposed it was the separation that was worrying her and the usual shortage of money and of work. As a civil servant, John had a good salary but while they were living apart, he made her no allowance. He still believed she was well off.

I don't know why we were so poor again so soon, for she had earned such a lot the year before. She had given £100 to the building fund, we had had a good holiday and she had bought some wedding clothes, but otherwise we had lived in our usual careful way. I can only think that most of it must have been swallowed up by ancient debts. It was all gone and she began to run up bills again. When John's posting was reversed and he returned to London, she was sure that she would be able to pay them all off.

She was constantly going up to Manchester to see him, and Mars and I went back to the same friend every time – until Miss Morison complained.

'Miss Morison telephoned today,' my mother told me one evening. 'She says that you never go to stay with her when I'm away. She is very hurt. She seems to think that *I* am stopping you. I know you don't like it, but I expect you ought to go there sometimes. It's never for long and she says that you can have Mars in your room. I've had to let her pay your school fees again this term and so we must do what she wants – and she is so kind. When John gets back to London we shall be peaceful again.'

About this time, perhaps to save herself the cost, Miss Morison put my case up to the School Council who waived the fees altogether, accepting me now as a charity child. And the next time my mother went away, Mars and I moved into the boarding-house. But it was not as bad as I had expected for whenever anyone came into my room he growled and so, nobody did. Miss Morison had several talks with me in her sitting-room.

'Now that your mother has married again your life will be very different,' she said one evening. 'You will not be with her so much, she will have John and the other children to think about. But you will soon get to like being in a larger family. You will be able to do many things that you couldn't do before. Your school life will be happier for you will not feel so divided. More of you, in time the whole of you, I know, will go out into the school and you will understand then all that I am trying to do for you and the self-deceptions that you suffer from and the mistakes that you have made. Your character will have a chance to develop in the right way, your life will take on shape and meaning and you will be at peace with yourself.'

'I'm sure that I shall never be any different,' was all that I could think to say.

At the beginning, she had believed it would be easy to detach me from my mother and win my love for herself. She was so sure of her power and of her money. My resistance and all my shortcomings she ascribed solely to my mother's baleful influence and she was sure that she was the only obstacle between herself and me. As time passed, she grew more and more frantic at her lack of success and casting round for other ways of separating us, she now jumped at the possibilities presented by the marriage. The only effect that these new revelations had upon me was to make me more careful how I spoke about my mother. Never again could I use her as an excuse.

In June we went down to Wingfield House again. The weather was hot and the garden, which we had only seen in winter, was now bursting with glory. There were acres of exotic flowers, vine-covered walks, rose trellises and lily pools and the air was filled with perfume.

After tea on the terrace, under a striped awning, the house-party broke up into small groups to wander among the flowers, the blazing quietness acting like some sweet contagion upon everyone. When my mother and Lady Caillard strolled away together to see some special border and exchange their secrets, Sir Vincent turned to me and I went with him, into the deep concealing wilderness of flowers.

He took my hand and, without speaking, we walked until we reached a distant arbour thickly covered with honey-suckle and bougainvillaea. Inside it was a wooden seat. We sat down, he put his arm round me and looked at me, looked first into my eyes then downwards at my body, then back into my eyes again.

'You are a naughty girl,' he said, 'to leave me for so long.'

'I couldn't help it,' I replied naively. 'So many things have happened to us.'

'I know, sweetheart. I didn't mean that seriously. But I've missed you so much. I've thought about you every day. Have you ever thought about me? I'm sure you haven't.'

'Oh, but I have. I've often thought about you,' I answered even more childishly than before.

'I know *how* you've thought about me. You've wanted to ask me about the political situation and to guess where the world is going.' I smiled at him.

'Yes, yes, I have. But not only that. I've thought about you in lots of other ways too.'

'Have you, darling? What other ways? Tell me?'

'Well, I've thought about you playing the organ. I've thought about you sitting in that lovely room, working, with all those books round you and ... and ...'

'Yes? Go on, sweetheart.'

'Well ... well ... I've thought about you and ... and ... me.'

At that, he swung round and hugging me tightly kissed me with such violence that my head bent backwards and I could hardly breathe. And again I hated it. His breath was rank and there was a sour taste to his lips and tongue. I felt nothing but repugnance and boredom. But I had to go on – and put up with it, receive his rancid kisses and pretend that I liked them.

He released me at last and leant back against the seat and, for a few minutes, talked about the garden. Then he bent over me again.

'You've grown a lot. Several inches I'm sure. You're getting quite a big girl.'

'I'm 14,' I said proudly. 'Next term I shall be in the upper fourth.'

'And soon after that you'll be in the sixth and then you'll leave school and marry a handsome young man and forget all about me.'

'Oh no. I like you too much. Whatever I do I hope I shall always be friends with you.' And as I said this the thought of my life's work, my high destiny, rose powerfully into my mind and the sweet smile that I gave him was really the smug superior smile of my secret certainty. With an impulsive jerk, he drew me to him again.

'I wish you liked me well enough to kiss me as I kiss you. Won't you try, darling? Let your little body go and kiss me properly. I know you can. But you don't try. You still resist me.'

He bent over me again and pressed his mouth to mine and I made a weak mechanical attempt to please him. But I disliked it so much that I soon stopped and grew inert again.

'That was a little better,' he said when he let me go once more, 'but not half good enough. My little sweetheart makes love with her big brown eyes and her smile and then stops. She's a naughty tantalising little thing. I would like to give her a good hard spanking, only I daren't. She would be so angry with me.'

Again I smiled at him while I tried to make sense of this baby love talk, half flattered by it, half bored with it. I didn't understand how one made love with one's eyes and one's smile. I didn't know I was doing anything like that. Then, feeling that it was now my turn, that I had earned the right to change the subject, I moved away from him a little and pushed my hair back and stopped smiling.

'There is something that I do so want to ask you,' I said.

'I can guess what it is, my little politician,' he replied quickly, half amused, half irritated, leaning back against the seat once more.

'How long do you expect the coalition government to last? Lloyd George is driving the country into some terrible dangers, don't you think?'

'I should certainly like to see an election and the parties standing separately again,' he answered. 'But for all its mistakes, it's a strong government and in disturbed times like these, with the country so divided, it might be very risky to change it.'

'If there *is* an election, who will lead the Conservative party?'

'That is hard to say now. The party is so disunited and unready.'

'I should like to see Austen Chamberlain at the head of a new government.' I don't know whether it was my friendship with Dorothy, but at this time I was a great champion of the Chamberlain family.

I kept this conversation going for as long as I could and then, suddenly, I stopped and my whole body froze. He was no longer listening to me. He was bending over me again. His left arm was round my shoulder again and his right hand, which for a few moments had been resting on my knee, was now travelling slowly over my dress up my leg. It seemed rude to push it violently away as I wanted to do. I grew hard and closed all over as I waited to understand what he was doing. And then I knew. I took his hand very politely and removed it. He gave way at once and sat back with an impatient sigh, staring moodily out into the garden. Then he tried again but this time higher. While he was kissing me, his hand moved up from my waist to my breast and I jumped away and roughly pushed him from me.

'Darling, why are you still so frightened of me? I would never hurt you. I only want to caress your lovely little body. Won't you trust me?' he said in a tone that was both coaxing and exasperated. I said nothing. I was too bewildered. Then he looked at his watch and stood up.

'Come, darling, it's getting late and I still have a lot of work to do.' He bent and picked me up and held me in his arms for a moment. Then we walked out into the sunlight.

We always went to that arbour; several times each day. On Sunday, before my mother and I left for London, we went again. He sat down first and held out his arms.

'Come and sit on my lap, sweetheart.'

'I'm too heavy,' I said.

'Rubbish! I shall think it's a fairy flown down into my arms, sitting on my knees.'

'Awkwardly I sank into his lap and he pulled me back and kissed me and then I felt his hand fumble with my dress and petticoat and then creep under them and up the inside of my thigh. I jumped out of his arms and stood staring angrily down at him.

'There goes my little fairy again, furiously leaping and fluttering about when she could be so happy if only she would stay quietly in my arms,' was all he said.

And my week-ends at Wingfield House were always like that now. Gradually, I learnt how to hold him away and at the same time please him and keep him always hoping that one day I would do everything he wanted. I still didn't know what that was and I was still too timid and unready to go further and find out. His never-ceasing attempts to explore my body always mystified and annoyed me and I was always thankful when the amorous days were over.

As soon as we arrived home, I hurried round to my friend's house to fetch Mars. It was so lovely to jump and race through the streets with him again, to be a child again and not an old man's petting thing – my father's mistress.

The entry lists appeared on the notice board and I had to give my Victor Ludorum cups back. Cynthia had returned from America and I should have been pleased. But I wasn't. She had grown a lot, she was much bigger than I was and I knew that I could never beat her. She was bound to be the champion this year. And I was so mad about winning now, so caught up in the passion of it all that, after the triumphs of last year, the thought of walking up behind her again and again, to receive second prizes every time – was unendurable.

I decided not to enter for the sports that year and then I changed and decided that I would, that I would go and face inevitable defeat. Then I changed again and then again and for the two long, terrible weeks that the lists were up, I lived in this divided, painful state. I couldn't sleep properly or work, the craving to win was like a raging fever and I could do nothing else but struggle with my cowardice. On the last day I was so paralysed by indecision that I let the lists come down without my name.

The visions of defeat, so vivid in my imagination day after day, faded into fog, the agony shifted from my mind and spread through my body and changed into a deep, all-over, incomprehensible ache. I was so dulled with exhaustion that I no longer knew what I was worrying about.

But when the grand exciting day arrived and the whole school and all the parents went flocking out to Richmond and I alone came home the pain flared up again, aggravated now by shame and regret.

A week or two later I won the swimming cup again. But the victory meant nothing to me. Defeat at Richmond would have pleased me more.

All this time John had been striving to get himself posted back to London and now, with his case still unconsidered, his letters grew despairing and my mother's trips to Manchester became more frequent until, in her usual dynamic way, she decided to intervene. She went to Mrs Baldwin and told her their story. The same day word went direct to the Minister and a week later John was notified of his recall, immediately after his summer leave.

One hot July day, near the end of term, Amy dropped in to see us. I was getting ready to take Mars for his walk.

'I'll come with you and we'll walk up to the park,' she said.

'Oh, I'd love that. Then Mars can have a swim in the Serpentine.'

There was very little traffic in the residential streets in those days and people seldom kept their dogs on their leads. Mars chased about and often ran out into the road. We had nearly reached the park when a limousine crawled silently up behind us, just as he was prancing back to me. But I felt no concern for the car was going so slowly. The next thing he was screaming and a moment later, with blood pouring out of him, he was lying in the gutter at my feet. The limousine stopped, the chauffeur looked casually down at him and then drove on.

My one thought was to save him. I rushed to a house and rang the bell, intending to telephone for a vet and I was sure that the people inside would help me. I waited, with Mars still screaming, but no one came. I rushed to the next house and rang that bell, but when I looked round I saw that a lorry had stopped and a crowd had collected. I went back and forced my way through the people. Standing over Mars was the driver, young and fair and huge.

'Shall I put 'im out of 'is misery, Miss?' he shouted to me, for Mars was still making a terrible noise, and writhing.

'No,' I shouted back. 'I want to send for a vet. Perhaps a vet can save him.'

''e's done for, Miss, there ain't nothin' yer can do – best put 'im out of 'is pain an' finish with it.' And I knew he was right and I couldn't endure his screams any longer myself and I nodded my consent.

He walked back to his lorry and fetched the starting handle. I turned my back. I could have screamed myself. I heard his skull crack. Then silence. When I looked again I saw him dead.

The man returned to his lorry and then came back with a piece of old lace curtain. He bent down and gently spread it over him – and then drove away.

When the crowd melted, Amy became visible again and we stood together looking down on the small, still, lace-covered body. In the doorways behind us two smart servants stood looking angrily out, summoned improperly by their bells. Then Amy rose to the occasion.

'I will carry him home for you,' she said. And I was grateful for I couldn't have carried him dead. She picked him up, all blood and dust, the lace dangling, and held him away from her as if she was carrying an offering and we walked back the way we had come. Mrs Just got him buried in the garden of one of her friends.

Soon after that, we went away for the holidays, all of us together now – John and the two girls.

10

Unlawful and Damnable

JOHN chose it. A hideous hotel dominating the cliff at Lowestoft. I shared a room with the girls but I kept myself apart, my bed was in one corner and they were together in another. It was not that I had grown into such a snob that I would not make friends with them, for I played with the boys in the hotel. They were just uninteresting and, as my new sisters – unreal.

At meals, we sat at a large round table in the big bleak dining-room like all the other happy families. But I felt no joy in possessing a family at last. I didn't feel that I belonged to them at all. I sat like a stranger eating silently, critically watching my step-father in his holiday clothes talking intimately to my mother, greeting the people round him, bursting with holiday spirits and newly-wed confidence. And I hated him.

He soon knew everyone in the hotel and spent most of his time in the bar with the other men, all of them rigged out in blazers and white flannels; chief clerks and sales managers, property agents and garage proprietors with bright, home-centred wives and lots of neat unenterprising children. And I was bored with them all.

I was hardly ever with my mother, only when we went down to the crowded beach to bathe, leaving John with his boon companions and the girls with the dull daughters of all these worthy mothers and fathers.

It lasted a month and then the girls went somewhere else, I went down the coast to stay with friends at Southwold (they had rented Miss Morison's cottage for the holidays) and my mother and John returned to London. I was thankful to be among cultured upper-class people again and away from my new family.

When I came back to London, too, I found the flat quite changed. The single beds in the room which I had shared with my mother had gone and a double one was in their place. I had been moved to the box-room. She had had a small bed built into it, for it was no bigger than a cupboard, with one side sloping over the staircase, piled with trunks, a ladder and window leading onto the roof and some steep steps with a door at the bottom, leading up to it.

When I got over the shock of my banishment, I rather liked it. I could escape there from John who resented me and soon showed it, I could lead a new independent and solitary life of my own up there in the roof. Miss Morison was right. My mother's marriage had changed my life completely. But she was also wrong, for it didn't turn me towards her and the school. It turned me into myself.

When we all went back that autumn, the demolition work was over and the foundations for the new buildings and playground were being laid. During lessons the noise was pleasantly distracting.

American children were all brought up on the story of George Washington yet when I was among them, I was never aware of his noble example being followed. It always seemed as if only *I* took his story to heart, as if only *my* conscience grew more and more tender, as if *I alone* was incessantly striving for moral perfection. It seemed as if his code was preached but never practised.

In England, on the other hand, one of the first things that I noticed was the regular George Washington behaviour of all the children. A mistress had only to say, 'who has done that?' and the culprit would own up at once and be punished. But, instead of admiring this, I was perplexed to find that I reacted strongly against it. And when, in time, I realised that the George Washington code and the public school spirit were one and the same, I was shocked and worried. It was not only preached but practised here and I had turned completely round and was rejecting it. And as the years passed my conscience, in this respect, grew more and more insensitive and stony.

Now, at the age of 14, I had the mind and heart of a criminal. I had pondered over the problem again and again but always come to the same conclusion. There would be no point to burglary and arson and all the other sins of the underworld, I argued to myself, if, as soon as the hunt was on, the criminal walked into a police station and gave himself up.

As the rules and ways of the school were impossible to live with, I continued, I had to break or ignore them. I was obliged to wage a form of covert war upon the school and there would be no purpose to it if, whenever I committed a crime, I owned up immediately and was punished. On the contrary, it was my duty to outwit the mistresses and conceal everything I could from them for they, from Miss Morison downwards, were the Police in a society which I hated and only endured because I had to. I thrust George Washington out of my mind and marched grimly along my amoral, anti-social road without him.

Life in the flat soon became very difficult. Everything I did, or didn't do, John criticised. One day, at dinner, when I was embarking on my usual second-helping, he jumped up from the table in a rage saying that I ate too much and took too long and he couldn't stand having to wait for me. After that I had my meals in the kitchen. And now, while the chances were so favourable, Miss Morison exerted herself more than ever before to win me.

She took me to theatres (to the popular plays), she showered me with presents, my shortcomings were overlooked, she flattered me and fawned upon me and there was a new confidence in her trying. Underneath the fawning I could sense elation, for victory seemed at last within her grasp.

One night she said to me, 'You can't go on living in that horrible little box-room, darling. Why don't you come and live at the boarding house? You can furnish that little room for yourself and soon I'll take a lovely flat and we'll live comfortably together. Your mother's marriage would be happier if you did this.'

Sometimes I loathed all this courting, sometimes I seemed to loathe and like it at the same time and sometimes I forgot my loathing altogether and was drawn towards her more strongly than ever before. Back in the box-room I would think about her in a sweet desiring way and about that flat that she would take and the life that we might lead together. And then, suddenly, the whole affecting fantasy would vanish, the old distrust and dislike would return and then I would resolve not to tell her any more about my life and what went on. When I disliked her, I was afraid that I was hurting my mother but when I liked her, in this tender way, I felt disloyal and guilty.

When I first came back to London I saw a change in my mother and now, after two months, I was sure that something was distressing her. And whenever I caught a glimpse of him I fancied that he looked different, too, and I wondered if Miss Morison was right and it was I who was upsetting them.

Then, one night, I was woken by a frightful noise. He came up the stairs underneath me shouting and banging all the doors and when he entered the bedroom, I heard my mother's angry voice, 'You're drunk again.' I jumped out of bed and ran down my little steps and stood behind the door at the bottom, thinking that she might need my help. They went on shouting at each other. At first, I couldn't understand what he was saying, his voice was thick and his words senseless. But I understood my mother. 'If you don't like it here you'd better leave,' and again, 'I won't put up with you like this any more. I can't stand your horrible drunkenness.' And then, in a voice that was suddenly distinct I heard him say, 'I can't stand that child in the house,' and my mother's quick retort, 'Well, I'm not sending her away for you.' After that, there was silence. He must have dropped into a drunken sleep. But I didn't know this and I was afraid to go into the bedroom and comfort my mother. Instead, I stumbled up the steps again horrified by what I had heard, but in my heart of hearts, glad. I knew that the whole thing was over.

In the morning, I didn't see or hear him. But I saw my mother. She looked at me hard and knew that I had heard it all. We said nothing.

A week or two passed and then, one day, when I came home from school I stopped outside the drawing-room door, as I always did, to listen. There was absolute silence and it seemed as if both of them were out. I opened the door and there he was, his legs wide apart, his arms dangling; sprawled half in an arm-chair and half on the floor – drunk as drunk. I stared at him with loathing and then closed the door again. Before long, my mother came home and I ran downstairs to meet her. 'He's in there,' I told her. She opened the door. 'He'll have to go,' was all she said. The next day he was gone.

'I should never have done it,' she said to me now. 'I wasn't in love with him. But I wanted a man to look after me. I was tired of fighting the world alone. He was comfortably off and I wanted his money. And he wanted mine! He never loved me. I was just a passable widow with a house in a fashionable quarter and behind me, he believed, a comfortable income. He married me for my money! That's what makes it so comic.' And she laughed in a bitter way.

'I couldn't tell you all this at the time,' she went on. 'I didn't want you to know that I was only marrying to get kept. For that's not the way to do it. And he certainly took me in. I was sorry for him. I thought he had suffered and needed looking after – and I thought he was good and kind. But when he discovered that I had no money, he was horrible to me. He's a beast and it's not he that suffered but that poor woman – his wife.'

Amy was the first to spread the news. Dropping in the same day, she soon found out that he had gone and later there was an excited telephone call from Miss Morison. She was incredulous. Her hopes and plans were dashed again.

The double bed disappeared. All traces of the disagreeable intruder were removed and my mother and I settled back into our old way of living. But not the same way. Too much had happened and I soon discovered that our relationship, itself, had changed.

I was setting off to a political meeting one night when she tried to stop me, telling me that it was too far away and I would get home too late. For the first time in my life I wouldn't listen to her. I turned angrily upon her and flung out of the house.

I could not concentrate upon the meeting. I knew now that nothing stays the same, that love can alter, even *my* love for my mother. Although I loved her just as much, I knew that the paradisial phase was over, that we stood as adults before each other now with all the claims and postures of my forceful ego likely, at any moment, to darken the air between us. And I wept for my lost childhood.

Every night now, she sat at her bureau writing out her story and working up the grounds upon which she meant to claim a separation allowance.

Secretly I disagreed with her. Although I detested John, I could not understand why, after only a few months of marriage which had not affected us materially at all, he should be expected to support, or partly support, her for the rest of his life. It seemed most unfair to me. But I didn't realise how worn out she was, how desperate for money, how much the experience had hurt her and how hard it had made her. And I didn't know until then how she could hate. I knew she hated Willie, but I hadn't seen and felt it. Now I watched her hating and fighting and 'getting her own back', upon John.

She needed witnesses for her case and the first person that she went to, of course, was Florence. And now, to her dismay, she heard the truth about her sister. John had always drunk too much, Florence told her, and her sister had been desperately unhappy and had died of drink herself. When my mother asked why she didn't warn her, why she had encouraged her to marry him, she replied, 'I thought him rather a pet. I thought he might improve if he made a fresh start. And the children needed someone.' When, finally, my mother asked her if she would help her by appearing in court as a witness, she was disillusioned altogether.

'I'm terribly sorry, my dear, but I really could not do that. Edward would not like it.' She was married herself now and her husband knew nothing about the sordid circumstances of her sister's life and death. She didn't want my mother to bring a case at all.

John resisted vigorously at first, but the more he did so the more implacable my mother became. And she won in the end. He agreed to a separation on the grounds of desertion and to payment of £100 a year. Her hurt and her hatred were assuaged a little.

All this took many months and the school year moved heavily on. I was now working for the university which was to be paid for jointly by Miss Morison and my godfather's widow, in Cornwall.

After leaving school, most of those girls went to a 'finishing' school in Paris and then 'came out'; were presented at Court by their fashionable mothers, went to balls and parties every night until they married, as quick as they could, the richest, most titled young men they could catch. A few, from the professional families with no special social position, went to the university. All other ways were despised.

Although university life always sounded rather fine, yet it didn't really attract me. But neither did my mother's way – the way of the artist. I despised it, too, for I was still bewitched by the glamour and importance of high society, still eager for the security which a place inside it would give me. The power and influence of that great grand world, in whose shadow I lived, was so strong that no other counter-force would at this time have drawn me away from it. I was fated to go after it, to scale its unscalable walls and know it, and the experience, as it turned out, was perhaps as rich a one as any, as good a university as all the other more befitting and conventional ones.

Not long after John left us, Miss Morison conceived another most surprising plan for me. She proposed that I should go to a boarding school. As my health was not good, she said (I was having health troubles for the first time) and as I could not properly appreciate her school and co-operate as I should, as I was thwarted and unhappy, she thought it best that I should leave and see if I could change and become the person that I ought to be – somewhere else. The fees, she assured us, she would pay herself. It was her last desperate attempt to separate me from my mother. With week-end visits and alluring holidays she would finally win me.

A year or two earlier I would have jumped at any chance of leaving. But now it was too late. My mother and I took several day-trips to the country to look at schools. I did not fancy any of them. They were surrounded by green fields and rolling hills, they were screened and shaded by beautiful trees and only bird songs disturbed them, they looked clean, pure and peaceful – they looked so boring.

I now preferred the grime and squalor of the city, the sound of traffic, the view of buildings, the living waves of people, the smoky highly charged, stimulating air. My home and my school lay close to the very heart of Westminster, within a short walk of St James's and a long one of St Paul's, shaded not by inanimate and voiceless trees but by Parliament and Palace. I had no real friends but I clung to them for their fathers, the cabinet ministers and generals, the dukes and earls and lords-in-waiting. For this whole, high, vivid world of London I chose to go on suffering. I had become my own gaoler – half loving all the torture.

Disappointed again, Miss Morison grew frantic and the interviews became more frequent. Several times every term we faced each other on the two chairs and afterwards, tussled inconclusively in Miss Kiddle's bedroom. I was stronger now and it took her longer to overcome me, but as she felt my resistance growing, so did her madness. Although the love scenes appeared so unsatisfactory, yet after each frenzy she always glowed with delight and I knew that only if I could withstand the first sadistic assault, could I thwart the ecstasy that followed.

When the confirmation season came round again, again I made no move and when she sent for me to tell me that she wished to confer a great honour upon me, to make me a prefect – I refused it. In every way I could, I went on trying to frustrate her and to save myself – often loving her at the very moment when I struck her.

That summer, the new playground and buildings were finished and a large dais, draped in red, white and blue bunting with a canopy over it, was erected in the middle of the asphalt tennis court, hundreds of yards of red carpet were rolled out everywhere, more chairs than ever before were hired, union jacks waved from a dozen flag-poles and with a fanfare of trumpets followed by the usual choir of angels singing 'God Save the King', one of the royal dukes arrived for the grand opening ceremony. It was the high-point of Miss Morison's career.

At the same time I was moving towards the high-point of my successes and my standing from which, then I rapidly descended. As the balance of her passion changed and hate grew up beside her love, it infected everyone around me and I felt encircled by spies and persecutors.

My friends, as they got older, came under her spell, changing into goody-goody little adorers, quick to sense her every mood, smug, obedient and conforming. As they strained for her approval and worked for honour and office, I despised them and when they had to speak to me, I answered rudely. Not content to lose them I made them hate me until, in the end, the whole form banded together against me – all except one.

Ione was that one – so clever and yet such a fool and now, when the rest of us matured, the eternal child. As if in a dream, I moved grimly through the school with that loyal and laughing clown by my side.

I handed back all my offices and honours and enjoyed seeing the dismay of the mistresses when I told them that I had no time to swim or play games any more. The unprecedented action infuriated Miss Morison.

When the summer came again, however, my system was still not wholly purged of the poison of competition and desire for prestige and I entered for the field sports again.

On the day, I felt unwell and my mother tried to persuade me not to go, but I was hysterical and half crazy. I went and was defeated in every event. And not honourably by a superior like Cynthia, but by Rachel, the silly, vain, flibbertigibbet. And when the cups were presented, again and again I walked up behind her and saw the delight in Miss Morison's eyes, the cold, pleased look on so many of the mistresses' faces, the mean look of those who had once been my friends and Rachel – gloating. I had still not reached the bottom but I did not have much farther to fall.

As the present became more and more oppressive, so did the future. As my sense of mission grew stronger, so did my fear of it. I knew that my adult life would be utterly different yet, in one respect, I was now certain that it would be the same, that it would be lived from one ordeal to another along a path of incessant anxiety and strain.

Although the experiences of the time may seem to have been the reason for my projecting this pessimism onto the future, yet the view was not just morbid and meaningless and passing, for the life that I ultimately gave myself, the natural continuation of the life which even then I was giving, or bringing upon myself, was just as I forsaw it.

I had gained a new important insight into myself. I had understood that the present was not just an unpleasant episode, a deviation from a paradisial norm and a theft of the bliss of childhood, inflicted upon me by the ill-judgment of my mother, the wickedness of my godmother and the imperfections of society. I had seen that I was not just a passive victim, but that life was a dual affair – what I, myself, made it and the storms of the present were already contained in it. It attracted them now and would always do so, for hell was my own nature – the passionate, self-proclaiming character which I believed must accompany me through the whole of time and space.

The next term, the autumn of 1924, exactly five years after we returned to England and when I was 16-years-old, I reached the sixth form and the final nightmarish months of my school life. Every day of the school week, Miss Morison sent for me and we looked into each other's eyes and our minds struggled for mastery. In between, I went to my classes, but the battle was the only thing that I could really concentrate upon. The daily battle was my life.

On the last day of the term, according to custom, we queued outside Miss Morison's office to say good-bye and I waited with an easy mind, believing that a month's respite was before me. But when my turn came and I entered her room, she didn't hold out her hand.

'I'm not going to say good-bye to you, Philippa. I want you to come to breakfast tomorrow and we'll say our good-byes then.'

The boarding house was strangely empty and quiet the next morning, for the children had gone home the day before. We hardly spoke during breakfast while the maids were waiting on us. Afterwards, she led the way up to her sitting-room and the fight began all over again.

She had plenty of crimes to roll off, my very attendance at the school now was an anomaly and a scandal, my person an expression of protest and unrighteousness. But that morning she excelled herself. Everything was remembered and everything was magnified. She was more forceful, her eyes more mesmeric and devouring. Yet, somehow, on this day, I matched her power with an equal power. I daren't speak but as long as I just looked at her in silence I found that I could hold her. At last I could hold her! Yet my strength didn't appear to disconcert her. On the contrary, she seemed more exhilarated and confident than ever – for she had something in reserve.

She didn't hurry. She let me struggle. She could see how hard it was for me.

She pressed and pressed, then stopped as if it was all over, then pressed and pierced again. And on and on she went, longer than ever before, more desperately than ever before – and then it came, the final stroke, the stroke to end it! The last word, the confounding word – the ultimatum!

'This cannot go on, Philippa. The school comes before everything, it stands above both of us and its honour lies in my keeping. I, alone, am responsible for it and you, you of all people, whom I love so and have tried so hard to guide into the proper path, you my godchild – alone disgrace it. And when the school is hurt – I am hurt. I have been patient. For years patient with you, always hoping that love and tenderness would soften your heart and bring you to understand how stubborn and mistaken you were. But now I can see that my patience has been exercised in vain and although I love you no less and I will continue to help you just as much as you will let me, yet I can no longer allow you to bring dishonour on the school and such pain to the staff. The pain that you cause me and have caused me for years I do not consider, that is something I must bear. But I can no longer condone what you do and protect you with my love. Unless you can change – you will have to go. I give you three months. If you have not conformed in that time, I shall have to expel you. And you know how grave a thing that is.' There was a threatening note in her voice.

It was curious how, from the very beginning, her passion and my resistance to it were never referred to directly but only in terms of my resistance to the school with which they were always equated. I was still baffled by this fusion and confusion of objects, the double-headed nature of this lurid relationship.

When before, she gave me the chance to leave I had not taken it. Now, she was opening the prison gate again, and although this time I longed to go yet, again, I could not walk out to my freedom. And she knew it. For in three months time I was due to take the first of the Cambridge examinations and I believed that to change schools at this juncture, and to change in disgrace, would not only upset my work but prevent my acceptance by the University. She knew before that I did not want to go. She believed now that I *could* not go. She was sure that she had trapped me.

As I listened, I knew that I could never change and would never conform. Hope and hopelessness were mixed together in my mind as I went on staring into her white tense face. And now she was sure that I would break. I could see the excitement in her eyes as she waited for it. But I didn't. In the same moment when I believed she had destroyed me, I had won at last – for I held and I held and I held her.

She waited. Her swollen face had a blanched look, even her tightly drawn lips seemed bloodless, the blue mark bluer. She was trembling. Then she stood up and pushed her chair back. I got up, too, and waited in the middle of the room cold and stiff and motionless. She came up to me and put her arms awkwardly round me and keeping her body away from me, held me limply as if she was holding a tree or a lamp-post. And neither of us moved. We just stood looking at each other and despair was in her eyes – and hatred.

Then she dropped her arms and still without speaking, I left the room. In the hall, I put on my hat and coat and then walked out of the house.

I had gone about 50 yards, then, without having heard her, suddenly, she was walking along beside me. She had crept up behind me and now she was bending and peering round into my face and she saw that I was crying, that I had broken in the end. After all, she had won. She made some clever excuse for following me and then, with a triumphant smile, turned and walked back to the house. I went on home, weeping then with rage.

That night, at about two o'clock, we were woken by three loud raps of the knocker on the front door. We jumped out of bed, flung up the window and peered out. In the light of the street lamps, we could see the figure of a woman on the door-step. There were three more reverberating crashes. We ran downstairs and my mother opened the door. With her hair hanging loose down her back and a coat over her nightgown which was trailing on the ground, Miss Morison swayed into the hall. Her eyes were shut and she spoke to my mother as if she was someone else.

'Louie will hate me,' she moaned, 'Louie will hate me. I adore her child. I worship the ground she treads on.' She repeated these words over and over, swaying all the time. My mother thought that she was sleep-walking and must be treated with the greatest care.

'Louie won't mind,' she answered soothingly, using the same third person. 'Come and wait here a moment and I'll get my coat and take you home.' And she sat her down at the bottom of the stairs. I was watching from the landing. When she was ready she took her arm and they left the house and walked briskly along the street while I watched again from the window. She returned in about half an hour.

'I put her to bed,' she told me, 'and then I woke Jessie' (her personal maid) 'and told her that she wasn't well and should be watched. She must be dreadfully worn-out to sleep-walk through the streets like that, poor thing. She might have been taken up by a policeman. But what was rather strange,' she added, 'was that when we reached the house, she took the latch-key out of her pocket and opened the door and then told me to take off my shoes and be quiet going upstairs so as not to wake the servants. She seemed quite normal then.'

Before breakfast, Jessie came round to tell us that Miss Morison was up and apparently quite well. She also told us that when my mother left her, she went downstairs again to bolt the front door.

Bewildered by all that had happened, my mother telephoned her doctor and then went to see him while I waited nervously at home. She came back utterly changed.

'He said she wasn't sleep-walking. It was hysteria – and you must never see her again!' At this my whole soul leapt. I was out of the trap I was free! I didn't worry about my work. I was sure now that I could change schools and still be ready for the examination – and change without having been expelled.

But my mother did not really understand and quite believe him. She was afraid that she might have misled him and been unfair to Miss Morison. If she had to remove me at once she wanted advice founded upon more than just second-hand evidence and so she had asked him to come and see her himself in such a way that she did not know that *she* was the patient.

Miss Kiddle had been taken ill and it was still not known what was the matter with her. She lay in bed weeping over the hurts inflicted by the woman she adored so. Tuberculosis was eventually diagnosed and she died very soon.

Now, my mother telephoned Miss Morison and, expressing concern for Miss Kiddle, said that she had arranged for her own clever doctor – the one Mrs Baldwin went to – to see her at once, that very afternoon and, falling into the trap, Miss Morison agreed to meet him at Miss Kiddle's bedside.

This time, I waited in terror. I was sure that when he met her he would be charmed and magnetised like everybody else and change his opinion, take back all that he had said and the freedom that I had won in the morning, I would lose again. And now I wanted my mother to see Miss Morison as she really was and to stop loving and admiring her so.

She returned even more distressed. She had had another long talk with him and learnt about things which were suppressed in those days and which dismayed and disgusted her. And to hear all this about her friend had shocked her terribly.

'She was looking awful. Her face was white and strained, her mouth swollen and that mark on her lip ... and her eyes ...! He said that her love will turn to hate.'

I was still awake when she came to bed that night and I could talk at last, tell her the truth – that I had never loved my godmother, never even liked her. I forgot about those sweet warm waves of attraction and even if I had remembered, I would not have spoken of that love, which was different and which I did not understand and felt ashamed of. But I told her about everything else. All the repressions and submissions of the years poured out of me and I felt no pity – only triumph. That night I gave her someone else to hate.

When I stopped talking, she said suddenly, 'I've just remembered something. Years ago she once said to me, "One day, Louie, you will find me out". I thought she was joking. Now I have – but all too late. And I thought she was so wonderful.' In the morning she had changed a little and from her came the pity which I could not feel.

'She leaves for Southwold today and she'll be alone in the cottage. I won't tell her yet that you're not going back to school. The shock might send her off her head. And I believe she drinks, too. Her father died of it. Do you remember the whisky bottle in the cottage when we stayed there the first time? I don't believe the plumber took it. There was a bottle on the floor by her bed when I took her home last night. Poor thing! I'll wait and break it to her when she's back.'

On the first day of the new term at five minutes past nine the telephone rang. My mother answered it.

'Why isn't Philippa at school?' the voice at the other end screamed wildly.

'I'm coming round to see you,' was all my mother said.

11

Godmother's Despair

WHEN SHE came to our house in her night-gown in the early hours of that morning, Miss Morison was quite conscious and only acting, the doctor said. Fearing that she had gone too far with her ultimatum and perhaps shaken my mother's blind trust, that was her hysterical way of making sure of it again. And she must have believed that she had succeeded, taking the silence that followed for her continuing blindness and sympathy. Now, when I did not appear her fears returned.

With the doctor's evidence to support her, my mother never thought of accusing her of perversion, nor did she mean to speak of it to anyone else for if it became known, she knew that it would ruin her career. She wanted to smooth over the whole affair and remove me without an open break. But she did not reckon with Miss Morison. She did not see that it would open the way to yet another completely false situation.

She went to the interview with only half the arguments – and the wrong ones at that – and, in holding back the truth she enabled Miss Morison to turn the whole thing upside down and place us where she should have been herself, in the weakest possible position, and she had to keep up the pretence of love and trust and friendship.

For five years my relationship with my godmother had been one long humbug and now my mother was assuming the same postures. Throughout that time, in all our encounters, the symbol which we used, the coded speech with which we communicated was always my resistance to the school, never the whole truth – my resistance to Miss Morison herself. And when they met that morning, they spoke the same double language to each other and all the same confusions followed.

Perhaps my mother suppressed the truth because of their long friendship and because she did not want to hurt any more than she was hurting already, or because she was still shy of the subject, or because the whole situation was too much for her.

As Miss Morison had told me that I would have to leave in three months time if I did not conform, my mother argued when she saw her that it was best for me to leave now since my health and pressure of work would make it impossible for me to do as she wished. And this mild saving message allayed Miss Morison's worst fears and played perfectly into her hands. She slipped instantly out of her proper part as the accused and became the accuser.

'Do you mean to tell me that you are taking her away now?' she burst out angrily. 'I didn't mean that she would have to leave altogether. She could have stayed on as a bye-student, attending for coaching lessons in the afternoons. Why didn't you tell me before that you meant to do this? You must have known weeks ago! Why didn't you consult me? Why couldn't you have talked it over with me in a friendly way? Why did you have to spring it on me like this? It is an unpardonable thing to do, to leave a public-school without giving half a term's notice.'

'I didn't want to spoil your holiday. You were worn out and needed all the rest you could get,' my mother answered.

'It would have been better to have had my holiday spoilt than for you to shatter the first day of the new term. I asked her, in the kindest and most loving way I could, to be more co-operative, to play her proper part in the school, to live up to its standards and ideals. Never would I have believed that such a mild reproof would make you snatch her away. And I thought she had more courage than to run away from her difficulties.'

This roused my mother and she hit back harder and more truthfully than she meant to.

'She has plenty of courage but she's tired of being criticised and always called a failure. Nothing she ever does is right. And so am I. I'm tired of having our home-life criticised. I know quite well that you think I'm a bad influence on her and that she ought to leave me and go to the boarding house or away to another school. We are both tired of being dominated by you.'

'Louie,' she gasped, 'how *can* you say such things to me?' She dropped into the chair before her desk and drooped forward, supporting her head in her hands. Watching her, my mother changed again.

'I am sorry. And I don't want you to think that I am not grateful for all that you have done for us. And her leaving needn't change things. Our friendship can go on as before.' She didn't mean this but now she had to say it.

'So she really *is* leaving?'

'Yes. I'll get tutors for her. Tomorrow, when you are feeling better, I'll ask your advice. And I'll pay for them myself. I shan't expect you to.'

'Oh,' she groaned. 'Have I ever minded what I paid for her? Paying makes me happy. I love to pay for her even though I'm Scotch and mean like all my race. So you've taken her away! She's left! Oh!'

'I'll go now,' my mother said, moving slowly backwards towards the door. 'And believe me, I really am so sorry about all this.'

'I had no idea that you were both resenting me all the time,' Miss Morison went on. 'I have loved that child. I have loved you both. I have only tried to help you, tried to make your life more easy, believing all the time that you loved me. I thought you were my dearest most devoted friend. How long have you been feeling like this? How could you accept my presents, write me those lovely letters at Christmas? How could you both be such hypocrites? Never in my whole life have I been so wounded.

Then, the truth rose to the surface for an instant. My mother had never said that I was not to see her again, but she already knew. She cried out wildly and imploringly, 'When can I see her? You can't take her away from me without even a good-bye. You can't be so cruel. Please let me see her. I know if I could see her I could put everything right. Just for five minutes, I beg you, let me see her.'

But my mother could not answer – so she fled.

Always before when Miss Morison complained that she was not seeing enough of me, my mother had cajoled me into going. Now, when she came home and told me all that had passed between them, she did not try to persuade me to go and say that last good-bye. She left it to me. And I was cruel and rude. I heard that anguished cry, but I had obeyed or been coerced too many times already and I felt I owed her nothing, not even five minutes more of myself – not even a letter. And I had the upper hand at last. I stopped my ears and did not stir.

About two hours later there was a rap on the door, the letter-box opened and a fat envelope dropped through onto the mat. It was the first of the storm of letters that, for the next three months, fell frantically upon us.

Without another meeting, a gracious letter or even a message, my relationship with my godmother was suddenly severed in a way that, as a rule, only death accomplishes. Her letters (which my mother endeavoured to reply to), her lingerings and pursuits and interventions were more like spectral antics and occult communications from the 'other side' than real, affecting actions. Both she and the school dropped out of my life as if they had never been in it, as if they had been only long painful dreams from which I had now awoken. In thrusting the whole episode out of my conscious mind, erasing it from my surface memory, I created a gap behind me in my life which has remained there until, with this writing, I dragged the drama up again and filled it.

What so surprised me at the time, was that my mother's experience seemed to be exactly the same. If for me it was like the dissolution of a nightmare, for her it was like emerging from a state of hypnosis. Her love and admiration for Miss Morison seemed to evaporate instantaneously. Only pity remained and flickered on for awhile. And then it, too, blew suddenly out. And immediately she cut this friendship out of her life I saw how it had affected our own relationship. When the subtle, demonic power vanished, the silence and the hiding and pretending, the constant feeling of disruption were all done with; the three-pointed line seemed broken and the two that remained were left in undisturbed communication.

Three and four times a day, week after week, the letter-box rattled and a bulging envelope dropped in – delivered by Amy, a servant or anyone else passing. And often, after dark or as the winter afternoon was drawing in, through our windows we could see the black familiar figure scurry along the opposite pavement, stop for a few moments to stare across at our house and then hurry on and wait again at the corner, to gaze back up the street. And whenever I went out I expected to be chased.

Once, I ran straight into her. I spun round and sped away and she came after me. We both walked faster and faster until, with the advantage of youth, I out-paced her and escaped down a side-street. And I felt no pity whatsoever – only contempt or curiosity, sometimes annoyance and sometimes even a horrible twinge of pleasure. Now that I was safely out of reach, I could feel flattered at being the object of so much attention and often gratified to see the strain and stress which I still caused.

In the letters, the same themes and phrases were repeated over and over again, wildly and pitifully or coolly and consistently; themes which, if the truth had been faced and brought out into the open in the first place, would have had no point and could never have been conjured up into a rational case.

On the level upon which she argues and pleads, she appears overwhelmingly in the right, the deceived and injured party upon whom the world's sympathies would naturally rest, while we are exposed for what, on the same concealing level, we certainly were – rude, ungrateful hypocrites.

This was the story she built up, believed in, and circulated and to which my mother, all unwittingly, subscribed. For years, out of pity and decency, she refused to speak and upset the whole edifice, change it from the simple tale of a child 'leaving school under a cloud' to a major scandal at the top. When she did speak it was too late, except that my disgrace had never really mattered for in reality, inner reality, it was not they who had cast me out but I who had cast them all away from me. She wrote:

> ... your interview was the most terrible and grievous that I have ever had in my whole career ... I can never forget it ... it revealed thoughts and feelings I had never guessed at ... 'the criticism of your life' which you so hotly resented was simply that when we all found Philippa

> falling far behind the other girls in public-spirit, in influence, in work and even in games we deplored it and I *longed* to give her greater chances ... whenever we asked her to join in things it was always home-ties that prevented her ... After I spoke to her so gently and lovingly, she told you that I was 'kicking her out' (she fastens on this phrase which I am sure I never used) ... *My* Philippa, for whom I have prayed ever since the day that she was born ... but all this will not make one bit of difference to my love and friendship for you both. It will always be a *joy* to come to the rescue at any time and in any way and I do promise you that if you die before me, I will share my last penny with her and my deepest heart of love and sympathy ...

In another letter:

> ... how could she bear to take presents from me if she really thought that I was 'kicking her out' and if all this resentment was seething inside her? ... it grieves me to the heart that she should leave under a cloud of offence ... why has she never come or written a line to say thank you and good-bye to me and the staff? ... can you conceive of any other child behaving so? ... why do you refuse to let me see her? ... why doesn't she come back to disprove what everyone is saying – that she and you have acted in a *horrid* way, contrary to the great traditions of the school? ... you say that everything is as it was ... to me nothing is ... you, my dearest friend, without provocation, have wounded me in my most vulnerable spot ... If you regret this hurt then, for the school's sake, make amends ... let her come back ...

And again:

> ... I only asked her to be more public-spirited ... why doesn't she send a greeting to the school from which she has received so much and where she has had so much happiness ... I have loved and cared for her in a way that I don't think you even faintly realise ... why don't you let me see her ... again I beg you to let her come to me ...

Another day:

> The ordeal is over*. Mr H. said, "This is the girl we have assisted all these years". Sir Clive said, "That is my friend Ariel" ... They asked if such a thing had *ever* happened before. I said *never.* Then the matter was dropped ... They saw I wanted no discussion ...

* Referring to the Council meeting.

Variations upon the same themes filled the pages of these letters, the dominant plea returning and returning like a scream, 'why don't you let me see her? ... I beg you to let her come to me.'

There is no conscious acting or dissembling in them. It may be that, through all those years, she never understood the truth about herself and so, at the end, when it was not revealed to her, she remained ignorant and confused, believing honestly that it was she who had been wronged and acting out her tragic part with genuine passion.

From the very first day when she caught me in her arms and whirled me round and round, I had humbugged and pretended and so contributed equally to all that followed. Now, in her pain, when she kept crying out, 'why were you not open with me?' her cry was justified and the answer is in the whole, long, muddled human story.

She not only followed me through the streets but, for years, wherever I went she tried to reach me and when she failed – to damage me. I had pushed her out of my life and consciousness but she kept returning, like a poltergeist, to rattle and break things and annoy and with every intervention, my mother's pity ebbed.

In due time, heaped with honours and panegyrics, she retired and as her violence lessened, so did my hatred and my hardness and I found myself thinking about her. Even tremors of the old attraction passed through me now and then and I wished that I could meet her – give her that five minutes she had once asked for.

As my mother grew bitter, the loves and hates shifted round but the line itself had not broken. One of its points had only been pushed out into space where it held the form together and, in an attenuated way, still dominated the others.

Many years later, when I was wandering through the streets of Westminster again, the Abbey close but hidden, I became aware of an old woman walking a few yards in front of me. Although I was only seeing her back yet instantly I sensed who she might be, and when my eyes travelled over her black clothes and reached her feet, pointed outwards in the same buckled shoes, I knew for certain who she was. And the knowing and the seeing brought back my fear and hate.

In the past I would have turned and run, but now I didn't. I dropped behind some people and, using them as a screen, followed her, just as she had followed me that morning, crept up silently behind me hoping to see tears. Now, unconscious of the past, I did the same; crept up after her wanting, wanting desperately, to see her face.

She leant upon an ebony stick and little by little, always keeping somebody between us, I drew nearer until I was just behind her. And now I bent, like she did, and craned my neck round, just as she did, and then drew level and walked along beside her. She was looking on the ground and I could go on peering. Then, she raised her head to see where she was going and I looked down straight into her face – and she looked up at me. But she did not know me. I had crept up in my cruelty to see her pain but when I saw it – in her eyes and in her face and in her failing body – I did not gloat as I had meant to. At last I felt pity. There was nothing to resist now and I could love her unequivocally, love her as my godmother. Yes. I truly loved her then as I walked on.

Afterwards, I was sorry that I had not spoken to her, had not given her, at last, that five minutes and said that good-bye. She had made me suffer, wrecked good years of my childhood but she had given me an experience which I must have needed and attracted – and I had made her suffer, too, and worse. And it was love, after all, that did it; unlawful and damnable but a great great love.

When she died, I believed that the three-pointed line was finally broken. Now I know that such points are not erased by death but remain indelible inside one.

Mrs Stanley Baldwin,
Countess Baldwin of Bewdley.
Water colour painted in the shop window.

Sir Vincent Caillard
The original is a life-size oil-colour.

Part III

1

Loneliness and Street Adventures

EVEN A prison is a little world, more intense and engaging for being enclosed, and when I escaped from mine, with no money, social position or family to fall back on, I was nowhere. Ione, the clown, and Dorothy the child, moving high above me, were my only tenuous links with the reality beyond my home.

At first I did not mind. I felt free and self-sufficient. My tutors came and, for the first time in all those years, I enjoyed learning. But soon, the isolation became oppressive and my mother felt it too, and on Sundays we began calling on people that she knew and we searched out distant cousins. Sundays were regular 'at-home' days then and a large tea party in a lovely house was exciting. But the door didn't always open. Sometimes they were *not* 'at home'. Then, disappointed and not daring to go back to houses that we had been to recently, we would stand out on the pavement trying to think of someone else that we could go to. If we went on hopefully to some remote acquaintance we were likely to be received with surprise and coolness. Generally, we went forlornly home to a late, dull, lonely tea with each other.

I had been lonely at school when surrounded by people. This was the other kind, the loneliness of isolation. But these conditions were not disabling privations, but springs for that inner law, and I soon resumed the adventure pattern of my life abroad. A good book was instantly effective in suppressing my need for a normal social life, but a journey through the streets was even better.

I loved the streets of London. I soon had friends in the markets and the pubs. I sat with night-watchmen in their shelters before their braziers and I got to know the tramps and buskers and the black-teeth children of Pimlico.

In a draughty, echoing arcade beside Trafalgar Square, a violinist played every night. There was no classical piece that he could not perform and although the tone was often atrocious yet, as the notes soared and sang above the raucous noise of the traffic circling the great imperial meeting and marching place, they sounded beautiful to me and his lonely swaying figure, pouring music over the meandering, clotted crowds, moved me.

He was not easy to know but, one night, I forced myself upon him, hung round him all the evening, and when the theatres closed and the crowds were thinning and he stopped and wrapped his instrument in a piece of silk and walked away – I walked with him. When he turned into a Lyons Cornerhouse he invited me to come, too.

He was soon joined by his busker friends coming in one by one from their stands in the West End. They were professionals of a kind, enjoying steady work and a rough respect and in the warmth of Lyons they relaxed and seemed happy in a grim harsh way. There was a scratchy quality about them which was new to me, as if the grit of the gutters had got into them.

I returned to the arcade again and again, and soon I was holding out the money dish and chasing stingy listeners. He had a woman who always joined him in Lyons, but I soon knew that I could easily displace her in his Kentish Town lodging-house and fall into his rich rough street life. But when I had seen enough I broke away abruptly and afterwards avoided that sweetly singing corner of Trafalgar Square.

When a bye-election was announced in the East End I travelled down to Limehouse to canvass for the Conservative candidate. The journey was an adventure in itself and when I arrived I was given an area and sent off with another girl. But we didn't keep together. We each took a street and I knocked on my first door, smiling in a friendly way when it opened and an old woman peered out. But instead of responding to my sweetness and charm, she lurched out onto the doorstep shaking her fists in my face. It was people like me, she yelled, who were the cause of all her troubles and she hated me.

I tried to talk to her but all my beautiful ideas for rescuing the world were useless. I was a vapid, inglorious Galahad, falling at the first encounter and I approached the next house warily.

The steps were worn away, the walls were cracked, the door warped and paintless, the windows broken. I knocked. A young woman with a baby in her arms then stood before me. Her hair was matted, her face dirty and so were the hands that clutched the dirty baby, and she was virtually in rags. A horde of thin chalk-white children peeped from behind. She looked at me for a moment then, with a curse, slammed the door – so hard that it nearly fell apart.

I did no more canvassing, but I went from house to house peering through the curtainless windows into the empty rooms where families lived on the floor like savages and when I saw an open door, I went into the dark stinking hall. The walls were stained and the floor boards soaked with urine and a mound of excrement was in a corner. When I heard someone moving, I ran. Then, staring like a traveller through the underworld, I walked all day through streets like these until terror drove me home.

These experiences intensified my passionate concern for the world and my openness to unacknowledged ways of knowing, expanded.

In spite of all my reading and the political meetings I attended, my understanding of Socialism was crude and simplistic. It was just the name given to a revolutionary plan to turn things upside down so that the workers would come out on top with their poverty relieved and, naturally, I approved of it.

Now, suddenly, concepts and propositions poured into my mind, day after day and week after week, and in ecstasy I caught them and arranged them as they came, until growing grander and grander, the whole great politico-economic system of democratic socialism was complete in my head. But I did not know that it was socialism. I thought I had invented a new, sublime instrument for changing society and finally redressing all injustice and I wanted to proclaim it to the world.

Then, something even more mysterious happened. Ignorantly selecting a book from the library catalogue without being able to see what I was getting, I came home one day with a treatise on socialism and when I opened it found that I knew it already, that line by line and page by page, I had been reading or receiving it for weeks – and the sensation was uncanny.

I was rather disappointed that, after all, I was not the original creator of this programme for salvation yet, at the same time, I was glad to know that it was already established in the world and that I could immediately become a passionate adherent.

When, later, I began to educate myself seriously and I was struggling hard to comprehend the world, most of my knowledge, nearly all the key ideas and systems, observed or created by the brain of man, came first to me like that, with the details and commentaries found afterwards in books.

Although these experiences became less frequent and the ecstasy less overwhelming when the first drive for knowledge was over, yet whenever I was moving on again and searching hard for something, a book, a teacher or a voyage might reveal it first, but just as often a message from nowhere.

Now that I was a socialist (in mind as well as heart) I began attending Left Wing meetings and one night, set off for a big one in Hammersmith Town Hall and, in my eagerness to hear and see everything, I sat in the front row and waited excitedly for the speakers to take the platform, turning round continually to see if they were coming and to stare at the people behind me. Then, at the last moment, just before they did, there walked into the hall, into the middle of that respectable crowd – a scarecrow! A hairy, top-hatted down-and-out, dressed in a filthy, greasy raincoat, carrying a parcel of old newspapers under one arm and a bundle of rags under the other.

I stared with astonishment, as did everybody else, and then watched him advance towards the platform, walk up to the front row and then along it until he came to the empty seat beside me where he stopped, let his bundles slither to the floor and sat down, half on top of me. There were several empty seats that he could have spread himself upon, but he chose to squash against me, the skirt of his raincoat falling over my lap, the hard, sharp contents of his bulging pockets digging into my side.

My first reaction was to jump up and change my seat. But immediately afterwards I knew that I couldn't do that, couldn't hurt his feelings, however much provoked, and as I sat there, choked by the smell of him, cringing away without showing my repulsion, surreptitiously pushing his raincoat off my legs, I recovered from the first shock and knew that I had wanted him – and must have attracted him. Out of this great crowd of a thousand people, to be singled out for all this stench and discomfort was my good fortune – opportunity dropping, quite literally, into my lap. After that, I became so fascinated by my extraordinary neighbour and my closeness that when the meeting began, I could hardly listen to the speakers and all their fine words.

He was utterly unconscious of me and of everyone else. Afterwards, I followed him out into the street and walked along beside him, talking, and when we reached a pub, invited him to come in.

We pushed through the swing doors together and I helped him with his parcels when his bulging figure stuck. By the time we were both inside, all eyes were upon us. When we sat down at a table and I ordered beer for us both he began to talk himself – and once started, never stopped.

He was a regular Tower Hill speaker with a brilliant, half crazy gift of the gab. He had no particular subject, he must have preached to the crowds about everything, just as he preached to me – from the abolition of the clergy, the bad manners of bus conductors, the futility of work, the corruption of barbers (he had stopped going to them for this reason), the usefulness of slot-machines – to 'fire in the trousers' (a phrase from an old Spanish proverb, he said).

We stayed until closing-time and then crossed the Broadway and took the Underground. When I got out, he got out too. He clung to me now and gave me his address, a well-known doss-house, and asked for mine. I gave him my telephone number and when, at last, I managed to retreat to the staircase and backed up two or three steps he followed me to the bottom and once more dropping his parcels, reached up, clutching the iron handrail and stood there, still declaiming, in his battered top-hat and his rags and his face all stubble and grime, looking up at me passionately in the perfect pose of the romantic lover. And his peroration, spontaneous like the rest, was one of the most lyrical, turgid, obscene and beautiful love poems that I have ever listened to, or read.

It must have taken at least 10 minutes to declare.

For months he used to telephone me and hold me, sometimes for an hour, while he preached salvation through the gifts and graces of eccentricity, rhapsody and sex.

These adventures continued, increasing in richness and range until, to refuse any experience would have been a betrayal of my nature, cowardice, lost opportunity, loss of stored-up power for the future. Sometimes I did turn back to save myself but always I went close enough to look over the edge and my life became more and more uprooted and unstable.

But as soon as I recognised this wild centrifugal force exploding within me, I became conscious of another, the one that held it and preserved me from disintegration, the golden thread that I could see and feel inside me – my Centre. I saw it now – at the start of another stage of the deep foreshadowed journey.

I had worked hard during those three months, but when Easter came and I went up to Cambridge and stayed in Newnham College, the examinations seemed unreal. There was an unreality about my whole life and the familiar feeling of not belonging, changed now to one of actual floating, as if I was not quite touching the world at all and was made of some immaterial substance.

I looked round Newnham and saw that it was just an extension of the school. The same notices and rules were pinned up everywhere (only Miss Kiddle's beautiful calligraphy was missing), the same bells clanged, there was the same rushing to noisy communal meals, hundreds of the same conforming women, teachers of the future, dull frumpish girls whose lives lay in the balance of that one stress-filled week. And when my turn came to appear like a worm before her, the same eminent, frightening, grey-all-over woman inquisitor at the top. And when I learnt that the gates were locked at half past ten every night my mind was settled. When I went home I told my mother that whether I passed or failed I did not mean to go. I wanted the world – as wide and high and free as I could have it.

In the meantime, with no work to do and nothing ahead – I was totally nowhere. I never thought of taking a job, just any job, for it would have been beneath me and so, without the money to make the world my playground, I could only sit and read and continue to roam the streets and wait for the next profound idea to reach me on the air and for several empty, demoralising months I ate too much and slept too much and grew fat and lazy – just like Willie.

I read *The Times* now, but not only for the political news. In the social columns, I followed the lives of the girls who had once been my friends; read about the balls that they attended every night, how beautiful their dresses were when their mother's presented them at Court. I saw them photographed at Ascot and Lords, watching polo at Hurlingham and whenever they were married at St Margaret's, Westminster, I could imagine their happiness as they walked beneath the arches of crossed swords, leaning on the arms of handsome titled bridegrooms. As I devoured this page every day, my genius, my great task and the rescuing of the world were all forgotten. High society was all that I desired.

We paid another of our regular visits to Wingfield House. Sir Vincent seemed to like my new voluptuous curves. The others just smiled in a knowing way. Young girls all go through a plump stage, they told my mother.

When we went to the arbour I still disliked his kisses and would not allow him to go further, yet at the same time in a strange perverted way, I found myself loving him. I could shut my eyes, make myself insensible to his foul breath and the bitter taste of his lips, imagine him a young, fresh, handsome lover and kiss him 'properly'.

When I returned to London, instead of acknowledging the visit in the usual, gracious way, I wrote him my first love letter and investing him with a Faustian youth, burst into rapturous, fanciful song. I wrote about birds and boats, their flight on golden wings, their gleeful voyaging upon enchanted seas – and I and my young Faust were in all this escaping. Aroused by these transports of imaginary love I discovered the delights of literary production and, combining them together, soared into a high, ecstatic world of feeling and creativeness – a world that resembled my early vision and which I had forgotten could exist.

He responded at once with lines as sweet and lyrical as mine and from that time onwards, until my life changed again, these letters kept me lifted and aflame, occupied me day and night and halted the ugly course of my degeneration.

In the meantime, my mother was grinding away at her portraits; keeping us alive and giving me the time and freedom to stumble from one inner experience to another, to muddle my way forward or backward or just stand in the same place – waiting.

She was worried about me. But she didn't know what to do and so she just talked about me to everyone she met in the course of her work. And this method of finding a solution to my future eventually bore results.

When her husband became Chancellor and then Prime Minister and they went to Downing Street, Mrs Baldwin decided to patronise the arts in a bigger way and she gave commissions to several struggling artists. My mother received orders for life-size portraits of herself, her daughters and her grandson.

But by this time, my mother had not only lost her power but her integrity as well. The problems of my growing up made the need for money greater than ever. She had to launch me, or so she thought, and when the choice was between me and high artistic standards – it was the standards that she sacrificed. Occasionally, in a fury, she would cut a canvas up but generally, if it pleased the sitter she would let it go and most of the sitters knew no better and only wanted something grand and life-like. The Downing Street portraits were all like that. But they passed as successful, brought in money and brought others.

One day, an official car stopped before our house and a beautiful woman accompanied by an important-looking man got out, rang the door bell and came in. They were the Prime Minister's and Mrs Baldwin's private secretaries and they had come to talk about a portrait. We supposed they were engaged.

She was about 35, petite, with large, grey, almond eyes and a slightly aquiline nose. She had an Eton crop and wore a leopard-skin coat and her hem-line was high – even for the prevailing fashion – well above her knees and she displayed her slim shapely legs with obvious pride. They were a striking pair.

The business of the portrait was soon settled and after lingering for awhile, admiring everything in the room as royalty do, Colonel Sir Ronald Waterhouse and Miss Chard departed, smiling and waving as they drove away. A few days later she returned for her first sitting.

There was an easy uninhibited 'something' about her which my mother found original and most attractive. While the work progressed they talked and very soon, of course, she was talking about me. Miss Chard evinced immediate interest and I was called in to meet her.

She greeted me like an old, familiar friend and when she had gone we felt that we were not just being patronised by smiling people in high places but treated as their equals. And every time she came, her friendliness increased. She told us about Downing Street, about all the exciting things that happened there and all the interesting, important people that she met. Her chatter was fascinating and her life sounded marvellous. Then, one day, she arrived with a proposal.

'Colonel Kinko and I had a great talk yesterday,' she began in her usual intimate, engaging way (Kinko was her pet name for Sir Ronald). 'It all started after a bit of a schemozzle in the morning.' (She used lots of amusing slang words and colourful phrases which I had never heard before.) 'You see, an important letter which should have reached the Canadian High Commissioner the day before – never did. I told Kinko that I just couldn't help it. I was out with Mrs Baldwin all the afternoon. We opened two bazaars, watched a dancing display, attended a committee meeting and ended up at a reception at the Japanese Embassy from which I just could not dig her out – she has an absolute pash for the Japanese. When we got back to No.10 it was too late to get the letter off – even by special messenger. I told him that I've just got too much to do – private secretary in the morning and lady-in-waiting in the afternoon. Things pile up. Then bang! Something blows up! Kinko put it right, of course. He always knows what to say. Well, when we'd talked it over we decided that I must have an assistant and, of course, the very first person that I thought of – was Philippa!' (She turned to me then.) 'Would you like to come to No.10 as my assistant?'

'Oh, yes, of course I would,' I gasped incredulously. The very idea of working at No.10 Downing Street in daily, intimate association with this fascinating woman took my breath away. And my mother was as overcome as I was. Then she addressed my mother again.

'Kinko hopes that you will lunch with us at his flat tomorrow and talk the whole thing over? I do hope you're not already engaged?'

Fortunately my mother had no previous luncheon engagement and she was able to accept. She didn't hide her feelings, she was thrilled to accept and when Miss Chard finally left, we felt like dancing together.

Sir Ronald lived at the top of a small building in Shepherd's Market, that already famous little oasis of quaint old shops and variegated life in the heart of Mayfair. The door was opened by an elderly woman in a white apron – his old 'Nanny' who looked after him. My mother was scarcely inside when Sir Ronald and Miss Chard hurried out into the hall to greet her. Here, in their own setting, how welcoming and agreeable they were.

'What a charming flat you have,' was the first thing that she said when they were settled in the tiny drawing-room.

'I've lived here for years. I'm one of the oldest inhabitants,' replied Sir Ronald, pouring out the sherry. 'You'd never guess that, except for my flat and Nanny's, the rest of the building is occupied by prostitutes.' And they both laughed. This was evidently the first observation with which every new guest was enlivened on arrival. And my mother laughed too. She enjoyed remarks like this.

They talked about the portrait until Nanny announced lunch and then, in the intimate atmosphere of the tiny dining-room, discussed the plan for me to work in Downing Street.

'We can't bother the P.M. about this,' said Sir Ronald. 'Neither he nor Mrs Baldwin would ever be convinced that another secretary is necessary. We can arrange it as if it was an official appointment. I can do any explaining that is needed.' Then Miss Chard went on.

'Philippa will have to learn to type but I'm sure she'll pick that up quickly and do as well as I do. After all these years I still only use two fingers!' And they laughed again. 'It's not haste that matters in this job but accuracy and the way the letters are set out, for of course, they're read by very important people.'

'The training will be invaluable for her,' Sir Ronald continued. 'A girl starting at No.10 can go on anywhere – all the prize jobs will be open to her. If she proves capable I will guarantee her future.'

'When can she start?' asked Miss Chard finally.

'Whenever you want her to,' replied my mother. 'She's not doing anything. She can begin at once.'

'Good! Then let her come tomorrow,' she cried gaily.

In a whirl of mutual esteem, satisfaction, excitement and gratitude, the little party broke up – and they returned to Downing Street.

Money was never mentioned. My mother would never have dreamed of suggesting anything so mercenary and vulgar. Just the honour and opportunity were rewards enough. She was ready to work on and support me indefinitely so long as I was settled in so splendid a position with the chance of meeting men of mark and getting married.

When she came home she recounted every word and described everything – Nanny, the flat and the prostitutes. Of course, I had read about these women, that their peculiar mode of life condemned them to an existence outside society and I supposed that their activities were much like mine with Sir Vincent in the arbour – but with a different lover every time who paid them for their kisses. When I heard that Sir Ronald lived among them in the slightly wicked neighbourhood of Shepherd's Market, I regarded him with even more wonder and interest. And then my mother added something else.

'From the appearance of the flat and the way she behaves I believe they're lovers,' and she smiled in an amused and knowing way.

The next day, on a fine hot summer morning, at the age of 17, with two long pig-tails hanging down my back, I walked up to the door of No.10 Downing Street and read the inscription on the brass plate – 'Prime Minister First Lord of the Treasury'. Then I rang the bell. When the commissionaire opened it and I stepped inside, I was acutely conscious of the moment, that the road was now clear and straight and lighted up before me, that I had only to keep on it to fulfil my high destiny while at the start, to obtain security and position, a fashionable marriage would not be difficult to achieve.

When the door closed behind me I was taken to my office.

2

10 Downing Street

THE Social Secretary's room was in a corner of the building on the ground floor. It had once been the dairy and looked out onto a small rather dank piece of garden enclosed by high walls. From one of our windows we could just see the Foreign Office and from the other, across the little patch of grass, the blank end wall of the Treasury. But in spite of these walls it was a large, light pleasant room and when I entered it for the first time and took possession of a huge desk – I thought it wonderful.

Miss Chard greeted me in her usual animated way and the first hour was spent in friendly talk – that is to say, she did all the talking and I the listening. She told me all that she had done since we last met, passed on the latest gossip about the Baldwin family and when secretaries came into the room, gave me colourful accounts of their characters and lives as soon as they were gone. When, at last, she remembered that she had some work to do and stopped, I was rather glad for I was longing to begin my job.

She knocked off two or three letters in a very few minutes and then began again although this time, in between the lively chatter, she did manage to show me what she wanted me to do.

She had been Mrs Baldwin's secretary for nearly three years but the work had been so overwhelming that she had never had time to do any filing and, in consequence, all the correspondence for that period lay in piles upon the floor along two entire walls of the room to a height of about two feet. When she needed to refer to some previous letter she had to plunge into the most likely sector of this long bank of paper, hoping to be lucky. As she seldom was, it was only natural that she should set me to the filing of this dusty buried heap.

She showed me the system and I attacked the long task of demolition and excavation with enthusiasm. But after a few days, before I had had time to make any impression on the bank at all, she decided to accelerate my training. I was to go on with the filing and learn to type as well and as soon as I was proficient I could relieve her by taking over this purely mechanical chore altogether.

I was delighted for I was avid for work and responsibility. The only thing that worried me was that I could never do enough, for at least half of every morning was taken up in talk. I had never met anyone so garrulous. Everything flowed out of her and she never knew when to stop.

I was too naive to see how much she was enjoying it, how superior it made her feel to boast and posture before a callow girl whom she herself had raised and whose position was not so different from her own. I did not know then how insecure and lonely she really was, why she needed an audience so much and into what dangerous indiscretions, as well as engaging honesties, this weakness could lead her. And the more she talked the more compulsive it became.

An entire morning was given to the story of her life. She had grown up in poor circumstances and, at an early age, had left home with a man friend and then knocked about from job to job and place to place with one friend after another. It was during the war that she met Sir Ronald.

'Of course, he didn't have his "K" then, he was plain Colonel Waterhouse. We fell for each other at once and he got me a job as one of his assistants. When the war was over and he went to the Treasury, he got me in there, too. But it didn't last long. There was a blistering row and we had to go. Then he became equerry to the Duke of York and I was soon the Duchess's private secretary. That was a marvellous job. We both had a whale of a time – until the King got to hear of us. God! Didn't he swear! He went purple in the facc and nearly had a fit. But he got his way, the old bastard! He had us sacked! But it didn't bother Kinko. He came on here and when the Baldwins moved in and she needed a secretary, well, naturally, he recommended me!'

This tale, of course, was filled out with a wealth of rich and racy and startling detail which, unfortunately, I have forgotten. I can remember sitting there entranced even if my fingers were fidgeting all the time with the typewriter.

It was only when she was out of the room that I could do any consistent work; when, after carefully combing her blonde, boyish hair and powdering her nose and painting her lips, she seized some papers off her desk and with an important expression and an attempt, in her short skirts and bangles, to look dignified, set off upstairs for her morning interview with Mrs Baldwin. Or, when she jumped up in the middle of a story, preened herself even more carefully and with a parting discharge from the door, 'I'm going along to the Chief' (this was Kinko's official designation), skipped away to the other side of the building to 'waffle' with Sir Ronald and the other men.

People came in occasionally on business but only Sir Patrick came regularly just to waffle and, sprawling on the sofa provided for our guests, dawdled for as long as he dared. He was a jolly, jokey man and over the top of my typewriter I was soon discretely flirting with him.

A well-known woman M.P. was often at No.10. One day, Miss Chard came bouncing back into our room with her eyes flashing.

'I ran straight into Fifi' (that was their nickname for her) 'on the stairs just now. She gave me such a look. Of course she's after Kinko again. She's mad about him. And he's just laughing his head off.' She sat down at her desk and was strangely silent for about five minutes. Then she continued. 'Kinko can't stand her. Old horse-face he calls her. She wears crepe-soled shoes and plays golf. She only got her seat because her husband is one of the P.M's best friends. Poor Kinko! He's having an awful time. He does nothing but dodge her all over the building. I told him he ought to pick her up and spank her.'

She got up from her desk and walked up and down the room for awhile in deep thought. Then she stopped and drawing herself up, looked charitably down at me.

'When I become the first woman prime minister you shall be my principal private secretary.' Then her expression changed again. 'I'd better go and see how Kinko's getting on. He may need rescuing.' And she whisked out of the room. She little knew that that was my ambition too.

I was not only kept informed of what she and everybody else at No.10 did from day to day, but I learnt about their health as well: about her periods every month, the condition of her bowel, Sir Ronald's bladder, the P.M's liver and Mrs Baldwin's legs. She found the body absorbingly interesting but I hated her accounts of what went on inside her – and always tried not to hear.

I had not been very long at No.10 when Sir Ronald received an unexpected visitor. Lord Wigram (I had known him as Sir Clive) came over from the Palace one morning with a private matter on his mind. It was about me. He had been sent to find out what I was doing in Downing Street and he didn't leave before he had described in detail all my failings and deficiencies at school and the disgraceful way I left before being expelled.

When I heard about this I was shocked and angry. I told Miss Chard the whole story and they both took my part. They had come up against the Palace themselves and were broad-minded and could appreciate my tale. Miss Morison didn't try again to harm me there.

'Oliver was here last night,' Miss Chard announced with glee one morning. (Oliver was the Baldwin's younger son.) 'He came in by the kitchen door and spent the evening with the servants. He won't use the front door and he can't be bothered with his parents. He lives in a slum among the working-class and writes revolutionary pamphlets. Everybody says he's mad and ought to be shut up. Kinko says that if you turn Red you're bound to turn insane.'

This information electrified me and in a secret, guilty way, I wished that I could meet him. My own passion for Socialism I kept concealed inside my second self and the double personality which I seemed to possess, mystified and worried me. For I was believing in and admiring two contradictory things at once – a radical proletarian movement and a Conservative upper-class. First one was in the ascendant and then the other. It was most confusing.

Then, day by day and week after week, I was entertained by the unfolding episodes of a most startling and enthralling serial story. I knew that Sir Ronald had a wife somewhere. I didn't know until then upon what friendly terms they still were.

She possessed many valuable jewels and furs which were heavily insured and a plan had been devised between them by which these would be stolen, their value claimed and the money equally divided.

After receiving an outline of this plot I next heard that the first part of the operation had been successfully accomplished. Without being seen by anyone, Sir Ronald had managed to remove the valuables from his wife's house to his own flat. Then I waited keenly for the day of the robbery, for an account of the way the thieves had entered through the unfastened window, then for the result of the police investigations and for the lamentations of the owner and sympathies of everyone in Downing Street, then for the arrival of the insurance people and finally, for their acknowledgment of the claim and maximum pay-out.

The plan and its execution had been perfect. For a few weeks, Sir Ronald's master mind had been diverted from its normally high preoccupations and the tax-free outcome made them both comfortable for life.

It was a fantastic tale but I became so interested and emotionally engaged myself that by the end, it seemed quite a natural happening in the story-telling world in which I was now living. For, although I caught glimpses of many people and I could feel the solemn urgent life going on all round me, yet I scarcely ever left our room and I never got to know anyone beyond it. I was shut away with this extravagant babbler whose pitiful mind created a whole new teeming underworld that soon enveloped me. I seemed to be in yet another prison, looking out this time through the distorting windows of Miss Chard's consciousness onto a high but peculiarly reduced and rather shabby, futile world.

She appeared very late one morning, hurrying in with a story which she especially relished.

'I felt dreadfully ill yesterday,' she burst out. 'I thought I was going to die. I dashed to Kinko's flat and jumped into his bed. When he came home that's where he found me. And I ought to be there still. I'm still feeling ghastly. But I had to struggle up and come. I couldn't let my job down.' There was a heroic ring in her voice as she watched me out of the corners of her slanty eyes.

She was less interested in sex than in all the other functions of the body. She enjoyed skirting round the subject, telling her little stories, hoping to shock me and arouse my curiosity, but I was growing bored now with her everlasting chatter and I hardly listened any more – just pretended I was hearing and still admiring.

In spite of the intensive extension of my education, I was soon typing all the letters and I managed to reduce the pile of papers.

I noticed that whenever a different kind of letter had to be written, a decision made or problem solved, Miss Chard went at once to Sir Ronald, coming back with the answer or the draft which she copied surreptitiously and then passed to me. I also guessed that all the standard replies which we used, marked A.B.C.D.E. etc., had, in the first place, been prepared by him. In fact, I knew that Miss Chard was incapable of writing an accountable letter or of forming a responsible judgment and that Sir Ronald was carrying her completely.

When the holiday months came, although I was no longer at school, we still thought it necessary, after the manner of the rank and fashion, to leave London for six weeks. But Southwold now seemed a dull and childish place – and Miss Morison was there. The grandest people travelled north in August for the grouse-shooting and we decided to do so, too – not to shoot but to be among them. We were still naive enough to believe that in a small country place some of the barriers would be down, life would be more natural, with opportunities for making friends and joining in the summer gaieties. And my mother was always sure that I only had to be seen to succeed – that once they glimpsed me, the young men would pursue me and everybody else would admire me. She had to learn that pretty but impecunious girls were not appreciated for their charms but, on the contrary, were hated, humiliated and quickly driven out. She did not understand the forces that create the gulfs.

I learnt that Aboyne, on Deeside, close to the King and Queen at Balmoral was the 'right' place to go and, as luck would have it, my mother remembered that she had some friends there – Admiral Sir Arthur and Lady Farquhar. She had stayed with them, long ago, and painted the whole family and they had been so hospitable then. Her memories were sweet and hopeful when she wrote and they replied as if they would be thrilled to see her again – and to meet her daughter. We engaged rooms, bought tweeds and brogues and travelled 3rd Class, herding with the proletariat, to our snob destination.

The success of this adventure was doubly assured when, on hearing that I was going to Scotland too, the Chamberlains invited me to spend a fortnight with them in Perthshire.

When we arrived in Aboyne we telephoned the Farquhars and were, at once, invited to tea. (That useful, non-committal meal.) They seemed as kind as before and made us feel so welcome and so happy. They didn't suggest another meeting, but we returned to our lodgings feeling certain that invitations would follow. We waited and we waited – watching all the fine distinguished people as they walked about.

On Sundays, we went to Church, to see them closer and to force the Farquhars to see us. We saw the dukes and lords and lairds with their matching ladies take their places in their private pews and read the lessons and hand round the collecting plates. We sat behind them, on the edge of the aisle, and could have touched them as they passed. We sang and prayed ourselves but we were not really participating for even in Church, we did not belong.

But this Highland play – a fragment of society cavorting on the banks of Dee – was so novel, so real and the individual performances so entertaining, so comic, that often I forgot that I wanted to be in it and just enjoyed the watching, scene by scene.

Then, leaving my mother in Aboyne, I went on to Kindrochit House, a large shooting-lodge on the moors at Struan, expecting to see Mr Chamberlain and to talk politics with him. But, again I was disappointed, for the very day that I arrived, he left, and I found myself alone with Dorothy and her mother and her little brother, Frank.

The first morning, I was woken by the sound of bagpipes skirling below my window as an Atholl highlander marched round and round the house – and I was happy, even without Mr Chamberlain, for here from the moment I arrived, I belonged. I was a guest of the great and one of them, engaging in everything they did, not left out – not just watching.

Every day, after breakfast, we set off with picnic baskets – walking or cycling or sometimes driving in a hired car. When we arrived at some beautiful loch or moor-top Mrs Chamberlain would settle down on a rug and take her shoes off and then take the pins out of her hair and let it fall round her shoulders. Where no one could possibly surprise her she could dare to look undignified and relax. Leaving her then to read or sleep, we children (I was still a child) climbed the hills or fished or bathed.

Even when she had nothing to do and plenty of sleep, Mrs Chamberlain had that same detached manner, the same half-dreamy way of talking and listening. But when we passed through a village or approached a crofter's cottage, she would rouse herself a little.

'Those look like new houses,' she would say, her voice high and slow and slightly affected – or, 'that cottage must be dreadfully small. I wonder if it has a bathroom?' and then, with all of us behind her, she would march up to the door and knock. When it opened and the woman looked out with surprise, she went on parade and with a charming ceremonial smile and carefully blended mixture of grandeur and simple friendliness addressed her, using the same words every time.

'I am Mrs Neville Chamberlain. My husband is the Minister of Health. May I see your house?' And always, without another word spoken, the woman seemed to melt aside and we all tramped in. We went from room to room, poked our heads into the cupboards and peered into every corner while the woman kept up a running apology for the dust, disorder and her unpreparedness. And we always left with the same speech.

'As I am sure you know, my husband is keenly concerned about the housing problem and by his policies is encouraging new building all over the country. He will be very interested when I tell him what the houses are like here. Thank you.'

When the husbands came home at night I am certain, very often, they were told that a very grand lady had called who said she was the wife of a Health Inspector or, was he a building contractor, anyway, she wanted to see their house and tell him all about it.

She was very interested to hear about my job at No.10. On the face of it it looked and sounded so important. And I let her think it was. I didn't tell her the truth of how I got there – not through Mrs Baldwin, as she believed, but through the side door of Sir Ronald's personal power and for the convenience of his personal friend. She would never have allowed Dorothy to do a job of any kind but she thought it an excellent start for me.

By the time I left, this grand secure existence had begun to pall and I was glad to return to Aboyne and my own precarious and peculiar life. I had none of the things, known or unknown, that I wanted but the visit taught me that poverty and exclusion were not wholly negative conditions; that a hungry sort of happiness, an uncomfortable contentment, a burdened anxious kind of certainty and excitement were contained in them while in my mother, I possessed riches which I never saw anywhere else. Even when my life seemed most empty it was never dull for my mind was always in a ferment.

We walked on the moors and watched the Highland Games – always alone, we never made a friend. In the evenings, when the music from the balls and parties came floating over the river, we sat in our room making up doggerel rhymes about the grandees whom we knew so well – yet didn't know at all. We were not so awe-struck and downcast that we couldn't laugh at them at the same time as admire them. And the time passed and we returned to London.

3

The General Strike

I DID not tell Miss Chard the truth about my holiday. Although we were both outsiders and social climbers we were not united in adventure. For all her friendliness and her confidences she always kept me at arm's length, deciding from the start, unconsciously perhaps, that we were rivals – not partners.

The office was in a state of disorder. There were unfiled letters everywhere and a basketful of unanswered ones on her desk. Although she was pleased to see me back, there was a hard resentful look behind her smile.

Before I went away, she spent the mornings with her dressmaker, her milliner or her hairdresser while I did all the work, but I still received no salary and could come and go as I pleased. Then, one day, after pacing up and down the room for a long time with her hands behind her back, in one of her Napoleonic moods, she stopped and faced me.

'Philippa, I've been thinking lately about your training. It seems to have come to a stop. There's a lot more for you to learn and many ways in which you could be more useful to me. For one thing, I ought to be dictating. It's time that you learnt shorthand. I will give you two afternoons a week off to attend one of the Pitman schools. It will be to your own advantage to become more qualified. I've spoken to the Chief and he agrees with me completely.'

The next day, the Chief paid us a visit. He settled himself on the sofa and a messenger brought in our morning cups of tea. They were both at their most charming and, after a few amiable remarks, he came straight to the point.

'Miss Chard and I have been discussing your training. I believe she has already suggested that you should now learn shorthand and should you do this, I've come to tell you that I would most strongly recommend that you then enter for one of the Civil Service clerical examinations. This would give you proper qualifications, a recognised position, a salary, increasing with your years of service, a fortnight's paid holiday a year and a pension when you retire.'

I did not want to learn shorthand or become a civil servant. But I trusted Sir Ronald, his knowledge and concern for me and I knew that they were both keen for me to do it. And so, I agreed to the whole plan – although with many inner doubts. For what else could I do? If I displeased them I might lose my job from which, in due time, I would advance to greater things. I already had my eye upon the political side of the building and my position now, on the social side, I looked upon as the first rung of the high ladder which I had to climb.

I found a Pitman school and enrolled for lessons and the winter months passed quietly and rather monotonously. Then things began to change. And the first change was in myself. I was grown up. I went to a hairdresser, put powder on my face and began to dress. And I was slim again. When Sir Patrick came into the room now, he looked first at me and addressed his jokes to me – and the change was not lost upon Miss Chard.

Then, we moved to Chelsea. We sold the remainder of our lease for a large sum and with a mortgage, bought a tiny terrace house where we could live without lodgers, have a bathroom again, a bedroom each and build a studio in the garden.

When we left that burdened house and the locality of the school and arrived in the bright little cottage with studios at one end of the street and the old rectory garden behind, we felt as if we had moved into another world and were starting a new life.

But even here we were not free. I walked in Battersea Park now and it wasn't long before Miss Morison was walking there as well. Coming round some bushes I ran straight into her one day.

'Philippa darling! Stop a moment! Stop and talk to me – just for a moment! Please!' she called out desperately as I walked rapidly on. I was angry over her intervention at Downing Street but I saw how she had aged in the year since the break. Her face was lined and drawn and her eyes – I went on seeing them for days. This love was like a ravaging disease which Time did not heal.

Then, the chance came to break out of my cage. Miss Chard came in one morning very excited. Her doctor had told her that she would have to have her appendix removed. This portion of the intestine was so entrancing! And the importance of it all and the prospect of spending a fortnight in a nursing home being petted up by everyone, delighted her. She talked of nothing else and I soon knew all about her ascending colon, her caecum, jejunum, peristaltic activity and a lot more physiology besides. And when she wasn't talking about it she was out buying herself a trousseau. When the great day came, she left in the highest of spirits.

I was quite confident about carrying on alone and if I found myself in any difficulty I only had to run along to the 'Chief', as she did; to that mysterious 'other side' of the building where the real work was done, the work of governing a quarter of the world. For a fortnight I had the freedom of Downing Street, power and opportunity.

The next day, I sorted the post and, after selecting those letters which directly concerned her, went upstairs for the morning interview with Mrs Baldwin.

Her private sitting-room, looking out over the Horse Guards Parade and St James's Park, was a riot of colour and collected treasures. Everything she'd ever fancied, inherited or been given, was in it. The walls were covered close with pictures of every sort and size; the piano and every shelf and table top were massed with ornaments, photographs and momentos; exotic birds flew out of screens in corners and fringed lamps and lacquer stools filled every gap; huge chintzy flowers bloomed on the chairs, classical figures lay upon the sofas and monstrous vines climbed up the curtains. It vibrated and one could scarcely move for the congestion. Everything leaped and clashed and then melted into a unity which was dazzling and triumphant.

It was the unwritten diary of her long and happy life with Stanley Baldwin and she loved this room so much and was so anxious to have a memory of it, that my mother strove to paint it. Although a trifle photographic, it was a great success – for everything was in it, rich and gay and recognisable.

When I came in, she greeted me as if there was nothing strange about my coming although I was very conscious of my new important part and shy. We discussed the letters, I took notes and then we talked about her programme for the day. It didn't take long. She was never very responsive but after about a week, she gave me the opportunity I longed for.

'I want you to come to my Thursday receptions, my dear,' she said calmly one morning. 'You can help me with the people; look after the lonely ones, hand them cakes and talk to them, introduce them and, when you see that I've had enough of someone, take him away. Can you start this week?'

'Yes, of course. I'd love to. And I'll help you all I can,' was how I answered restrainedly, all excitement inside.

The next day I missed another shorthand class (I was constantly missing them for I hated them) and went off to buy myself a dress and hat and when Thursday came I made my way upstairs to the reception rooms and reported to her and then turned keenly to my duties. And now, I was not just watching all these interesting important people but going up to them and talking to them – with a right to be there, a job to do and a place among them.

I visited Miss Chard in the nursing home. Her room was stacked with flowers but the only thing she cared about and looked at was a bottle, standing on her bedside table. When I came in she snatched it up and held it out for me to see.

'Look! There it is! Look at the condition it's in! Have you ever seen anything like it?'

I never had. It was her appendix preserved in alcholol. She then launched into a long account of everything she had observed or been able to find out about the operation and only when she had exhausted the subject did she ask about the work at No.10. I gave her all the news and, at the end, mentioned casually, that I was now helping Mrs Baldwin at the receptions and I could see that she didn't like this.

When she came back she brought the bottle with her and she'd no sooner flung off her hat and coat than she was gone again, clutching it in her hand, to show it to everyone she could. After that, she kept it on her desk and whoever came into the room had first to admire it and then hear all about it.

When she asked me about my shorthand and I made her absence my excuse for missing classes, she looked at me suspiciously.

On Thursday afternoon, I changed in the cloakroom as usual and went upstairs – and we met. She had never seen me dressed like that before. With a glance she took me in from head to foot, muttered something, then turned and disappeared. I went and stood by Mrs Baldwin, expecting her to do the same. Eventually, I caught sight of her, talking to someone in a distant corner and at that moment, suddenly, I saw her as she really was.

She was always so brisk and confident with Sir Ronald, with the secretaries and flirts who came into our room, when giving complimentary tickets to her milliner or dressmaker, or when alone with me. But now, among those high, sure, established people all her confidence had left her. With no presence, style or manners, she had retreated into a corner with some little nobody, like herself, and she looked cheap and pathetic – just a common little street girl.

She saw me at once and so I couldn't stare. But that moment was enough. I slipped away and went on with my job.

The next morning she came in very late. She didn't look at me but kept her eyes on the papers on her desk and soon she was able to find fault with me, find something that I'd not done right. Then she left the room and was gone for a long time but when she returned, she was in a better mood.

'Aren't those receptions the most boring things on earth? I can't think why people trouble to go to them. I wouldn't if I didn't have to. Of course they're something new to you, you still find them amusing. I've had so many they just give me a pain. You'll feel the same very soon. You looked smart. Black suits you.' With this last remark she shot me a quick dangerous glance.

Mrs Baldwin gave us tickets for Ranelagh and during the summer months we went there every Saturday, to watch the polo and eat an expensive but delightful strawberry tea. And the scene fascinated me. The ponies and the stylish, virile men who rode them, the grooms, the coloured horse-blankets, the pails and brushes, the shining harness and the marvellous boots – the whole jingling, steaming, sweating, vigorous world of upper-class aggressive sport. My father had played polo and must have ridden like these men, looked like them, been one of them – and I watched them. I watched them.

Fewer people were coming into our room. Sir Patrick who had dropped in daily and whose joking and flirting I looked forward to, now stopped coming altogether and Miss Chard had stopped talking and was hardly ever in the room. There was something ominous about all this and I would have worried if the world outside had not grown even more disturbing.

After several years of Mr Baldwin's healing policy and apparent social peace, the country was splitting apart again, constitutional government was being challenged and the old rumours of revolution were in the air. It was the early summer of 1926 and the long-drawn-out stoppage in the coal fields now threatened to end with a general strike. When it did, things changed for me as well.

On the first day, when all public transport had disappeared from the streets, a large official car fetched me from my house and drove me in solitary grandeur to Downing Street. I felt like a Cabinet Minister as I sat back in one of the soft comfortable corners, gliding past the people tramping to work. I had been too young to take part in the war but now I could serve England in a hundred ways and destiny had placed me at the centre of it all. When I arrived and the chauffeur jumped out and opened the car door for me, I enjoyed the gaze of the big crowd waiting anxiously in Downing Street and when I walked into No.10, I was burning to embrace the high historic hour.

The hall was full of people and there was a tenseness in the air. The door-keepers and messengers looked at me with a new responsiveness, reaching out to me, a new closeness and at that moment my solidarity with Downing Street seemed absolute.

When I opened the door of our room I was amazed to find it full of women and Miss Chard already there, prancing from one group to another, inflated with new power and grandiloquence. When I reached my desk through the crowd she came up to me and explained rapidly that, inspired by Mrs Baldwin, a women's convoy system was being organised at Downing Street – and she was in command. Then she frisked away to chatter to the volunteers again, a mixed collection of Whitehall typists, debutantes and friends of her own, rounded up in a wholesale way. I recognised her intimates among them, her hairdresser and milliner. They were all her inferiors or so young that she could act before them as she always acted before me. A few of them could drive a car.

I was apprehensive the moment I came upon this scene. The women lolled on the sofa, or sat primly on the hard chairs which had been brought in for them, or leant against the walls, or propped themselves against our desks, or just stood – and more kept coming, until the crowding and the talking made the room unbearable. Then, after a trip upstairs, looking still more pleased and important, she addressed the gathering.

'Ladies,' she began, 'I have a message for you from Mrs Baldwin. She wishes me to thank you for responding so splendidly to her appeal for volunteers and to tell you how confident she is that this convoy organisation will play a vital part in breaking the strike and frustrating the attempt to overthrow constitutional government. By taking out the cars and bringing the people in to work the business of the country will go on. The country will not stop and starve and then surrender for you, Ladies, have answered the call. You will keep London working, London moving, keep the great heart beating and while it beats the country and the empire cannot fall. This is the message of gratitude and confidence, Ladies, that she has asked me to deliver. And now, may I add a few words on my own account.

'Mrs Baldwin has put me in command and, conscious of the honour and of my great responsibilities, I shall work night and day without rest or relief until the Reds are defeated and victory is ours. And I know that you will do the same. Working tirelessly and selflessly together we shall turn the tide of revolution and make history. We shall save England, Ladies!

'But as this has all come upon me so suddenly I cannot give out jobs to you at once. I shall need the day to prepare a plan. Therefore, will you come back at the same time tomorrow when jobs will be ready for you and we shall go into action. That is all, Ladies. Thank you.'

The women stirred and, murmuring to each other, turned towards the door and moved slowly out. From their blank expressions I could not tell what they really thought of this speech, but upon me its effect was devastating. Some of my keeness had evaporated the moment I came into the room and now, it was gone altogether, punctured and poisoned by that ridiculous performance. My attitude to the strike was already ambivalent and at this moment, the peculiar balance in my mind shook violently and swinging from one inclination to the other, dropped heavily – upon the wrong one. A hot, strong wave of sympathy for the strikers and their criminal revolutionary purposes swept through me – and I froze to my desk. I daren't look at Miss Chard. I sat silently and sullenly pretending that I was working. But even if I had been, that was not what she wanted, which was flattery and admiration. Annoyed, she made some sharp remark and flung out of the room.

When she came back, I flattered her enough to please her and told her that she could leave all the office work to me while she got on with the great task of commanding the convoys and I expected her to remain rivetted to her desk for the next 24 hours. But she did nothing of the sort. Lit up, in a veritable ecstasy, she dashed about the building all day long, talking to anyone and everyone; to butlers, commissionaires, porters, typists, even the housekeeper who came into the room with some domestic question.

The next morning, the limousine fetched me again and, this time, I told the chauffeur to stop and pick up some of the walkers. Five or six people jumped with alacrity into the big empty car and, squeezed into my corner, I no longer felt like a Cabinet Minister. Instead, I felt and behaved exactly like Miss Chard. I showed off. I wanted these unimportant Londoners to think that I was grander than I really was. And so I talked, just as she would have done, and let them know that they were riding in the Prime Minister's car, let them wonder if I, myself, was his daughter or, better still, his confidential secretary.

Fortunately, only about half the number of women patriots reported for duty that second morning. The rest were found wanting at the crucial hour. The Transport Office sent the drivers off on common chauffeuring jobs, some of the others hung about all day and the rest went home again.

On the third day, I was banished from the scene altogether. With a grim expression, Miss Chard conducted me to my 'operational post' and after explaining what I had to do, left me. And there, in solitary confinement, I stayed until the strike was over.

My 'post' was a small telephone room close to the Cabinet room. In it was a table, a chair, a telephone and directories of every kind. At first, it felt like another prison, a miniature one this time, until I realised that it was a vantage point, a secret spying place, for the window looked out onto the Terrace – the famous Downing Street terrace – and at various times every day the Prime Minister paced up and down, sometimes alone, sometimes with his colleagues. And whenever he passed I peeped from behind the curtain. If I had opened the window a crack I could have heard what they said. I enjoyed being hidden there while the P.M. walked up and down – and England was being torn and tested.

Although I was now firmly on the side of the strikers yet, as a watcher on the terrace, I grew more and more detached as the days went by and in the end, I was sitting in the centre, the great play going on all round me, like a mute, underground spectator.

My job was to look up certain names and numbers in the telephone book and write them down on long sheets of paper. I was certain that it served no purpose whatsoever, that she had shut me in a box with some spurious work just to get me out of the way for the duration.

One of the door-keepers was my only real friend at No.10, and I depended on him now for the news, and the first thing that he told me was that Mrs

Baldwin's convoy organisation had been taken over by the Women's Emergency Corps and was being worked from their headquarters.

When my window life lost its savour and my work became too boring to endure, I took to going home early. When Miss Chard found this out she stormed into my box.

'From the very first day,' she shouted, 'I couldn't help seeing that you lacked the right patriotic spirit and enthusiasm for the cause and that I couldn't depend upon your loyalty, and afterwards I knew that you were not carrying out your task here with the eagerness that I expected of you and now, without asking my permission, I find that you are leaving early every day. It is a pity that you, alone, in Downing Street have failed.' I didn't reply. I had heard all this before.

When the strike was over we settled down again as if nothing had transpired between us. She chattered as confidingly as in the early days and I decided that everything had been forgotten and that we were making a fresh start. And the next surprise came when, without further mention of the Civil Service, she told me that she and Sir Ronald had decided to pay me a salary of £100 a year – starting at once. I was earning at last! Soon after that, I heard from the door-keeper that her name would be included in the next Honours List when Sir Ronald drew it up.

Only one incident stood out in the peaceful weeks that followed. Going through the morning's post one day, she looked suddenly across at me in a bright and friendly way – a letter in her hand.

'Would you like to sit on a committee?' Then she read the letter. It was from a well-known charitable organisation asking if Mrs Baldwin would care to suggest someone from the Downing Street staff. 'You'd be very good on a committee,' she went on, 'I think we ought to propose you.'

I longed to sit on a committee. Every day I was handling letters with grand names at the top of them. If I could climb onto one of these I would be in high society at once, I thought. I didn't see that she was only baiting me.

I waited several weeks until all the rational judgment I possessed was burnt away by the fever of desire and I decided to take the matter into my own hands. Why shouldn't I propose myself, I thought, and when I told my mother what I meant to do she supported me with enthusiasm. She always loved action, just as I did, and would do the wildest things herself and encourage them in me. For all the strenuous living we had done we were still so foolish in the ways of the world.

I telephoned. A woman answered and listened and seemed to be agreeing with everything I had to say. At the end, I thought the matter was settled and I said good-bye in a gay, intimate way. I was sure I would soon be meeting her.

But again, the weeks passed, my hopes finally withered and I let the brilliant picture fade.

July was the last month of the London season. The pace was hectic; the balls in the great houses clashing and people going from one to the other on the same night, at Hurlingham and Ranelagh the polo finals, the Oxford and Cambridge and Eton and Harrow matches at Lords, the racing season reaching its climax, and luncheons, dinners and garden parties crowding the calendar and competing for the grandest guests. At the end, when all the brilliant parties had been given, the jewels and gorgeous gowns displayed, when all the cups and trophies had been won and all the dazzlement and triumph were over, the Court moved to Balmoral, Parliament went into recess, the great town houses were shut up and the awesome people scattered to their castles and their country mansions.

The Downing Street Garden Party was one of these high points. I had become quite an accomplished aide to Mrs Baldwin and, taking for granted that she would need me, I bought an expensive lace dress and fashionable hat and looked forward to the event.

I thought it strange that Miss Chard never talked of it and sensing a doubt about my own position, I referred to it casually one day, letting her know that I was coming. She looked at me quickly, then down at her desk again – and that look was frightening. Then the day before the party, a letter came to our house by the early post before I had left for work.

'I've just spoken to Sir R.,' she wrote, her spelling even worse than usual, 'about your coming to the garden party as he has "vews" about too many of the staff turning up at official things and we dont want to get a rebuf from him. The position is a little delicat as he says there is no necessity for any staff to be there except in atendance on the P.M.

'In the circs I think it would be better for you not to be there (as there's nothing to do) but cheifley because it might cause advers coment and also becaus the question of who goes to what is under discusion and there is internal feeling against Sir R's vew. As he is Chief of Staff it would be tactful to meet him in the matter. I'm so sorry to disapoint you, this is to catch you in time to prevent your canceling your shorthand lesson.'

I did not believe any of this and my mother and I agreed that I could not be stopped like that and we thought up a most extraordinary plan – designed to prove that I had not received the letter. My mother telephoned to Frank, one of her awful brothers whom she hadn't seen for years, and asked if we could come and spend a night or two with him and his wife Martha. We couldn't waste money on a hotel and we could think of no one else. We packed my garden party clothes and went to Sidcup and from the post office there, sent a telegram to Miss Chard regretting that I had been called away from home the night before, but would be back in time for the Garden Party the following afternoon.

Frank's little villa was filled with beautiful things from Campden Hill and Henry Moore's studio and frightful things – Martha's acquisitions. Great, grim Martha, monolithic product of the East End clothing industry, and in the grotesque little parlour, over cups of tea, we were soon listening to the story of her life. How she had raised herself from the rag trade to a machinist's job in a factory and then set up in a little business on her own. That was when Frank married her. When she had some money.

When he came home, he was as pleased with us as she was and we spent the evening together, talking about Campden Hill and the family. It was like a peculiar dream, the hours spent in that peculiar house.

The next afternoon, I dressed up and, waving to Martha and my mother at the hideous front door, both of them admiring me in their different ways and for different reasons, walked down the suburban road and took the train to London.

Downing Street was crowded with cars, taxis, policemen and spectators. I was nervous. I hated playing this trick. But I hated the tricky letter even more. I had to come. I couldn't let her get the better of me as easily as that.

I was soon moving slowly with the crowd up the main staircase towards the great drawing-room where the Prime Minister and Mrs Baldwin were receiving. I was half-way up when – I met her! She was making her way down. I tried to smile naturally but her look of hatred appalled me. She never paused and, jostled by the people, we almost touched as we passed.

The encounter was over and I felt free now to go on and do my job. I went straight to Mrs Baldwin and caught her eye and a few moments later she left her husband and came up to me and bent down beneath my hat and looked into my face and whispered, almost affectionately, 'Tell your mother, my dear, you're looking lovely.' After that, I felt safe and happy.

I had one friend in all that crowd, an Irish peer who came to the receptions every Thursday and always waited in the same place until I was free to come and talk to him. I didn't like him very much but he was important and, like all those men, stylish and self-assured. My mother was certain that he was in love with me and I wondered when he would propose. He was not quite so old as Sir Vincent and I decided that when he did I would marry him – for his title and the grand wedding I would have. When I met him that afternoon I flirted with him hard and felt as if I was really living at last. I did not see Miss Chard again.

I travelled back to Sidcup and recounted my adventures to an excited and admiring audience. It was a typical Luker trick that I had played and it appealed to Frank, and the snob majestic setting thrilled them both. While, on my side, there sprang out of the drama a feeling of recovered kinship, lawless and bizarre; a sympathetic oneness with these dreary failures of my artist family. If I had met Frank and Martha anywhere in the neighbourhood of Downing Street I would have cut them dead, but hidden here in Sidcup, I could talk and laugh and feel affection. And talk I did. I bragged and boasted and entertained just as Miss Chard would have done had she fallen suddenly among left-behind admiring relatives in a despised suburb. And my mother did the same. The rich stories that we told them brought us comfort and were compensation for our unsatisfied outsider lives. They thought our lives were marvellous because the whole truth was never in our stories.

The next morning, I was in the office at the usual time and when Miss Chard arrived, very late, in a cold and silent mood, I acted out the next scene of the play, after much rehearsing to myself.

'It was a great surprise and shock to me when we returned to Chelsea to find your letter waiting there,' I said, looking her straight in the eye, without a blush, as I lied monstrously.'Had I received it in time I would not have come.'

'It didn't matter. I was able to put it right for you with the Chief because as soon as I saw you I left and so, when he asked me why you were there, I told him that I had had to leave early and you had come to take my place. I was glad to be able to get away.'

The next few days were very strained and the weather made them worse. A heat wave was covering the country and our room, half buried behind the walls, was particularly airless and oppressive. Miss Chard kept out of it most of the time. Then, after lunch one day, she returned and, spreading some papers out upon her desk stayed, hardly moving, for the rest of the afternoon. But she wasn't working. She just stared at the papers and occasionally pushed them about. Her silence was as heavy and sultry as the weather.

'There'll be a storm tonight,' I said, trying to break the horrible calm. She started and looked sideways at me for an instant, then down again with a sound that was something like a grunt. I had never seen her sit so still before or sit so long in one place. I wondered if the heat was affecting her, and I thought I could see her trembling.

'Are you alright?' I asked her after awhile. 'There's no air in here at all. It's a wonder we don't both faint.'

'I'm not going to faint,' she muttered angrily. I said no more. Every five minutes I looked at my watch, desperate for the moment when I could leave my desk and go. But in that room, even Time had stopped.

At six o'clock I tidied up my desk, drew my handbag and gloves out of a drawer, then crossed the room and took my hat down from a peg. When I turned to say good-bye – the storm broke. Not the storm outside but the one which had been building up within the room. She came suddenly to life. Her slanting eyes narrowed until only two hard points were looking into mine. Her mouth was taut and thin and cruel.

'Why are you going now? You shouldn't leave before I do, walk calmly out like this! I can never trust you. I never know when you're going to run off home leaving all the work to me. Why did you come to the Garden Party? You had no right to. I never gave you permission. What made you ever think that you could come – all dressed up in heavy lace! The Chief was furious and everyone was pointing you out and laughing at you. You push your way in everywhere. Isn't it enough to be working here? What more do you expect? I suppose you'd like to take my place?

'I've brought you here and given you this wonderful start, but you aren't grateful. You show no proper respect for me – your Chief – and you're always letting me down. You don't know the meaning of duty and loyalty and team spirit. You're just working for yourself all the time. And you went behind my back, didn't you, and proposed yourself for that committee! Ha! Ha! That *was* a clever thing to do! Who *is* she?' they asked me. I had to get you out of that. If you want to make a laughing stock of yourself how dare you make Downing Street look silly as well. You ought to have been dismissed for that. I only let it pass because you were still young. Now I'm sorry. You're not worth all my kindness. You're just a rotten little chit of a girl – worth nothing, nothing, nothing!'

She was screaming at the end of this and her face was red and her whole body shaking. But before she could recover her breath to start again, I opened the door and left. In the hall I smiled at my friend, the commissionaire, and walked out of No.10 for the last time. A few hours later, a tremendous storm broke over London.

When I came home and repeated the words of this tirade to my mother she wanted to hit back at once. But to appeal to Mrs Baldwin was difficult, for all her letters passed through Miss Chard's hands and she still admired her. And so did Sir Ronald, of course, yet, all the same, she wrote to him. His reply was slippery and fatuous and it got her nowhere but she had only wanted to test him and lay a little poison. 'It is something of an anomaly,' he ended, 'that while most get away at the start, there remain those few who do so only after continuous practice.'

I wrote a formal letter of resignation to Miss Chard and received, in return, my first and last salary cheque. I also wrote to the Irish peer and told him that I had left Downing Street, hinting delicately that it would be nice to meet him somewhere else.

He replied on House of Commons notepaper, but the pleasure he expressed at hearing from me and his hope of seeing me as soon as the pressure of his work allowed – meant nothing at all. I never heard again and when I looked him up in *Debrett's Peerage*, I found that he had a wife and family.

Again, I was virtually expelled as a failure and again I did not really mind for I was always so sure of myself and of the golden thread which received me, whenever I fell back. And Miss Chard was right to hate me, for in me she saw herself. There were too many of us in Downing Street. Someone had to go. And I was bored. I had even lost interest in the political side. So why not me?

I was again back in my groundless solitary home without a friend or any prospects. I seemed to have gained nothing. I was no nearer to my task. I still moved everywhere except the way I had to go.

My mother waited to see where she could strike again. And while I waited to find my true road, I longed to go to dances and meet young men and because it seemed as if I never would, I decided to give a ball myself. Not in a grand house, of course, but a charity one in a hotel. Subscription dances were fashionable and popular, as I knew from my work at No. 10 and from my reading of the newspapers.

My mother loved the idea and we decided to give one for 'Our Dumb Friends League' because we happened to know a woman who was dedicated to the cause and we were sure she would be helpful. My own love for animals was purely incidental.

We booked the ball-room of the Rembrandt Hotel and advertised widely. The tickets sold well and I bought my first evening dress and when the night came, we went early to the hotel and waited excitedly for the band and the guests to arrive.

Still so ignorant socially and believing, and feeling, herself to be the hostess, my mother stood waiting to receive them. But no one took any notice of her. The dancers came in couples, never looked at anybody else and stayed glued together all the evening.

As I stood about, not dancing, my mother became more and more desperate. She even tried to break up some of the couples, but they wouldn't be broken. At the end, they left with sparkling eyes and the dance was acclaimed a great success. My only dance was with the old husband of our 'Dumb Friends' supporter who, taking pity on me, did his best to give me a turn.

At my first dance I was a mystified, unhappy wall-flower believing that the young men didn't like the look of me. We had hired a room and hired a band and assembled 500 people but what we didn't do and should have done — was hire a young man!

4

A Parliamentary Candidate

I STILL loved people and believed that most of them were good and kind, regretting only that due to some mischance or inner leaning, I never met that sort, for they still dwelt in a city on the horizon, as in a mirage, while the place in which I stood was always shadeless, waterless and cruel. My school had been like that – and Downing Street. But they were exceptions, I was sure, disappointing aberrations from the real and now I would have to try again to reach that city and those people – and find my task there as well. I worried all the time because I had not found it although I knew that when I did, my job would be over-laid with pain and it would drive me, from that moment on.

I did not waste time. I was 18 and the disease from which I had been suffering for so long, political schizophrenia, had reached an advanced stage. I wrote to someone high up in the Conversative Central Office and asked for an appointment. While I waited for the reply I read Karl Marx's *Capital*, received knowledge through the air and resumed my walking.

It was the London markets that I went to now for in them I found a warmth and simplicity that I had never known and that I loved. I seemed to understand them, the stallholders and their customers, and I felt easy and unafraid.

In Walworth Market, one day, I stopped before a bookstall and as I ran my eyes over the titles, the young girl watched me and presently came forward.

'Is it love yer wants?' she asked me.

'Yes. Love is what I'm looking for,' I replied.

At that, she flung herself upon the books and pulled out one after the other and handed me some half a dozen. She would have gone on if she had not been concerned for my purse.

'I've read 'em all. Them's the best. I'll keep all the good ones for yer until yer come again.'

I paid for them at tuppence each and left them on the bus seats as I travelled home. And I went again, for the love that the young girl gave me as we sat together talking in the street.

When the reply came from the Central Office I went for the interview and

The Rani of Mandi
The original is a life-size oil-colour.

The Red Fort (Purana Kila), Delhi

and below

Dal Lake, Srinagar, Kashmir
Both water colours, much reduced.

told the important person that I wanted to become a Member of Parliament and would like to work in a constituency to gain experience.

I didn't say what *kind* of Member. I wasn't too sure myself. But he was and he took me on at once, quite pleased by this accession of strength to the party and the next day he introduced me to the woman Member for one of the Hackney divisions, another of those gaunt, grey disciplinarians. She told me that I would be under her wing for training and she arranged for me to work in the agent's office.

The agent (or perhaps the Member) had decided to modernise his organisation by introducing a card-index system. The fortuitous arrival of slave labour enabled him to go ahead with this ambitious project and, shut up in a room alone, I spent long boring days. When I asked him if I could go out into the clubs and homes for at least part of my time, he told me that all that would come later, but I must first serve in his office.

It was this character business again and I suspected that the Member was behind these counsels. Months of boredom was their way of testing for backbone, grit, tenacity of purpose, that same old thing – the proper spirit. I was being schooled again and I wanted to live. After three months I wrote to the grim, grey woman Member withdrawing myself from under her wing and she replied with another of those censorious letters, meant to hurt and always containing a sting. But I felt up against the world now, battling for a place in it and what my character was like didn't matter any more – and politics didn't matter either.

I knew before I went what politics were like, I knew when Mrs Baldwin first told me to read *Hansard* and the debates in *The Times*, I knew at Downing Street. But all this knowing was not enough, I had to see and feel and through the blank, enclosing walls of the agent's office I finally learnt what I already knew – that politics were not my road.

In the meantime, my mother composed a full account of the Downing Street affair and sent it to one of the Baldwin daughters (whom she had painted). She showed it to her mother who believed Miss Chard's tale – not ours. But the story spread all the same until it reached the Prime Minister. Then, Miss Chard was dismissed and Sir Ronald went soon afterwards – both into the wilderness. It was the last of their high posts. It was also the end of Mrs Baldwin's friendship. She never forgave us for depriving her of her clever little secretary.

When I left the agent's office, knowing that politics had failed and that the high fine world I so desired was unattainable, I would have dropped into a state of despair had I not discovered at that moment, a new independent way of holding back the void. I shut myself up, hardly slept or ate or talked, and for several months lived on the wings of an exciting revolutionary world, pouring out into a novel the lived material of my own short stormy life – enlarged, lifted and enlivened.

But when the book was finished – I was finished. I was not just nowhere this time, but beyond it, in a dark unthinkable dimension where my genius could never be fulfilled, where my task was undiscoverable – and I stopped trying.

I didn't read, my channel closed, I didn't walk – and I couldn't see or feel my golden thread. I ate and slept and in between, fell into frenzies of convulsive weeping. And this went on for weeks and weeks until, one night, I woke and knew that I had to go on trying – and knew the way. I woke my mother and told her that India was where I had to go. When the morning light came through the window we were laughing and, in our minds, preparing for the journey.

I had neither read nor thought about India but now, I was suddenly aware of that authentic segment of high society, shuttling back and forth, which ruled the orient; aware of the glamour and romance of the great shimmering sub-continent; aware that after eight hard, chilling years of punishment I could escape there from the narrow mean prison that was England; aware that the world was open and made for adventure – and I was certain that my task would be discovered there and, less consciously, that in India hung the loose related end to join my golden thread to.

We were only just settled in the pleasant little Chelsea house. For the first time in her life my mother had a real studio and didn't have to work so hard and we could live in a small mean way without worrying. In a flash it was all given up!

But we could not start at once. While my mother was finishing some portraits, I took over the management of our affairs and raising money now became my job. And I was ruthless.

By turning on my charm and talking, I let the house for seven years at £200 a year – far more than it was worth – to two simple women who liked and trusted me. I sold them the furniture at a price at which they could have bought it new. I raised a double mortgage on the freehold and then insured our lives and borrowed on the premiums. I grabbed every trick and sold the earth beneath us and amassed enough to buy us clothes and pay our fares, keep us in the best hotel when we arrived and provide us with a small basic income for as long as we were there.

I found an undistinguised but initiated person who, for a modest fee, was willing to present us both at Court, a formality we believed essential to success and every week we went to have our dresses fitted, we practised curtseying and when the time approached, ordered a private car. Then two days before, a letter came from the Palace informing us that our Summons had been withdrawn. On information furnished by Miss Morison (about my mother's legal separation) Lord Wigram had acted swiftly and, this time, successfully.

Clothes were very important and we bought wildly and gorgeously, cramming our tin-lined trunks with lovely things, for we didn't mean to go in the old casual, unassuming way, like artists. Even if the Court had withheld the magic passports we meant to go like queens, live at the top and stay away for years.

My mother's early preaching, exposure and conversion, all the infant trying and defeats, the whole long misbegotten passion had grown and blown into a madness. Art I despised now and my mother's talent was just something to be exploited to gain my own confluent yet disputing ends. And she acquiesced.

Perhaps she was glad to have all the thinking and deciding and business taken off her and to be left to live just as the earner. I had always gone my own way but now, when I grew into a commanding 'know everything about everything' character, she let me go completely. I was already a genius and now I was an intellectual giant. Whatever I did was right. And the wrongs I did were not wrongs. She was all heart and art. Willie had been a genius who could do no wrong.

After the Court defeat, letters of introduction became even more important and, ignoring the break, she wrote to Mrs Baldwin and although the reply was not friendly, it was fair and generous. She recommended my mother's work to the Viceroy, Lord Irwin, in a strong convincing way, which was all that we needed. And we loved her for it.

Not until the spring of 1928, when I was 20, were we ready to embark. In the purser's office I found a telegram – a farewell, good-luck message from Miss Morison. Her dangerous love still followed me.

It was the wrong time and the boats were empty, most people travelling in the opposite direction to escape the hot season and we met no one influential who might have helped us on arrival – only some R.A.F. short-service officers who talked with half-erased provincial accents and looked like grocers when their uniforms were off. But I used them. I spent the voyage practising upon them, learning how to make men fall in love with me.

After Suez the time passed quickly. My mother was optimistic as always but anxiety disturbed my joy and when, from the sea, I first saw the Gateway of India and the flotilla of sailing boats and glinting pinnaces moored before the Bombay Yacht Club, I was conscious of the strains that lay behind them.

When the ship reached the jetty, it was the noise that first struck me. Above the grinding of the winches rose the yells of the coolies, the crack of the coolie-master's whip, the shouts of the native agents and the harsh pleading voices of the beggars. But when we went ashore it was the smell. The heavy, holding, musk-like scent of India which I loved at once.

At the station we took possession of a large reserved two-berth compartment into which our luggage was stacked without noticeable diminishment of its space and we soon learnt that it was customary for travellers to be accompanied, not only by their personal baggage, but by their household goods as well.

As we stood on the platform, waiting for the train to leave and letting the high dark tide lap over us, we noticed that all the white passengers had their own servants, smart uniformed bearers who looked after their baggage, supervised the coolies, ran about the station buying fruit and bottled water and newspapers, dragged the sweepers into the compartments to dust the ledges and clean the floors and, spread out their bedding rolls, while the Sahibs and Memsahibs did nothing for themselves – nothing but give orders.

The R.A.F. men had already acquired them, picked them up when they swarmed onto the boat and there were more of them there, going up and down the train, soliciting work. It was all we could do to support ourselves and to find that life was insupportable without a servant, made us anxious.

To prevent *dacoits*, or robbers, from boarding them and then moving up and down to do their work, Indian trains have no corridors. Throughout the long journey my lovers jumped in and out of our compartment whenever the train stopped and their bearers fetched our food from the station restaurants. As for bedding rolls – we didn't have them. We rolled our coats up for pillows and with our travelling rugs, made the best of the hard seats. And we soon learnt how to call in the sweepers.

I did not want my lovers now. I had played with them on the boat, feeling and using my untried powers and now I could not cast them off. And I liked partings to be artistic and not unkind and so, when they left the train in ones and twos along the way, I was thankful. At Kalka we boarded one of the open cars of the mountain railway for the exciting zig-zag climb.

Simla was built upon a long tree-covered ridge with spurs leading off it, sloping gently downwards. The single road, The Mall, ran along the middle of this ridge and the buildings clung precariously to the rocky slopes each side. Only the Viceroy, the Commander-in-Chief and the Governor of the Punjab were allowed to use their motor cars. Rickshaws and horses were the general means of locomotion in this yellow-brown township balanced serenely upon the knife-edged mountain top.

Rickshaws pulled us up from the rail-head to The Mall and then rolled us, one behind the other, to the Cecil.

The Cecil Hotel was the great social centre of Simla, but when we entered we were astonished to find it full of painters perched on bamboo ladders and armies of servants hanging curtains, laying carpets, cleaning and polishing. We had been misinformed about the date of the great annual move to the hills and had arrived a month too early. This was a shock. Four weeks of high hotel bills – money squandered just on waiting. And we were nervous and impatient to begin.

We engaged a cheap room in the annexe and when asked if we wished to reserve a *go-down* for our bearer, said that we would do this later. The servant question was now a serious challenge for we knew that it was not only a matter of practical convenience but that imperial prestige was involved. As adventurers, that was something that we had to be particularly careful about and, at once, we did the wrong thing. When we reached our room we checked the baggage and paid off the coolies ourselves. Then we looked at each other – we had arrived!

We went to the window, looked out – and all our petty worries vanished before the sight that we beheld. Thick forests rolling down and up and down again, wave upon wave, like a vast undulating sea and beyond them, far away, rising high and sharp and shimmering in the sunlight – the long white, deckle-edged mass of the Himalayas. And we gazed and gazed upon this wonder of the world.

Eventually, we dragged ourselves away and went over to the main building for a meal, leaving the window open and the wire screen as well, which we supposed was for flies. When we returned a great noise was coming up from the room below and when we hurried to the window to recapture the view, we saw things flying out beneath us, crashing and breaking on the stony slopes. We thought the occupants must be quarrelling violently or else had gone mad. Yet there were no voices.

For a long time we leant out, watching boots and shoes, coats and hats, silver-backed brushes and combs and mirrors, bottles and boxes being emptied out of the room. At length, we telephoned the office. A few moments later we heard voices and immediately two small monkeys leapt onto the window-sill and, chittering and chattering, ran down the drain-pipe, crossed the litter-strewn clearing and disappeared into the trees. Now we knew what the screens were for.

We chose a window table in the vast oriental-style dining-room and settled down with delight to this new exotic life, to being waited on by turbaned, white-gloved servants, to elaborate meals, to indolence and the illusion of position and permanence. We had enough money to live like this for two months. After that, if my mother didn't earn we would have to move to somewhere cheap and squalid and, if still her work did not catch on, take the next boat home, although we had no return tickets and no money in reserve to buy them. But we only thought about such things in fleeting frightened moments – and kept the thoughts to ourselves. We were certain of success and even waiting was exciting.

Box-wallahs (business men) came and went, otherwise the hotel was empty. Then, one of my R.A.F. lovers telephoned from his station in the plains, announcing that he had three days leave and was coming up to see me. He was the most plebian of them all. But I couldn't stop him. He meant to come and he came – and in that grand exposing place he looked more rough than ever. If anyone of importance had chanced to see him sitting at our table I was sure we would be damned.

I didn't like him when he came. After three days I loathed him and when, on the last night, he proposed to me, I was cruel. He left in the morning cowed and resentful. My first proposal was depressing.

I bought a Hindustani language book and a copy of the Army List and studied them both for several hours every day. Then, towards the end of April, people began to arrive, looking white and wan from the heat below. We watched them from our window table. They were all so sure of themselves and their positions in this official and hierarchic society and I envied the young girls their guaranteed lives. They could look forward to a long, carefree intoxicating summer.

As social adventurers it was important to make friends and we picked out people whom we liked the look of and manoeuvred ourselves into their orbit or spoke to them across the tables, radiating charm. We had to be careful not to attract the wrong ones and fall into the wrong set for, although crowded together in the hill-stations, the many sub-divisions and levels of British society were kept strictly in their places.

As soon as I learnt a name I looked it up in the Army List and if I found that it belonged to an inferior regiment or corps, I proscribed it at once. And civilians, the Civil Service, could be shunned altogether without any researches. And I seldom made a mistake. When I did we retreated quickly and effectively with the piercing politeness that I so hated when it was used upon me.

In England the Church, the aristocracy and the professional class, the three upper estates of the realm, had long ago lost their separate and exclusive identities and duties. The power and influence of the Church had declined and the aristocracy had inter-married with the upper middle-class. In India, however, the old divisions were intact, with the military-aristocratic class at the top and the civil administrators below. Each felt superior and despised the other, only mixing on the highest levels. (My chosen road climbed steeply and passed out of sight of the more interesting route below.) In the Indian society which the British had supplanted, the Brahmin or priestly caste, had always been at the top, but to restore the missing element and reverse the order was more than could be expected from a humanistic imperial power.

At the apex of the pyramid stood the Viceroy, combining in himself both the military and civil powers and round him, contained within the same narrow marches, moved the high society that we had come to capture. But climbing the pyramid was not the way to reach the top. That was the very way *not* to. The steps had all to be avoided. To jump was the only way – and we knew it. That was why we trod so carefully at the Cecil.

Mrs Gyle-Chattery was the stout warm-hearted wife of a red-faced, dreamy-eyed general (he was always in a state of partial coma). She painted herself and was thrilled to meet a fellow-artist and soon she took possession of us and, striding across the dining room after every meal, plumped herself down at our table and puffing cigarettes in a long holder and drinking cup after cup of black coffee – offered us the world and all its scandal as a garnish.

She was so perceptive and sympathetic, she knew exactly what we wanted and she had it all to give. She would introduce us to all her friends from the Commander-in-Chief downwards, obtain invitations for us to visit the Maharajahs with whom her husband had great influence, she would give parties for us, secure commissions and her daughter, Lavinia, would look after me. She would launch us into Simla society and whenever there was time, she and my mother would go sketching together.

Growing more intimate, she burst into our room every day and hour after hour we listened to her fascinating tales, lapped up her promises and glowed in the warmth of her friendship. But the introductions and parties and commissions never quite materialised – and Lavinia ignored me. It was hard to understand. But we went on hoping and responding until doubt followed disappointment and then disillusionment overtook them both. Later, we learnt that Mrs Gyle-Chattery was Simla's arch-bore, avoided by everyone, without a friend anywhere.

From the beginning of May when the season officially opened, there were dances at the Cecil twice a week and, on Saturdays, the famous prawn-curry lunch; an exotic piece of fun designed, it seemed, for the especial delectation of the older and most exalted members of the community – the generals and judges, the princes and pandits, the high handful of excellencies and even the Viceroy himself. Once or twice during the season the red carpet was unrolled and into an atmosphere of awesome expectation, he stepped gracefully and grandly to honour some high host and the worthy purveyors of the crustacean banquet.

From half past twelve onwards long lines of horses and rickshaws came winding along The Mall from both directions and converged upon the hotel, causing traffic jams of an entangled, turbulent complexity most entertaining and picturesque to watch.

Both the guests and their hosts streamed out of their fine bungalows scattered about the spurs in beautifully cultivated clearings. Their private rickshaws were embossed with their crests and monograms and painted in their special colours and their coolies wore the eastern counterpart of English livery. Here was high society transplanted to the orient, clinging to this rough preposterous ridge and raising up upon it the life and all the fine observances of London.

We watched them take their places at the large oval tables and the smaller round ones, watched them talk and laugh and drink champagne – and eat the prawns.

Several hours later, when the successes and satisfactions were still being counted, the slips and omissions still being deplored – the prawns began to do their heinous work and by the evening the thudding hoofs of the doctor's charger could be heard along the Mall. At least a quarter of the company of gourmets were regularly poisoned.

He was a great big red-faced R.A.M.C. colonel, the jolliest of social companions but in his professional capacity – murderous. People congratulated themselves each time they got out of his hands alive. And all night long he thundered up and down as if he was carrying the good news forever backwards and forwards between Aix and Ghent – not just antidotes for prostrated proconsuls. And Sundays, too, he worked full-time. The calls did not abate. Yet no sooner were the victims snatched from death's door and set upon their feet again than back they came the next week, by special election, to the high compelling ritual – and the sacrifice.

By the middle of May the summer capital was full but still the Viceroy had not come. My mother did not wait. She put her usual notice up and several intrepid people came to our room to sit. These oil-colours were small and cheap, just head and shoulder size at £25 each and they made us safe for several weeks, although no great rush of people followed as in the old days of the little water-colour sketches.

When he arrived at last we presented Mrs Baldwin's letter. It was answered at once with an invitation to lunch and when the day came we dressed up in all our finery, signalled to two rickshaws waiting in a row like taxis, and were whirled away to Viceregal Lodge.

It was built on a flat knoll at the extreme western end of the ridge with the mountain falling steeply away on three sides and The Mall circling round it in a loop. An Indian sentry presented arms as we passed through the gates and our coolies slowed down as the long drive, twisting through fine trees and flowering borders, turned sharply upwards.

The building was like a large, very ordinary English country house with tiers of balconies stuck onto it all round. When the drive levelled out the coolies made a last spurt and drew up with a flourish before the steps where an A.D.C. was waiting.

He helped us from the rickshaws and the coolies trotted on to the servants quarters to rest and wait. We walked up onto the verandah and through the great front door and then to the A.D.C.'s room, talking all the way, filling the silence and our passage through the house with the cool amiable words expected of us. Young and tall and handsome in his black, braided, undress uniform of the Guards, he looked like a god.

The room was full. We were introduced to the Controller of the Household, the Military Secretary, the Captain of the Bodyguard, their wives, the guests – and the other A.D.C.'s, all chosen for their looks and stature, all like young gods.

The room was like an officers' mess with military portraits, battle prints and sporting trophies on the walls, cups and prizes on the shelves and heavy enduring masculine furniture. It was a bachelor establishment now for Lady Irwin had gone to England for the summer.

I sipped my cocktail, the young men bending over me, lifting their glasses, flicking their cigarettes, turning and swaying, their manners and movements all so restrained and I gazed up at their handsome faces and noted their beautiful hands and fell in love with them all – the critical parts of my mind utterly drugged.

We were soon taken to the high oak-panelled hall where, at the bottom of the great curving staircase, we waited for the Viceroy. After a few minutes, punctual to the time-table, we heard the sound of muffled footsteps and looking up, saw him coming. Tall and dignified he descended gravely with an A.D.C. behind him, the light of the staircase window striking his figure when he turned at the bend and came down towards us. Our names were announced, we curtseyed and smiling gently he shook our hands. Then, with the principal guests on each side of him, my mother on his left, he led the way into the dining-room where dark-skinned patriarchs in scarlet coats, golden cummerbunds and white gloves stood behind each chair.

I had learnt to hide my nervousness behind an assured sophisticated manner and I had become very loquacious, with strong opinions on every subject. At the Cecil I held forth upon a variety of semi-intellectual topics and now, to the men each side of me, I did the same. But sensing quickly that serious conversation was not the thing, that women were expected only to amuse, never to presume upon men's intellectual territory (especially if the men were not capable of entering it themselves), I subtly reduced the weight of every argument, softened it with a delicate submissiveness and humour, even splashed it when I could with the colours of comedy. I turned every subject, however profound, into light entertainment and with my gay laughter and the daring use of my eyes – made it acceptable. Perhaps I only made myself acceptable.

After lunch, Lord Irwin took my mother round the house to show her all the pictures. He knew a lot about art and must have had a fine collection in his Yorkshire home. He rejoined the other guests for a few minutes and then disappeared to his work with the same quiet, lonely dignity. The next morning, an emblazoned bearer knocked upon our door and handed us a large envelope. Inside was a letter from the Military Secretary requesting my mother to paint a portrait of His Excellency. We were saved! A future suddenly unrolled before us, secure and rapturous – for the Viceroy was behind us!

Within a few hours the news was all round Simla and my mother was a celebrity. She was interviewed and photographed by the press and soon all India knew that an important artist had arrived from England and the commissions flooded in. The Commander-in-Chief asked to be done and the Governor of the Punjab and princes wrote from every part begging her to visit them. She had work which would keep us there in comfort and security for years. Suddenly we had status. She was the official painter to the Viceroy with a place on the establishment. We belonged.

And not only commissions but invitations, too. The grandees angled and contrived to meet her and the hostesses gave lunches and dinners in her honour and included me in all the dances and tennis and gymkhana parties. Night after night I whirled round the ballrooms in the arms of all these gods. I had arrived in high society.

We moved into a suite and the large sitting-room, facing north, my mother turned into a studio. But we still did not engage a bearer. The very idea was repugnant. We were too mean and still too frightened to pay or suffer waste where we needn't. I supervised the sweeper every morning and once a week did all the washing and the ironing. The laundrymen were notoriously destructive. They slapped the clothes on stones or banged them with truncheons in the nearest streams. My mother the painter – I the servant, secretary and manager.

Lord Irwin was usually a lovely sitter, sensitive and calm, talking quietly all the time. But one day he was fidgety and difficult, so impatient that he could hardly stay on his chair. Gandhi was coming!

He loved him, accepted him as a saint and could think and talk of nothing else. He was a very religious man himself. My mother did not keep him. She worked on alone for awhile and then packed up her things and servants carried them to the door. There was a crowd there. The staff were gathered on the veranda with servants mustered behind, peering and craning excitedly. And on the steps stood the Viceroy himself. Gandhi had come! My mother watched them meet, watched him defer to the little wizened man in the *dhoti*, his political opponent, watched them pass in together smiling and talking, well pleased with each other.

Chris Birdwood was my first love. He was sensitive and charming, a delicate edition of his father, the Field Marshal. He played the piano beautifully and was mildly unhappy in an Indian cavalry regiment. For several days he pursued me, danced with me and me alone, held my hand and looked into my eyes and under the soft trees in the scented lamp-lit gardens, tried to kiss me in a weak, half boyish way. Then, just as suddenly as he had loved me he deserted me for a dull mousey little girl with not half my vivacity and allure, I thought. I was heart-broken and for a week, wept and mooned and dragged myself about. And I was sure it was my own fault. My mother had told me that I must not let men kiss me all at once. 'You'll get a bad name if you do,' she was always saying. Now I wondered if I had been too prim and *should* have kissed him. I knew nothing about men.

The time soon came when the sum of all this hospitality had to be counted up and returned. We knew that it wouldn't go on forever even under the special patronage of the Viceroy. The system, as in London, was one of carefully calculated giving and taking and, after the first excited explosion, we could see the giving already weakening. And it had to be kept up. We were in it now and we couldn't stop.

I planned lunches, dinners and dance parties and sent invitations to everyone, flinching only at the Viceroy. The acceptances came swiftly back and we plunged into an orgy of entertaining.

The rickshaws came rolling to the Cecil, even one of the privileged motor cars drove up to the door, one Saturday, discharged its immortal occupants, the Commander-in-Chief Field Marshal Sir William Birdwood and his wife, and then waited like a lonely juggernaut while, inside, at one of the round mystic tables, they partook of the poisonous prawns proffered by us with so much social pride and satisfaction.

My mother was now a successful hostess as well as a celebrated painter, we rose even higher – and so did the bills.

This leap to the top and drunken, giddy balancing upon the heavenly summit lasted about two months and then the whole thing shook, our foothold went and we looked over the edge into the void.

Disquieting things began to happen as my mother's health broke down. For the first time in her life she suffered from insomnia and, not her old familiar giddy attacks, quick to come and quick to go, but constant gastric trouble.

She blamed the altitude and then, for awhile, became obsessed with the idea that she was being poisoned. Other fantastic notions followed, she grew more and more hysterical as her work first deteriorated and then stopped altogether.

Lord Irwin's portrait was not going well. In her younger days she never worried about failing because she never failed but now, every picture frightened her until it was half finished and she knew that it would pass. And, naturally, the Viceroy's was the most frightening of them all. So much depended on it. Everything depended upon her. If she failed, we could expect little pity from this high, hard, indifferent world from which we should just drop and no hand, however regal, would be concerned for long to save us. And in official India there was no halfway place to fall, no independent middle station, nothing between the mighty rulers on their thrones and little traders and, after them, the outcasts – the Anglo-Indian half-breeds repudiated by both races, detritus of empire flung out and down to rot. The whole adventure was staked upon her failing powers and even if we both refused to see it, subconsciously she knew it.

The Colonel came galloping along and gave her sleeping pills and stomach mixtures, strong to start with and then stronger. One morning she never woke at all. When I came back from breakfast she was sleeping still. I put her sitter off and half-way through the morning tried to wake her. After lunch I telephoned the Colonel.

'Don't worry,' he boomed out gaily, 'just let her sleep it off. I'll look in later on my way back from polo.'

When he came, redder than ever, tousled and sweaty, his boots covered with dried lather, his white breeches stained with the rub of saddle polish, he strode over to her bed, took her hand in his great hot fist and felt her pulse, then let it drop like something inanimate.

'Noth-ing wrong at all. Noth-ing to worry about,' he then told me, almost singing the words and loving the first syllable of 'noth-ing'. 'Just what she wants – a good long sleep. She'll feel frisky as a filly when she wakes. I'll look back in the morning.' When he came she was still sleeping and still 'noth-ing' at all was wrong.

We had a lunch party that day and up to the last minute I hoped that she would wake and feel 'frisky' enough to entertain her guests. But she didn't and I received them alone. Afterwards, of course, the news of her sleeping was all round Simla. And the Viceroy also heard.

That evening, slowly and heavily, she waked. But she didn't feel frisky. She felt terrible and she was days recovering from the Colonel's over-dose of the poisonous drug.

As soon as she was well enough she asked for another sitting and went with a new canvas. Lord Irwin was most concerned about her ordeal and before the sitting was over, had invited us both to spend a fortnight at Viceregal Lodge, until he went on tour again. The change, he hoped would do her good. We were dropping now and he, alone, did what he could to save us. The next day we left the hotel for the supreme experience.

We were given a suite each and when we opened the doors and walked out onto the balcony we were once again shocked out of ourselves by the prospect that lay waiting there. The trees surrounding the house had been cleared giving an Olympian view of the plains of the Punjab.

We stood, pressing against the rail, gazing down upon that shimmering, yellow-brown, sun-covered world with the Indus and its tributaries, the Sutlej and Chenab and a hundred lesser ones, cutting their way through it, tumbling from the roof of the world to flow in winding grandeur through a thousand miles of plain and desert. And I longed to be getting down there. I knew that Simla was not really India and now Hindustan lay spread before me, mysterious, seductive, sublime. If we felt like royal guests when we arrived – we felt like gods now.

My mother slept naturally at once and ate all that was served to her. She was made well by the feeling of protection, she said afterwards.

Our lives, for every minute of each day, were determined for us. When breakfast and the newspapers were brought to our rooms, embossed sheets of paper with our programmes beautifully set out, were laid upon our writing tables. Our work was to study them and decide what clothes to wear for each event and tell the servants what to press and prepare. We had walk-on parts in every scene of the Viceroy's life. We dressed, stepped out onto the stage behind him to act and speak our unimportant lines and then withdrew when he did to change our costumes for the next appearance.

The Court in India, it was said, was even grander and more lavish than the monarch's Court at home. The conquerors competed with the kings they had subdued and felt they must surpass their extravagant displays. In the two weeks that we were there we had only one quiet night which we spent alone with Lord Irwin and his staff.

It could have been the most exciting of them all for, to me, he was another, but greater, Sir Vincent; a father-teacher from whom I hoped to learn so much. But he refused to play his teaching part for me, preferring easy chatter and then bridge. At the end of dinner when he asked me if I played and would like to make up a fourth, madly I said yes. When we cut for partners I was paired with him.

I had only played once and then in a frivolous way. In Simla, when I saw that bridge was a social asset which might help me, I learnt the rudiments of the game – and that was all. And now, I was sitting at a green baize table in a pool of yellow light and the first hand was being dealt – I was playing with the Viceroy of India!

I had the confidence of the fool but not the luck of the beginner. I played both cautiously and recklessly, winning tricks and losing them. Sometimes he told me gently what I should have done but for most of the time he was silent. All of us were silent, only my mother across the room, talking quietly to the others. I never thought about the score and I didn't even know that I was playing for money. On the first of the month when we were back at the Cecil, I received a colossal bill for my losses that night.

Before our visit ended and Lord Irwin left Simla, a State banquet and ball were given. The Indian Bodyguard with lances and pennons were mounted in the hall and doorways and the dinner guests assembled and were marshalled into a circle by the A.D.C.'s. The English women wore their Court dresses, their tiaras and their jewels; the Maharanis their rich saris of gold and silver thread. Most of the men were in scarlet mess-kit with different coloured facings, orders and decorations; the turbans of the princes were plumed and heavily festooned with pearls and their brocade coats shimmered in the light of the chandeliers.

Subdued conversation rippled round the circle until the doors opened with a fanfare of trumpets – and the Viceroy came in. Dressed in black wearing the single Order of the Garter and followed by his retinue, he advanced into the circle and moved slowly round it, shaking hands. Then, the most important lady took his arm and the company moved in procession into the banqueting hall. Another fanfare sounded, the banquet opened and an army of emblazoned, scarlet-petticoated servants ran noiselessly to and fro serving every course on solid gold plates while the band played in the gallery. Upon the third fanfare the guests rose to drink the health of the King-Emperor and then, moving in line, bowed to the Viceroy across the table and one behind the other, left the hall. At ten o'clock a scented, dazzling multitude arrived for the ball.

I danced every dance – even the State Lancers. I flung myself crazily at everything as if this was a new birth and I had done it all before, done it in some former life, and the glory of return went rioting to my heart as the champagne went to my head. A few days later we were back at the Cecil and the Viceroy was on tour again.

During the visit I fell in love with one of the A.D.C.'s, an auburn-haired

Adonis, seconded from the Grenadiers. He held my hand and sometimes put his arm limply round me and on the night of the ball, I let him kiss me. When he left and I knew that it was all over, my heart collapsed again. I did not see that he was much too shrewd and calculating ever to love unwisely.

With the departure of the Court at the end of July there was a general exodus. Most of the people went to Kashmir for the remainder of the hot-weather and the character of Simla changed. Students and delegates came up out of the heat for courses and conferences and the hotels filled up again.

Although she recovered her health at Viceregal Lodge yet my mother still had difficulty with Lord Irwin's portrait and she didn't finish it before he left. With relief she turned now to all the others on the waiting list.

Sir William Birdwood, and his family stayed on in Simla and while she painted him again their house became the focal point of all our friendships and pleasures. The first portrait was so successful that he had ordered another to leave behind in Snowdon, his official residence. It was the scarlet tunic that he loved and the plumed hat beside him on a table and the Field Marshal's boots and baton and the medals and orders covering his chest. He didn't care about the face and the ostentatious figure overwhelmed it. It was a magnificent life-size representation of all his badges and regalia.

Into the Cecil now came the 'backward boys'. They were, in fact, the bright boys of the army, picked by the selection boards for the Staff College and sent up to Simla on a month's final course with an examination at the end of it.

They were scarcely through the door when a handsome gunner major, older than all the men I had been loving and losing, made a rush at me. He was as ardent and in earnest as the others had been limp and I fell in love again and abandoned myself to the joys that he brought me and the dreams that he inspired. The pace grew faster every day and my heart's condition more delirious. I could see myself married, my mother free of me and both of us – safe. And then, someone told me that he had a wife in England. I thought the shock would kill me. But he didn't give me time to die at his feet or even be indignant. He first fled into the examination hall and then was gone altogether. When I recovered I remembered my Irish peer and understood now that this was a trick men played, which one had to look out for.

Suddenly, our world and the world beyond were shocked by the news of the attempted assassination of the Viceroy. His train was blown up by terrorists. Fortunately he escaped uninjured and my mother and I rejoiced at his deliverance and, siding with our own, bitterly condemned the subject people, daring to rise and strike and almost kill. And the act was disavowed by all the Indian leaders.

Many years later I met one of those terrorists, both of us having travelled by a long and circuitous route to the encounter. They had all been caught after the outrage and he spent seven years in prison. But they were the most valuable years of his life, he said. He studied for a university degree and got married. His fiance used to visit him regularly and when the wedding ceremony was held in a nearby temple, the governor of the prison was the principal guest. That terrorist is now Yashpal, one of India's leading writers.

It was now that I killed the spiders. We were staying for a few days in a bungalow with the usual bucket and jug and hole in the wall bathrooms. The first evening, I was sitting in my tin tub when an enormous spider walked slowly across the wall in front of me. Its round body was at least two inches and the span of its legs, at least six. I liked small spiders but this one frightened me and I didn't like the idea of meeting it there again, perhaps in the dark, and I decided to kill it. Stepping out of my bath, I picked up a towel and hit out at the monster. But the soft blow didn't hurt it and it ran rapidly up to the ceiling and from there attacked me, swinging down at my face. As I jumped about defending myself with the towel, it swung and swung at me on the end of its thread, pursuing me round and round the tiny room. And the battle went on and on. Of course I overcame it in the end, but the strength, intelligence and courage of the creature amazed me. I regretted its death but, at the same time, was glad that I had killed it. I couldn't have kept such an implacable enemy in my bathroom.

The next evening, at the same hour, I had scarcely opened the door when another, even larger one, waiting to revenge the death of his mate, came swinging down from the ceiling – and a second battle started, far fiercer than the first. Fighting back with everything that I could snatch, I leapt and dodged and hit out wildly feeling like a bulky, culpable Goliath before this tiny swinging David. When I killed it I grieved for them both. And perhaps I need never have done it for it was I who struck the first blow and made them into my enemies. I – the human race.

A short time before we left for Delhi I met Reggie, a high-ranking Air Force officer, mature and deep and strong – more magnetic than them all. I fell desperately in love. Every afternoon we rode on horses along the brown paths that threaded through the trees and dipped and rose and curled about the mountain. Often the monkeys followed us chattering and screaming and throwing things at us and when we heard the singing of a priest in a temple far below we stopped and listened to the lovely, lonely, siren voice.

Every evening we danced together and at week-ends he got his car out and we drove down the Kalka road until we saw an open bank upon which we could picnic and spend the day. When he had searched the ground for snakes and scorpions he would spread out a rug and then the lunch. Afterwards, he would take my hand and draw me to him. The first time I was frightened and drew away and he was disappointed and annoyed. The next time I let him take me in his arms and kiss me. I knew that he was married but I did not care. I was sure he would divorce his wife, sure that our love had never been surpassed and was eternal. I was certain he was mine.

The government departments were moving down and Simla was emptying. We fixed a day to travel and Reggie received a posting to Karachi. He left first and on the day of his going we all lunched together and afterwards I walked down to where he kept his car. It stood ready for the long journey piled and roped with his baggage and his bearer was beside it. He took my hands. I was still sure that he would make me some proposal. He said something kind and sweet and kissed me tenderly, then got into his car and drove away.

I had lost them all, one after the other. I could attract them (I had learnt that), but nothing more. Yet, when I thought about them afterwards it was not the lightness of their love which really hurt me but the fickleness of my own. That I could love so greatly, lose, grieve for a little and then love again, astonished me and made me frightened of myself. I didn't see that I hadn't loved a man at all yet – only men in general and love itself.

A few days later we left too, without being able to pay the hotel bill. All the money that my mother had so hardly earned and the remittances which came from home were not enough to pay for our mad leap and attempt to live beside the rich and mighty of the world.

5

The Gordon Highlanders

MAIDENS Hotel, in the residential part of Old Delhi, was not only a social centre like the Cecil, but a tourist centre and one of the landmarks of the East. Officials had their winter quarters in it and whenever a world-cruise vessel docked at Bombay hundreds of American tourists soon poured through its doors and dropped limping and exhausted onto the comfortable settees.

We arrived there from Simla – but not to stay. We had the Cecil to pay off and Maidens was even more expensive. But where else to live we didn't know. We couldn't afford any of the European hotels and the Indian ones were primitive and out of the question.

We walked about and rode in *tongas* getting our bearings. The public transport system was not designed for Europeans and after the smallness and simplicity of Simla, the very distances were a major problem for the new city was almost finished, most of the people had moved out into the fine modern bungalows and much of the social life was already centred there. And these great twin-cities, each spreading carelessly outwards, eating up the jungle, were five miles apart. A motor car was the first necessity of life.

After several weeks, with neither of our problems solved and having to do something quick, we left Maidens and went as paying-guests to a *box-wallah* family in New Delhi.

Mr Harvey was a plump, placid, contented little man but Mrs Harvey was the exact opposite. After 20 years in India and bringing up several children, she was nervous, unsatisfied and unhappy. In England they would have lived in a suburb, she would have cooked and cleaned the house all day and he would have mown the lawn on Sundays. There, as Sahib and Memsahib, they kept eight servants, a car and two horses.

When we first arrived she was dressed up all the time, even for breakfast she put on her imitation diamond ear-rings and all her rings. The servants wore newly washed *puggarees* and tunics every day and she ordered them imperiously about except when she thought we couldn't hear or understand – and then she nagged them.

In her determination to impress, it was the meals that she worked hardest on and lifted highest and enjoyed most. In the dim, sun-protected dining-room, she and her husband sat at each end of an enormous mahogany table (its feet set in bowls of water against the white ants) and when the two white-gloved, bare-foot butlers were not hurrying anxiously in and out with the dishes, they stood solemnly behind the Sahib's and Memsahib's chairs in grand viceregal fashion.

Matching her voice and manner then to the splendour of it all, she entertained us brightly and the pride and pleasure which she felt and all the hopes that we aroused relieved her taut-strung nerves, animated her haggard rouged-up face, lightened her despairing eyes and charged her whole thin, pinched-up body with happy expectation. And the mean pretentious meals went on and on for as long as she could drag them out.

We soon realised that it was not shortage of money (they had plenty) which had brought us into the house but Mrs Harvey's desperate loneliness and social ambitions – and we were bored and more annoyed than compassionate. We saw our own degrading struggle being repeated on another level; repeated and repeated all the time on all the levels.

They both lavished cordiality and kindnesses upon us and we took everything, returning in exchange the same false friendship that we gave to Frank and to Martha; expedient, capricious, stopping at the boundaries of the bungalow, a relationship of which we were ashamed and had to keep concealed.

When Mr Harvey drove us about I always managed to sit beside him so that I could watch him drive and learn about cars – for I knew that I must have one. And soon, because Mrs Harvey could no longer ride (her nerves were so bad) he invited me to go out hacking with him every morning before breakfast. We cantered along the ridge which ran close to their house, the famous Delhi Ridge which had figured so often, always so heroically and bloodily, in all the old battles for the city. Or, we crossed over it and dropped down into the jungle beyond and broke through the scrub between the trees and galloped over the hard brown clearings. I loved those morning rides and I loved the big horse, Autumn.

My mother still had the Viceroy's portrait to finish, two or three small orders, and a third full-dress picture of Sir William Birdwood, this one to be hung in Flagstaff House, his official residence in New Delhi – but nothing more ahead.

Before we left Simla much of the excitement over her work had subsided. She had not only failed to deliver the Viceroy's portrait but even those which seemed so successful were, in some way, disappointing although it would not have occurred to anyone to call them photographic or mechanical. If she had still been in her prime painting as she once could, the enthusiasm would never have abated and the commissions would have gone on flowing in.

When the orders stopped – so did the invitations. At first, we thought it was our isolation and the disruption caused by the move down from the hills. When the people were settled we were sure that they would look for us, invite us to their parties, bring us back into their lives – and order more pictures. But the season opened, the gaieties were once again in full swing and none of these things happened. And we didn't know why, didn't realise that because we had lost the power to maintain ourselves in it, we had dropped out of their world and were already forgotten, that we were where we were – down among the *box-wallahs*.

A motionless silence fell round us and however much we resisted, we were thrown more and more upon the Harveys – and we didn't know how to change things, how to get back into 'our' world. I just drifted on hoping that something from outside would save us.

I soon knew that Mr Harvey liked me. I could feel his eyes following me about and he often touched me as if unintentionally, but I knew it wasn't. I didn't want love to develop but I wanted his companionship and favours, the riding and driving. I remained as cool and distant as I could but at the same time went wherever he asked me.

One morning, we stopped our horses on a rise and waited for the sun to come up. The scents and sounds of the jungle were so lovely. I just sat on the big horse drinking them all in. Then, suddenly, I became aware that he was looking, not at the sunrise but at me, and the next moment he jumped off his horse and tethered it to a tree and then came and stood beside Autumn and took his bridle.

'Won't you get down, too?' he asked.

'I can see better here,' I replied as gently and politely as I could.

'Please get down. I want to talk to you.'

'But why? Can't we talk like this?' I knew now what was coming. I'd been waiting for it and doing my best to prevent it.

'Please,' he asked again and took my hand as if to urge me and I knew that I had to do what he wanted and face what was happening. I slipped my feet out of the stirrups and swung myself down. I had hardly reached the ground when he flung his arms round me. When I pushed him away, he let me go.

'I'm sorry,' he said, 'I shouldn't have done that. I didn't mean to. But I love you so. I've loved you ever since you came and I had to tell you. Please forgive me.'

'Of course, and I'm so sorry,' I replied. 'I didn't want this to happen for even if I loved you too, nothing could come of it. I shall have to go away. It's awful, awful.' I was overcome myself now with pity and I felt that it was my fault for having allowed it to go as far as this.

'Don't go away. I don't want you to. I'll never bother you again, I promise. I'll never do anything to annoy you. But stay, please stay and let me go on loving you.'

I didn't answer and he went on raving, pouring out his love. Then, suddenly, he returned to his senses and looked at his watch.

'Good God, I'll be late for the office and my wife will be in hysterics.' Then he took my hand.

'May I kiss you before we go? Just this once, never again. Please?' He looked at me imploringly and, taking me in his arms, kissed me gently and respectfully on the cheek. Then we mounted our horses and galloped them back to the bungalow, saying that we had lost our way.

I told my mother what had happened and we both agreed that we could not drift on any longer. Several times a week the Birdwoods sent a car from Flagstaff House and the huge canvas, easel and paints were loaded into it. On other days she travelled long distances in a *tonga* to her other sitters. But this resumption of work did nothing to change our lives. She went just as a worker now and I might never have existed and when the Viceroy returned to Delhi and she went on with his portrait he, too, had lost interest. I knew now what had happened. I understood it all.

Mrs Harvey was in a dilemma, too, but she found an excellent way to solve it. She may not have been aware of her husband's hopeless passion but she was soon aware of the hopelessness of her own. When she understood what snobs we were, what humbugs and how out of reach, she first sulked, then grew angry and then disappeared. She locked herself in her room and took to her bed and we never set eyes on her again.

The house reverted to its normal state. The servants' clothes grew dingy and crushed, the white gloves and ceremony vanished from the dining-room, the food became still meaner and more badly cooked and a look of dismal sloppiness came over everything.

Most of this was a great relief and if it hadn't been for that locked room with the half-mad woman languishing inside discharging her neurosis through the doors and walls, we could have lived in the seedy house with Mr Harvey – love and all – quite pleasantly.

Then I thought of something I could do. I took a *tonga* into Old Delhi and bought a second-hand car for the equivalent of £20 and drove it away. Somehow, I got through the narrow streets, the bullock wagons, sacred cows, donkeys, goats and milling crowds of the old city and when I reached the broad straight highway leading out to New Delhi, I was cruising confidently along. I drove into the compound and stopped in front of the bungalow. Mr

Harvey and my mother were astonished. Fortunately, no driving tests were needed in those days and I bought my licence later.

Now I could escape. I drove about everywhere and soon discovered that the new Gymkhana Club was finished and that bungalows in the compound could be rented for the season. Already, even before the official opening, the club was the centre of New Delhi life and the attractive buildings and lively atmosphere made me long to live there.

When I found that the bungalows were already taken by important people I persuaded the manager, much against his will, to let us live in tents and two immense Public Works Department marquees were erected side by side, one for sleeping and the other, with the roof folded back, as a studio.

Until the twentieth century, tent life in India was a high form of living. Comfortable, well-equipped quarters could be created at a moment's notice and the British were quite content with canvas homes. The new Viceregal Lodge was not finished and tents still surrounded the old house, accommodating the Viceroy's staff and guests.

They were always large and high with double, specially ventilated roofs and netted windows. Electricity was laid on and the sweeper-type bathrooms were the same as prevailed in all the old houses. They were carpeted and often sumptuously furnished and always cool.

All the conquerors of India had built themselves a new Delhi and then been overwhelmed. When the British, in their turn, built the 7th capital city the native prophets cried their doom and the people smiled knowingly. And their city spread wider than all the others, their buildings were bigger and higher and heavier and they pushed away more of the jungle than any of the others and covered it with so much concrete, steel and stone that tents were no longer needed. They became despised antiquities, like wattle huts, and air-conditioned rooms and flush toilets were demanded by British and Indians alike. And this time, it seemed as if the prophecies were not to be fulfilled for the conquerors remained and appeared as strong as ever. But the subject people dressed in *khaddi* cloth and gathered passively, made bonfires of Lancashire cotton and disobeyed the laws and fasted and prayed – and knew what they knew.

Mr Harvey helped us move, loading his car with luggage and then, when we arrived, doing a bearer's menial things and all the time that he was fussing round our tents I was afraid he would be seen and I wanted him to go for, like the R.A.F. man who followed me to Simla, I was ashamed of him. But when he went at last, looking so pathetic – I was sad myself.

The club messing charge was only eight rupees a day and the rent of the tents, almost nothing. I had found a way of living at the centre of the world –

'our' world – within our means. If my mother never painted again and the hostesses ignored us I could still succeed for I knew that I had power over men. As my mother always said, 'I had only to be seen …' And here I would be seen. As an adventuress I would make my own way now and rise again upon the nature and indulgencies of men. I didn't give myself that name but I was one – unskilled, clumsy and still innocent.

Happy and excited, our good fortune seeming like a dream, we walked from our tents to the clubhouse for our first meal and when we found the tables filled with families from Simla, we rushed at them with joy. After the lonely months I wanted to embrace the girls I knew. They all smiled, enquired where we had been all this time and said how pleased they were to see us. But they weren't. They didn't want us. I was only an unwelcome competitor now in the ruthless Delhi marriage market.

On the first dance night, we sat alone at our table watching the gay dinner parties just as we had watched them when we first arrived in Simla. Afterwards, when the couples took the floor, I watched again. But not for long, not long enough to lose my pride – just long enough to be seen.

When Lady Irwin returned from England with a fashionable house-party, the Viceregal Court became more closed and grand than before and the A.D.C.'s reflected this in their tightened cautious manners. The ones I knew tried not to see me as I stood there. It was the men I didn't know, the Gordon Highlanders, who looked.

The regiment was quartered in cantonments in the jungle several miles outside the new city and the officers drove in to the parties and gathered for the great drinking hours before dinner every evening. It was they who chased the girls, were stalked by their mothers and who set the pace and gave the social life of Delhi its spirit and sparkle.

The next evening, I dressed carefully and went over to the club and sat down at a table and ordered myself a drink. They were all round me, aware of me, looking at me slyly but without a formal introduction, not daring to speak. And I kept my reserve. I finished my drink, flicked through some magazines and then got up and walked away.

The next day it was easier, we could dare to recognise each other and say 'good-evening' and before long, say something else. The unnatural code broke, they moved their chairs up, we talked – and I was 'in'. On the next dance night they left their parties and danced with me and the one they called Harold, came again and again. I was back in high society and once more I flung myself at everything.

Twice a week the Delhi Hunt met before dawn and a large and stylish field turned out to follow the hounds over rough jungle country. As soon as I heard about it I asked Mr Harvey if he would sell me Autumn. He wouldn't part with him but he offered to hire him out at five rupees a time – just something for the *syce* and the extra oats. I joined the Hunt, the prestigious game, mounted by the little *box-wallah.*

The night before my first Meet I danced until one o'clock, slept for three hours and then got up at four. It was icy cold. When the sun went down, the winter winds off the Himalayas brought frost to the Delhi nights. No one else from the Club was going and I had no bearer to help me start the car. I swung and swung the handle and drove away at last. I passed through the old city, dark and silent, the sleepers wrapped like mummies in their blankets, stretched out upon the pavements and the steps. When I reached the jungle road on the other side I saw first the reassuring lights of other cars and then, through the trees, the camp fires and hurricane lamps of the *syces.*

They had set off the day before and walked the horses and now, in little groups, they squatted round the fires with the blanketed horses tethered round them. They looked like cavalry waiting silently in the darkness before a battle and as I walked between the fires looking for Autumn, I felt as if I was going into battle myself.

I shivered with cold and fright. Other muffled figures were also searching for their horses or standing beside them, patting them, testing their girths and talking softly in Hindustani to their *syces.* When, for a moment, a lamp lit up a face that I knew I spoke, said something foolish, anything – just to draw courage from somebody.

I found Autumn and gave him sugar and stroked his head – and waited. When the first faint glimmer of light appeared the hounds were let out of their travelling box, the word was passed down and people threw off their top-coats and mounted their horses. I swung myself up onto Autumn.

It was still very dark as we filed through the narrow jungle paths and came out into a clearing. Then in the dawn light, I could see the Master out in front and the hounds padding round with their noses down, already picking up scent. We had two hours before the sun would rise and kill it.

The Master and Whips moved slowly off, the horn blew and the field, spreading widely out, went after them. Autumn was straining on the bit and shaking his head and snorting, his neck taut with excitement. We were already too far forward but he wanted to be up with the Master. He couldn't bear to have anyone in front of him. He always wanted to win and he looked like a beautiful steeplechaser.

I held him back and, nursing my joy and my terror, was conscious of everything; of his hoofs striking the ground, the jingle of his bridle, all his movements and the strong sweet smell of the jungle.

The Master broke into a trot, then into a canter and before I knew any more we were away at a gallop and the horn was blowing a find. Then the hounds veered and the ground changed, trees and thickets came and after that, some rocky terrain and a *nullah*, and Autumn plunged and swerved and galloped through them all and when we reached the next clearing we were level with the hounds, ahead of some of them, and one of the Whips shouted at me angrily.

But I was happy now as we galloped on. I didn't know how to ride. I had never learnt to grip with my knees. I rode by balance like a jockey. But I had kept on, even if I'd had to clutch the saddle-bow.

When I heard the horn again the sun was rising over the horizon, a great round staring face of fire. Autumn slackened at once when I pulled him up. He knew the run was over. I patted his neck. He was wet and white with sweat and needing a rest. We cantered gently to a clearing where the Whips were calling out the names of hounds, ordering in the stragglers. For the first time, in full daylight, I saw the whole Hunt. The Viceroy was there in pink coat – he was an M.F.H. himself in England. And Lady Irwin was beside him and Anne, his daughter and one of his sons, and all his staff and guests. And they drew together and kept themselves apart.

It was not a kill. Only a check and when the hounds were all back the Master drew away once more. The next moment, crashing through thick undergrowth, they began baying, the horn blew and we were galloping again. The sun was getting high now and the scent was failing as we approached a wide belt of thick impenetrable trees and I looked from side to side wondering which way to turn to get round it. Then, I caught sight of a narrow gap in the middle and a rider near me saw it, too, and spurred his horse and drew ahead. Autumn raged, his muscles leapt and he raced to overtake him. Then as he drew level, I saw what was coming. Deep in the tangled wood was a wall of prickly scrub, four feet high, completely closing the gap. And I had never jumped before!

I pulled him up and stopped him winning and let the other horse leap first. Then, as I gave him his head and tried to grip with my knees, he rose like a flying beast and I landed lying over his withers, my face on his neck, the stirrups dangling, my topee on my back. And he galloped on through the glade.

The horn blew again and the hunt was over. As we rode slowly back to the lines I bowed to the Viceroy when we drew near him and he spoke, praising Autumn. And I praised Autumn, too.

We never missed a Meet. Although we were always in the forefront I only once saw a jackal killed, saw the hounds despatch it quickly. It was not the chase that I cared about but the ride; two hours of galloping with horse and rider one, both straining together, both playing and loving the hard hazardous game. I was blind then to the meaning of the sport – blind to so many things.

Autumn taught me to ride and we shared many comic and a few quite scarifying experiences. He unseated me once and dropped me into a thorn bush. On another occasion, coming suddenly upon a deep wide fissure in the ground, he sat down on his haunches and slid to the bottom of it and then scrambled up the other side. On the day that we got lost we should have wandered forever if I hadn't dropped the reins and let him bring us back.

We were riding one day, towards the high, built-up bank of a *nullah*, or dried-up water-course, with a line of closely planted trees growing along the top of it and only one place wide enough to ride through. One of the A.D.C.'s was ahead, making for this gap and when he reached it he passed through it and disappeared. But when Autumn and I neared the top and I could see down into the *nullah*, there was no sign of him and when we gained the top there, beneath us, was an enormous crater with horse and rider at the bottom of it. I jabbed my heels into Autumn's flanks and he jumped it – hole, horse and man. It was his greatest jump of all – and my greatest moment.

6

Harold

THE Viceroy's portrait dragged on until, in despair, my mother again abandoned it; then, finishing the others, she retreated into herself with nothing else to do but watch protectively (as she thought) over me while I, forgetting my task and losing all sense of my golden thread, advanced ever more surely towards ends which seemed demented.

The Club was the ground of the Gordons. When I fell among them I fell into a clique. But even if I had seen how narrow it was I would not have tried to change it for I loved it and was proud of it – it made me feel safe and belonging. It was another, inner kind of narrowness that I was first aware of.

At the beginning, I knew that several of the subalterns were interested in me yet, only one of them advanced. As if by agreement, as if they had drawn lots for me, the others all retired leaving Harold alone in the field. I tried hard to break this boycott but their sudden indifference, albeit friendly, was as firm and unshakeable as a battalion order and in the end I had to give up trying. Their solidarity was absolute.

Without any skirmishing, Harold pressed relentlessly forward and I was driven into the position of having to accept his attentions or offend the whole regiment. I was in a trap yet the kilts and the pipes were so dazzling, the romance of it all so powerful that they clouded my senses and transformed my situation and made me glad as well as troubled to be inside its splendid bars. And there was nothing outside it. The trap was the only life I could envisage. I had been caught and claimed and now I waited to be taken, my right to be myself already gone.

Soon we were all paired off. Each man picked a girl for the season and his choice was sacrosanct. I was caught and didn't like it but the others did and tried their hardest to draw their men on into marriage while the men, for their part, cared little about the girls, ran them down and laughed at them behind their backs and only used them as dancing and sleeping partners.

I looked them all up in the Army List and Harold's name did not impress me. He was not aristocratic (his father was only a doctor), he had not gone to Eton or to Harrow, he didn't dress well, he had no money – and he was not even good looking. But he had strength of character and his status and stature were enlarged by the magic of the regiment and when he was in uniform he was transfigured. Then I saw, not the commonplace little man but a proud Highlander and the power of this myth still affected me.

I danced with him and followed him round Delhi because it was exciting to have a Gordon Highlander pursuing me; because I always looked for experience and knowledge, always forced myself a little further, through pleasure or through pain towards an end that was either good or bad – and because he would not let me stop. If I had I would have been down among the *box-wallahs* again.

He could not afford to keep both a car and polo ponies and one night, sitting late with me, he let all the others go without him and I had to take him back to cantonments and then return alone through the jungle. After that, he expected me to do it every night. Another girl did it – so why shouldn't I?

My mother objected at once. It was dangerous, she said. The car could break down and it wasn't right for a man to let a girl do such a thing. I resented her interference but felt bewildered. I wanted to take him and yet I didn't. It wasn't right and yet it was. And if I hadn't he would have been annoyed. The world was different now and girls were different. I went on doing it and these night rides became fixtures like everything else. But in that close tropical environment the fixtures changed quickly and remorselessly.

Every night, when the dances ended, the couples got into their cars and drove to some wild spot which they had made their own and I supposed they did what we did – embraced and kissed and talked. When Harold did more than that, when his hands began to roam about my body I didn't like it and I pushed him away. Just like Sir Vincent then, he sat back and sulked and then tried again. Then, on one apocalyptic night, I learnt the meaning of it all. He taught me what Sir Vincent had been wanting all the time and what the other couples did and what I would have to do now and learn to like.

We were in our favourite place, a glade beneath the walls of the Purana Kila, the old fort lying along the banks of the Jumna. We had first climbed up onto the wide, grass-grown ramparts and looked down upon the tangled Mogul garden lying forgotten and neglected, the dried-up, dust-filled marble ponds still white and dazzling in the moonlight. Now, we were inside the car again and Harold was kissing me and holding me so tightly that I could hardly breathe. Then, stopping, he looked hard into my eyes with an expression that was brutal. 'Do you want me as much as I want you?' he asked.

I didn't know what he meant. I supposed it was an odd way of asking me if I loved him and liked being with him and wanting to please him, I said – yes.

'Take your dress off,' he said excitedly and he began unhooking it and pulling it over my head. I couldn't think why he should suddenly do this but his intensity was so communicative that by the time he had taken all my clothes off, although I knew nothing, I knew with my whole body-mind what was going to happen to me. And I didn't want it – but I wouldn't turn back. I wanted the experience, the knowledge, an end and a conclusion and for these I let him force me onwards.

'Darling, do you want me to undress, too?' And when again I gave him the answer that he wanted, he jumped out of the car and tore off all his clothes. Then he spread a rug under a tree.

'Get out, darling,' he ordered me.

I crept out, trying to cover myself foolishly and lay down. The moon was at its full and he stood for a moment in its sharp light looking down on me and I looked up at him – looked up at his nakedness. Then he fell upon me and in spite of my foreknowledge, what he did was so unexpected and so shocking that when it was over I was stupefied. It was more than an end, it was a very centre I had reached and the knowledge that was waiting for me there, tore and shook me.

We dressed and sat a long time in the car and then, in a half-conscious state, I drove him back to cantonments. I let him keep me there again, still submissive and receptive. There was no stopping for at the centre was a new beginning. Knowledge danced ahead upon each point of Time, at every turn and within every form and situation. I was already setting off again.

It was nearly five o'clock when I got back to the club. The light was on in the sleeping tent and my mother was up, in a frightened angry state.

'What have you been doing?' she cried out. 'I've been worried to death. I thought something awful had happened to you. I daren't wake the Grimshaws to find out if Barbara was late, too. I was afraid of giving you away. It would have been all round Delhi today. But in the end I rang up the Police.'

'I'm sorry,' I said in a sulky resentful tone. 'We were talking and I didn't notice how the time was passing.'

'Have you been making love to him?' she went on. 'If you do that he'll soon give you up. A man soon tires of a girl he's once made love to. And they'll all know. They tell each other. You'll get a bad name and no one else will look at you. Men don't marry second-hand girls.'

I was shocked by this outburst. I thought I was free and now my mother was constantly criticising me, trying to control me and giving me advice which made no sense in the context of the life that I was leading. I got into bed without saying another word, my mind in a turmoil. I understood now how all the other couples spent their time together. I understood the jokes I'd heard, the giggles and the stories. If everyone was doing this how could it be so wrong? And even if I didn't want to do it how could I be different from the others and say 'no' to Harold? And if this was the first law of living, the basic fact of existence, the thing that moved the world – Nature's Centre – it was grotesque and abominable and that I should have to descend and go from one terrible centre to another, appalled me.

Harold expected to make love every night now. He praised my beauty and pressed his own demands and flattered, intimidated, inquisitive, I bent before these forces and made myself accept him, calling it the inescapable act. Sometimes, however, it got so on my nerves, the physical dislike which overlaid my anguish, that I pushed him away and wept.

On one of these occasions, incredulous and exasperated, he remarked, 'I like to see you cry. It shows you *do* have some feeling. You always seem so cold.' But soon he moved things on again. He asked me to marry him.

I was glad. He had not grown tired of me as my mother said he would and I felt a little less inferior, less helpless and less used. I was still in the trap but I was caught with dignity although my dilemma was now even worse.

To have accepted him at once would have ended all my social struggles. My mother could have rested and the security and status would have made me free to go on to the next goal. But the pity was that I didn't want to marry him. I didn't love him. I only loved the regiment and if I turned him down I knew that I could never capture one of the others.

I gave no answer. But he didn't mind. He was too confident to care. He waited cheerfully until the next night and then asked again.

There were moments when I felt strong enough to reject him and break my whole life up again and others when I was weak and ready to make the best of him and take all the material things he could provide – and endure his love.

When I still gave no answer he wasn't so patient but he waited again and in the meantime, I told my mother.

'Can't you keep him dangling?' she said. 'He's a nice little man and a Gordon Highlander would be a good marriage. You might not get anyone better.'

She had criticised Harold so much and I was sure she didn't like him and would be sorry if I married him. She, herself, had not married for love but for her own special reason, yet she had always hoped that I would. I saw how frightened she, too, must be. But I didn't know how to keep him 'dangling'.

'Darling, why can't you say "yes"?' he demanded on the 3rd night. 'Why do you go on making me wait? You know all about me now, you know I'm not a wet' (according to him nearly every other man was). 'You know how I adore you and we get on so well together. You really *must* say yes and settle it.' His vehemence paralysed me more than ever.

'But, darling, I can't. Because I don't know yet ... I'm not sure yet ...'

'Why don't you know? You love me. You like me making love to you. When we're married we'll do it all day long. Please, please make up your mind.'

I was silent altogether and felt like crying. We parted early that night and when he got back to cantonments the mess was still full. He went straight to the Colonel and stood stiffly before him. He described this scene proudly to me later.

'Sir,' he said brazenly, 'I'm engaged to be married.'

'Congratulations, old chap!' the Colonel replied heartily, slapping him on the back. 'I'm glad to hear you've fixed things up at last. That girl of yours will make a splendid regimental wife.' Then he turned and called out sharply to a mess orderly. 'MacGregor, bring a bottle of champagne.'

The other officers gathered round and they drank Harold's health and my health and the health of the regiment. And that was how I got engaged.

Early the next morning I was woken by girls' voices and the next moment they came bursting into the tent.

'We've heard the news! It's all round Delhi! Congratulations!' they all cried out together, envying me – not for marriage itself, not for security and status like me but because there was nothing else for them to do. And the pace and pressures were severe. If they were unsuccessful the first season they were already considered stale and after a second season they had to look lower, take whatever they could get, or try somewhere else. When one of their number succeeded and a wedding was announced their joy was genuine for it increased their own chances by removing a competitor and turning her into a friend and helper, vibrating all existing relationships and making the very atmosphere suggestive.

I was flabbergasted and I didn't know what to say. And so, once more, I said nothing. When they had gone I dressed and went over to the Club for breakfast and the fathers of the girls, the generals and the colonels, their mothers and everyone else rushed up to me smiling, and throughout the day people came, all smiling and acclaiming me, for there was nothing dubious about me any more. I was marrying into the regiment, marrying a Gordon Highlander – I was really one of them now! And my silence all day long sealed the lines of that absurd affair.

It was a few days before my 21st birthday and, in the same week, I received a letter from Miss Morison telling me that when I did not go to Cambridge, the money for the college fees had been placed by my sponsors (of which she was one) in a bank and would now be paid to me upon my coming of age. She hoped that I would spend it wisely. She hoped that I was happy. She loved me still and hoped that I had changed and was now the person that I ought to be and that she had longed to make me. A cheque came from a solicitor for £300. Not enough to set me free but enough and just in time to buy my trap and re-gild it.

I paid off all our debts and then entertained and ran up new ones, I bought a better car and then put the rest aside for the grand wedding that everyone expected and I, myself, wanted.

I rejected Cambridge and chose another university which also had its fees and this money helped to pay them. Who can say which fees were more proper, which path was more wise for there are fees for every path and wisdom lies along them all.

Our engagement was the event of the season and Harold and I were feted everywhere. All the people who had dropped me now entertained me and in the new car we sped from place to place, banqueted, toasted and embraced. Even the Viceroy took new interest and summoned us to dine.

'Has he money?' he asked my mother when he saw her later.

'No,' she replied, 'but that doesn't really matter.'

'It matters very much,' he went on solemnly. 'In every marriage money is a most important thing.'

The noise and whirl of the merry-go-round stopped me thinking and bouncing up and down upon the painted horses made me believe that I was happy.

Late every night, when these celebrations were over, we drove to the Kutab Minar, an ancient tower rising high out of the jungle (still used, from time to time, by high-caste Indians for delicate murders) or to our favourite spot by the Red Fort. Often, when the moon was large, we crept through a gateway into the abandoned garden and walked along a path, bathed in the heavy scent of flowers, to a dainty pavilion paved round with wonderful mosaics. The Mogul emperors had lived inside this fort and strolled about this garden with their wives. Sometimes, we sat down upon a low marble seat and sometimes went on further to a doorway that led out to the river, the quiet and fallen Jumna flowing sluggishly between its muddy banks. And the beauty and mystery of these places tricked away reality and lifted me somewhere beyond.

In the daytime I went about with the Delhi girls. Judy was one of those who burst into the tent that morning. She was fat and exuberant and her affair with Robert was not going well. In her case, my mother was right. He was tired of her but she clung to him despairingly and he cursed and complained every day in the mess and even asked Harold how he would shake her off. It was all very touchy for her father was important and so was Robert's military career.

Her cousin, Clara, had been invited out for the winter by her illustrious relatives to help her to escape from a dull life at home – and find a husband. When she arrived, she looked such a simple, dowdy little country maid but soon she was the most abandoned and scheming of us all.

One day, several of us were wandering listlessly in an old garden, picking mangoes as we talked when, suddenly, she shot off like a missile and with her head down, tore round and round as if she had gone mad. We stared at her in consternation, until a tall attractive boy gave chase. She smiled when she saw him coming and flew on even faster, circling the trees and darting in and out among the flowers and bushes. Then, she slowed her pace and let him gain on her but when she was nearly caught she threw her head back, laughed and sped away once more. And this went on and on, this running, pursuing and wild laughter – until she dropped exhausted. When the satyr picked her up and carried her away, the nymph screamed with joy.

Jane lived at the Club. She was one of the colonels' daughters, big and bony with chunks of jet black hair, black-brown ogling eyes and an enormous devouring mouth. Her mother thought her marvellous and was always pushing and priming her, never having noticed how stupid she was. At first she never spoke, not because she was young and shy but because she had nothing whatever to say.

'Jane, my darling,' we often heard her mother telling her, 'you *must* learn to talk. You'll never get on unless you talk. When you go to a dinner party the only thing you need to do is *talk* to the men each side of you. It doesn't matter what you say so long as you keep talking.'

Jane lapped up these lessons slowly and when she learnt at last to talk she never stopped. She talked and she talked, the most inane, insane, unutterable rubbish. And just as her mother had told her she became a dazzling social success, although she only married a Tank Corps man – very low on the pyramid. I suppose a colonel for a father-in-law outweighed the torture of her tongue.

Occasionally Anne Wood, the Viceroy's daughter, joined our parties accompanied by an A.D.C. and a chaperone, a kind of lady-in-waiting. But she always kept aloof, conscious all the time of her position and the Court that ringed and cushioned her, surveying us with cold critical eyes, her mouth hard and unsmiling, looking as if she felt that she had fallen among riff-raff. And in that clearly graded society, she had. Even the illustrious regiments of the Highland Brigade were a shade of a shade lower in degree than the Guards or the Cavalry Corps. Even the Scottish peers were a shade of a shade less grand than English ones. The nearer to the top the finer and more subtle became the distinctions. It was never persons in themselves who were regarded but the forms and families they represented.

One night, about this time, I woke hearing my mother shouting.

'Go away! Go away at once or I'll call the *chowkidar.*'

I heard bumping, grinding noises and I jumped up and sprang to the centre pole where the lighting switch was fixed and turned it on. Lurching from side to side, foaming at the mouth and biting and snapping at everything it bumped into, was a rabid jackal. Horrified, I watched it roll about until the light drove it finally away.

It had woken my mother biting at her bed and we found the sheets in ribbons round her pillows and blood and slime everywhere. In spite of the pink coats and tireless galloping of the Delhi Hunt, the jackals roamed in constant numbers round the outskirts of the cities, often penetrating the gardens of the bungalows. I used to lie in bed at night listening to their barking and eerie, wake-like howls, rising and falling in waves as the packs came close and then receded.

My daily conversations with Harold were rather limited in range. We never over-stepped by so much as half a thought the line drawn heavily around the people that we knew, the life we lived – and the regiment. And of these, the regiment of course, came first. Harold could talk of it for hours on end, recounting what went on every moment of every day. At first, I was intensely interested for it reminded me of the delirious months of my childhood spent with the soldiers in Victoria. As I listened, I could see the kilted Jocks, catch the liquid lilt of their speech and rub against their strength and lively natures: I could perform every duty, obey every order and even give the top commands until soon I had so identified myself with the regiment that I felt that it was mine as much as his.

I shared this passion with him for a long time and even when it became harder and harder to respond, to live totally inside the regiment like this, I did not admit to myself that I was bored. The only evident change in me was my attempt to introduce other topics. I tried everything. I even questioned him about his boyhood and family and related incidents from my own life. But nothing roused him. He never even listened but just waited politely until I stopped and he could start again – get back to the regiment.

I had never revealed to anyone, anywhere, my addiction to socialism. I would have lost my job at Downing Street even sooner than I did and here, in high and low society alike, had this heresy been known to be secreted inside me, like some loathesome micro-organism, I would have been damned at once.

But this secret now began to worry me. The man I was going to marry must know everything about me. I couldn't let him find out afterwards what sort of woman I really was. The great task lying concealed ahead of me was still so vague that I decided not to mention it – at least not for the present. But my socialism, yes, that I had to confess as soon as I could and I was certain it would stun him. If he wasn't interested in anything else I talked about, he couldn't help being struck by this, so heavily perhaps that he would break off our engagement. The next night I waited nervously for an opening.

'Darling, I've got something very important to tell you,' I blurted out at last.

'Have you, my sweet? What is it?' he replied in the jolliest of tones.

'It's ... it's something about myself that I feel you ought to know.'

He changed at once. 'Another chap?' he asked sharply.

'No. No. Nothing like that,' I answered, glad to be innocent at least in one respect. 'It's about politics.'

'Oh!' His guffaw was almost hilarious.

'I think you ought to know, darling, that I'm a socialist. I think that a society in which there are poor, some terribly poor, and rich, some terribly rich, is all wrong. It isn't fair that a few, the capitalists, should exploit the many, turn them into wage-slaves and expropriate the surplus value. And socialism is the only way to stop this. Only by nationalising the means of production, distribution and exchange shall we be able to establish the good society in which everyone is free and equal and happy. That's why I *have* to be a socialist.'

I rattled off all these Marxist clichés passionately, hoping that their power would move him and induce him to take a tolerant view of my near-criminal opinions and then I looked at his blank face and waited for it to turn purple with rage. When it didn't and he went on calmly staring at me I was afraid that I hadn't made it clear enough.

'When you really understand how strongly I feel about the poor I know you'll agree with me that socialism is ...'

'Stop! Stop! My darling girl! Let's not talk about this any more. Of course I'm sorry for the poor. But why do you worry so? When we're married you'll forget it. Now let me kiss you. My kisses will settle all these problems and make you happy again.' And he put his arms round me. But I didn't respond. I could have cried with humiliation and fury. But what could I do? Rebel and break it up? I swallowed it down and with everything else it lay protesting inside me.

The winter was moving on and although my life was so enclosed and hectic I knew a little of what was happening beyond; that Gandhi had arrived in the old city and was burning cloth and stirring up the people, that there was rioting in places. I knew that it was the month of *Ramadan* when the Muslims fast from dawn to sundown and their tempers are uncertain but as I dashed about in my car I saw nothing and didn't worry.

The polo ground had not been moved yet. It was still on the outskirts of Old Delhi and to avoid going through the centre of the city I used to take a road which ran along the outside of the great wall behind which were the temples and mosques, the huddled houses and bazaars and the teeming crowds of the ancient Indian quarter.

One afternoon, I took this road as usual. There were few people about, they were all at work inside – and no traffic at all. The only thing ahead of me was a stationary *tonga* on the near-side, with the driver and a friend standing talking at the pony's head and a little girl playing in the dust behind it.

As I approached it, the child ran out into the road but I braked hard and she got safely across. I accelerated again and drew level with the *tonga*, then level with the horse and, as I did so, her little brother ran out from behind the horse and the two men – straight in front of the car.

I could have swerved to the left and avoided him but then I would have hit the pony and the two men. I swerved violently the other way, the child hit the radiator and fell between the wheels and I ran over it and then crashed into a tree on the other side of the narrow road.

I scrambled out of the car and saw the child lying as if dead. My one thought as I rushed towards him was to get him into the *tonga* and race to the hospital. As I reached him, a small crowd sprung from nowhere, and the next moment when the child moved, sat up and yelled, they were pouring through the gateway and I found myself surrounded by an ever-growing multitude. Then, again like magic, a young Indian doctor emerged.

'Can you help me get the child into the *tonga*?' I shouted at him.

He smiled in a sweet friendly way, the *tonga* was dragged through the packed mass and he clambered into it and the child was lifted up to him. But by that time, I was being so jostled that I couldn't get near it and as it moved slowly away without me, I called out helplessly, 'You look after him. I'll come later.' Engulfed I stood watching them go.

The people had only me to look at and think about now and their mood changed from concern for their own – to revenge. My Hindustani wasn't good enough to speak to them, explain how it had happened and express my own sorrow. I could only stand there in the middle of them, in the heat and smell of their bodies, the shouts growing louder, their arms waving and hate in their eyes.

Then, another miracle occurred. Two Englishmen (plain clothes police I learnt afterwards) pushed through to me and stood each side of me, using their bicycles as barriers.

'We've got to get you out of this quick,' one of them said. 'They're shouting murder but they're always slow to get worked up.'

We fought our way to another *tonga* which stood surrounded and they helped me climb into it, people trying to stop me, pushing and clutching me. I sat behind the driver, facing backwards, and looked down and round upon the crowd. The whole city must have emptied out. But we didn't move. They were shouting at the driver and holding up the pony. The policemen shouted at him, too, and one of them forced his way to the pony's head and pulled him forward. Slowly then, we moved and with my two escorts and their bicycles I sat raised above this black angry sea, knowing that at any moment I might be torn from my seat.

I knew that I mustn't show fear and as I sat without moving, without changing my expression, I was sure that I could dominate and hold them and I turned my head imperceptibly from side to side and went from face to face, picking up their eyes, speaking to them, commanding them, fixing them – with mine. And I planned what I would do if this should fail.

At the first sign of a surge or if one of them came at me, I meant to jump over the seat, seize the reins and whip from the driver and push him out, for he was small and weak, slash the horse into a gallop and make a run for it. But I never had to for soon they were quiet, marching passively all round me and when we reached a crossroad at the end of the city wall we picked up two uniformed Indian policemen. Part of the crowd then melted back inside the wall and the pony moved a little faster. The procession went on dwindling and when we reached the police-station, only the fanatics were left.

I wrote out my account of the accident and then looked for my rescuers but they were gone, once more patrolling the inflamed areas. When I returned in an open truck filled with armed police and two inspectors, the place was as empty and innocent as when I first drove through it and my car, embedded in the tree, was untouched.

When the measurements had been taken and my recapitulation was concluded, I was advised not to go to the hospital at once and, if asked, not to give any money. The child was alright, they said.

I took a *tonga* to the polo-ground and found Harold still playing. When his game ended and I told him what had happened, he showed little concern. He found it hard to imagine that such experiences were real.

I went to see the child a few days later. He was sitting on his *charpoy* with his little sister, both of them quite happy in their solemn Indian way. I was being dunned for money by their father, a *mullah*, but I could take them sweets.

The Delhi Horse Show and Highland Brigade Week brought the season to a brilliant and exciting close. Around the Lion Rampant of Scotland, drooping from its flagpole, a great camp arose and, first horses and then competitors from the Scottish regiments in India, converged on Delhi. From dawn to sundown the skirl of pipes blasted the pensive posture of the *maidan* and then floated off into the jungle, stirring the heavy air and easing the dark troubled ground, and a host of stalwart stamping Jocks and a variety of tartans turned the flaking dried-up city into a little Scotland and the dusty polo ground into a cool, mist-laden moor – gathering-place of the clans.

The Gordons were the host regiment and when Harold was the officer-on-duty and I watched him walking round among the people in his heavy swinging kilt, his sword with its great red tassle hanging straight at his side, I was proud of him. Even my mother remarked how fine he looked. And when he bent over the back of my seat and talked to me from time to time, showing the world that he was mine, I glowed with satisfaction. At last I was sitting in the special enclosure with the right coloured badge pinned to my dress – possessing the man who possessed the show.

The glittering fortnight ended with the Highland Ball. For days beforehand we had been practising the reels and when the great night came I wore a new white dress with a sash of the Gordon tartan round my shoulder and Harold wore his dress kilt and scarlet tunic. And the Colonel danced with me and paid me homage and with bands and pipes and dancing and the smiles of all the approving people, I was formally and finally received into the regiment. I was the darling of the night and at the zenith of my popularity and importance.

After three years in India, Harold was due for home leave and he didn't want to lose it. He wanted me to return to England with him and get married there. But I wouldn't. This was my last chance to be alone again, myself again, to see and think and feel without him. And so we planned for him to spend half his leave in England and then return to Simla for our wedding.

When I saw him off at the station he was happy and confident, looking forward to seeing his friends, buying clothes and having a good time and he was sure that the wedding preparations would keep me busy, that his love would keep me happy and that my waiting time would not seem long. We embraced cheerfully and waved until the dust obscured us.

When I got back to the Club, I found my mother talking to some new friends. These people were spending a few weeks in India visiting their son, a subaltern in the 4th Huzzars at Meerut. I had seen them all at the Club before but never met them. My mother had somehow picked them up that morning and liked them, and they were joining us for lunch.

They were very grand and aristocratic – and they looked it. The Colonel was a little senile and she was not impressive in herself but her money (she came from a great industrial family) and her manner masked that easily, for her clothes, her jewels and her captivating arrogance would have fitted any duchess. As for their son, John, with his close, grey, apprehensive eyes, sensitive face, beautiful hands and pale smooth skin – he was the most patrician of them all. I thought him fascinating and I enjoyed the lunch although I did not expect to see any of them again.

Now that I was alone and could think once more, it was not the tyranny of my situation and desires; not the tyranny of love – for I was not in love; not even the tyranny of the unknown task and all the questing and experiencing; not the tyranny of existence itself – but the tyranny of men that troubled me.

I had trimmed my speech and actions to fit the attitudes and predjudices of high society as soon as I climbed into it. I had done the same at No.10 and before that at school. I had come to accept that the instrument of pretence was needed in every society for maintaining personal relationships and a modicum of social harmony and not since I was a child, abroad, had I been truly myself. And now the disabling hand lay even heavier.

I had not just pretended all these months but, chained to Harold, I had lost the power to speak at all – and move. Owned and ordered, I had spoken with his voice and moved as he pulled me and all the girls had been like that with their men, puppets dancing on their strings in the show which was written and played as they wanted it, for the open employment of their power. When the train moved that morning and we broke apart, the strings were cut and, when later I met John, I thought I saw a man who would not want, and would never try, to play with dolls.

It seemed to me now that woman's beauty was just another trick of nature to expose her, like a bright berry, and make her tempting to devour.

The weather was very hot now and we joined the crowds going up to Simla. Not to the Cecil again but to one of the cheap hotels, the Grand, for I did not need to be seen and make a show now.

I knew the girls that I wanted for my bridesmaids but I did not ask them; I knew the *durzi* who would make my dress but I did not go to him; I knew the church that we would marry in but I did not call upon the vicar; and when Harold wrote every week asking for the date I replied with clever vagaries. While I procrastinated, with everybody waiting and watching and entertaining me, the presents poured in. From all over India and from England too. (Harold had put an announcement in *The Times*). Miss Morison sent something fine and Amy delivered up the family silver tea-service which she had appropriated years before from Campden Hill. I opened the parcels as they came and looked coldly at their contents as if they had nothing to do with me and the pile in the corner grew bigger and bigger. Sometimes I felt that it would bury me before I had decided what to do. I did no conscious thinking but just waited in a numbed, uncomfortable state. Then, suddenly, I knew. I saw my golden thread.

I telephoned Judy and asked her to come to see me and she dashed excitedly along. When she came into the room and saw the pile in the corner she gazed at it with envy and then slopped into a chair and waited to be told that she was chief bridesmaid. I remained standing and looked frigidly down on her.

'Judy,' I said, 'I've asked you here to tell you that I'm not going to marry Harold. I've changed my mind.'

When she left she rushed to the Cecil and flung her fat self upon the cocktail crowd and gave out the news and within an hour, it was all over Simla – and I was out. Angrily and viciously pushed out. I wrote to Harold and began posting back the presents.

About a fortnight later, when the worst of the uproar had died down and a ring of silence had grown round me, I was walking along The Mall when, riding towards me, was John of the 4th Huzzars. He jumped down and talked and seemed in no hurry. He had just arrived from Meerut on 10 days leave and had not had time to hear my news and all that was being said about me. When he rode on and I walked on, I turned to look at him again – and he turned, too. I was in love.

7

Simla and John

I KNEW that Harold would never be heartbroken and I struck as gently as I could. I wrote a long wordy letter saying that I did not feel like getting married yet and as it would not be fair to keep him waiting, I thought it best to break off our engagement. I even said how fond of him I still was. I did not want him ever to know how he had been taken in by all my acting and pretending. And so I went on pretending.

He was shocked and upset, certainly, but still confident. He had read my letter over and over again, he said, trying to understand how I was feeling and he was quite willing to postpone our wedding but he could see no reason for breaking off our engagement.

He was so sure that he could easily change me round as soon as he saw me again but he did not upset his leave and hurry back to do it and it took several more circumlocutory letters from me and dull, ill-written replies, to make things absolutely definite. His world had crashed, he said then, but only his vanity and pride were really hurt and the real cry came when he told me that he was trying for a posting somewhere else as he could not return to Delhi to face the regiment.

Although John was very distant when we first met, I was sure that he liked me and when he dismounted from his horse in The Mall and talked and then turned afterwards to look at me again, I was even more sure. Yet, when he heard that I was free, even if he didn't listen to the gossip and didn't care that I was ostracised and isolated, I knew that he would never advance and that I would have to do the chasing. He was more than just shy; he seemed frightened, suspicious and elusive and it was these mysterious things together with a sad, lonely expression which so attracted me. I had always hated having to make the first advance but as an adventuress I had had to make myself into an attacker and so, I now disposed all my powers for the pursuit.

The first move was the difficult one. From any direct approach I knew he would recoil at once and so make a second attempt still harder and another fortuitous encounter seemed impossible to devise. So I decided to give a party.

On the ragged fringes there were a few young girls and men still pleased to be entertained by me and I arranged a small party and sent a formal invitation to John. To my delight he accepted and the hope that this gave me increased the nervous force that I was summoning up and using.

The Grand Hotel was a boring, second-rate place yet I planned to hold my party there for I didn't want to be seen and talked about anymore. I wanted to keep my life as secret as I could. Then, at lunchtime on the day, a note was brought to me. I recognised John's handwriting and knew, before I opened it, that he was refusing after all.

That morning, he wrote, he had been licked by a dog suspected of rabies and he was leaving at once for the Pasteur Institute at Kasauli and regretted so much having to miss my party.

There was a lot of rabies about and everyone was scared. I knew that the treatment took several days and that by the time it was finished John's leave would be over and unless I followed him to Meerut, I might never meet him again. For a few moments I felt as if my life had collapsed once more. Then, I remembered the trick that I had played at Downing Street and, instantly, I decided to play it again.

'I'm going to Kasauli too,' I said to my mother. 'Why can't I say that I've been licked by a rabid dog and must have the treatment and when I meet him there I'll pretend that I never received his letter, that I left before it came.'

My mother loved this sort of drama and she threw herself into it excitedly. I ordered a car and while I was packing she telephoned to the guests cancelling the party, explaining in agitated tones the terrible thing that had happened to me. Within half an hour we were on the road to Kasauli, a thousand feet lower in the Simla hills.

At first, as we drove along, I felt buoyed up by the boldness and brilliance of my plan but as we neared the place I grew more and more frightened and by the time that we arrived, the whole plot seemed utterly crazy. I thought I must be mad and if it hadn't been for that demonic thing in me which always drove me on to the end whatever the end might be, I would certainly have ordered the driver to stop the car and return to Simla. But if I had, I would have loathed myself. I would never have forgiven myself. My mother sat smiling beside me and jumped out happily when we got there.

It was a very small hill-station, just a handful of bungalows but, to my dismay, there were two hotels – both much the same in appearance. It was imperative to stay where John was staying and I could hardly ask before I booked a room for I wasn't supposed to know that he was there and they might have thought it helpful to tell him of the enquiry. I made a wild guess – I called it my intuition – and led the way towards one of them and we walked in. I looked quickly round for John and then went up to the desk.

'I want a single room for a few nights,' I said to the Indian receptionist.

'Will you give me the register to sign, please?'

He opened it and before he had turned it round and placed it in front of me I had seen John's small but striking signature standing out like a magical figure, a few lines up from the last name.

I pointed to it silently and my mother nodded and smiled. Then I signed my own name, trying to make my signature look as fine and distinguished as his. After that, we had tea in the empty lounge and then we walked out to the car and I watched her drive away. I was alone now with my mad adventure.

I unpacked and settled myself in my room and then dressed carefully for dinner, all the time rehearsing the scene to be played. If my acting talent failed me now and John saw through my desperate plot he might well be more frightened of me than of rabies and run from the place at once.

I went into the lounge early and, choosing a favourable chair, ordered myself a drink. The people staying there were all taking the treatment and I was glad to be able to talk to someone. And then, in the hall outside, I heard voices, young men's voices – John's voice. I was thrilled. I was terrified.

They came in together, three of them, and I looked up boldly, straight at John – and John looked straight at me. And then I acted and I lied as I'd never done before. He came up to me in a bewildered way and my bewilderment was even greater. He could hardly speak for astonishment and my surprise was so intense that I could only gasp.

'But … but … what are you doing here? I … I … thought you were in Simla … giving a party?' he said.

'But I thought *you* were in Simla? What are *you* doing here? I had to cancel the party. Didn't you get my message?'

'No. But didn't *you* get mine, saying that I couldn't come, that I'd had to leave suddenly for Kasauli?' he answered, still more bewildered.

'No. I must have left before it came. I was licked by a rabid dog in The Mall and had to leave at once. All the dogs have got it. It's raging there.'

'But so was I. I stroked the dog at the club and it licked my hand and then it gave me such a queer look that I was sure it wasn't right, so I wrote you a note and came straight off here. I'm terrified of rabies – aren't you?'

'Yes. I am. Who wouldn't be? But isn't it extraordinary that we should both be licked by mad dogs at the same moment.'

He was sitting beside me now, animated and happy and I was happy too, for I had played my part successfully and I knew that the rest would be easy.

He ordered drinks, then several more in quick succession and our talk grew so exciting, our friendship developed so rapidly that we forgot all about dinner and were left sitting in the lounge by ourselves. Then, we both woke up.

'Can we dine together,' he asked. 'I was going to eat with those two fellows. They're here for treatment, too. But they won't care. And I'd much rather dine with you.' And he bent forward and looked into my eyes. And I adored him. He was the most fascinating man I'd ever known, ever seen, ever imagined.

We went into the dining-room. The other diners had nearly finished and some were leaving. We sat down and he picked up the wine list.

'We'll drink champagne,' he said. 'We couldn't have the party in Simla – so we'll have it here. I hated this place until I found you. I was feeling so unhappy. But now I love it and we must celebrate. Drink to this meeting in Kasauli!'

I was already a little drunk and I nearly added, 'let us drink to the mad dogs that sent us here,' but the idea was too bitter and grotesque and I had the sense to stop myself.

Alone in the dining-room, the meal was a long-drawn-out delirious affair. We talked and drank toast after toast and when it was over, walked out into the woods. It was a marvellous star-crowded night as we strolled along a path which led through the scrub to the edge of the mountain. We stopped talking. The warm, dry, fragrant air was like a seeing, hearing, conscious thing about us and I sang and danced inside. I sang the sweet song of my success and the shrill one of my power and turned and turned until I was giddy with love and the frenzy of my dancing and with my feet, my hands, my heart, my whole glad whirling body, prayed that this mad mountain dream might go on and on forever.

The path ended in a scrub-covered bank and we peered over it, down onto the night-hidden plain. Some lights were just visible far below – beyond them, soft brown-black infinity. Small night-sounds rang sharply out from the jungle slopes all round us. Then I spoke.

'How long have you been in India,' I asked.

'Two years now and I've another year to go.'

'Do you like it – the country and the life?'

'I hate it. I don't like the Indians and I don't like the British in India. The Indians are stupid weaklings and the British are stupid up-jumps. Give me the Arabs – they're the people that I love.'

'Arabs?' I said with surprise, 'do you know them?'

'I was stationed in Cairo for a year and I learnt Arabic and lived in the desert. They're men, really men – hard, brave, honourable and loyal. I mean to go back there. As soon as I can get out of the army I shall join the Sudan Political Service.'

'You don't like the army either?'

'No! At least not the 4th Huzzars. I liked it once – when I was in Egypt.'

'But why was it different in Egypt?'

'Because ... because I wasn't *in* the 4th Huzzars then. I was in the 15/19th Lancers.'

'Why did you change regiments?'

He didn't answer. He only looked at me and the expression of agony that was in his eyes and the drawn lines in his face and nervous twitching of his mouth, frightened me.

'I'll tell you,' he said at last. 'I've never told anyone but I want to tell you.'

'Please do. I want to hear,' I answered softly, timorously.

'I was married – once. I'm divorced. I was still at Sandhurst when I met a girl ... she was older than I ... she had red hair, flaming red hair ... I hate red hair now ... she was fascinating and I fell madly in love with her. You're not allowed to marry when you're at Sandhurst. You're not expected to marry until you're a senior subaltern. But we did – secretly. No one knew. Not even my parents. My father would have been wild. He would have cut me off. When I passed out, I was gazetted to the 15/19th and I joined the regiment in Cairo but I daren't take my wife – and she hated me for leaving her. But I had to ... I had to ... If I'd appeared before the Colonel with a wife he would have sacked me. After six months, when she'd slept with every man in London and she was bored, she began to think of me again and wrote to say that she was coming. I said she mustn't, that if she did she'd ruin me. But she went on saying that she was coming and I didn't know how to stop her. When I never heard from her for several weeks I was more frightened than ever and then, one day, I was sitting in the mess and a servant came to tell me that Mrs Gage was on the telephone. The other chaps thought my mother had arrived but I was half dead when I reached the phone-box. She'd just disembarked and was at Shepherds Hotel and I rushed there at once.

'She wasn't pleased to see me and although I adored her I was too shocked and frightened to embrace her and when I told her that she couldn't stay, she screamed and shouted. I thought the whole hotel would hear – and I knew that there was nothing I could do for she meant to destroy me. And I knew that she had never loved me, that she had only married me for my money and my family. I ran from her; out of the hotel, past my friends sitting on the terrace, I ran wildly to the Nile and when I reached the middle of the Kasr-el-Nil Bridge, I stopped and stood there ... stood and stood ... trying to find the courage to throw myself in.

'The Scots Guards were in Cairo then and she knew them all and soon all Egypt knew that young Gage of the 15/19th had a beautiful red-haired wife and I was hauled up before the Colonel.

'He told me that I would have to leave the regiment and my father was informed. But I didn't go at once. I wish I had. They were a long time deciding what to do with me. I left the mess and lived at Shepherds with my wife and we quarrelled all the time. I followed her to all the parties, watched her get drunk every night and came back alone while she came in the morning. She made scenes wherever she went. She kicked a man once and he was six months in hospital. She smashed a man's glasses into his eyes and scratched a woman's face. She swept all the bottles off a tray and another time, beat up a servant. She had red hair, a scalding temper and a burning ravaging lust. She was fire incarnate, a red devil, lawless and demented and all men adored her. I hate everything that's red.

'I was sent back to England. There was a dreadful row with my father and divorce proceedings were started and soon after that, I was transferred and sent out here. That's why I've never liked it. That's why I shall never like anything anywhere again.'

'Oh but you will, you *must*!' I burst out. I was almost weeping, the story had so moved me.

He looked down on the ground and seemed to be trembling. Then, I turned and stared over the bank into the void and very softly, for I could hardly speak, I told my own little story, simplifying all of it and leaving out the parts I was ashamed of.

'I never loved Harold. I tried to and I thought I did. He rushed me into an engagement, he was very forceful and strong and somehow, so long as he was here I could never break away, he seemed to mesmerise me and I let it go on. But as soon as he left I knew I had made a mistake, a terrible mistake, and I broke it off. It was only the regiment that he really minded about. He's not coming back to Delhi. Everyone thinks me awful.'

When I stopped he looked up quickly and, very shyly, took both my hands.

'I don't. I understand.'

My hands responded to his hands and for a long time we stood gazing into each other's eyes. Then, very timidly, he asked:

'May I call you Philippa? No, Phi? I'd like to call you Phi.'

I was surprised by the name and I didn't like it much but I would have let him call me anything. Then he bent forward and kissed me very gently and when I responded he let my hands go and took me in his arms. And I worshipped and exulted as the dream rushed madly on.

'I love you. I loved you when I first saw you in the club and I loved you still more when we met at that lunch. But I thought you were out of reach and I wouldn't let myself think about you.'

'And I've loved *you* ever since I first saw you,' I answered. His whole body became taut and strong and confident and I kissed him as passionately as he kissed me.

'My darling. Oh, my darling Phi, why can't we marry and both be happy at last?'

It was getting light when we walked away with everything settled between us. The great plain was changing colour, turning from black to violet and from violet to rose and then to yellow. The trees were shaking with chattering birds. The hotel was still locked up and the *chowkidars* had gone and John climbed through a window and then let me in through a door. He took me to my room and we tore ourselves apart. Now the dream had carried me to the very gates of heaven.

We rushed together the next morning and, after a late breakfast, hurried to the Institute. With any other man I would have confessed my plot, knowing that he would be flattered and would even admire me for my daring. But with John I couldn't. I didn't know what irrational fears and misgivings such a disclosure might arouse. I had to go through with it.

The Institute, which was some distance from the hotel, was a long low white building and a great crowd was round it. People came from all parts of India, camping under the trees with their bundles and cooking pots, building fires inside little rings of stones and between their treatments, squatting patiently all day. They came alone and whole families came. Some stayed only a few days and some were there for weeks. The scene was very moving and I looked into their solemn expressionless faces as I passed between them.

John and I were interviewed together. I was questioned first. After all that had happened, I found it hard to go on lying and pretending and my performance was very poor. But the doctor helped me with my shaky yet alarming story.

'Where did the dog lick you?' he asked, 'and how?'

'It ... it sort of rolled against me and seemed to lick or ... or slobber on my leg.'

'What did it look like?' he went on.

'It ... it couldn't walk properly. It lurched about and its mouth was open all the time and ... and there was froth on its lips and its ... eyes were wild ...' I was thinking all the time of the jackal in our tent.

'Did it seem to see you, or did it just roll into you as if it was blind?'

'No, I'm sure it couldn't see me. I'm sure it was blind,' I answered with alacrity.

Gravely, he wrote my answers down. He may have thought me frightened and silly as all women were supposed to be and my story vague, but at least he believed it. He didn't guess the truth. He looked up, at length, with a sympathetic smile.

'You will have the four-day treatment,' he said. 'Two injections a day –

one at ten o'clock and the other at four. You have nothing to worry about. You were not bitten, your contact was limited and you have come in time and the treatment will give you full protection.'

When John's turn came, his story was as vague as mine. His dog didn't sound half as mad as mine, in fact, it didn't sound mad at all. But I questioned nothing. If only fear had driven him here, fear of dogs and other fears, I didn't understand them then. We both received an injection in the stomach and then walked happily away.

If I had known then all that I know about serums now – especially the rabies one – I do not think I would have done what I did. But if I had been so wise I would never have known John. Eight shots of toxic material into my blood-stream was the dangerous price I paid so gaily for his love.

I felt light with joy and utterly at rest. Not only was the strain of conquest over, but the strain of the whole Indian adventure, too. Everything I'd wanted and fought for I had now obtained – love, position and security. But it wasn't long before new strains and anxieties arose to take the place of the old ones.

All that day we scarcely separated a moment but the next morning, when I was getting up, a note was brought to my room. It was from John, telling me that he was ill and would have to stay in bed and begging me to come to him at once. I hurried to his room where, in a mangled bed, he lay tossing. He greeted me with a wan suffering expression and risking whatever odious disease he might have contacted, I kissed him tenderly and anxiously.

'Darling,' he said, 'I've got fever again. I'm always getting it. It's this damned country. I never had it in Egypt. I'll have to stay in bed all day. Isn't it bloody! Just when I want to be with you.'

'But I'll stay with you, my darling. I won't leave you. Don't worry about that. But first I want to know what's really wrong with you. I want to get a doctor.'

'No. No. I'm not having any damned doctors. I only want you.'

I put my hand on his forehead and felt his pulse. 'Can you get hold of a thermometer?' he went on, 'I'm sure my temperature is very high.'

'I'll buy one at the chemist's,' I answered and I hurried out. When I returned, after carefully disinfecting it, I put it in his mouth and while I was timing it, watched his face anxiously. When I took it out – it was normal. I shook it down and put it back and this time, left it longer. But it was just the same and when I showed it to him he wouldn't believe it.

'The damn thing's no good – like everything in this country. They've sold you a dud one,' he burst out querulously.

'I'll go and change it.' And I ran back to the shop and complained and they gave me another. But when I returned and we tried it again – again and again –

the results were always the same.

'They're all rotten,' said John at last. 'The whole stock's defective,' and he threw it angrily onto the table beside him. 'Anyway, it wouldn't have helped. Just knowing what my temperature is wouldn't bring it down. So let's forget it. Sit down on the bed, my beloved, and let's talk. But first let me kiss you.' And I bent down to him on his pillows. After that we talked, but not for long for suddenly he sat up.

'I say, it's nearly time for our injections. I can't miss that. They're terribly important. I'll have to struggle to the Institute whatever I feel like and then come back to bed afterwards. Wait for me in the lounge, darling, while I get dressed.' A few minutes later he joined me.

'Forgive me, my sweet, but I didn't have time to shave. If we're late they might not do us.' And he hurried out of the hotel and we walked away rapidly. He seemed alright and he was even better when we returned, yet I still expected him to go back to bed.

'As soon as you're in bed I'll come into you,' I said. A surprised look came over his face.

'Oh ... oh, I don't think I need to go back to bed at once. A short walk won't hurt me. It might even do me good and I'll rest afterwards.'

We went for a walk, not a short one but a very long one and were out the whole morning. As we approached the hotel, he stopped dead.

'I've just remembered my fever. I think it's gone. You've cured it my darling,' and smiling shyly, like a little boy, he bent and kissed me. For the rest of our time at Kasauli he was well and happy and I floated beside him, deep in the heavenly folds of my dream.

I had telephoned my mother and told her, discreetly, that my adventure was succeeding, but when I returned and recounted every detail of those four fantastic days, she was overwhelmed. And soon, she loved him too. She thought him so sensitive and handsome and aristocratic-looking and when he told her that he painted and had always wanted to be an artist, she adored him.

When his leave ended and he left I shut myself up like a recluse, devoting all my days and half my nights to writing. My love and my letters became my life. And John did the same. When his military duties were over (and they were not very onerous) he spent his time composing the love letters which touched every nerve and answered every thought and sweet fastidious sentiment in mine and lifted by this rapturous communion, I moved like a seraph across an ocean of ever-deepening love and creativity. It was like my correspondence with Sir Vincent – only this time the young man was real.

He had many passionate interests which, together with his new-found love, provided the themes for his letters and he built them up and filled them out until I was familiar with every facet of his mind and the world in which he lived. His hatred of India and the English in India was one of these themes.

> Darling, darling little beauty, I cannot bear to think of you in daily nearness to all the harridans and hoydens and tarts in that most terrible of all abominations – an Indian atmosphere. The noxious germ of Indiana enters the human mind insidiously and nothing is more deplorable than the domiciled-in-India Englishman or woman. Ignorant of the world outside, contented with small mercies, they are paralysed when they return to England where India has never been heard of. Oh God! how I am straining at my leash for next year when together, we shall leave it all behind ...

And another time:

> We English, in this graft-ridden country, are striving after an end which destroys itself like the silk-worm moth. As this moth succumbs to its labours, so does the 'Kwai-hai' die his social death on retirement, with his life's labours lost.

And about himself:

> Beloved angel, the days drag on with their dry, dusty, uncompromising heat. This afternoon, I hung up all my sea pictures to prevent myself getting 'cafard'. The heat does not worry me so much as the awful emptiness of everything. This stagnating, mind-destroying existence makes me so irritable and thankless. I should go raving mad were it not for the constant visions of your sweet face ... No, darling, not a damned person in this world has ever cared very much for me. Certainly no woman. And whenever I've discovered their pseudo-love the shock has well-nigh killed me. Disillusionment is the cruellest thing in the world and I have had so much of it ... but you really care for me, my wonderful girl, my gem amongst women ... I know that you do and that is a marvellous feeling ... All the flesh-pot huntresses that I have known may now be in their graves for all I care. Mine own, we will smash every difficulty to hell and the thought makes me feel twice the man.

He adored the sea and again and again wrote long imaginative accounts of ocean races and the sea-faring life. Gradually, he built up an ecstatic picture of the life that we should live in England among the great and grand.

> Mix with the damnable herd you must, my beloved, but don't be

> depressed by this brutish land. Keep thinking of England ... Next year, at glorious Goodwood, we'll stroll together in the paddock and note the form and watch the races from the royal enclosure. I'll take you to Firle, my cousin's place, and then to Cowes in August where I can see my little flower, my beauty, walking in the squadron gardens among the smart yachting people and she the smartest and most beautiful of them all – and he so proud beside her ... I'll get you onto the Britannia if our poor king is still alive and well and if he fits her out. Heavens! how she will love that ... the berthing of the royal yacht, her escort man-o-war, every yacht in the station 'dressed ship', launches, small sailing craft and steamers full of trippers. After that, I shall be sailing in the Ocean Race where my darling cannot come ...

He goes on to describe the race, his own rugged salty part in it and his pride and joy when he wins it and I meet him at the finish. At the end of this sea dream he asks the question, 'do you like my style of living, darling heart?' and then he drops back into the awfulness of reality.

> The lilt of an old sea shanty gnaws at me now as I sit here in this grave thinking of my golden darling and my goddess the sea.

Another day it is a race that he actually sailed in:

> I remember so well 'standing down' Channel in Neptune in the Fastnet Cup race. We were off the longitude of Cap Hanoise and about forty miles from the Lizard and it was my watch. The sun's lower limb bore W¾N and I took a compass azimuth to correct our standard compass. The wind had fallen off and as I looked upon that awe-inspiring vastness, I thought of the Pilgrim Fathers, Drake, Frobisher and all those glorious sailor characters who made the same passage westwards. They, too, must have taken a sight at the setting sun to correct their astrolobes. I shall never forget it – the great loneliness of the ocean at sundown when the sailor is in communion with – God. I'd never thought of Him before that night and I was frightened ... then, for a few moments, my soul became one with the universe and – Him. I want you to have that same experience, my darling one ...

And the Delhi-Simla girls:

> Jerry, I believe, was quite a nice girl before she was ruined by a heterogenous collection of men. Having a certain sanguinary attractiveness, she made use of it and played fast and loose with every man and boy she could enrol, becoming lewd and loud ... Jane shrieks and yells like forty parrots when a dance is under way. Pam is the same,

> a bovine, brainless, unkind school-girl, like a servant in appearance and men rate her 'a good sort'. These surface judgments make me sick.

And discord in the regiment:

> I arrived back to find a volte face in the regiment. Bernard, (acting C.O.), in a row with Peter, told him that certain subalterns could not get on with the rest. Peter slimed up to me then to ask if this was true. It is the discord and intrigue, I told him, against which we cavil. There is surface peace now but we are terribly on our guard.

And again and again his own wretchedness and the love which alone relieves it:

> A heavenly, heavenly letter greeted my gladdened eyes in the mess this morning when I returned from stables. Darling thing, you do write so beautifully and I have cried aloud for you again and again in this waste of grey mud, scorching and relentless sun and putrescent wog ... In very truth this Indian station life is a living death ...

Another day:

> ... Most of the fancied things in life leave me utterly cold ... I may be called an aesthete but I'm damned if I become practical to suit the whims of accurates who want results and efficiency. Heavens, how I long for you and your lovely ways and vagaries. How wonderful to love someone who is staunch and true and not a monetary opportunist, a jazz character in the world of surface lives ... With all my poor heart-strained resource of love for you, my adorable one, my dream of love – with 'embraces et baisses a toi, mon ange intime' ...

For a long time all this rapture and exquisite rage and the grand, inspiring future, painted brighter in every letter, enthralled and satisfied me, the vagueness corresponding with my own ecstatic state.

My mother was excited, too, but she had never left the earth as I had, she was dreaming with her eyes fixed firmly on the calendar and she soon began to nag me for something definite about John. I was indignant, telling her how unworthy her thoughts were, how assured my future was and how objectionable it would be to pin John down to dates and stupid conventional arrangements. But, after awhile, I began to wonder myself why he didn't at least tell his parents and, very delicately, I lowered the tone of my next letter by asking him when he meant to do this. I knew he was frightened of them and after the shock and shame and bother of his disastrous marriage they were watchful and suspicious. But he had to tell them sometime, so why couldn't he do it at once, I thought, and get it over?

'Darling beloved,' he replied, 'I haven't told my parents yet because my mother has not been well and I didn't want to spring any surprises on her, even a heavenly one like this, until she was quite recovered. But in my next letter I will tell them. They liked you when they met you; when they know you they'll adore you almost as much as I do.' A few weeks later I asked if he had heard from them.

'My angel one,' he answered, 'I haven't written to them yet because they've been away and I thought it best to break the glorious news when they came back. In my next letter I'll do it. They shall know, they shall know about my heart's great love, about the jewel that I have found and may clasp and call my own ...'

But the distasteful business was shelved again and then forgotten altogether when he announced ecstatically that he had got 10 days leave and would soon be rushing up to Simla. I was overjoyed and thankful, too – for another reason.

The daily love letters I had pushed up and up in style and content until their production was on such a high emotional and literary level that I was finding it a strain to keep them going. But I couldn't let them drop in quality; my pride as an author prevented that. Now I looked forward to 10 days rest.

He arrived looking white and ill and terribly nervous. My mother was most concerned about him and I longed to comfort and restore him. His thinness and pallor made him look more handsome and aristocratic than ever and hanging loose upon him, his well-cut suits and fine grey-blue shirts that blended with his Old Etonian tie, looked superb. Every day, after breakfast, he came straight to the Grand and stayed until late at night. We went for long walks or rode and, at first, we all ate together in the dining-room. But he soon grew dissatisfied with that.

'Can't our meals be brought up to your sitting-room?' he asked, 'so that we can eat together in private?' And after that, heavily loaded trays were carried up to us and my mother ate alone.

On the first night, at dinner, he insisted on drinking champagne and I ordered a bottle.

'Let me sign for it,' he said when it came, making a weak movement.

'Oh no, you're my guest,' I replied proudly, snatching the chit from the *khitmagar*. And we drank it every night. He loved it so. I couldn't refuse him. I daren't refuse him. I had to pretend that we could afford it, pretend that we were rich. If I hadn't, if he had suspected how poor we really were he would have been terrified and run from me, convinced that I, too, was a flesh-pot huntress.

Every night, I dressed with the utmost care and took great trouble to make the table elegant, spreading it with lace mats and other little furbishings. Because the lighting was so ugly I bought some brass candle-sticks in the bazaar and with the *khitmagars* serving and the champagne flowing, we dined ceremoniously in the soft transforming candle-light. And John adored the deceptive grandeur and seclusion. Afterwards, we sat on the sofa with our arms round each other alternately talking and kissing. But after a few nights, this grew a little boring and John's hands began to roam. I knew that this was bound to happen but I still didn't know what I would do. My mother would have given me the same advice as before. 'He'll tire of you – and even if he doesn't, what will be left to the marriage when it comes,' she would have said.

But if the world had been like that she would not have aided, as she did, the situations which produced the new behaviour. Released and flung together, our relationship advanced and already riveted with trust and understanding, how could I be cold now and refusing?

That first night, uncertain of myself, I held him gently back but the next I gave way and lay down on the sofa. He bent over me then and looked at me hard.

'Phi, my darling, you *are* a virgin, aren't you. One can't tell when a woman rides astride.' I was astonished by this question but I knew on the instant that I had to lie to him.

'Yes,' I answered.

He lay down beside me but I was agitated now and nervous of what I was doing and, in an obscure way, nervous of him. Even while surrendering I went on resisting. We stayed there for a long time and I tried so hard to help him but, in the end, he broke down and wept.

'It's this accursed country!' he cried out. 'I've never been like this before. I'll not be able to marry you. My life is finished. I might as well be dead.'

'You'll be alright again. You're just run down,' I kept telling him. But he groaned and wept and clung to me like a suffering child. After he left me, I didn't worry about him but about the lie that I had told him. I couldn't bear it and I made up my mind to tell him the truth.

The next morning, I went to the chemist and bought several tonics and when he arrived, made him start on them at once and then swallow them at hourly intervals. He was not so depressed as I had feared he would be and the day passed quite happily.

He drank more than ever at dinner, not only champagne but spirits as well. He liked taking the tonics but his faith was in alcohol, he was sure that it was the only real cure. Afterwards, on the sofa, things were not quite so disastrous as the night before and he was full of hope that in a day or two he would be normal. Then I spoke.

'I've something serious to say to you, my darling,' I began. He looked nervous at once. 'When you asked me last night if I was a virgin I lied to you. I'm not. Harold made love to me. I had to tell you the truth.'

He flung me violently away from him as if I was diseased and leapt from the sofa with a wild look.

'Then I can't marry you. I can never see you again,' he shouted angrily.

I thought I'd lost him. I had made a mistake which I might never retrieve. I was desperate and ready to lie again, to employ every verbal contortion I could to reverse or alter the meaning of what I had just said.

'No. No, he didn't really make love to me. I didn't mean that. I meant that he just ... half made love to me, do you understand ... never wholly and completely ...'

I twisted frantically about with this feeble explanation. I had to make it save me. I had to convince him that I hadn't actually been deflowered, that only my approaches had been ravished and then persuade him to accept me in this soiled, half ruined condition. And I seized his hands, imploring him to understand and forgive me. I grovelled before him and as he stood looking down at me, his eyes were like screaming points of pain.

'I don't know what to say now. I'm too upset. I'll have to think,' he said at last. 'I'll let you know tomorrow whether I can still marry you.' And coldly he turned away and left me.

I was in despair and utterly confused. Was my mother right when she told me that men won't marry second-hand girls? Had I lost the only love that would ever satisfy the high ineffable demands of my mind and heart – by doing what all the others did? And if I hadn't – what would I do now? Make John stand back and wait? Yet my compliance he took for granted. It was the natural outcome of our love and all our pledges. Yet this right which he claimed for himself he would not concede to Harold to whom, after all, I had been formally engaged. Or did this inconsistent claim spring only from the disordered depths of his unhealed frightened soul? Now, when I thought that I might lose him I adored him even more and longed to prove my love and with my strength and constancy, dissolve away his fears and give him trust and rest and happiness at last. I lay awake in misery and waited for him in the morning meaning to fight again, to fight and fight – before I let him go.

I watched from the window, hoping to know the answer before he reached me. He arrived in a rickshaw, he never walked, and stepped slowly and wearily out of it – usually he left it with a jump and ran up the steps at once. I couldn't see his face under his topee but when he had paid the coolie, he stood for a few moments staring down the bank across The Mall. He seemed reluctant to come up. He was dreading what he had to do. I knew the answer. I had lost him.

A few minutes later, the door burst open and he came smiling into the room and rushed upon me, enveloping me in his arms and smothering me with kisses and I clung to him weeping with surprise, relief and joy. Distressed, he asked me why.

Those 10 turbulent but entrancing days ended all too quickly and we dined in state for the last time, my imitation pearl necklace and earrings and the imitation hotel silver glowing and sparkling in the deceiving candle-light. We finished one bottle of champagne and then ordered another. With the *khitmagars* coming and going, we drank and kissed continuously across the table and our talk became more and more extravagant and when the coffee cups and brandy glasses had been cleared away and John's cigar was burnt to a sucked and flavourless stump we moved to the sofa which that night became, in truth, our nuptial bed.

Early the next morning, I went to Kalka with him in the little mountain car and then watched the mail train carry him away into the dry burning life-less heat soon to be swept by the pullulating tides flung down by the monsoon, advancing now across the continent. A few days later, my rapturous memories and blissful confidence in the future were disturbed a little by the fantastic food and wine bill presented by the hotel, which we could not pay. But we had learnt how to live on credit now and I soon dismissed this ugly irruption into my beatific path as irrelevant and of no importance. Later, John asked me to send this bill to him. But how could I? I was as sensitive and apprehensive about my poorness as he was about his wealth.

The daily letters were now resumed. Refreshed by the interlude and inspired by so many new ineffable sensations I wrote with ease again and an even greater eagerness. John's first letters were filled with the anguish of the parting.

> I cannot express, my most beautiful, the overwhelming horror of my loneliness when that appalling train steamed out of the station and I realised that my Phi had left me to pursue her darling way up that infernal mountain ... Heavens, heavens, how my distracted soul cries out for her ... I am utterly unstrung and cannot bring myself to realise that I am in this prison settlement once more ... but we must both be strong and think of England – the pleasant land. Fair breezes, fair tides, glistening white sides and flaxen sails of my darling Solent. Marvellous visions can I conjure up even as I sit here in this blazing sepulchre ... On no account must she follow me (*I had suggested joining him*) to these hellish plains ... no rain yet and the temperature 110 degrees. It would be utter cruelty and I value her too much ...' A few days later he added sarcastically, 'Today is a charming day – 115 degrees and so sunny! ...'

He was playing cricket at six o'clock every morning and polo in the evenings, going pig-sticking regularly and exercising hounds twice a week (he was 1st Whip of the Meerut pack) to fill the hot awful empty days. And then the rains came.

> ... Meerut is like a ghastly greenhouse now, far worse than before. Damp sticky heat, snakes and scorpions in every hole and crevice – fabulous and unnatural. I am as restless as a twenty tonner in a gale of wind ... God! what would I not give to be at the helm of a racing boat with my darling at my side, the spindrift tearing from the lee-bow and racing canvas thundering overhead ...

And another day:

> Darling love, I'm in such a state about my affairs and leave and one thing and another that I feel physically and mentally incapable of dealing with anything ... It rests with my little bog-rat of a C.O. (in England is the little devil) as to whether I go to Poona or to Saugor in the autumn. If to Saugor, I can get some leave first and come to you ... I don't know what to do. Whether to fling away my commission and buy a French fishing boat, or hang on until next year and then go to the Sudan. My family require me to do something and it is a pleasant land and would get me away from the army ... yet the sea is what I really want ... but there's no job there, no future in it. If I had no parents and you approved I would say to hell with all these people who annoy me – and clear off to sea. I *hate* military society and have meddled with cavalry snobs long enough. Hurlingham, Roehampton and Deauville polo make me retch! I've done it all and met only rudeness from the graspers and climbers of the Cavalry Corps and their hot, horse-coping friends ... Phi, my beloved, I am worried about everything and a great wave of discontent sweeps over me ...

And I was worried, too. His sufferings seemed intolerable, his whole life was so uncertain (just as my own was and had always been) and I longed to be by his side comforting him and giving him my strength. If only we could marry at once, I thought, that would at least make one thing firm and fast and, I was confident, settle all the rest; fix and clarify the shifting perspectives and remove all the hateful, desolating impressions. But I daren't suggest this in a direct way. He might have thought I was rushing him. He was still so frightened and suspicious, always looking for underlying motives. And so was I, always looking into myself, conscious that my motives were not pure. So I only hinted and asked again when he was going to tell his parents. His regiment knew all about me, the secret was leaking out in India – but still they did not know.

He answered:

> ... I too dream of the day when we shall be together always ... But not yet, my darling heart, not yet. Never would I ask you to submit to these conditions ... never will I claim you while we languish in vile India ... I've thrown out lots of hints to my parents. Next week I'll tell them everything. They're going to love you so ... and now, my angel, think about the journey home next year ... my father's chauffeur meeting us with the Rolls at the P. & O. dock at Marseille ...

A week or so later.

> I changed my mind about telling my parents. It's best to wait until my plans are more settled.

I did not mention it again but left him to resolve the future in his own way and time. And it didn't really matter, for my future could hardly be more shaky and obscure than it was already, even in his hands. But I still ached to be with him, to begin my work of healing him.

He lashed out continuously at his brother officers and the Delhi-Simla girls:

> ... The regiment is extremely quiet. Peter sublimely oily to Bernard and the others actually said good-morning to me when I came into breakfast ... Bernard is a most human man. I had a long talk with him today. However much they intrigue against him he means to win and will oust the scum. What joy when all these devils from hell have gone ...
>
> ... I suppose Pam is competing for the Crown of Simla – that heartless and debauched kingdom! To teach her manners, she needs a four-year course of London society under the direction of some fabulous old hostess with an iron will and sense of humour. After that, she might not be a bad girl. In the meantime, I hope you are continuously rude to her ...

He did not know that I was too isolated to be rude to anyone.

As an outsider, looking up and around, I was a critic of society and a snob before I came to India. Now, living fully in a community for the first time since my school days, I began to study people as individuals and to condemn them. I still wanted to change the world by legislating against poverty and suffering and now I wanted to change people's characters as well and this, too, I believed could only be done by over-turning society.

As an insider, neurotically conscious of his position, John looked down from the ancient bastions of property and the agreeable walls of the high holy places upon the 'climbers' and the 'graspers', the 'crashers' and 'insinuators', the rising, raucous, infiltrating masses – frightened and refusing.

But in the new, real world in which he had to live, hating and rejecting everyone, he had become an outsider himself, dreaming all the time of escape – to the sea, the Sudan and now, to me; an insinuator with the powers of a serpent for he believed that among all my 'diabolical sex' I was different, unique, a paragon with the features of a goddess. I, alone among women, was pure and true and good.

To keep this dream unbroken, to save him from another 'cruel disillusionment', to protect myself and my love for him and to please him, I now pushed my judgments harder, I went beyond my own evaluations and moral balance; disparaging, condemning, rejecting all the people round us – and all India. I became like him.

He didn't want to manipulate me. It was the force behind and within him which drove him and degraded me; which made me write about the 'dregs of Britain', 'unpalatable upstarts' and 'board-school adventurers'; and when I wasn't invited anywhere, made me let him think it was because I didn't want to be; and sinking still lower, made me drop remarks about my own lordly relatives, of whom I knew nothing – fearing all the time that he would see through the blinding veils of love and seeing, know that I was a 'climber' and a 'grasper' too.

My mother was painting again in a desultory way and earning a little but there was no real need for us to stay in Simla where living was expensive and I was an outcast and so, when the season ended, we decided to follow the smart world (as always) to the playgrounds of Kashmir. And John was pleased. He had never been there and when his leave came through, he said, he would join us.

At the end of another sea rhapsody, he wrote:

> ... mechanical progress has bred a robot-like human with no feeling for God's mighty oceans and their mystery. To pit one's strength and cunning against a million tons of water, gales, tides and splitting masts and spars is surely a finer, truer occupation than splitting characters in a narrow, revolving shore-going life ... The conversation in the mess is so brainless that I want to hurl every plate, knife, fork and spoon at these demons who so disgust me. And then I think of my little Phi in the hills, miles out of water like this poor fish ...

In the last letter that I received before we left, he wrote:

> ... I know that I am emotional and introspective and that years of self-hatred have given me an inferiority-complex but I am getting over this,

> now that somebody really cares for me – for you *do* care, my darling one, and that strengthens me like the triatic stay of a schooner's main and fore top-mast heads ... One must accept a deity and I hate and despise my fellow humans for jesting at the Great Unknown ... with a sailor's heart of love for his angelic one, until we are bilged upon life's reef ...

Perhaps he was neither an insider nor an outsider but an artist, uncomfortable in all positions and belonging nowhere – an artist who searched in vain for his art.

8

Kashmir and John

UNNOTICED by anyone, without telling anyone, without anyone to tell, we packed and left. The only person we said an uncomfortable good-bye to was the hotel manager, when we could not meet the final bill. Once again, we had to beg for time and promise monthly payments. But when we got away with all our baggage we relaxed in our rickshaws and thought no more about it. India was indulgent to the imperial race, even to the outcasts. We took the mountain train down to Kalka and dropped into the monsoon heat.

Once more, we struggled with porters and reservations and provisions, all the muddle and clamour, all the sweating jostling business that a bearer would have saved us – and the steamy heat was overwhelming. Once inside our compartment we switched on the *punkah* and then collapsed onto the wooden bunks. The fan whirred noisily and the punishing air bombarded us, without relieving us. When the train started a boiling gale drove in through the windows. But I liked it. I loved it. I had been longing for this experience for one would never know India until one had known India's heat. And John had been suffering this for months and I wanted to suffer, too.

I lolled stickily upon the seat and looked out through the screens at the mud and glistening pools and vivid green rice shoots of the flat unchanging landscape and at the heavy tropic clouds passing like regiments of temple dancers between Earth and the eternal sun.

We reached Lahore the next day and then went on to Rawalpindi where we hired a car. There was no mountain railway and all the traffic used the one narrow but magnificent road. We gained the foothills in an hour or so and then began the climb and, at dusk, stopped at a *dak* bungalow where the air was already a little cooler.

All the trunk roads of India were studded with these post-houses. They were usually just large wooden huts with benches round the walls and a servant in charge who could be called from his *go-down* at any hour to open up and attend to the traveller. Sometimes, it was possible to get a rough meal but at most of them, only boiling water for tea and a tubful for a bath.

Other cars had stopped there for the night – it was the busy season – and we brought out our food and ate together at the communal table and afterwards, slept together round the walls. Before dawn, we were all up and making ready to drive on. Later in the day, we reached the changing-place for Gulmarg, just a clearing by the roadside, a crowd of coolies with their *dandies* and the start of a foot-track leading up through the trees.

They jumped up when they saw the car coming and when it stopped, began pushing and shouting and, speaking Hindustani which they didn't understand, we pointed and gestured and haggled. When the business and the loading were at last finished, we set off with a long line of coolies in front, each with a trunk or bundle roped to his back while we brought up the rear, swaying and pitching in our litters, each carried by two handsome, eagle-nosed ruffians in ragged robes with beautifully embroidered Kashmiri caps covering their greasy heads.

It was a long steep ascent between the trees up a narrow, winding track pressed flat or beaten into steps by generations of human feet. It took many hours, for the plodding wiry upright beasts had several thousand feet to climb. We often walked a stage.

At the top, the trees soon ended and our ancient cavalcade levelled out, straightened its line and trudged over the last stretch of rich green sward to the hotel. We were 12,000 feet up now in cool, clear, mountain air.

The hotel consisted of one large wooden bungalow with a collection of small ones scattered about the flowery slopes all round. We were taken to one of these and, excited by the beauty and novelty of it all, we settled happily into our own little house.

Gulmarg was a concave plateau which, looking like a large green saucer, sealed the top of a round mass which buttressed the still higher mountain rising in great cliffs upon its northern side.

The golf course was in the middle of the saucer and trees fringed the edge, obscuring the world outside, holding us in some rare unexperienced location. The club, another hotel and some private bungalows were scattered here and there. In spite of the altitude, the difficulty at first of breathing and moving, we soon went exploring. We crossed the golf course and dragging ourselves up the other side, took a path which plunged into the trees. We walked for a long time, until we reached the edge of the saucer, the edge of the mountain, where the path turned and followed it round and the trees dropped over the sides. But still we could see nothing. Then suddenly, they cleared, there was a gap where they grew and the doors of heaven opened! The Simla views had electrified us but this was greater – the greatest in the whole wide world!

Below us, far below us, was a golden valley with a river winding down the middle and walls like monstrous cliffs on either side and beyond the valley, just beyond it, was a mountain range and in the middle, rising from the middle, was one mountain that was higher than the rest; one that rose up and up, thrusting through the floor of heaven to serve as a crystal seat for God Himself.

We were spell-bound. I felt that I was looking out upon a lost land, the land of Prester John, a hidden, secret, sealed-up valley which no one before me had found; a valley made of gold, its walls set with precious stones and a mountain like God's sentinel behind. It was not an overpowering inner vision this time but an outward revelation, a seeing with my open eyes, an actual view of Earth and Heaven where they meet.

When we got back to the hotel, we learnt that it was Nanga Parbat, the second highest mountain in the world and the valley was the 'Happy Vale', the Vale of Sprinagar and the river was the Jhelum, upon whose banks 4,000 years ago, when the Aryans were advancing into the Punjab, the seers or rishis (some 30 of them women) composed many of the hymns of the Rig Veda.

John's letters now grew desperate. The distance dividing us and the heat and the discord in the regiment seemed almost more than he could bear. He could not get the date of his leave settled. The only thing he knew was that he was going to the Cavalry School at Saugor in September.

> ... By the time my love gets this she will be miles and miles and miles away in the high unattainable heart of Hindustan. Although we are together in spirit yet thinking of the awful distance drives me to the depths of a most terrible depression. My little dream divine, I am writing with your photos under my eyes, I cannot let them out of my sight for three seconds and I shall follow you, like Pharaoh, at all possible speed – but *when*, oh when? I can scarcely write for love and worry ... They are plotting Bernard's downfall and a lump comes into my throat when I think of the injustice of it all. The meanness, the underhandedness of these men. I cannot stand much more and if Bernard doesn't get command – I go ... I am writing home about us, this mail, although perhaps it is a risk ...

He grew so frenzied and I so anxious that again I said I would go down to him.

> No, darling, no. You must *on no account* come down to this red screaming morgue of bitterness and ill-health ... it would kill my little golden one ... even love itself would fall away among the ashes of this heat and discomfort. And there's nowhere for her to stay – not a woman in the place, thank God! No, no, no ...

Later:

> ... after flaming, detestable Simla, she will adore Kashmir. Yet what a debt do I owe to Simla and Kasauli. The memory of those precious hours will go with me, gratefully, to eternity for she has given me back my happiness ...

Another day:

> ... When I gaze upon your photos they take my mind away from these hell-fiends incarnate; from blasted Peter, the super haemoglobin, the man of little blood but yet so b-y! ... Bernard has not been given a chance. The bog-rat was determined to down him before he arrived in India ... I cannot describe to you the marvellous monotony of these days. No work, no play, no sport, no insobriety! Nothing! One just exists. My only intellectual activity is writing to you and feverishly brushing up my Arabic ...

And the next day:

> I think I had a touch of the sun yesterday for I had a fearful headache ... The blasted bog-rat returns on August 3rd and I must, at all costs, get my leave and avoid him ... Unjust, weak, vindictive and self-seeking, terrified of superiors and powerful subordinates *and* unforgiveably common! Can one give a commanding officer a worse character? How can I serve under one so vile? Take darling Bernard – just, handsome, clever and forgiving, a man-of-the-world and – out of the top drawer! The bog-rat hates him from sheer jealousy ...

Then, at last, his leave was settled. He was coming on the 26th of July.

Every night, in the sitting-room of our bungalow, I sat writing and my letters took longer and longer. Without realising it, I was writing now like a professional, carefully choosing every word, feeling the rhythms and working over every line and passage until each one was a finished prose poem, sublime in my own estimation then, although lacking, I am sure, much of the slap-dash brilliance and spontaneity of John's letters to me. I thought I was writing only rather special love letters. I did not know that I was at the start of an immense, never-ending literary enterprise.

Then more trouble came to him:

> My love, my love, I am in a terrible state of disease. From my foul and filthy bearer have I caught scum-pox and do all that I can, I am unable to remove its malign traces from my face and neck and I hardly dare be seen in public, let alone by you. I shall arrive next week smothered in

grease and bandages ... I shall soon be stowing kit for the voyage, then breaking out my hook for my little sea-going sweetheart ...

A thousand miles away she is and a feeling of sadness and finality comes over me until I am nearly driven mad. Why should you be so far from me? My face and the back of my neck are covered with filthy sores and I find it difficult to write one word of sense. Ten thousand curses on these wogs and their disease-breeding bazaars ... If only I am in a fit state to meet her ... I am unholy to look at now!

On the 21st July he wrote from hospital.

Sweetheart, I thought it best to come in here and get the job done properly rather than hang about in my own bungalow with filthy servants and a million flies. I shall arrive in a putrid condition I fear and shall not want to come near you ...

And the next day, the 22nd, he wrote again.

I am still in this accursed dog-hole and so far there is little change in my condition. I've got prickly heat as well and everything has gone gangrenous. But I am going to start on the 26th. The M.O. says the change will do the trick ... This damnable summer is now nearly over, the winter will pass as in a flash and then home, my darlingst, home – to the sea, Thalassa, the sea! ...

And the next day, the 23rd.

This foul disease will not dry up. If I'm still in a putrid state I shall not start. I cannot arrive with oozing fabulous sores all over me. Oh, my darling, I do wish she was down here now. I want her so terribly, terribly badly ... I now resemble a character from the sea. A Drake's beard mingles with my straggly ends of moustache ... Nature on land depresses me but nature at sea is beautiful and awe-inspiring ... Angry seas, southerly busters, black and white squalls and El Pampero, the 'devil wind' of the Rio de la Plata, knocks houses flat and raises a nasty broken 'popple'. We'll cruise in those latitudes one day, my sweet ...

And on the 24th.

I'm still trussed up from head to foot, can't shave, sleep, eat nor bath and the whole time wanting to scratch like a frenzied dog! But I'm coming, I'm determined to come ... This hospital is dull but it's a change from the mess which is divided now into two hostile camps. I don't believe this has ever occurred in any regiment in history ... Farewell for a short time only, my darling, for your John is coming, he *means* to come ...

And he came. If he hadn't, I would have gone to him.

9

The Kashmir Flood

HE arrived as he said he would, bandaged and bearded and he looked very ill. He was given a bungalow close to ours and I unpacked for him and ran round him like a nurse, in a delirium of having and loving and caring. But within a few days, sores broke out all over my face, too, and then we both went about greasy and disfigured. But I soon recovered – and so did he.

We played golf every morning and went for walks and in the evenings, although John never wanted to go to the club, yet we always did. The crowded cheerful tables were magnetic and although he criticised the people afterwards, he seemed happy while he was with them. He drank a lot himself, round after round, and wanted me to drink too, like everybody else and to please him, I did. Afterwards, we went back to his bungalow where I spent half the night.

I loved being with him but we were both nervous and I hated creeping back in the early morning to the room I shared with my mother, always hoping not to wake her, afraid of her reproaches. If we could be away together I was sure that we would learn to love and I would come to like his loving. After awhile, these nervous unsatisfactory nights became a strain and I made excuses and tried to leave him early. But he wouldn't let me. He would have liked to have me there all night and he always wanted me to stay until he fell asleep. And how could I refuse him.

He brought all his pictures; beautiful little pencil sketches and water-colours of sailing ships and some clever and amusing pen and ink caricatures – 'impressions of Cairo' – he called them. My mother put them up round the room and when she told him how talented he was, he beamed with pleasure and began to think seriously of becoming a professional artist – when he left the army.

I wasn't interested in golf now but I played because he wanted to. One day, topping another ball, he banged the ground angrily with his club and broke the shaft and then began to shout. There were players coming up behind but he didn't move. For several minutes he stood in the middle of the fairway in a paroxysm of rage, his eyes wild, his face white and twitching. Then, just as suddenly as he had started, he stopped and taking my arm and looking at me with an entrancing smile, picked up his clubs and walked on.

'That was the Gage temper,' he said proudly, 'and you came through it very well, my love. It's something you'll have to get used to.' He kissed me and we went on with our atrocious game.

He was soon bored with Gulmarg. He did not feel god-like on this high, lush playground, this imperial Mount Olympus – but claustrophobic. He felt he couldn't move without falling over the edge and there were too many other gods resting from their labours and disporting themselves upon the green golf pastures in their usual upstart, bovine way. I told my mother and she agreed, at once, to leave. She always agreed to everything and I never knew whether she was pleased or sorry. The next day, we travelled down to Srinagar.

The old, crowded, picturesque city lay huddled upon the right bank of the Jhelum behind a high *bund* (to protect it from flooding when the river rose with the melting snows every summer). There was one European hotel, Nedous, and a few shops. Most of the British lived in houseboats moored end-to-end alongside the *bund* or on the lakes beyond.

The social climate was luxurious. It was the one spot in India where the lines were all rubbed out and people mixed with each other in a gay, gregarious way, released and uninhibited, exploiting every corybantic moment of this heaven before recall to their dull defined stations and the purgatorial heat. From Nedous to the club, from the club to the bathing rafts and back again to Nedous, they swooped round and round like a cloud of chattering starlings. The few exclusives and crowd-haters went trekking up the flower-strewn valleys, or climbing in the lower ranges, or fishing in high, unvisited lakes and streams. But in the 'Happy Vale' the crowd reigned and was happy and into it John and I now plunged.

My mother rented a house-boat on the Dal Lake, moored close to the shore, with a gang-plank dropping straight onto a path between the rushes. It had five splendid rooms, not to mention the kitchen, and a ladder led up to the flat roof. It was ornately carved and very beautiful and from it we set out every day upon an unending round of pleasures.

After breakfast, we were paddled by one of our boatmen in our own *shikara* to the middle of the lake where we dived from the rafts and swam about in the warm brown water for most of the morning. After that, a specially ordered taxi waited on the shore to take us to the club. There, we drank for an hour or so and then drove back to the house-boat, often very late, with the lunch drying up in the oven, the servants sulking and my mother waiting. In the afternoon, we swam again and then again went drinking at the club. Once more then, we returned to the house-boat to dress and have dinner and then set off for Nedous to dance half the night.

My mother sketched to pass the time and paid several visits to the palace. The Maharajah had seen one of the portraits of Sir William Birdwood and commissioned her to paint the Maharani and himself. Although he seemed to have changed his mind now, she was determined not to let him and she kept writing and calling. Her letters were never answered but the Military Secretary was always charming when she went there, however exasperatingly vague he was about the portrait. But she kept on going.

John met old friends and made new ones and was soon the life and soul of all our drinking parties. He had such charming manners and such a distinguished air, all the women loved him and the men admired him, for he told good stories, was a tough drinker who could hold a lot and – he had plenty of money, standing round after round however big the circles grew.

And the circles all grew and became more gripping and the sessions more abandoned; every day they lasted longer and our meals got correspondingly later, sometimes we missed eating altogether and just sat on and on drinking, talking, laughing – the laughter exploding in obscene bursts and fading upon a silly titter, the talk a frightening cackle. We became so welded to these drinking crowds that we could not leave them and order went out of our lives and half-besotted all the time, we slid through the dreamy, shapeless days. And the nights were spent in fuddled fornication.

What my mother thought about all this, I could not tell. Perhaps, in a subconscious way, she had given me up now, given me away to John whom she loved and trusted, although she still went on asking me why he did not make definite plans for our marriage and I went on trying to reassure her and to convince her of his difficulties.

For awhile, John seemed perfectly content. When we were alone he criticised these crowds, of course, but in a detached, light-hearted way. Then, one night, after the last dance at Nedous and the last round of drinks we stumbled into the taxi and flopped onto the back seat. But instead of embracing me quietly and tenderly as he always did, he jerked himself upright and there was an expression of despair in his eyes as he flung himself upon me and clutched me as if he were drowning.

'Oh Phi, my beloved Phi, I've got you to myself at last! Those swine, those dogs, those repulsive uncouth devils! I can't bear to see you among them, sitting close to them, see them talking to you, looking at you, leering at you, longing for you and licking their slavering lips as they toss and take you in their thoughts – you, you my little beauty, my jewel, my lovely treasure, my own, own darling, you who should be kept a mile from where they sit and soak! No, no, five thousand miles from where they run and rut! And there you should be laid in a golden barque upon the pellucid undesiring sea and with me at the helm and all canvas spread, carried before the breeze into the glorious unpeopled paradise of Ocean! Oh, my beloved, let us sail away together. I can't bear this any longer, I can't see them any more!'

Surprised and desperately moved I responded with gladness.

'And neither can I! Oh, my love, my love, let's leave them!' I cried. 'Let's go off on our own. We can. We're quite free!'

'We will, my sweet, we'll start tomorrow. We'll go fishing at the end of the lake. We'll not meet one of them again.'

He was calm and happy when we reached the house-boat and the hours that followed were sweet and tranquil. The first thing that I talked of in the morning was our fishing.

'We'll have a swim first,' he said, 'then go into the city and buy some rods, come back, have an early lunch and set off afterwards.'

We swam but we never went into the city.

'Let's drop into the club on our way, darling, just for five minutes. We won't stay. Nothing would induce me to stay. But one quick drink will do us good.' And he smiled at me like a little shamefaced boy.

When we reached the club we were greeted with shouts and cries of delight and a chorus of questions.

'You're very late, both of you? Where've you been? What have you been up to?' And John smiled and waved his hand with pleasure. We had one drink and then another and another. I kept trying to make him move.

'Just one more, my sweet, and then we'll go. Does she mind?' He kept whispering with that same engaging smile. And he looked so happy. I didn't know what to do. We sat there for the rest of the morning and got back for a late lunch.

'We can still go fishing,' I said as soon as we were alone. 'We can borrow some rods. The servants can find some while we're having lunch.'

'I think we'd better go climbing instead,' John replied. 'I've been told that the fishing in the lake isn't much good, anyway. Supposing we take the car and drive to the bottom of that mountain,' and he waved his arm vaguely in the direction of a giant with an embroidered skirt of lesser ones dropping one below the other into the far side of the lake. 'We can scramble up one of those quite easily and the view from the top will be marvellous.'

'Alright,' I replied, trying to be as enthusiastic as he was and we sat down to lunch and talked of nothing else but climbing. Afterwards we drove to the nearest mountain and stopped the car and set off up an easy slope among pleasant trees and flowering shrubs, but after a few minutes the way grew steeper and he began to puff and pant and look unhappy and after half an hour he stopped altogether and we sat down and rested.

'We've chosen the wrong place,' he said. 'We couldn't possibly get to the top of this today. We're still in the foothills. We haven't even started on the mountain. We'll have to give it up. The only way to tackle this sort of job is to start at dawn.'

'Alright,' I said, 'let's get up as early as we can. We won't go to Nedous, we'll go to bed and get some sleep for once.' We set off down the hill and soon reached the car and John was silent as we drove away.

'I don't think I like mountain climbing,' he said at last, rather querulously, 'I'm not cut out for it. I ought to be on the sea. We ought to be sailing in the Solent now, not getting pricked and scratched and pestered by flies and bitten by mosquitos climbing these hot beastly hills.'

We stopped at the club on our way back and went to Nedous that night as usual. Afterwards, in the car, he burst out again.

'I can't stand that great red-faced dustman who was in our party tonight. He ought to be emptying garbage, not playing the lord out here and giving lip to me. Did you hear what he said when I happened to mention that my father belonged to the Royal Yacht Squadron? He asked if Cowes was the place where the cows ran about in sailor jackets? And did you hear how that great bitch sitting beside him laughed? God! what swine! What boorish unlicked louts! these proletarian gargoyles with their servant wives and chasing, used-up tarts!'

'But, darling,' I protested, reacting with a sudden inconsistent contrariness to this violent outburst, 'they're not *all* so awful. I think Roger and Lucille are dears and Tubby Read is sweet and I like Dick Parker, I like lots of them, if only one could take them out of those awful drinking parties.'

'Oh, yes, some aren't bad, I agree. Young Melville of the 21st is a corker and right out of the top drawer. But most of them are just climbers and graspers, bridge fiends, horse copers, petty fiddlers, office idiots and infantry bumpkins! Underbred grotesques! Scum!'

I was silent and the next moment he embraced me frantically.

'Phi, Phi, my darling heart, do you love me as you did? Tell me, please darling, tell me that you love me. Tell me *how much* you love me?' And I held him as closely as I could and kissed him ardently and assured him over and over again that I adored him more than ever and would go on adoring him until the end of all things.

The next day, we went to the club as usual and in the evening to Nedous. The taxi drove up to the door of the hotel and we jumped out and it moved away. The people getting out of their cars and walking up the steps greeted us cheerily and I walked up with them. But John didn't. He stopped where he was and I waited for him. Then I went down again.

'I can't go in. I just can't go in there tonight,' he whispered to me. 'Let's go back to the boat and spend the evening quietly by ourselves.'

'Yes. I'd love to,' I answered vehemently.

We looked for the car and then drove back. All the way he clung to me wretchedly, needing help, needing strength which I longed to give him but didn't seem able to, didn't know how to. I supposed I wasn't strong enough myself.

When we reached the boat, he went straight to the dining-room and poured himself out nearly half a tumbler of whisky. I drank nothing and we sat for awhile talking calmly and more happily. Then he jumped up and came over to me and took my hand and smiled in that irresistible way.

'Shall we ... go to Nedous after all, my love? Let's go. Come along, let's go.' And he pulled me out of the chair, we recalled the taxi and set off for the second time that night.

And all the days were like these days until the three weeks of his leave ended. The last night we didn't sleep at all but spent it locked in a sad prolonged embrace, talking, imagining and inventing, jumping from one fine distant vision of the future to another, kissing and weeping and weeping and kissing. We got up before dawn and I went with him to Nedous where the car was waiting to take him down the mountain and I waved him finally away from all the tangled pleasures of this fairyland, this vale of love and dreams and drunken revels, this other inner secret side of the British Raj and the ruling race set far away from all the rigid seats of government, set high upon the white and golden roof-top of the world – the 'Happy Vale' of all the conquerors who had ever marched or sailed into Hindustan.

I was exhausted when he left but greatly as I missed him it was a relief to be alone again, to be able to think and live in my own way, be myself again. But I didn't worry, for I believed that it was India as much as John's weakness that I had been struggling with and that when we were married and living in England I would be able to heal and strengthen him and go my own way.

He paid up his enormous drink bills before he left but the enormous taxi bill he left for us to settle although it meant defaulting on our crop of monthly payments. But we couldn't expect credit in Kashmir. And we moved at once for we had learnt too much about the lake.

There were no latrines on the shore and everything went into the water which was like a sewer all round us and almost solid. There were stand-pipes of clean water at intervals along the banks and the servants were supposed to fetch and use it. But we knew that they didn't. We supervised the boiling of our drinking water and the washing of the fruit but we couldn't stop them dipping into the lake for everything else and this, together with their dishonesty and rudeness, made us glad to leave. Our new boat was moored to the *bund* in front of Nedous. We didn't feel so isolated and when an elderly colonel came and shared it with us, we felt happy and very secure.

It was a magnificent river, broad and strong and winding with splendid trees hanging over the water, sheltering the boat from the hot sun. The *bund* rose high above us. There were steps up to the top of it and down the other side to the road below and one could walk on it for miles and boats were moored along it.

Then John's first letter came.

> I have arrived, sore, lonely and unloved with not a single soul that I can talk to. The little bog-rat's back from England and in command again and my most beautiful and adorable is a thousand miles away. I couldn't bear the sight of your tragic little figure standing in the doorway of Nedous. Oh, my ownest, I hope never to have to witness that again; and how I loathed the damnable and cheerless drive to 'Pindi' ... As soon as Bernard's family arrives from England I shall arrange for you to stay with them ... I am off to the courts to hear the Meerut conspiracy case ... Have just heard the most wonderful duel between the criminal prosecutor and one of the witnesses for the defence. His sarcasm was marvellous to listen to. Never have I beheld such fiendish countenances ... little half-wit Bengali baboos, all Communists. They arrived in two lorries singing the 'Red Flag' ...

And the next day:

> A divine letter from her this morning, full of wonderful ethics and phrases but oh, my darlingest, so sad ... but very soon she will come down to Delhi and be closer ... Heavens how glad I am to be getting away from this god-damn place for seven months. There are no hotels there, so I will arrange for one of the Saugor wives to take charge of my precious ... I am painting another large water-colour for the Srinagar exhibition.

A day later:

> I've had a long letter from my father – about my debts. He is severe but kind and he has given me my last chance and I respect his words. I have been unsystematic and dreadfully extravagant over the last six months and it has been very worrying. I owe the local cavalry officers' money-lender a most infernal amount. But all this will now be settled and I

shall try to keep the bills down at Saugor. How is the old colonel? Rather a bore I expect, but we must feel for the old boy ...

The old colonel was more than a bore – he was an old satyr, living on cocaine, from whom I was always fleeing. He took me to dance at Nedous when he came and after that, I never had a peaceful moment. I even had to lock my door at night. But these games on the house-boat ended very soon when retribution overtook us all. Perhaps it was the god of Israel again, affronted as before by the sins of his children and using the same vengeful weapon of chastisement upon them. For the waters rose and engulfed us – and flood covered the land.

It was raining heavily in the mountains and the snows were melting and we heard that the river was rising fast at the head of the valley and our own part rose a little. Then, we heard that it had overflowed its banks and was flooding meadows and carrying away the peasant dwellings and the bodies of animals began to float past. Our own river rose still more and there was a rush on the shops. And still it rained in the mountains. Then it came to Srinagar.

The water rose rapidly and the current became tremendous. Extra ropes were needed to keep the boats from breaking away and all day long, with their punt poles, the men were pushing away whole trees, planks and the bodies, not only of animals, but of people as they swirled past. We looked up nervously at the overhanging branches. And still it rained in the mountains and people asked each other if the *bund* would go.

Then, we heard that nearly all the banks had burst, that the whole valley was flooded and Srinagar was now an island in the centre of a rushing sea several miles wide, an island with only a small mud bank to hold it against the mighty pushing torrent. And still it rained in the mountains and still the water rose.

Food ran short and an ineffective rationing system was introduced. A watch was kept on the *bund* although nothing was done to raise or strengthen it and the Maharajah sailed round and round in his powerful motor boat, creating a wash which people said would weaken it.

We helped the boatmen push away the debris although, at first, we left them to saw the branches off the trees when the boat rose and touched them, but when we went up one night and found no one there and the roof grinding against a branch, we never trusted them again and we stayed up sawing them off ourselves. The colonel had fled at the first hint of danger. And still it rained in the mountains and still the water rose and people were certain that the *bund* would go.

The waters came within a few inches of the top and the waves from the

Maharajah's boat broke over it. We were lifted up until we floated level with the roofs of the houses. And still it rained in the mountains. Finally, to save the city, the Maharajah ordered the cutting of the last piece of unbroken bank above us, the waters flowed still deeper over the meadows engulfing the few remaining farms which, built on higher ground and only half submerged, were still holding out – and with this last release of water came the last gruesome wash of corpses.

Then, when the water was level with the top and lapping over it and seeping through and the Maharajah was still racing round and round (his palace was on a hill outside) and the people stood waiting for the city to go – the rain stopped in the mountains and the waters fell.

This was the great Kashmir flood disaster of 1929 when the 'Happy Vale' was turned into a vale of tragedy.

When my letters stopped and before the news had reached the outer world, John grew frantic. When the mails got through again I received a packet of desperate letters.

> Has she got my telegrams? My darling, darling, I am extremely worried because I have written hosts and thousands of letters ... Yesterday, I drove over to Delhi. It is cramfull and I don't see why my darling shouldn't come down next week. Meerut is still unbearably hot but Delhi is quite cool – or at least Maidens is. *Do*, darlingest, come down and see him before he goes. Oh, it is a crime to think that all my letters have been lost. Hateful, hateful, brutal country ...

And another one:

> Does it mean she is ill? Does it mean that she has started down the hill for the plains? What is it, what is it, my darling one? I am wiring you again. It is raining down here and cooler. Oh, do come to me, mine own. She *must*. I will book a room at Maidens ... I am going to take the bull by the horns and tell my father all about us this mail. I *must* ... Oh, that the days were here when we need never separate again ... Oh, come to me, come to me, do come to me. The world has gone completely wrong all of a sudden ... Write, darling, write for God's sake ...

And this time, at long last, he did tell his father.

And then:

> Thank God for her telegram and now three glorious packets of letters. When the news got through I thought of all the most dreadful

> happenings and I scanned the papers for the tragedies. She is well! My love is well and not drowned in the Nigim Bagh! Your story of the floods is amazing ... *Do* come down, my beloved, before I go to Saugor ... I have had several shots at a schooner in a gale but I cannot get the feeling and atmosphere in this terrible place and I've had to tear up all my efforts ... Come down, come down to him, she *must* come down ... Farewell for the moment, my queen. All, all, all my love a thousand times over for a thousand years, from her ownest worshipping John ...

But I did not go. The road had been washed away and was under repair and traffic was restricted. But that was not the reason. That would not have put me off.

I had no money. We had just paid that taxi bill. Yet this was not the reason either. I never considered money when I really wanted to do something and I could have run up another bill at Maidens.

To be dragged to Delhi in the heat just to see him once or twice was unreasonable and there were limits beyond which I had to protect myself from his wild demands. But this, too, was not the reason. I had never thought about myself before. Again and again I had wanted passionately to go to him and been ready to travel twice that distance just to be with him for a day, an hour, a single minute!

The road, money and John's wildness were the excuses which I marshalled in my surface mind but the truth was that I did not go because ... I did not *want* to, because ... because now ... I did not care enough. And subconsciously I knew this.

He left Meerut at the beginning of September with a small private army of orderlies, bearers, *syces*, horses and forage and it was 10 days before I heard from him again – from the Equitation School.

> ... work and bother and *bandabasts* and I haven't had one second to write to my beloved! This is a grand place. It's like being back at school, chivvied from pillar to post with small aggravating parades ... I am already busy with a young remount which I have to lead along the roads without letting him bolt into the blue or come down on my head like a cartload of bricks and I have to groom him every morning ... Oh, my most beautiful, my little darling, how he longs and longs for her. At the first possible moment I will get you down here. It's not a bad station and the surrounding country is beautiful ... green, undulating hills covered with tiger and panther jungles, with pig-sticking about six miles out ... Besides which, my sweet, there's an

> awfully nice crowd of fellows on the course and I'm extremely happy.
> My only worry now is *you*, my darling. You mustn't get snowed up …

Snow was now falling heavily in the high mountains and the temperature in Srinagar had dropped sharply. But we could not come down now for my mother was on the point of succeeding with the Maharajah and we hoped to be invited to a guest house and then to accompany him to Jammu when he moved down to his winter capital.

The next day, in another cheerful letter, John was planning to take a 40 mile block of jungle and arrange a Christmas shoot – just four of us. He and I and a young married couple. But the day after that, the tone of his letter was very different.

> My sweetheart pet, my darling, I do want you so badly especially as things are not going well with me. I had a spasm of heart yesterday which frightened me … I was riding round the closed school and suddenly felt weak. This morning, the doctor told me that I've got high blood pressure and must be careful. I believe I shall be boarded out of the army on medical grounds and I'm in a mighty bad mental state. I told you that I had overspent myself and was forced to write to my governor for support, which he gave me, with many reservations and restrictions. Well, I thought things were now alright. But his letters, since then, have all been hostile and estranged. Poor darling, I am terribly sorry to have to tell you all this but I cannot contain it … On this forlorn day I can write no more. I hate everything …

The news about his heart was worrying and our plans seemed shaken up again and as for his father, all the signs there seemed ominous. Mail took three weeks to reach England then and he would not have received John's letter yet, breaking the news about us. It might be another month before we should know his reaction. Then that night, a telegram arrived and the next morning, another. The first one read:

'In hospital heart groggy should like darling see you at once trying to get home all love J.'

And the second one:

'Desire you come immediately all love J.'

I thought he must be dying and quite frantic with shock and anxiety, I hurried to Nedous and scanned the notice board where people advertised spare seats in cars going down the mountain. A Captain Field was leaving the next morning with a seat and I settled with him what I regarded as a purely business arrangement. Then I wired to John telling him that I was leaving at once and would travel via Delhi and be with him in four days – that was the quickest I could do it. I packed my trunks and saw them onto the baggage lorry, discussed the future with my mother and at five o'clock the next morning, drove away with Captain Field.

I hated leaving her so suddenly, alone and rather stranded. My last view of her, like John's of me a month before, was pathetic. It seemed as if the impetus of this great Indian adventure was carrying me farther and farther into the unknown and leaving her behind. In the cold darkness before my last Kashmiri dawn as I started on this uncertain journey, I was fully conscious now that I did not want to take it.

The first hours were glorious as we drove through the mountains over the Banihal Pass, the highest in the world, and then wound slowly, always turning, forever turning, down that marvellous road.

Captain Field was a nice safe little man – a safe driver and a safe companion. He talked all the time. A bit too much. I wished he would be quiet and let me think, for I needed to think. I was not only worried about John but bewildered and apprehensive about everything. I think I knew already how all this would end.

At midday we stopped at a dak bungalow. It was warm now, the air of the plains was already touching us. After that, we drove relentlessly on. He was anxious to get down before dark and the last hours were a slow, cautious race against the going light.

Covered in dust, we reached Sialkot and drove to a small hotel. The steamy heat was overwhelming and there was a dreamy other-worldly air about the place. Three men and a woman – a great fat helpless jelly – sat lifelessly on the veranda with *burra pegs* (large whiskies) on little brass tables beside them. A native boy squatted on the floor and pulled listlessly on the rope of the *punkah* which waved over their heads with a soft swooshing sound. The woman had a fan, as well, which she held inertly in one hand and jerked across her face occasionally. Her fat white arms were stuck to the arms of the chair; her clothes, which looked like thin wet rags, were moulded to her body and her face was utterly expressionless. They all sat in silence for not one of them had the energy to speak.

With an effort, we hauled our night-bags out of the car and stumbled up the steps, and passing between the phantoms, went into the hotel. I felt drugged by the heat myself and the oil lamps, each with a cloud of buzzing flying creatures round it, cast a dim yellow light which made the place seem even more unreal – and still hotter.

I went straight to my bathroom and this, too, was alive with creeping things, come in through the drain hole in the wall in search of water. I tried not to tread on them with my bare feet, not because I was humane or filled with reverence for life, but because I did not know which of them would bite or sting. The tin tub was full of warm water, even the springs were hot or the water got hot on its way. I washed off the dust and then joined Captain Field in the dining-room where an elaborate badly cooked dinner was served in a slow languid way. Even the Indians were only half alive. I couldn't eat. No one could.

When we went to bed, I crawled under the mosquito net and lay sticking to the sheet inside, stifled, almost expiring. I could not sleep. No one could. I am sure that that poor fat woman hadn't slept or eaten for months. But on the banks of this Lethe she could exist on whisky and doze day and night on that veranda with open staring eyes.

Again we started at five o'clock and for the first few hours were confident of reaching Lahore well before the midday heat. Then, when we had only 90 miles to go, a tyre exploded and poor Captain Field had to change the wheel, with me trying to help in a useless way. Soon afterwards, another one went and now the dry burning heat was fearful when we stopped again on the dusty road, the plain flat and desolate all round – not a car or habitation to be seen. But that wasn't all. They went on bursting every 10 or 15 miles. He had plenty of inner tubes but no more spare wheels and he then had the awful work of prising off the tyres. We could see Lahore when the last one went and when a car appeared and stopped and I was offered a lift, I accepted it, feeling rather mean at leaving Captain Field behind still struggling. But an army lorry pulled up soon afterwards and helped him get the car in. It took us six hours to do those 90 miles with the temperature reaching 110° and it was tea-time when I was dropped at Faletti's.

When Captain Field arrived we had tea together. We were friends now and shyly he revealed to me how much I had hurt him because I had treated him, at first, just as a driver and the whole thing as a petrol-sharing transaction whereas what he wanted and had really advertised for, was a companion. I apologised and tried to make up for this insensitive blunder but when he asked me if he could call me by my Christian name and come to see me in Delhi, I wasn't slow to take advantage of this favourable turn of events and when it came to proffering my petrol money I did so with the utmost diffidence – desisting the moment he demurred. For what was I but a 'grasper'?

I reached Delhi at eight o'clock the next morning and was met by the stationmaster with a telegram. I was sure John must have died.

'Quite well again don't come yet cholera raging all love J.'

I was frightened before I opened it. I was stunned when I did. Then, coming towards me smiling, I saw Jane's boy-friend. After I left, my mother had wired to one of the Gordons to meet me but as he was on parade and couldn't, he had sent Rupert instead. They were now quartered in the Fort together. I had always looked down on him but now I was pleased to see him and during breakfast at Maidens, he gave me all the news of Delhi.

I did not know what to do. I did not want to stay in Delhi, the scene of all last winter's triumphs and injuries and I was sure that I would be an outcast – and besides, I couldn't afford it. I had hardly any money now. I was living on my wits and the only way of doing that, the well-known way, was to live upon one's friends, play Molly's game, the girl who lived for years in India and hardly spent a thing, cadging visits everywhere. But if I had no friends – how could I do that? I was surprised that Rupert was so friendly but he didn't count for he was only Tank Corps, pulled over the social line last winter by Jane and her colonel father. But even if I had *one* friend, if Judy liked me still – she wasn't here yet. There were no women down in Delhi yet, Rupert told me – at least, just one, one married couple whom I hardly knew, out in cantonments.

When Rupert left me I collected my car which had been repaired after the accident and drove about the whole morning searching for somewhere cheap to stay and seeing what I could sell. I returned to Maidens for lunch and afterwards wrote to my mother and John.

In my letter to him, I didn't entirely conceal my annoyance, for I was annoyed by the needlessness of it all, even with him. To my mother, after describing the journey and the shock of the telegram when I arrived, I wrote:

> ... I tried to make the manager of Maidens reduce his charges – but he wouldn't ... my *banjulele* will fetch something and they say that the car should sell within a fortnight. In the meantime, using it restores some of my self-confidence ... I am counting on staying with Judy when she arrives. John has always said that he would arrange for me to stay with Bernard and his family. Perhaps I shall go there. Anyway, don't worry about me. I shall soon get settled, borrow horses and become a hot-weather queen! ... This afternoon I am driving out to tea with the Andersons and I'm hoping to make immediate arrangements with them. I don't want to spend a single night in Maidens! ...

And I did. They were hard up and bored and glad to have me and by the evening I was cheaply and comfortably settled – once more among the Gordons.

I could not judge things by them – a detached, indifferent couple – and I was nervous of meeting the others again. But I was ready to put up with any number of snubs so long as I could save money while waiting to go down to

John in Saugor. Then I wrote to my mother again.

> ... the Andersons are both rather stupid but very kind and the others are one and all most friendly. How unexpected! At a regimental concert, the other night, the Colonel came up to me and shook my hand! I sat next to Andrew, just down from Simla. 'Your name is mud there,' he told me and roared with laughter, greatly entertained ... It amuses and interests me to be here again under such peculiar circumstances. ... At six every morning and again every evening we bathe in the new Viceregal swimming pool. It has marble pillars and is lovely, far more alluring than the muddy waters of the Nigim Bagh ...

I had injured one of them and been dropped by society yet the Gordons were indifferent and it seemed, once again, as if it would be easy to climb back, if I wanted to, through the autonomous and self-governing society of men. I still did not understand how uneven were the terms in a slave-using kingdom, highly charged and exciting – an open brothel. Nor did I see how small were the chances and how soon the slaves grew stale.

The next day I wrote to my mother again. I wrote daily to them both now.

> ... Hugh and Madeleine have a three-months-old baby. A dear little thing but terribly white and limp and covered with prickly heat. They could not keep it in the hills, they hadn't enough money. An English nurse looks after it ... I can't borrow a horse. All the subalterns are quartered in the fort now and it's too far ... A swarm of locusts came over yesterday. The sky was brown with them and the compound and the roads were a shimmering carpet. Today, there is an appalling dust storm and always, every conceivable sort of insect, reptile and rodent crawling, flying or hopping everywhere and into everything. A large lizard dropped from the ceiling onto my shoulder the other night and gave me such a shock. I thought it was a cobra, at least! ...

Then John began writing again and his letters upset me.

> ... I am now quite well. I am terribly sad about this temporary derangement of your plans to come to Saugor but you must please try to understand the situation. Yesterday, I wrote a very snappy letter* to you, mine darling, and I am very sorry but my nerves were all on edge and I couldn't explain fully to you what I am going through now. My sweetest, this is a monastery, an institution of labour. The instructors

* This letter has been lost.

watch you like cats ... When your work is finished they want to see what you do afterwards and if you don't school a pony or charger or play some game, they give you a bad chit. Such is the system which must be obeyed. The days are full; remount parades and equitation, lectures and sword drill, polo and school, school and again school. If you came down I could do none of these things ... so I should be far happier if you would stay in Delhi for some time. I did badly want you when I was ill because I thought I was going to 'kick the bucket' but my heart is perfectly sound ... it was only from playing too much squash in the heat of the day ... I wish you weren't living with those beastly Gordons, poodle-fakers of the worst description but I suppose there is nowhere else ... Darling, darling Phi, we shall see each other soon but *not now*. I hope you can see the sense of this ... and cholera rages in the bazaar, another reason why my darling must not come ...

He then gave me a number of errands to do; guns and ammunition to order for his Christmas shoot and crash helmets for his pig-sticking.

Thank you, my sweetheart. Do write to me more practically and then you will be a first-class girl. You must, my darling, ride energetically each day and for a long time without stirrups ... Oh, my Phi, cheer up and play the game. On this course, I have given up thinking deeply and live as Rome does – and it pays. But the community that you are living in is very different and I fear you will get the wrong ideas if you lash around with that mob ...

It was a new shock to hear that I could not go to Saugor yet, that it too, like all John's plans, was pushed away into the vague future. I understood the reason well enough. The course was intensive and his life was full and I accepted that. Cholera had nothing to do with it. There was always some disease raging in the bazaar wherever one was. He seemed to think that I hadn't the sense to understand things and needed frightening as well. And he didn't like my letters now – they didn't suit the mood of Saugor. And he deplored my living with the Gordons but he never mentioned the abortive journey which had landed me among them, nor did he remember his promise for me to stay with Bernard and his family. I was to cheer up and play the game, *his* game and as for ordering me to ride every day – how could I when I didn't have a horse. His new life was carrying him away from me already and when I replied – I was critical.

My darling, I have nothing to say and I can sympathise with you. But Saugor hardens one. The place is most unromantic and if I have written in a different strain it is because 'Saugor is as Saugor does' ... I don't

> wish to hurt but I *have* changed my outlook and you cannot possibly appreciate why ... I hate the type of woman who goes 'jungle-ising' and brags about her experiences in male sport. I do not, however, mind a woman who is modest and filled with wonderment. It was because I thought *you* would be like that, that I asked you to come on the Christmas shoot ...

Then, with clever comic illustrations, he described the mounting of a raw four-year-old horse.

> The first stage is to lie across the saddle. The next, to put one's foot in the stirrup and cock one's leg over. The first day, I crept up to Anna May Wong, another fellow gave me a leg up and all went well. I did it twice but the third time I was in a maelstrom of hind legs. Today, I got my leg over but again both my trusty assistants (*syces*) who are supposed to prevent the horse from bolting forward, fled their posts and I received thirty bucks which, however, did not unseat me ... I enjoy it. It would do some of those Gordons a power of good to come down here ... I should never have asked you to come. The most crazed thing I have ever suggested ... I suppose I am a creature of moods ... no policy, and I deeply deplore every damn thing I do. Always and forever your ownest John with all his tender love for his darling Phi ...

He ended his letters with the same rapturous phrases but their tone was different and his apologies, I felt, were not real but only cool, impatient words and when he said that the place was unromantic he was really saying that he cared less for me. That arrogant, critical, terrible mind was now turning upon me and as a woman and an outsider I felt suddenly inferior and tossed aside and I wondered if his love would survive Saugor, survive marriage and life – or whether it was as weak and unreliable as he himself.

If he had changed and I did not like it – I had changed too, and he must have felt it. But I did not admit it to myself. If I saw his weaknesses and was wary and critical of his wild ways, I still believed that I adored him and would take him as he was and love and cherish him forever. But did I and would I? Would *my* love survive Saugor and marriage any better than his? The hot-weather idyll was over and we neither of us knew it.

In the meantime, these critical, hurtful exchanges ended, the cloud of misgiving which had blown to the surface dissolved, his weakness and my fears were forgotten as our lives settled into their new more strenuous patterns. His letters became short, breezy and less regular and mine grew lively and confident.

Madeleine and I were still the only women in Delhi. No one knew about

John, and I became, in truth, the hot-weather queen – as I had gaily predicted. After the long monastic months, not only the Gordons, but all the men of Delhi fell upon me wherever I went and although I was conscious of John all the time and I kept them at arm's length, nevertheless, I enjoyed my reign. After apologising one day for not having written, John went on,

> ... one hasn't even time to blow one's nose (to be vulgar!). Remount Anna is now alright be'ind! I mounted him (Anna is a 'him') for two days in a Baldock tackle which is an apparatus by whose action no horse can move horizontally, vertically or laterally and, after this, he let me get up on his back without any more trouble ... I'm glad you are feeling happier but I wish you weren't living where you are – in suburbia. Can't you break and live somewhere else? ... My darlingest, I must fly and get on board my charger ...

In a letter to my mother at the beginning of October, I wrote:

> I am most relieved that you have found someone to share a boat with but if you don't move to a State guest-house soon, you must go to Nedous. Their out-of-season prices will be low and you will be safer and more comfortable ... John's parents treat him like a child and keep him dependent for every penny. After the money quarrels, I told him that when he leaves the army we can *both* earn, live carefully and become independent of their much-grudged bounty. This would bring them to their senses and they would respect him ... I do wish I had brought all my old clothes down. I could have sold them to the Jocks' wives for *enormous* sums! ...

When I wrote to her again, after several pages of anxious advice, I went on:

> Here's drama for you! A few days ago, I went into my room and found Madeleine there. 'You must help me' she said, handing me a letter. I read it. It was a letter of discovery, finish and farewell. Then, she dropped onto my bed and poured it all out. She had never loved Hugh and now she was desperately in love with another man and had been carrying on secretly with him for months – until his wife found one of her letters. At this point, she collapsed completely, sobbing and crying – and Hugh came in. He couldn't imagine what was wrong. For two days she kept up this hysterical weeping until he was quite distraught. And her lover didn't really care for he relinquished her so easily and when she telephoned him in despair, all she got was a hard, indifferent 'cheerio' – which set her off again. I was now afraid that she was going to do something foolish and I advised her to tell Hugh (he is the kindest

and most forgiving of men) and have it over. She must build her happiness here, upon a rock, I told her – and not upon a heartless shadow. The next night, after a dinner party (Hugh, strained and white went to bed before the guests departed) we talked it all over again until 2 a.m. when I forced her to go into him and tell him – and she did. He paced the room for the rest of the night. But it is over. That was why she did not keep the baby in the hills – not because of poverty but because her lover was waiting for her here ...

Rolled up in one of her trunks, my mother had been carrying that nightmarish portrait of the Viceroy about with her and now she was struggling with it again. Also, she had at last clinched the commission to paint the Maharani and sittings were soon to begin. All this was good news yet I was worried about her, for she had been ill again. She had been moving from boat to boat, sharing with a succession of unsatisfactory people, trying to save money all the time. Our income from home was about £8 a week and when the monthly debt payments were deducted, we were left with hardly anything. Now, I begged her to move to Nedous and then, when the portraits were finished, to return to England and leave me behind with John. After pressing this course upon her, I wrote:

I have sold the car and tomorrow, I will put the money into your bank ... I shall get some rebate from the insurance and I still have the banjulele to sell ... I have heard from Harold again, a rather agitated letter. He says that nothing will ever make him change and he will marry me whenever I say the word. I am sure he will meet some nice girl in Poona and marry before I do ...

Then I wrote again:

No letter from you for three days. I hope this doesn't mean that you are ill again? ... A diverting incident in the bungalow yesterday. After breakfast, I heard a scream and then another. I rushed out of my room and saw Madeleine, clutching the baby, dash into her bedroom and slam the door as a huge rat ran across the hall and into the box-room. At the same moment, all the servants fled to their go-downs and the nurse and I were left looking at each other! Rats carry plague, rats eat babies, rats are our enemies, rats must be killed ... I picked up a golf club and followed the rat and the nurse followed me! Heroics!

I chased it round the room among the trunks and boxes vainly trying to hit it while the elderly nurse stood stolidly in the middle encouraging me with her presence! This went on for a long time and then, when I stopped for a moment, wondering what to do next, it shot across the floor between us and I struck wildly at it, but when it ran on and disappeared under a huge wardrobe, I was sure that I had missed it again. The only thing to do then was to get it out and I got down on my knees with my face almost touching the floor and peered underneath. Rats, when cornered, fly at your throat, I then thought, removing my face from the floor and poking and rattling the club about. 'We must move the wardrobe' I said, and together we prised it an inch or two from the wall and I pushed the club down behind it. But still it stayed where it was. 'We must move it right out' and we heaved and tugged and dragged it clear. Then, holding the club poised for attack, I peeped round the back. And there it was, unmoving and easy to strike – unmoving because it was dead.

I killed the rat just as I had killed the spiders and hunted the jackal, without a moment's consideration for lesser lives, for life as such, without a thought for an alternative to killing or regret at having killed. I knew little about Hinduism and nothing at all about the Jains who revere and preserve all living things, even an insect. These barbaric attitudes I shared with my race.

My mother now had a psychic experience. She woke in the night and saw my hand, just my hand, in front of her. And I wrote:

> I can't interpret that experience and I hope no other parts of my anatomy will appear to you! ... It is wonderful the way you have stuck at that portrait and finished it at last. If you send it to me in a roll I will stretch, varnish and deliver it. To have that money in the end will be fine ... I am glad the portrait of the Maharani is to be small – easier to do. You will soon go down to Jammu with them ... You must not be ill again by poisoning or starvation. Avoid rich food and supplement your diet ... I have sold the green sequin dress for Rs.8, the dyed peach one for Rs.2 and the blue coat for 10 – so do I scratch for money like a barnyard hen while I reign as Queen of Delhi!

When I wrote again:

> I am very worried about John. I've not heard from him for 10 days and I'm always expecting to hear that he's been thrown on his head or broken a limb. I have been told that there is an accident every day on that course and even a death, sometimes. As for the horses – the place is a shambles ... Next week, the Simla influx begins. I shall have to feel my way about and find *someone* to stay with when the Andersons leave for England next month ... All my clothes are in rags. I mend and patch and fuss over them continually ...

Two days later, I received a telegram from John saying that he was leaving for Delhi that night and asking me to meet him at Maidens for lunch the next day.

Madeleine saw the telegram arrive and although I tried to hide my excitement she was an inquisitive, sharp-eyed woman, and for the rest of the day she watched me with a knowing, jealous expression.

10

The End of the Mad Mountain Dream

IT WAS two months since we had seen each other, since those Bacchanalian weeks in Srinagar. There was a trance-like quality about the hot-weather period but now, the temperature was more natural, we were back in the real world of rigid social codes and imperial power and purpose and much had happened to us both. I wasn't even sure what he would look like, fit and well from the healthy rigours of the course or ill and strained as I had so often seen him. I was deliriously happy for my love leapt up as strong and sweet as in the beginning yet when I reached Maidens, I grew desperately nervous.

He was waiting just inside the main door and he could see me as I came up the steps and when he jumped up to meet me, I saw at once that something had gone wrong.

He looked wild, dishevelled – agonised. And so dirty and unshaven, his clothes so creased and crumpled that I thought he must have just come off the train. When he told me that he had arrived early that morning and taken a room in the hotel for the day, I was utterly shocked. I wanted to tell him to go up at once and have a bath and shave and change his clothes – but I didn't. I could never treat him like other men and I could see how he was suffering. He had been drinking while he waited, of course, and now he ordered another large whisky and something for me. We hadn't embraced or even kissed, only shaken hands – and he didn't speak. And I didn't ask what had happened. I was sure that he would tell me during lunch.

It was Saturday, the great luncheon-party day (as at the Cecil) when all the smart people down from Simla and back from England poured in to entertain each other.

He wanted to go on sitting in the hall drinking but when, at last, I persuaded him to go into the dining-room and we walked in together, I felt so dowdy now and, even with John beside me, suddenly so unsure again and inferior – and he looked like a tramp. With the orchestra playing, the *khitmagars* scurrying about, and the gay chatter and laughter rising and exploding all round us, we sat at our table detached from it all in a little pool of gloom, not eating, just playing with the fine food and scarcely speaking.

'Have you got your car?' he asked me presently.

'Yes.' (I had borrowed it back for the day.)

'Then let's drive to somewhere quiet where we can talk. I can't stand this.'

'Alright,' I answered and we sat in silence after that.

Although he couldn't stand it, he didn't hurry to get away and talk and he let the courses come and go whether we wanted them or not and the whole elaborate meal spin out its convivial time. And afterwards, we sat for a long time in the lounge over coffee and brandies. In fact, he seemed to be dawdling deliberately as if he didn't want to go and I grew more and more mystified and anxious. When I saw him about to order yet another brandy, I couldn't bear it any longer and I got up. 'Darling, do let's go.' Reluctantly he got up too, and we walked out to the car.

It was very hot outside but by this time, I was almost as distraught as he was and I never noticed that he came without his topee. I drove out of Delhi to a road on the outskirts that I knew well. It ran along the edge of the jungle and was always utterly deserted. When we got there I slowed down.

'This will do, won't it? It's a nice quiet place.'

'No. No. We must get off the road – into the jungle. We've passed several tracks.'

I drove on and at the next cutting turned off and we bumped over the rough ground between scrub for about a hundred yards and then I stopped.

'Go on a bit further,' he protested at once. Still humouring him I drove on another hundred yards, then stopped again.

'Can't you go on a little further?' His tone was desperate now and wheedling. I tried to help him.

'No, darling,' I answered gently. 'We can't go on and on. There's no point. And I can turn the car here.'

He gave up and without saying any more, sat staring through the windscreen, his face set, his hands clenched, his whole body tense. I had hoped that as soon as we were alone he would embrace me. But he was even colder and harder. I stretched out my hand but as soon as I touched him he jerked away.

'Tell me what all this means?' I said desperately. He did not answer but went on staring out of the car. For a long time we sat in silence with the sun beating through the canvas hood and not a breath of air inside those dry, thick, tangled walls. Then with his head turned away, speaking not to me but to the jungle, some words – strangled, stuttering, hardly audible came from him.

'I've ... I've ... heard from my father.'

'I thought it was about time you did. Is that why you haven't written for 10 days?'

'Yes. I didn't know how to. I was nearly off my head. I thought I was going mad.'

'But, darling, there was no need to get so upset. Whatever he wrote, you could be sure I'd understand.'

'He's furious. He wrote me a terrible letter.'

'But you always thought he'd take it badly. That's why you were so long telling him.'

'If I marry you he'll cut me off without a penny.'

'That's just what he would say. That's the threat he's always using to control you. And even if he means it, what does it matter? You're free, aren't you? You don't care about the Army which needs money. You can get a job and so can I. We can stand on our own feet and live very well without his bounty and when he sees how independent and happy we are he'll change his tune. And if I can once meet him he'll change it even quicker. I've said all this to you before.'

'We could never do that. It's impossible. I couldn't keep you. I couldn't keep myself in the way that I am used to.'

'You care for money more than you care for me.'

'And so do you. That's just what my father says. It's not me that you love. It's my money that you're after. You've not loved me as I've loved you. If you'd really loved me you would have come down to Delhi to say good-bye to me before I left for Saugor. You're a climber and a grasper just like all the others. And your mother's only an artist. She's brought you out to India just to get you married well. In England you'd have no position at all. And when we met at Kasauli it wasn't just by chance. You weren't licked by a mad dog. You made it up. You chased and caught me there. My father says you did and my father's always right. I admire and respect him. He's the only person in the world that I can trust and when he tells me not to marry you I'm going to do just what he says.'

He was shouting at me now. The sweat was pouring down his unshaven face into his dirty crumpled collar and his eyes were wild and cruel. He looked mad. I started up the engine and turned the car and drove back along the track. When we reached the road he leapt out.

'I can find my own way back,' he shouted angrily, slamming the door and because I was angry too, I drove away. But when I had gone about a quarter of a mile, I looked back. He was walking in the opposite direction, not towards Delhi but out into the country and I noticed, for the first time, that he had no topee. I turned and drove back to him.

'Don't be a fool,' I said. 'Get in and come back with me. You'll get sunstroke next.'

'I don't care if I do. I can look after myself. I'm not coming with you.' And he went on walking and I drove away for the second time.

I returned the car and then, hoping that Madeleine was out and not peeping from the windows, crept round to the back of the bungalow and into my room through the sweeper's door and the bathroom. I went to the table where I wrote all my letters and sat down before it on the upright chair. And while I sat, I could see myself from the outside, see my mind stop, my spirit vanish, see my body droop and shrivel as if I had been murdered and was now being buried and I remained in my room, sitting on that chair, for the rest of the day, all that night and the whole of the next day. For 24 hours I was as dead and then, my life flowed back. When I moved and looked round and heard the sounds of the world I felt as if I had not only returned from the grave but as if I had left there, left buried behind me there, a great and oppressive burden. I was not only alive again but light – and free! I was myself again!

The mountain dream had started with a madness, a heaven-lit wild colliding, and carried me on and on, and down and down into a dark concluding madness, a violent pure repulsing – and a dying. Then, my golden thread had sought and found me in my grave and pulled me back.

That night I wrote to my mother:

> My world has exploded and fallen round me, and I give thanks – for I am free and can go on ...

I then recounted all that had happened, ending,

> You threw up everything and went to Africa to find the man that you already knew and you married him and, afterwards, you lost him and went on. I had to come to India and become a 'climber' and an 'insinuator' to find John but, unlike you, I had to lose him before I married him – and go on. He was a man to love inside a dream but not to marry in the waking state – and I think I am the same ... It is he who suffers now, another 'cruel disillusionment', and until he finds himself, he will be caught in this pain ...

Madeleine knew what had happened. She could read all the signs. There was nothing she didn't know about the advances and reverses of love – especially other people's. She watched me fascinated.

A few days later, I wrote to my mother again, on a practical level now. She had moved down to Jammu and I planned to join her there.

> Everything is the same here, lively and distracting, people in and out all day. Living in an Indian cantonment I can see, as John did, how deadly

and devilish it can be; all the quarrelling and denigration ... a soldier's life is awful and the life of a soldier's wife worse still. One would have to be terribly in love to be able to wander the far-flung garrisoned corners of the empire with a soldier husband ... What an extraordinary role women do play in men's lives! How they change, become like their men, become their alter egos and their slaves. First I was Harold and then I became John! Do all relationships do this, change men as well as women? Can we never be ourselves? But now the gates have been opened, the slave has been liberated and the road is outside, the road which I keep losing and mistaking – my road, my *true* road! ... I will join you as soon as you can arrange it with the Maharajah ...

A day or two later, at the beginning of November, I wrote again:

Your postcard has relieved my mind. Thank goodness that you are moving to the State guest-house tomorrow. I am taking for granted that H.H. will welcome me and planning to leave here the night of the 8th ... The last months have been so disturbing. I left you so suddenly and so unprovided for and it worried me a lot ... I know that I have used you and used your talent and made you suffer. Youth is a rash ruthless time ... But I have changed, sown my wild oats and never before have I felt such relief and such a lofty and easeful sense of security and confidence ... the fog has dispersed and I can see ahead, get back onto the road, knowing exactly what I want to do ... settle down in London, look for a good job, make friends and build a rich, intellectual life – while you, with your health restored, will paint, not for money, but for yourself at last ... The people coming down from Simla now are still *most* unfriendly. Judy almost rude. I could never have stayed with her and I shall be glad to leave ...

I did not mention my task, that was still my secret, but I was sure that in London, after all, I would find it.

I delivered the Viceroy's portrait, packed and then, to celebrate my release, indulged in a little adventure which harmonised with my poverty and my habitual interests but which, in India then, was almost an act of treason. I bought a 3rd Class ticket to Sialkot, believing that I was making my first daring attempt to touch and experience the Indian people. On another, less conscious level, it was an act of defiance against the Raj and the society which I had loved, hated and so thoroughly experienced.

At the station, when I stood among the low-caste natives in front of my *purdah* compartment with the white race walking up and down staring coldly and curiously at me, I cringed and hoped that no one that I knew would pass and recognise me. I had to stand there until the train started. I couldn't take my seat and hide inside for the tumult within was horrifying. In fact, now that I had done it, elected to travel 3rd Class and mix with the people, I could hardly bear the prospect. The encounter was too sudden and extreme.

On five of the six wooden benches five fat, veiled, voluminous women sat cross-legged, each with a baby in her arms and a bevy of wriggling, chattering children around her. Every bit of floor space was piled high with tin trunks, baskets, bundles, cooking pots, water jars and bedding. The five husbands tangled with each other and the children, as they leapt in and out fussing over their wives and adding more and more goods to the stack already there.

I went and bought some fruit and then came back and stood, in a cowardly way, in front of an empty 1st Class compartment but when a white man and smart servant came to claim it I slunk back to the brown attentive husbands, shouting through the window now and pushing sticky sweets up to the children through the door. Not until the whistle blew and the husbands scurried away to their own parts of the train, could I bring myself to climb in.

Such floor space as was left was already covered with big red sploshes and I picked my way between them as I went to my bench. There was a strong peculiar smell and the heat and noise were appalling. Counting the babies there were 22 of us in the compartment. I sat down, determined to learn all I could and make friends.

One after the other, they let down their veils revealing dull, ugly faces and red mouths, for they were all chewing *pan* or betel nut and squirting it over the floor. I smiled and tried my Hindustani on them but with no response at all. They just stared heavily. If they were thinking anything, they were probably taking me for a 'poor white' or a Eurasian and despising me. But their stares looked quite mindless and before long they lost interest and for the next few hours, until we turned out the lights and tried to sleep, they screamed incessantly to each other and to their children while they fumbled in their baskets and muddled about. My bench was next to the lavatory door and the constant trailing in and out and the escaping stench were detestable. When I had to go in there myself the flood, filth, dust and soot were the final horror.

These families were not dirty in themselves. They were very clean, as Indians, even of low caste, invariably are. It was only their strangeness and primitiveness from which I recoiled. The next day, at Sialkot, my mother met me with a State car and I was thankful that my next attempt to learn something about the people of India would be on the very highest level.

She was well and very pleased that I had decided to return to England. She had heard from the Viceroy. He liked the picture and had told her that if he didn't take it home with him when he left India, it would be hung in the new Viceroy's House.

She had never before had quite such a long hard struggle over a portrait and although it was like him – even now she never failed with the likeness – yet it was laboured, lifeless work. That fine commission, begun with such professional pride and confidence, ended as another grand impressive pot-boiler handed over with relief and a despairing unconcern, the cheque being all that mattered.

Jammu was a picturesque old city in the Himalayan foothills and the State guest-house was a bleak but comfortable bungalow, clinging to a rocky slope. I settled down happily to several weeks of interesting idleness, free of all anxiety about money.

The Maharajah had recently taken unto himself a new wife. After many years with many wives but no son and heir, he had consulted the priests and been told that, according to the auguries, he must first espouse a tree and then a woman of the people. The ceremony with the tree was duly performed and afterwards a peasant girl was searched for and another wedding celebrated. It was this girl that my mother had been commissioned to paint.

The sittings, which were begun in Srinagar, were now resumed and a car transported her, with all her paraphernalia, to the Palace every morning. But the portrait was not going well. The girl was dull and plain and inanimate, slumping on her throne in all her jewels and gold-thread saris like a sack of potatoes. Again, my mother grew nervous, fearing that she would never be able to produce the ravishing queen that His Highness was expecting.

They could not talk to each other which made it still more difficult and I suggested coming too, to see if my kitchen Hindustani would serve to wake her up. As it was not so far beneath the level of her peasant speech, we got on quite well and my mother was able to catch some expression and finish the head, the anxious part, and after that the clothes were easy and it was soon completed – and approved.

My mother was looking forward to returning to England, but already I had changed our plans. It seemed a pity, when passing, not to stop and see the sights of Egypt and climb another social ladder, if I could.

Before we left Jammu, I received another worried letter from Harold, asking me to meet him in Bombay before I sailed for home. I arranged to see him at the Taj Mahal Hotel, wondering how he knew that I was going home. He was waiting in the hall when we arrived.

He was different. Not only were his new London clothes better cut but he himself had changed. He was less confident, almost shy, and his expression was serious and thoughtful. We all lunched together in the vast, interior dining-room with the orchestra playing, the tables occupied by wealthy tourists, wealthy Indians, international businessmen and British officials. The Gateway of India, close by, was built and kept for kings; this was the gateway of the peoples, and the music, the heavy scent, the cosmopolitan throng and a man still loving me, all of it – went to my head. Two years before I had landed here a penniless nobody, an outsider, with nothing but my mother's art and my own wits and her art had soon failed – yet I had conquered India! I had lived at the top, lived and loved, done everything, risen and fallen and risen again but always kept inside, kept up, kept living – living at the highest pitch. But as I sat there triumphing, at the moment of leaving, I knew all the time that I was still an outsider and would always be one. But I did not care now for I had learnt that the only thing that mattered was to live, to experience – and go on.

After lunch, Harold and I went upstairs to the big lounge and settled ourselves in two comfortable chairs in a quiet corner, looking out to sea. As soon as the coffee was brought we began to talk and he came straight to the point.

'How did you know that I was leaving India?' I asked at once.

'Madeleine told me. I've had several letters from her lately – since you've been staying with her.'

'Madeleine!' I answered surprised. 'She never told me that she was writing to you and I didn't know that you were on writing terms.'

'No, neither did I,' he replied, 'but I suppose she thought she had something to write about.'

'What did she write about?'

'She told me you were in love with another man – a cavalry chap at Saugor.'

'That's true, Harold, I *was* in love with a man at Saugor. But how did she know that? I never told her anything about him. I never told anyone. And now it's over.'

'She told me that it had been going on for a year, that you'd been writing to him all the time we were engaged. Is that why you were so often cold and I so often wondered if you really loved me? How *could* you do that? How *could* you play such a double game?' I was flabbergasted.

'But Harold, that isn't true!' I protested. 'I didn't meet him, or even see him, until the day you left for Bombay and it was several weeks after that, up in Simla, before I got to know him. I had already asked you to postpone our wedding. Madeleine has made it up. She's been telling you lies. And now I can see what she was doing – reading his letters. I never locked them up. I never thought that there were people who went into each other's rooms like spies. Now I understand why she was always looking at me so knowingly, so nastily – all the time writing to you just to hurt you. I suppose she couldn't hurt me. She could read his letters but she could never know his second name, so she couldn't write off lies to him.'

During this outburst, Harold had changed completely. He was smiling now and bending towards me.

'Darling, I'm so pleased you've told me that. I've been feeling so miserable. I couldn't understand it. I couldn't believe it, yet she was so sure that I thought it must be true.'

'You must have thought me awful. I'm so sorry.'

'I've never stopped loving you and I don't know why, but all this misery has made me love you even more. Can't we start again? You must be ready to marry now? You were going to marry the other chap. Couldn't you marry me, after all?'

'I'm sorry, Harold, but I still don't want to.'

'I've been doing a lot of thinking and I can see now that I took it all too lightly last winter. I know I did. I didn't value you enough. But I do now and I shall never love anyone else. I know I could make you happy. Oh, I know, I know I could.'

'Please don't go on pressing me. I don't want to marry – truly, truly, I don't.'

We rejoined my mother for tea and afterwards we went for a walk along the water-front and in the evening I went with him to the station. He had to be on duty the next morning. The platform was as crowded and noisy as always but he had a compartment to himself.

'Let's sit inside a moment, darling. There's plenty of time.'

I climbed into the train, he pulled down the blinds and switched off the lights, leaving only the blue night light burning. We sat on the bunk and he took my hand and for a few minutes we were silent. Then he spoke.

'I don't know when I shall see you again – perhaps never. Will you let me kiss you – just once, just once before I go?'

I took his other hand and turned towards him and he kissed me, not once, but again and again and when I felt his tears on my face, I wept myself.

'Can't you change your mind? Oh, please, please change your mind.'

I liked him more than I ever had but still I could not love him. And it was true – I did not want to marry.

The whistle blew and the train left. The next day, when I stood on the ship's deck and watched the coastline of India receding – I knew that I would come back.

In Cairo, we stayed in an exclusive pension near the Gezira Club. We had no introductions yet, within a few days, I was dancing at Shepherd's, watching polo at the club, drinking cocktails at the Semiramis — and making friends with everyone of consequence.

We called at the Residency and were entertained by General Sir Peter and Lady Strickland. And Billa, their daughter, became my best friend. Had I been a duke's daughter come out to play and seek a husband, and my mother a duchess, I could not have flashed faster and more dazzlingly upon that fabulous scene — nor my mother been received with more deference.

After the Christmas gaities we stayed on another month and then decided to return the following winter. Restored in health, exhilarated and confident that she could paint again, my mother signed the lease of an unfurnished flat — and we sailed, at last, for home. It was 1930 and we had been away two years.

My grand-mother had died and left her money to Amy, Miss Morison had seen to that. And the Chelsea house was still let. We stayed in various cheap lodgings, secreting food in our trunks in defiance of the landlady, or sharing a gas ring on the landing with the other tenants. We went 'underground,' avoiding chance encounters overhead and, living on nothing, found the money for new clothes, steamer passages and the smart flat in Kasr-el-Doubara where we meant to entertain the haute-monde. It was not only a time of passionate preparation for the next leap out into the world but it was restful — and creative. I wrote again.

We had taken the flat for six months and as we needed at least a month to furnish and equip it and find servants and the Cairo season opened in October, we booked passages on a Dutch boat leaving Southampton at the end of August. We would have left earlier but for our fear of the heat.

My mother looked forward to the fun of a flat in Cairo and to the important part which her painting always played. Forgetting the loss of her powers in London, we were sure that the climate and conditions of India were the cause of her breakdown and her struggles there and that now, with a fine room to work in and our good food, she would succeed again, our position would be assured and my earliest ambitions realised — to marry into the only pleasing world I knew, to relieve her of my support and to support her, in my turn.

We set off without a fear or doubt of any sort and when we found ourselves in the crowded second-class, the only English people among the fat, pale, cheese-eating Dutch colonials going out to jobs and homes in Indonesia, it seemed at first like the last humiliation, the last ordeal of the 'underground' before we burst onto another high imperial stage. But when I got to know them — I loved them. I loved everybody now, for the world kept me in a state of perpetual excitement and this fortnight on the high seas among them, became yet another absorbing experience.

The flat was one of the finest in the diplomatic quarter, comprising the whole upper floor of a large two-storey mansion standing in a beautiful garden and the owner, a distinguished English widow, lived below.

We didn't waste money on an over-night hotel but slept on the floor and picnicked, sitting on our trunks. The next day we bought beds and chairs and cooking pots and beautiful patterned pottery in the bazaar and ordered quantities of the light and lovely peasant furniture.

Although the Delta heat was still severe, we tore about with an energy which was frenetic and, within a week, were living in luxury with woven rugs upon the polished floors, curtains in the windows and the telephone installed.

At the same time, my mother wrote to Lady Strickland, in Alexandria, asking if she might paint her when she came back to Cairo. And when she replied, 'delighted,' the future seemed assured. Our climb to the top would be easy in our own elegant flat beside the Nile. I was bound to triumph.

A few days later I woke in the night to find my mother ill — her old nerve trouble come on again. But I didn't worry very much and nor did she. She'd been overdoing it and I had been foolish to arrive when the Delta weather was still trying but, with every day getting better, she only had to rest and she would soon recover. I didn't even call a doctor.

Every few days a boy arrived with a new consignment of furniture on his head and the flat was filling up and beginning to look grand, with hand-beaten copper trays on shelves and ledges and lovely coloured glass, made from melted down beer bottles, arrayed upon the side-board in the dining-room. And the total cost was £50.

I was going about now and at the races I met some friends, leaving soon for England, and I asked them to pass on their cook. A few days later, Abdul arrived with young Mahomet to do the housework and wait at table. He was a wonderful cook and a sweet old man. They were both Nubians from Upper Egypt. The servants quarters were on the roof.

We were ready now to entertain and make our debut but still my mother lay in bed, eating nothing and swaying about whenever she got up. And I called in the foremost doctor. After he had examined her I went to his consulting room. A large volume, lying open, was on his desk.

'Your mother's condition is very serious' he began. 'She has middle-ear disease and must have an operation at once.' At this he passed the medical dictionary over to me and after I had read the description of the disease, he went on, 'The operation is an extremely dangerous one. In most cases it proves fatal. But nothing else can be done for her.'

That night, as I lay in bed, it seemed as if she had only a few more days to live, but in the morning, I disbelieved everything that he had told me. I thought him a pompous, ignorant fool who enjoyed scaring me and as for his book of diseases, well, anyone I thought could find whatever they wanted to in that. And I would not let her have the operation.

When Lady Strickland wrote to say that they were back in Cairo and she was ready to sit for her portrait, the news made her worse, for it was not just the weather that was causing her illness but also, fear of the portraits which, subconsciously, she knew she could no longer do. We went on waiting for the weather.

I was surprised not to hear from Billa. We had been such friends and I went to the club to watch the polo in the hope of seeing her. And I saw her at once, walking with a girl just out from England, Russell Pasha's daughter, and I waved and walked towards them. But Billa scowled, said something to the girl — and they giggled and turned away. Astonished and hurt I sat down alone.

Afterwards, they went up to the players, whom they knew, and were greeted warmly. I pretended to admire the ponies, hoping I would be noticed and the men would be friendly. They glanced at me superciliously and then ignored me and the girls, watching out of the corners of their eyes, smiled to each other. And I walked away. Walked and walked down the whole length of the polo field, with the eyes of the girls like daggers in my back and their mocking smiles following me.

This incident upset me but my confidence in myself was such that I quickly rebounded and began looking up my other friends. But most of them had gone. A new Guards battalion had arrived and subalterns, surfeited with Mayfair beauties had come. And the mood of those still there had changed. I was no longer a novelty, new girls now took their fancy. I had only been a passing comet and when I reappeared I had been seen before — and I was stale.

A shuffle of the cards, a break in time, a deadly mood, a spiteful word or glance were enough, singly or combined, to blow anyone away without money or position to hold them fast. I was so sure that I had conquered Cairo, yet I had conquered nothing — only an appearance which had shifted like the desert sands.

But I did not accept defeat at once. Remembering our successes at the Cecil, I decided to give a dinner party and I invited everyone I knew. About a dozen accepted — although not the ones I wanted.

My mother could move about now and on the night of the party she stayed up and I helped her dress. It was the first time in my life that I had entertained in my own home and I was proud and excited.

The guests assembled in the splendid drawing-room and my mother received them in a limp, tired way and to make up for her silence I chatted foolishly while I shook up the cocktails. Then, at the right moment, as graciously as any London hostess I helped her up and led the way into dinner.

Fine lace mats, sparkling silver and amber-coloured glass (all from the bazaar) covered the flimsy table and in the dim, yellow candlelight everything looked beautiful and grand. And as for Abdul's dinner – there had never been such a meal!

My mother sat at one end of the table and I, at the other. But by this time she felt so ill and was so weak that she could hardly sit upright on her chair and I should have taken her away. But I chatted and laughed even more to try to make the party 'go,' although I knew already that it had failed. Afterwards, it seemed like a tragi-comic dream, as well it might have been, for I heard nothing more from any of my guests.

Realising what had happened and to try and save me from utter defeat, my mother now wrote to Lady Strickland. She came at once, rolling grandly up to the house in her official car with the G.O.C.'s flag fluttering from the bonnet.

In her fine studio-room, my mother set up her easel and canvas and the camera, which she was now using, was on a table. She took some snapshots of different poses and then sat down behind her canvas, silent, struggling — and then just pretending. Lady Strickland was animated and talkative and should have been easy to do. When she left, my mother fell onto her bed. But, still, I was sure that she did not need that operation.

Although the weather was good now, the Delta was below sea level and the time had come to put my obdurate, near-criminal intuition to the test — and end her suffering. With the help of the driver, I got her into a taxi and, with more help at the station, into a coupé on the night train to Luxor.

After two months of illness, anxiety and inaction — I had at last acted. She would be cured or the exertion would make her worse — and perhaps kill her. In the morning I would know.

When dawn came, I leant over from my top bunk and saw that she was sleeping peacefully. When I climbed down and dressed she woke and when I helped her to get up she was stronger, and when the train reached Luxor and we clambered out — she could walk without my help.

From our window in the Luxor Palace Hotel we looked down on the Nile with the feluccas sailing by and, over on the other side, we could see the Pyramids. We spent a happy, restful day and the next morning when we crossed, she was riding on a donkey. It was the air that did it — and the escaping.

It was Christmas and the hotel was full of British officers and agents from all parts of Egypt, and tourists, and once again I danced and flirted and my happiness returned — and so did hers. Those two weeks were like a still and smiling pool in the middle of a turbulent river — the anxious, striving, ridiculous life which I kept creating for myself — and for my mother.

Back in Cairo, she tried again to paint Lady Strickland — and failed again. And now, we had no money to pay the rent. I had spent it on the trip to Luxor and our landlady was not the sort to confide in and let us stay — or go — without paying.

With just enough to pay our homeward passages, I dismissed the servants (Abdul begged us to take him with us to England) and we spent the last fortnight hiding all our movements until, leaving the flat just as it was, we slipped away one night. I was terrified that she would hear us, call the police and stop us.

When we reached Port Said, the harbour sounds, the sight of ships, the smell of the sea and, when we went aboard, the sense of escape, escape from everything, made me dance inside with joy and relief. I was just 23 when we landed back, once more, in England. As soon as we could, we sent the rent to our landlady.

11

Life in England

THE Chelsea house was still let and bringing in a good rent but it was not difficult to find somewhere else to live for it was 1931 and the economic crisis, when property was slumping and unemployment was already severe.

We found a charming little house in Kensington with a studio in the garden and the owners were so desperate to get rid of the lease that they surrendered it without a premium. When we installed some tenants on the top floor we could live comfortably on our income and, to be in England again with a home of our own, was restful and pleasant and the future seemed good.

But when I began looking for a job, it was not so good. I went to agencies and exchanges and studied the columns of the newspapers and wrote to all the influential people I had ever touched on. Polite but regretful replies came back and the employment clerks laughed at me when I told them the sort of job I wanted, advising me to go away and get myself some qualifications, shorthand and typing to start with. But even then, they said, I would stand little chance of obtaining anything, with so much unemployment. Domestic work, however, was still in demand, they told me.

I joined political groups and little intellectual societies but I found them all so dull. I wanted to entertain in my beautiful new home but I knew no one to ask. I searched for people I had known in India but they all lived in worlds of their own, remote from mine. The friendships were meaningless now, just momentary touchings in space and the re-encounters led to nothing. I even looked up my old school friends, hoping that time would have changed them, but they ignored me. I did go to lunch with Dorothy Chamberlain and I met her father for the first time and talked learnedly about India (giving him much useful advice) but she was getting married soon and she wasn't interested in me any more.

I tried hard to work and make a life in London but I found everything was out of reach or drab and mean. I sat alone admiring my elegant, empty home which soon became a hateful vacuum or I ran about from one trivial thing to another, leading a broken-up, boring, unsatisfying life which seemed to be getting me nowhere. It was all just the same as before. Nothing had changed; not even myself, for all my travelling and trying. Again I hated England for nothing good ever happened there – always she rejected me and I gave up all attempts to conquer a single height or even a low-lying common strip of the measureless, meaningless, incohering ground of London, I shut myself up and wrote poetry, love-hate musings upon England in the style of the 19th century poets which was all I knew – and then a book. A most peculiar work which was better sung than read but which kept me busy and happy for a long time although I didn't take it seriously and when it was finished and the creative fire went out, the emptiness and desolation were even worse. I felt at an absolute standstill. Then, quite by chance, we were given tickets for Roehampton Club and we went out to watch the polo.

The big match of the afternoon was between an Indian team, Jaipur State – led by the young Maharajah, and an English cavalry regiment. I loved watching polo then and as the ponies turned and twisted and I heard their furious panting and the rapid clatter of their hooves and the sound of the struck ball and saw the vivid carven pairs of riders race together, pushing against each other with sudden blasphemous shouts, the game and the vigorous antique world of space and flowing form which it proclaimed excited me and when it was over, I went up to the Maharajah. I would never have dared to accost an Englishman like this. I would have been certain of a snub. But with an Indian it was different and he was an engaging, approachable young man.

'May I tell you how much I have enjoyed watching Your Highness play,' I began.

'Have you? I'm so glad,' he replied smiling. 'It was a good game.' I liked his deep voice and the slow delivery of his words.

'That goal that you hit in the second chukka was magnificent.'

'That one went in but I was furious when I missed the last one, just before the whistle.' And he laughed in a pleased, simple way.

'That was very bad luck. You missed it by inches. Wasn't your pony good then? I've never seen such a turn. He literally jumped round. You have a wonderful string.'

'Yes, I have. I'm glad you admire them.' We were walking towards the pavilion now.

'This is the second time I've watched you play. The other time was in Delhi two years ago.'

'Oh, have you been to India?' he asked with new interest and pleasure. 'Where? What part?'

'All over the north.'

'But not in Jaipur.'

'No. I never got there. I wanted to. I heard so much about it, how beautiful it is.'

'Why don't you come to India again and visit Jaipur?'

'I wish I could,' I replied.

'Are you alone?' he asked then as we reached the pavilion. 'Won't you have tea with me and then we can go on talking about India?'

'I'm with my mother. May I bring her and introduce her to Your Highness?'

'Please do. I'm with Colonel Tanner. He was my tutor and he still lives with me in Jaipur.'

I fetched my mother and when the introductions were over we sat down to tea and were joined a few minutes later by the other members of his team. We talked about the places I had been to and of the people we both knew. Only when the Colonel reminded him that he had an engagement, did we all get up. But that was not the end of it. He drove us back to London and dropped us at our door and invited us to dinner two days later.

I lived again. My depression had vanished the moment I talked to him and when I sat down to tea all the grey, monotonous, stunted little lives of London which pressed continually upon me, disappeared and plains and jungles, great rivers and great mountains, bright sun and a thousand scents and sounds – all the rough primal grandeur of India rose up before me like a sweet sweet vision. That night I decided to return. My wild oats were not all sown.

I would go alone and look for a job. I wanted to work. I was tired of fluttering about. I knew it would be difficult because all the jobs were official. But I didn't worry about that. If there was nothing ready-made for me I would create something. Something must be wanted that I could supply.

We lunched and dined together constantly; always the four of us, always with our chaperones. And we entertained them. At last I had someone worth inviting to my home. He was only a boy really, innocent and rather shy, with respectful charming manners and his movements were as slow and lethargic as his speech. Occasionally, he came alone and took me for a drive in his open racing car and he was always polite and proper. The affection which we so quickly felt for each other was that of brother and sister. I couldn't conceive then of any closer relationship with an Indian.

When we dined at the Berkeley or at the Savoy, Colonel Tanner controlled him carefully. He wouldn't even let him dance with me, so anxious was he to observe the strict prevailing code of race relations.

In London high society then, the races met continually in sport, politics and at social functions, but if a white woman showed favours to an Indian it put her immediately beyond the pale of her own race and even an innocent friendship like ours would have been suspect and condemned. My success, therefore, was really only another defeat. I had dropped and damned myself still further for even with a prince I was down among the black men.

The summer months went by, the Maharajah left, and the plan changed a little. In her beautiful studio, my mother had completed several large and very successful portraits and they so renewed her confidence in her powers and she felt so well in health that she decided to come back to India too. She knew that if she could paint successfully out there, my way would be made so much easier. I knew it, too, because although I was drawn back to India, I didn't know to what I was really drawn. I could still only see the India of the British Raj, the worst possible environment in which to experiment with freedom. Weakly and foolishly I agreed.

Her courage was undiminished. If she did not understand what I was really after (any better than I did myself) she understood the obsessive driving thing at the centre of my nature which never ceased to press its crazy pattern of adventure on my life. And her love changed to a desperate, concentrating force, drawing nothing to itself, of a kind which grows and grows until it cages and punishes the loved and extinguishes the lover. Yet how could she have been different? What else could she have done? This love-force grew out of our situation and out of her own past. She had been bound and driven herself when she was young and all her family too, and now, I kept her bound to a wheel of endless journeying towards a destination still unknown.

The new Viceroy, Lord Willingdon, had been Governor-General of Canada and my mother wrote to Martin for an introduction. Then, we bought clothes, sold the lease of the house and, to conserve our health, spent the remaining summer months on the Belgian coast, where living was cheap.

Everything had gone the same way and I found myself repeating, move by move, the pattern of the first Indian journey – and I knew it was not right. I did not want it to be like that again but I had slipped too far into the future, into the streams of new experience, to stop it.

Avoiding the popular, expensive resorts, we went to an isolated market garden district and took a room in a little house standing on the long straight road which ran between the gardens and the beach. We provided our own food and cooked it in the family kitchen. Two or three miles away was a small country town to which we walked to do our shopping. The place was cheap and healthy but unutterably boring. When we had walked to the beach and bathed and walked back there was no one to talk to and nothing to do except stare out upon that inland sea of vegetables, surrounding us. But the steady contemplation of that sea soon inspired me to explore it and when I did I entered a new illicit world which gave me an occupation and a purpose – the world of amorality and petty crime.

I learnt from the cabbages how to go beyond the permitted places and to know and feel what it was like; they freed me from restraint and taught me what I was myself; they led me to where I was not just a reject of high society but an outsider everywhere, a reject of the world – and the experience was exhilarating. Their green peace stirred up in me a raging fire.

It all started very simply. We wanted a lettuce for supper but the shops were shut. I slipped out (subconscious memories of Andy!), looked up and down the road, darted into a lettuce patch and cut and carried one away. The escapade was quite enjoyable and so was the taste of the lettuce and to have saved 20 centimes gave me great satisfaction. I was so money conscious. I wasted half my time and strength finding money for our debts and journeys and now I counted every sou.

A few days later, I waited until it was dark and then went out again and stole another. It was so easy. And 20 centimes a day was one franc 40 a week and that was five francs 60 a month. And while I was taking a lettuce, why not take beans and peas and cabbages, I thought – and multiply the sum. And it was rather fun. My evenings were so boring. It would be something to look forward to – entertainment and new interesting sensations.

I stopped my mother buying vegetables and provided them myself. Then, I expanded my business to include the shops and for this I had to teach myself new techniques and assess new risks. As my skill developed and my confidence grew and my successes mounted, so did my pleasure and my pride. Supplying everything we needed became for me a duty and if I went into a shop and came out empty-handed, I felt despicable.

I stole from the big stores in the town and from the little country shops where the patron and his wife lived and slept and cooked at the back and a smell of cabbage soup came wafting out into the shop and they peeped through a hole among the goods every time the opening door rang a bell. Or, where an old woman wrapped in a black shawl, sat behind the counter knitting all day long. I worked them all indiscriminately and the easier they were to rob the more often I returned.

The world around me changed. People all looked different and I looked differently at them. I no longer smiled wherever I went in a friendly way. I saw suspicion in all the eyes that met my eyes and detection in every movement. I was not ashamed. It was only guilt that I felt – and fear. I soon disliked everyone and felt cut off and alone in a shadow world, moving within a new profane consciousness.

Several times I set a date for stopping but when it came, went on. I had to push this new experience as far as I could; maintain this act of insolence towards the world, as long as I could. I laughed to think that I, who would soon be dining with a Viceroy and visiting a prince, was just a common thief, loitering and robbing on my way. And when I reckoned up my takings and saw how much my nerve and expertise had saved – I gloated.

Slightly anxious all the time, my mother accepted this new madness as she accepted everything. I only stopped when we left for Brussels – exhausted. Purged of this pitiful passion I came slowly back to myself, to my golden thread, as if returning from a sojourn in Hell.

We spent a fortnight in Brussels, in another cheap lodging, so that my mother could have an evening gown made by an exclusive model shop. The fittings, right from the start, caused us anxiety and the final one was catastrophic. My mother protested excitedly that the dress was unwearable, Madame was called and all the Mademoiselles of the House dropped their work and gathered round in an angry circle and soon, they were all screaming and shouting at once while my mother stood helplessly in the middle in the awful dress, with me beside her. But we couldn't get out of it for the shop had made us pay in advance. And there was no time or money to buy anything else.

As the women dispersed sullenly and the dress was being folded in sheets and sheets of useless tissue paper as if to make it right and worth its price, I stood watching, in silent powerless rage. Then, when it was finally put into a box and handed to my mother and ignominiously she took it – I acted.

Shocked into instantaneous movement as if by an electrical impulse and drawing upon the trembling skills and sharpened senses which I had developed, I reached for a large bunch of fine pelts (they were furriers as well as couturiers), slipped it inside my coat and walked nonchalantly out of the shop, followed by my mother. Outside, I whispered, 'Go on home, I'll meet you later,' and I darted up a crowded side street and a moment after that jumped onto a tram, any tram, just to get away. And I got away. I got back to our room at last and showed her the weird bunch of skins.

They were peculiar things to sell. It took me several days to find a dealer in a low quarter who would consider buying them. I didn't hawk them round, I only talked about them and when I decided to trust the man and take them and I was walking back with them, carelessly wrapped in a piece of brown paper – I met Madame! I was terrified. I thought she would set up a hue and cry and I would be caught there and then with the booty on me.

I spun round and dived away from her into the crowd and was gone before she had time even to think what to do. When I recovered from that fright and walked on, I grew more and more nervous that the dealer would betray me and that when I arrived at his little back street shop, I would find a policeman waiting.

I went in cautiously and looked into the dark corners of the dingy, dirty crowded room. When I unwrapped the parcel he took the pelts and stroked them and squeezed them between his fingers and then held the bunch for a few moments, as if trying to assess its weight. And his expression never changed. Then he told me how poor in quality they were and how little was their value. I knew it wasn't true but he was knowing and I was frightened. When he made me an offer I protested, but I took his money and slipped rapidly out of the shop. I was glad to get anything and be rid of that awful burning parcel. I had no desire to experience a Belgian prison.

We had a pleasant room but a horrible landlady. She persecuted us in little ways and a few days before we left, locked us out of our room. I had to climb out of the landing window and walk along a parapet and get in again through ours and then open the door from the inside. We had another row on the very morning of our leaving but this time, it was my mother who took revenge. She locked every door on our floor – bathroom, lavatory and bedrooms – and took the keys. While the luggage was being carried down, I was terrified that the woman would run upstairs and discover what she'd done and call the Police. But we got away and while we were driving over a bridge, she leant out of the taxi window and hurled the handful of keys over the parapet into the river. And we both sat back and laughed. We travelled 3rd Class to Marseille and caught the boat from there.

12

Life in Jaipur

A STATE car met us at Jaipur station and drove us to one of the luxurious guest-houses which stood together in a row facing the new palace in which the Maharajah did all his entertaining. He lived in an old palace in the city. A few minutes later, an A.D.C. came to escort us up the wide marble steps, to lunch.

In the middle of a large, beautiful but sparsely furnished room with richly coloured, heavily jewelled ornaments standing on gold and mosaic tables, the Maharajah stood waiting for us. Beside him was his cousin, Bimbi, Colonel Tanner and several A.D.C.'s. His welcome was of the warmest. He was as charming and boyish as ever and to see him again and to be back in India, delighted me.

Soon Colonel Tanner's daughter, Zenia, came in with her girl-friend, Angela, just out from England and staying with her in Jaipur for the winter. Although Zenia smiled at me and pretended to be friendly, I knew at once that she disliked me. After that, the Maharajah made a move and we walked through a wide marble passage into a vast shimmering dining-hall and took our places at an enormous table, the Maharajah in the middle with my mother on his right and Zenia on his left. Colonel Tanner was on one side of me and Bimbi on the other and courtiers and relatives, springing suddenly from nowhere, filled it up from end to end. All were men. Their women were in close *purdah.*

After lunch, the Maharajah asked me to go for a drive with him; he was so anxious to begin showing me his state. It was wonderful to have a friend like this, bestowing such rich hospitality and with it, simple kindness. As we set off, I caught a vicious look from Zenia.

We drove into the jungle in his open Rolls which was specially equipped for hunting and could crash through the bush like a tank. The country was not flat like the plains round Delhi, but hilly and very beautiful. He was proud of his wild lands and when we stopped to look at a view or to stare into a dark tangled glade and he jumped out of the car to search for animal tracks, he was not the same young man whom I had dined with at the Berkeley and the Savoy. All that schooling and tailoring had dropped from him and as he leapt and looked and tore through the pathless, sun-filled clearings, he was one with his native jungle.

When he thought I had seen and admired enough for the first day, he stopped the car again under a giant deodar tree and without a word, or any warning, he flung his arms round me and kissed me violently.

'No, Jai! Please!' I said, pushing him away as politely as I could.

'Why not? You love me. You've always loved me,' he replied slowly but fiercely and when I saw that he was exposing his virility, I jumped up and stood holding onto the windscreen. He pulled me down and we struggled.

'I won't. I won't,' I kept crying out. Then, just as suddenly as he had started he stopped and slid back into the driving seat, angry and sullen. Our brother and sister friendship had dissolved at the first real touch and in my heart of hearts I knew it would. His colour and position did not make him different. It was only the speed and violence that took me by surprise. We drove back without speaking.

While I was dressing for dinner and thinking about my new situation, I saw what a fool I had been to look forward to this visit and to count on it so much. I should have known that in every jungle one must adapt oneself – or immediately retreat.

I wore one of my new dresses and took endless care over my toilette and when we were both ready we climbed the marble steps and appeared before the crowd of men, all dressed in gold and silver and rich colours, their turbans trimmed with jewels. They were *Kshatrias* and *Mahrattas*, the warrior caste of a warrior race. But I felt equally striking and as proud as they and the Maharajah looked at me and smiled once more. Zenia's expression was devilish. Four British cavalry officers, come to play polo, had arrived and I was pleased for, in an obscure way, I felt that they would protect me. But I saw very soon that they only despised me.

The scene in the hall was like a picture of some fabulous Biblical feast; oriental lamps upon the table, a multitude of servants carrying in the food on golden trays, the Maharajah in the middle dressed in white and gold, dark faces with flashing eyes and deep voices echoing round and round the marble walls. I would have loved the picture more if I had not been so painfully in it.

The next day, before breakfast, a beautiful saddled horse arrived at the door and an A.D.C. took me riding in the jungle. The Maharajah spent the morning at polo practice and we met again at lunch. He was still smiling and friendly and hospitable.

'I'm expecting the Nawab of Bhopal here next week on a State visit,' he told us, 'and I'm arranging a two-day tiger shoot for him in the jungles where my cousin lives, about a hundred miles from here. I hope you can stay on till then and come? I'm sure you'd enjoy it.' We accepted gladly. Later, he said to me, 'I'd like to show you something of Jaipur city this afternoon. Will you be ready after lunch?'

It was a city of palaces. Rich, intricate, many-storeyed, old ones and new ones – palaces for wives, for dowagers and for princely guests. We passed a high delicate building with rose-coloured walls. It looked too beautiful to be a prison yet the gratings over the windows were so grim.

'What is that?' I asked.

'That's the Purdah Palace where the Maharani lives,' he replied.

'The Maharani? Your mother?'

'No. My wife.' And he grinned.

'I didn't know that you were married.'

'I've been married a long time. I've got two children.'

'But you're so young. How old were you when you married?'

'Quite old – about 15. My wife's a lot older than I am.'

'Does she ever go about?'

'No. She would never come out of *purdah*. And she doesn't speak English.'

We drove on. Although it was only palaces and gateways and temples that he pointed to, I couldn't help seeing the crowded squalid alleyways behind them and the wretchedness of the people. We heard later how highly taxed they were. To maintain a polo-playing prince and a superstructure of palaces, they had to live in hovels.

'Now, I'm going to take you to see where the treasure of Jaipur has been kept for a thousand years. We shall have to climb most of the way.' And he looked so pleased and proud.

We left the car at the bottom of a steep, scrub-covered mountain. When we reached the top we looked down upon the soft reclining city and the quiet, unbroken, limitless sea of jungle which enclosed it. I followed him then, along a narrow secret path until we reached an immense rock in which a heavy door was set.

'I'm sorry I can't take you in,' he said. 'Only the ruler is allowed and I've only been in once myself.'

'When was that?' I asked.

'After my investiture. You go down and down into a great cavern, every inch of which is filled with treasure. I was allowed to take one thing and I chose a vase set with diamonds and sapphires – worth several *lakhs*. It's in my room at the palace. I'll show it you. No one knows the value of all that is inside there.'

'What a pity it can't be sold to relieve some of the poverty in the world.' I did not say – in Jaipur. I had to be tactful. He didn't reply but his soft dark predatory eyes fell suddenly upon me and the next moment his arms were round me and his sensuous mouth was swallowing me.

This time, I tried to make a joke of it. I laughed as if I thought it was a game and when I managed to wriggle away I ran gaily along the path, shouting nonsense back at him. But when he caught me I felt as if a wild animal was upon me and as if only my wits could save me.

'No, Jai, please – not now! Another day! I'm tired. That climb has made me tired. Wait – please wait!' I cried out desperately.

There was no reason why I should not have done what he wanted. He was young and attractive and I had already lost all consciousness of colour and buried deep in the jungle, as we were, there was no fear of detection and damnation. But I did not want to love like this and, if I wouldn't, I did not want to have to leave at once. I wanted to go on the tiger shoot and living free was so lovely. Men could have this hospitality for nothing but a woman had to pay. It may have been fair in the economy of the world but I would not accept it. I still believed that there was something else – another way.

I urged him along the path, distracting him with my talk now, praising and admiring everything he was and did and possessed until his arms and hands were snared in the honey of my words, as I lured him down the mountain. In the car I stopped talking, he pulled my hand towards himself and as we drove slowly back to the palace, I pleased and propitiated him a little.

The next day, for the 3rd time, he took me out and tried once more. But that was all. That was the end of it. He barely looked at me or spoke to me again. And Zenia was so happy.

The only relationship with a woman that he understood was the sexual one and now it seemed to me that sex was the prime concern of everyone, the single centre and the meaning of life, and because I was always struggling to evade it I began to feel peculiar, as if I did not belong to life, as if in life itself – I was an outsider.

Immediately, Bimbi took me up. Again, he sat next to me at dinner, smiling and giggling in a stupid childish way and afterwards he never left me. He was a heavy savage youth of 17,

The next morning after breakfast, I was reading in the guest-house sitting-room when he came tearing in and flung himself upon me. When I pushed him away he became still more violent, then, when I saw that he, too, was exposing himself, I lost my temper and shouted at him. He drew back, surprised, his sensuous mouth half open – and then slunk away. For several days, at different times and in all sorts of places, these obscene assaults were repeated – like a dog after a bitch in season – and sometimes, if I'd had a whip I would have used it. Then, like the Maharajah he gave up, turned his attentions to Angela, and never noticed me again.

The next morning, the Military Secretary came to take me for my ride. He was a handsome man, older and more sophisticated than the princes, and I was glad to have his company. He was very talkative and confiding and I had to walk my horse so as not to interrupt him. His troubles were all to do with his wives. When we reached the top of a pleasant knoll and felt a breeze, he reined in his horse. 'Shall we dismount here and go on talking for awhile and then canter back?' he said. I slipped off my horse and we sat down on a rock. For a few minutes he continued with his tales and then, when he became less coherent, I looked up and met his eyes – met the same dark ravenous eyes and the next instant, his arms were round me, his lips were fighting for my lips and everything else was happening as before. And again I struggled and, breaking free, jumped onto my horse and galloped off. And so it went on, with sex descending from one hierarchic level to another until the Nawab came and brought some respite.

Banners of welcome and flags were hung out all over the city and when he arrived he was received by the Maharajah, a guard of honour and a salute of guns. The first four days were given over to feasting and jousting followed by a vast exodus into the jungle for the tiger shoot. In spite of my personal failure with everyone from the Maharajah downwards, there was no indication that our departure would be welcomed.

The Nawab was a Muslim, quiet, dignified, disliking show and noise and extravagance of every kind. He was President of the Chamber of Princes then and high in the councils of the Viceroy. With his modest retinue he was given a whole palace and his daily programme was crammed with a succession of polo matches, military displays, processions, elephant fights and endless banquets and we followed eagerly in his turbulent congested wake.

Without intervals for rest, the music of classical instruments, brass bands, the explosions of fire-works, the detonations of 12-pounder guns and the trumpeting of elephants shook the city as it lay inert and the waves of the fierce fantastic carnival washed round it. The subtle, sumptuous barbarity characterising the life of the state, reached its height during these four sated boisterous days.

These celebrations were not universal. No happy holiday crowds came out to welcome the Nawab when he arrived and watch the games and displays and processions and claim a share of the feasting. The people cowered in their rags and peeped from their hovels like frightened animals while the whole thing passed and re-passed over their heads.

On the 5th day, the Maharajah, his principal relatives, his courtiers and his guests, with servants following, set off in powerful cars for the 'little' camp, as he called it. We followed a rough track for several hours and then turned off into pathless scrub and forest. Late in the afternoon, deep in wild, waterless, impenetrable country we came suddenly upon a beautiful canvas habitation, rectangular in form, with a green lawn in the middle, flowers growing round it and a pond with a fountain playing.

Over the gateway was a banner, 'Welcome to His Highness' and a gravel drive led through it, round the centre garden and past the entrances to all the tents. It was unbelievable, this green delectable creation in the middle of parched, formless jungle.

The living tents were placed close together along the two sides of the rectangle with a large dining-tent at the end, opposite the gateway. We walked between the flowers and lawn of our own front garden and through the doorway. Inside, was a huge lofty reception room with an equally large bedroom leading out of it and a bathroom. The whole suite was luxuriously furnished, with rich carpets covering the brick floors and candelabra hanging from the roofs. At the touch of an electric switch, the cool canopied rooms blazed with light.

There was another banquet in the dining-tent that night with no concession made to our situation. Course after complicated course was served just as if we had still been in the Palace. The next day, we rose long before dawn and drove in darkness still deeper into the jungle. Then, leaving the cars, we walked in single file along a narrow path until we came out into the clearing. It was light now and I could see the long straight belt which had been cut and which stretched away in both directions.

We were divided into pairs, in a somewhat haphazard way, and then ordered off to occupy the widely set *machans.* During this rather muddled process, everyone received a partner except the Nawab and I. But when I stood wondering where to go, he settled the matter at once.

'You come with me,' he said in a decisive tone and, delighted, I followed him to his *machan* and climbed nimbly up the tree ladder and onto the platform and sat there waiting for him.

Throughout these days I had never been able to talk to him alone. I admired him and now was my chance, I thought, to enjoy hours of uninterrupted talk with a new father-teacher. He hung about down below for awhile speaking quietly to a few excited, restless individuals still dashing up and down. And then up he came.

He was a reserved, unresponsive man and it was some time before I realised how bored he was with everything – including me. He was reputed to be the best shot in India and to have killed more tigers than anybody else. But now, he was tired of killing and in his own state, had set up 'hides' from which he photographed the animals instead. When he was placed in the *machan* towards which the tiger would be driven and given the supreme honour of shooting it, he was just uninterested and weary. He didn't want to shoot – nor did he want to talk to me. I never said another unnecessary word. Two hours passed before we heard the first faint cries of the advancing beaters.

A square of jungle, about a mile wide, had been marked out and a kill placed every night for months in the middle of it to attract and keep the tiger. Two sides of the periphery of this square had been cut, forming an angle or trap and *machans* built at intervals all the way along. The purpose of the beaters was to drive the tiger out at the point where the Nawab was waiting or, failing that, at some other point from which it could not fail to be shot.

An hour later, when the beaters drew nearer, the Nawab picked up his rifle. We spoke in whispers now for the tiger might be close, just beyond the clearing. After awhile some buck came out, looked up and down timidly and then sprang lightly across and disappeared into the thicket behind us. They were followed by two hyenas. Another hour passed and the Nawab grew impatient.

'I doubt if it'll come out here and, anyway, I'm going down,' he said. 'I don't like *machans.*'

He climbed down and walked out into the middle of the clearing and took up his position on a great black rock and stood there, still and tense, with his rifle ready. The beaters were getting closer now, dangerously close, right on the heels of the tiger. Then, I saw them, turbans bobbing up and down out of the scrub, barely a hundred yards away. And still they came, still yelling and beating the bushes with sticks. On and on until they were close to the clearing, getting closer and closer, then out, the whole line straggling out – and the shouting and the beating stopped.

They had driven him wrong. He was moving out at another point where someone else would get him. The Nawab lowered his rifle and came down from the rock and I climbed down from the *machan*. Then, when I was walking out to join him, there was a roar as the tiger broke cover in front of me and bounded past me over the clearing. The Nawab fired twice but the beast went on, escaping wounded into the scrub.

Immediately, there was pandemonium. Up and down the line they leapt and tumbled out of the *machans* and, too impatient to wait for the elephants, ignoring the danger, Bimbi and several others tore recklessly after it. When the elephants arrived and were brought to their knees, the rest of us clambered into the *howdahs*. My mother and I were together now and an old man, an uncle of the Maharajah's, climbed in with us. The *mahouts* prodded the animals and they rose and lumbered off. The hunt was on and the noise of snapping trees, the trumpeting of the elephants and the cries of the hunters rang through the jungle. Soon, our elephant began to tremble.

'Why is he doing that?' my mother asked nervously.

'They always tremble when the tiger is close,' the old man replied calmly. And it was then that I noticed that he only had a shot-gun. And tigers, especially wounded ones, leap onto elephants.

'What good will that be?' I asked him then. 'If you pepper it with shot you'll enrage it more.' He smiled gently but didn't answer, swaying in his seat happy and relaxed.

We crashed on and the elephant continued to tremble. It was growing dark when the hunters straggled back to the cars. Three days later the *shikaris* tracked it down and killed it. They only took this trouble because wounded tigers become man-eaters and move to the villages.

The next day we were out on elephants again circling aimlessly about, while they shot at anything they saw. In the evening, Bimbi gave a banquet in his palace nearby. There was no slackening in the hospitality. Up to the very last, the Nawab had to be diverted and kept happy by pastimes and pleasures ever more lavish and spectacular.

We started very late, each car cutting its own path as before, and all along the way the eyes of animals glowed in the headlights and a buffalo stumbled out in front of us. When we arrived at last, feeling rather tired and hungry, the scene which appeared out of the night and out of the magical heart of the jungle made us forget ourselves and, once again, just gaze and gaze – and marvel.

A single towering building, more like a castle than a palace, rose shimmering into the sky, lit by the filaments of a thousand hidden lamps and, huddled at its base, were tiny houses and narrow winding streets lit by strings and strings of fairy lights. It seemed like an illusion, the vaporous structure of a dream or the enchanted realm of a child's imagination.

The cars stopped outside, for the streets were too narrow to drive through and we walked beneath the fairy lights, peered at all the way by the people in the houses. Then, standing before the palace, we looked up at the high windowless walls and at the immense flight of stone steps leading from the ground to the roof where Bimbi stood waiting to welcome his guests – a tiny luminous figure dressed in silver, the ends of his turban flying out in the breeze.

We climbed. Halfway up it was frightening for the steps were narrow and the balustrade was low. We reached the top and stepped onto the roof. It was the size of two tennis courts with rich rugs spread all over it and *shamianas*, gorgeous in colour, erected or suspended in the middle with cushions piled beneath them. At one end, a square tower rose still higher with several rooms at roof level and above them a second storey, with a single heavily latticed window, where Bimbi kept his wife.

We strolled about, delighting in the miracle of just being where we were. Presently, servants came with trays on which were tiny glasses containing strange delicious drinks. The roof was crowded now, new faces had appeared, relatives of Bimbi's and retainers, but still a world without women.

We sipped the tiny ever-changing drinks and waited. The food had been brought from camp and was now being cooked, Colonel Tanner told us. It was one o'clock when we took our places at the rough unpolished table in the long, narrow, white-washed room in the tower, bare of ornament and colour. And then began a pure and uncorrupted Indian meal without a compromise or concession of any kind to England. For England had conquered India but not the jungle. England had never reached the place that we were in.

Dish after dish came on, each more complex and undefinable than the last, with scores of tiny saucers accompanying them as auxiliaries, containing unmet, mysterious substances with obscure and subtle scents and flavours. The rajah meal, symbolic of India herself, was a formless, fantastical culinary masterwork. And it lasted hours.

When we came out onto the roof again we were told that the party was not yet over, although it was thought that the older people might be tired and would like to return to camp. At this, the Nawab, my mother and Colonel Tanner left us and we were led into another white-washed room, containing only carpets and cushions.

We lay about talking. The Maharajah and Zenia and Bimbi and Angela sat together against a mound of cushions. They laughed as they talked and glanced at me occasionally, as if from far away; Zenia with triumph in her eyes. The polo-playing Englishmen also sat together, ignoring me and looking bored and sleepy. I was surrounded by a crowd of men most of whom I hadn't seen until that night and when I asked them what was going to happen next, they told me that musicians and dancers were on their way from the capital.

Eventually, they arrived – three men with instruments and half a dozen brightly dressed *nautch* girls with earrings and bracelets and anklets jingling and without hurrying, without any sense of time or urgency, they arranged themselves in the middle of the room. Dawn was already breaking but with the windows shuttered no one knew it and no one cared. It was endless night inside that room.

They danced and sang for about an hour and then stopped abruptly and sat down. I didn't know if they were just having a rest or whether this was the end of the party. The single light went out. I thought it must have fused and addressing the darkness, asked some silly question which no one answered.

There was utter silence, then movement – small, rustling tinkling sounds. A hand touched me and I drew away. It followed me, then two hands, then arms were round me. I pushed the unknown body away. I had dropped from the top to the bottom of the eastern stairs and now, with the *nautch* girls, I was a free-for-all.

For a few moments I lay by myself, curled up defensively, listening, listening. Then a match was struck and I saw it all. In the middle, sitting on a chair, was an old man with a match box, a voyeur, and all round him on the floor was a heaving mass of lovers. I looked round at the Englishmen thinking that now they would protect me but they were all asleep – drugged. Then, the match went out and a moment later hands were feeling up my legs and other hands were groping round my waist and still other hands were clutching at my breasts and I heard the breathing of three men as they crawled over me together. Then anger made me mad. I kicked, with my sharp-heeled shoes I kicked and kicked, not caring where nor how much I hurt. Then, when another match was struck, I jumped up and stumbled over the bodies, opened the door and ran out onto the roof. The door opened again and the voyeur followed me. I recognised him now. It was the old man with the shot-gun.

'You must get me a car,' I said angrily, 'I'm going back to camp.'

'You can't. There aren't any. They won't be back for a long time.'

'I don't believe that,' I answered.

'Wait a minute,' he said then, 'I'll see if I can find one.' He disappeared for some time and then returned.

'I've found one and I'll take you back to camp.'

'Thank you,' I said coldly and walked to the steps and as I stood at the top for a moment, something made me look back and up at the window in the tower and, behind the bars, I saw a young sad face.

When I reached the ground I walked quickly away, the old man struggling to keep up with me. In the morning light it was not a fairy castle but a dull, plain crumbling fortress, nor were they fairy houses that we walked between, but wretched hovels even poorer than the ones in Jaipur city. The whole place looked derelict and miserable with the jungle lapping round it and only waiting to reclaim it.

As we drove away, I wondered why the old man had left his fun to come with me. I trusted no one now and watched him out of the corners of my eyes. But I was wrong. He was harmless and by mid-morning we were back in camp. In the afternoon the orgiasts returned and soon afterwards we left for the capital.

That 'little' camp and the two-day shoot had taken six months to prepare and cost £50,000. We left for Delhi the next day and when we said goodbye to the Nawab, he invited us to visit Bhopal.

13

I Find My Task

THE free-living guest-house life was over and the struggle to go on began again. I did not want to repeat the club experience and Old Delhi was the most likely place for jobs and because we were still aiming high, Maidens was where we had to be. We went there when we arrived but we could not afford to stay for, this time, we had less money saved. However, we soon conceived a brilliant way of overcoming this first obstacle.

Across the road were some large houses standing in large gardens, all occupied by Indians. We called on them one by one and soon found an owner who was willing to let us a room. As in most Indian homes everything was rough and bare and primitive. But we did not mind for it was near and cheap. We could have our meals and spend our days in Maidens and then slip across the road to sleep. And Maidens would be our address. This seemed a splendid plan.

With our mode of living settled, the next thing was a car. I went to my old garage where I was welcomed warmly and told them that I was going to buy another car and would like to try out one or two before deciding. They offered me several and I chose the best and drove it away.

With everything organised and the appearances impeccable, even to the use of Maidens' notepaper, we now presented Martin's letters of introduction to Lord and Lady Willingdon and were immediately invited to lunch.

We drove out to the Viceroy's House in New Delhi, now part of the complex of government buildings designed by Sir Edwin Lutyens. Monstrous in size, a veritable palace, with impressive rooms and staircases and balconies and powerful views along each broad processional avenue, each leading outwards as from the hub of a vast wheel, together stating the grand design and purpose of the new imperial city.

The Willingdons and their staff were all very charming and a week later we were invited to dine. They did not order portraits, which was disappointing but they gave us the usual social start. Without assets of our own, however, unless my mother began painting, this was not enough to establish us in society – and nothing more happened. My mother could have employed her old tactics and forced her way to the top with a presentation portrait. But now she could not do this and I was more keen to find a good job than to become a social success again.

I went to ask advice from Major Metcalfe, the Military Secretary and another of Martin's friends. The only job that he could suggest was that of companion to a Maharani. But I did not fancy this idea. Now that I knew something about the native states I did not want to live in one – even an advanced one.

I talked of jobs to people whom I met in Maidens, I advertised and wrote to the newspapers asking if they had any journalistic openings. They sent me books to review, unpaid, and that was all.

Then, while I was going uselessly about and my mother was still thinking how best to start her work and earn some money, she fell ill once more and I had to call the doctor and reveal where we were living, hoping that our secret would spread no higher. But he could not cure her. She lay in that sordid room and such food as she could eat had to be brought across the road from Maidens. And soon I was sure that the cause was not only anxiety, this time, but the place that she was in. The house stood in a hollow, below the level of the road, surrounded by thick trees and bushes and our room was airless and stuffy.

Regardless of the fact that we could not pay for it, I took a room in the annexe of Maidens and moved her. And she was better at once. Not well enough to paint – but better. And now I really had to do something.

If I had had the money I would have sent her home. And I would have gone myself for I was already bored and disillusioned. This second journey to India was a mistake, I thought – a terrible mistake. I knew it was before we started. So why did I come? For what experience? Just finding the money to get us out? But instead of searching even harder for a job, I stopped altogether and just drifted. A week passed and then another before I knew what I meant to do, knew how I could earn a lot of money – quick! I went to see Major Metcalfe again.

'I can't find a job here that I want to do, so I have decided to work for charity,' I told him. 'I am very good at making fudge, chocolate fudge – you know what I mean – that heavenly stuff that you can't stop eating, which you can't get here and everyone would buy. There would be an insatiable demand and I would give the proceeds to some charity and I have come to ask you if there is any particular one that Lady Willingdon is interested in? If so, I would approach them with this project.'

He was a severe, humourless man and he did not smile or change his expression but he took me very seriously for my scheme was not so dotty as it sounded. I knew from my Downing Street days that charities played an important part in the lives of all society women. And, as a money-bringer, why shouldn't fudge rank just as high as a bazaar?

After discussing the scheme in detail, he told me that Lady Willingdon was extremely interested in the Red Cross which was very active in India and, before I left, he wrote me a note of introduction to the Secretary. That was all I wanted.

I knew all about the racketeering side of the charity world of that time, that half the donations and subscriptions disappeared into the pockets of professional organisers and impoverished peeresses long before they reached the victims. And if they played that game successfully in London, why shouldn't I play it here? I was desperate for we could neither stay nor go.

Of course, I could have sold the stuff for myself in a straightforward commercial way; become a *box-wallah*. But I was still sensitive about my standing. I had no friends – or enemies – in Delhi now. They had all changed yet I didn't want the Viceroy and the same icy watching world around him, to see me fall, and besides, the Red Cross would make things easier. I would sell twice as much. And, after all, I meant to give them *something*.

I went to see the Secretary. She was most suspicious of my scheme and if it hadn't been for Major Metcalfe's note, I would have failed with her at once. She liked neither me nor my project yet I came away with her full permission to use both the name and the emblem of the Red Cross.

The same day, I drove to the bazaar and bought an enormous copper pan, a veritable witches' cauldron, a dozen flat ones, a long spoon, a powerful paraffin cooker and a weighing machine. Then, at wholesale prices, a sack of sugar, half a hundred weight of butter, a gross of tins of condensed milk and a quantity of chocolate powder. And lastly, I ordered boxes to be made in different sizes and on each I had printed 'Philippa's Fudge – sold in aid of the Red Cross', with a red cross in the centre. All this raw material and equipment was carried up to our bedroom. I set up the factory in the bathroom and as soon as the boxes came, began operations.

I had cooked fudge successfully in small quantities but when I began producing it in bulk I found it either turned to toffee or never set. However, I soon got the trick of it and production went ahead. My mother was well enough to help stir the cauldron and weigh and pack. Every morning, I loaded the car and set off for my selling points – hotels, shops and clubs – replenishing stocks and collecting the money. Every afternoon, with a tray round my neck, I visited the polo ground, the tennis courts and the golf club.

I stood by the pavilion or on the steps of the club-house smiling and swaying up to people as they arrived or I walked up and down the rows of seated spectators. 'Won't you buy a box of fudge sold in aid of the Red

Cross?' I would ask them coaxingly, bending forward with such charm. They never failed to buy but when I had passed I was quite aware of the quizzical disdainful looks that followed me and the whispered comments. But this personal business, however painful, doubled my sales and selling had become a passion – fudge had taken hold of me. Night and day I dreamed and thought of nothing else. It was another madness.

The Saturday luncheons at Maidens were my best selling hours of the week. Missing lunch myself I dressed, nevertheless, as if I had been invited to the grandest of the parties and wafting round my loaded table in the entrance hall, I accosted everyone.

As they crowded in; high society and low, tourists, *box-wallahs*, princes, the whole world passing and re-passing me, the demonic power that was in my smile made them buy. My best customers were wealthy Indian businessmen emerging from rich curry lunches. They were so pleased to take their boxes and hand me hundred rupee notes and wave away my weak attempts to give them change. It was all for the good cause and I was white and incorruptible and the soft look of a white woman was so pleasant and compelling, the whole thing so cheering to their self-esteem and national pride.

In Maidens I became a new institution – a fudge hostess. And throughout Delhi I was soon notorious. A freak strain in the ruling race had appeared; a new talented type of charity worker, a fanatical maker of fudge. There had never been an imperial representative quite like this before and they did not know what to make of me. They understood what I was doing but not the way I was doing it, for when it was not suspect, my passion was unseemly. But when they looked at me now with amazement and scorn and whispered to each other I didn't care – for I had changed.

I was timid when I started, holding on to what was left of my position in society, trying to keep what I was doing within the bounds of my situation as it was. But when the enterprise succeeded and carried me away, I found that I had created a new independent role in the world for myself which, in spite of its idiosyncracies, I liked and was proud of. Then, freed of my sensitivity, I could go on smiling and swaying and selling with all the confidence of a duchess opening a bazaar.

With success came expansion. I extended the factory into the bedroom, engaged a bearer to help me and worked still longer hours myself. But uneasiness came, too. Nemesis drew near. The Red Cross Secretary began to murmur and show too much interest in the proceeds. I told her how heavy were my overheads and costs and how little was the actual profit and I sent her another hundred rupee note to keep her quiet. In the first month I cleared £75 but to pay the weekly bill at Maidens and our fares to England, I needed more. I had to keep the mad dishonest business going.

My social life was all contained in Maidens. I was queen of a variegated, kaleidoscopic hotel society of men. As they came and went I made friends with everyone, regardless of their class, their colour or their caste, dancing and playing about when I was not cooking or selling. And this drove me even lower.

One night, I was dancing with a subaltern from Lucknow. 'Why don't you come down for Lucknow Week?' he asked me. 'I'll introduce you to everyone and give you a good time.'

'I'd love to,' I replied, for I wanted a holiday. These weeks of carnival were held throughout the winter in all the big garrison towns, like the Highland Brigade Week when I was engaged to Harold. The polo teams and athletes and girls went the round and the regiments and clubs and hotels gave balls and the hostesses filled their bungalows with guests and entertained madly. I left double stocks in all my selling places and dashed away to Lucknow.

I stayed at the best hotel, unchaperoned, and when my subaltern arrived with all his friends, the sport began. They took me to the balls, the parties and the polo and they lent me a horse. They were hard-riding, hard-living cavalrymen. In Jaipur, there was a softness inside the savagery. These Englishmen were hard all through; beneath their style and a veneer of good manners, they were brutal and I was unfair. But the world was brutal and unfair, a place designed for predators and prey – east and west a jungle.

Between dances, in their cars, they tried to make love but I laughed off each attempt, leaving them angry, and ran off to the next one. It was like Jaipur over again and the women were as venomous as Zenia. 'Look at George with his Turkish Delight!' one whispered loudly to another as I passed. I still felt these stabs and the cruel, scornful looks of all these vaunting cavalry wives. But I was irrevocably outside and beneath them now and I spun and whirled and slipped blithely through the wild 'Week', ignoring them. Refreshed from my holiday, I returned to Delhi.

Not long afterwards, a charming, sensitive man arrived at Maidens on short leave and we danced and went about together. I was on the verge of falling in love with him and when, on his last night, he suggested that we drive to somewhere quiet and talk, I was sure that he was going to tell me that he loved me. I drove to the Kutab Minar, we moved into the back seat and I waited. But he didn't talk. After a moment of hesitation, he flung his arms clumsily round my neck and tried to kiss me. I stopped him. If he really loved me this was not the way to tell me. A moment later, he tried again.

'Please,' I said, 'I don't want to kiss you. I thought you said you wanted to talk?' He drew back, surprised.

'Yes ... yes ... I do ... but ...'

'But what?' I said.

'Well ... I thought you'd like it.'

'No. I don't. Everybody does that but I thought you were different.'

'But ... but I thought *you* were different. They say that you'll make love to anyone. The chaps all boast that they've had you.'

I was staggered.

'But that's not true. I don't let them. They're lying if they say I do.' I was angry now.

'I'm so sorry. I do apologise. It's all a mistake. Can I explain? You see, I'm engaged to a girl at home but she won't marry me yet – not until I'm more experienced, she says. I hoped that I could get that experience with you. But I made a mistake. I really am so sorry.'

Now I knew what I was. A high-class tart! My mother had always said that if I made love to men I would get a bad name. I'd got the name – without the love.

A well-dressed, middle-aged, good-looking Muslim began frequenting Maidens. He came for occasional meals and to sit about and he always bought a box of fudge and stopped and talked for a few moments in a soft, unhurried, pleasant way. I liked him and looked forward to these sympathetic sales until, having nothing else to do apparently, he took to sitting in the hall every day, at the very times when I was selling there, always choosing a chair from which he could observe me.

I resented this and didn't greet him in such a friendly way, showing clearly that I did not like being watched. But when, after that, he stopped coming – I was sorry. And when, a few days later, he came again – I was glad. Now, to my surprise, I found that I liked him sitting there. He was so perceptive and unaggressive and I no longer felt that he was just waiting to pounce. I began to trust him and to feel that I had someone there supporting me – a friend.

He never advanced beyond the purchase of his daily box of fudge and I grew so accustomed to his presence that I scarcely noticed him. I liked him there and that was all. Then something most annoying happened. My car disappeared. And it was on that very day that, for the first time, he approached me personally, without buying any fudge. He asked me to sit down and rest for once and allow him to give me a cup of tea. I was wanting to talk to someone at that moment and I blurted out what was on my mind. I didn't tell him that the car wasn't mine and that the garage had lost patience and taken it back. I said it was out of order. He listened so sympathetically and when I had finished, offered to lend me his. I could hardly believe my luck. He could not possibly have known what had happened or, had he perceived that I was in trouble and come forward then to help me?

After that, we were not just friends – but partners. He was really interested in what I was doing and how I was doing it and he didn't want to drive me to some desolate place. I could talk to him and turn to him.

The fudge sales went up and up and the profits mounted in the bank. I went on sending token sums to the Red Cross but all the time I was expecting the Secretary to take some action and Major Metcalfe, too, for his honour was involved. And the atmosphere in Maidens seemed cooler. I wondered how much longer the management would turn a blind eye to the establishment of a fudge factory in one of their bedrooms – even if it served a noble cause. I felt, not only that the avenging forces were awaiting the moment when they would close in on me and show me up for the fraud I was, but that everyone, wherever I went, suspected me. I carried my tray about less confidently.

I had made a lot of money but still I could not stop because Maidens was such a drain. We needed to live for nothing again, not touch what we had and wait for the next draft from England – and we thought of Bhopal.

My mother wrote a gracious letter to the Nawab reminding him of his invitation and asking if we might come. But while I was waiting for the reply another letter came, the one that I was dreading, from the Red Cross Secretary, asking me to come and see her. I fixed an appointment for the following week but when the day came, instead of receiving me, she received a note regretting that I had been called away from Delhi. We did not go to Bhopal for we did not hear from the Nawab. We went to Meerut.

When I made that appointment, giving myself a week to wind up my business and get out of Delhi my friend, Ali, seemed to sense the dilemma I was in and without asking any questions he immediately invited us to visit him in Meerut, where he lived. He rescued me again. But during that last week, while I was packing, collecting my monies and disposing of my equipment and supplies, my feelings became curiously equivocal once more. It was so wonderful to have a friend like this and yet ... and yet I could not believe that all the divination and giving, all the instant, miraculous gestures were really as simple and selfless as they seemed. When we left for Meerut I did not set off blindly. We would live for nothing but I was sure now that that 'nothing' would have to be paid for. But I was desperate. I had to escape from Delhi even if it meant becoming, in truth, the thing they called me and the mistress of a black man – not even a prince but a middle-class Punjabi – sinking as low as a white woman could, to the absolute bottom of the imperial pyramid.

I was desperate, yes, but curious too. I wanted to see what I had to see – and drop into the depths.

The night before we left, when I was dressing for dinner, I looked in the mirror and saw that my face was covered with red blotches and I thought I must have caught some skin disease. The nervous rash subsided later except for a patch which stayed – the mark of these wild years.

Ali appeared to be a man of some wealth and we were surprised to find how poorly he lived. But then, most Indians did – even the well-to-do. His house, in a crowded native quarter, consisted of two small rooms and some ramshackle huts in the compound. The bedroom was furnished in western style but the sitting-room had only rugs and cushions. He gave up the bedroom to us and moved into one of the sheds.

When my mother caught sight of the filthy cook and what was called the kitchen, a few bricks assembled in the middle of the compound and one dirty copper pan, she refused to eat anything that came from it and unpacked her old methylated spirit lamp. At once, with complete understanding, Ali dismissed the cook, kicked over the kitchen, improvised another and allowed her to take over both the cooking and the catering. And here we settled down, buried in the grey pullulating depths of native India, well hidden from all high righteous pursuers.

Ali looked after us as if we were his family. His tact and restraint delighted me and I forgot all my fears and doubts and was happy to be with him for awhile. We wrote to the Nawab again giving our new address and repeating our request and we were sure that now, an answer would soon come.

Every night for the first week, after my mother had gone to bed, Ali and I remained in the sitting-room propped against the cushions – just talking. It was unbelievable. We had been adopted, as it were, and it really seemed as if all this generous hospitality sprang from pure altruism. I had looked for friendship everywhere and here, at last, had found it – just where I least expected it.

He knew that we were leaving for England before long and hoping to go to Bhopal very soon yet, he behaved as if we meant to stay with him. He changed the furniture round in the bedroom and brought chairs into the sitting-room and did little homely things; gave me flamboyant ties, had my boots repaired in the bazaar and talked of buying me a new riding coat. And then horses appeared, from his estate in the country, he said, and we rode every day, always leaving the native quarter and passing through the British lines. But I did not stop this. I let them stare if they wanted to, cold and incredulous and I knew what they were thinking.

The 4th Huzzars had left Meerut a year ago and I supposed that John had come back here after Saugor and then gone home with the regiment. It was to Meerut that I had addressed so many of those rapturous letters, it was here that he had suffered so many of his miseries and it was here that I had hoped to come and stay with Bernard and his family. And here I was – regretting nothing and preferring the irony of things as they were.

Then, one evening, when we were sitting on the hard chairs in the sitting-room, he suggested that we should move to his room outside which would be more comfortable, he said. My suspicions were aroused at once and I protested that I was perfectly comfortable where I was – and he didn't insist. The next day, he found another present for me and in the evening, again suggested moving to his room – and again I told him that I liked being where I was, the room was so charming now with all the chairs. He did not seem to mind but the next night, when he returned to it once more, I knew that he meant to keep this up, that he was playing a slow and subtle game with me and I made up my mind to play it, too. And I meant to cheat and win it.

This time, I did not refuse outright. I said how much I was looking forward to seeing his room and spending an evening there. But there was plenty of time, I added, and while I was settling down I preferred to stay where I already felt at home. This gained me several days and when he tried once more I said that I would certainly have come that night if I had not felt so tired. I was going to bed at once, I added. This time, I caught a hard look. In the morning, he sprang another surprise.

'I want you to have this horse,' he said. 'From now on you must regard it as your own.'

I was astonished – and glad, for I was out to get everything I could from him now. I couldn't take the horse to England but I could sell it. I looked it up and down wondering what it was worth. That night, I could not put it off any longer.

We walked across the compound and entered the shack which was lit by an oil lamp and contained nothing else but an enormous Indian plank bed. Animal skins were spread over it, cushions were at the head of it and a large, black, long-haired fleece was the only covering. With the rays of the lamp falling onto it and darkness all round, it looked beautiful but savage. I was in the jungle again. I sat down on the edge of it.

'No, not like that,' Ali said. 'I brought you here to make you comfortable. You must climb up and lie back against the cushions.' As he bent to help me his dark face came into the lamp-light and, for the first time, I saw him as he really was – another handsome, cunning, predatory animal.

I kicked off my shoes and climbed up. For awhile he lay in his shirt sleeves beside me. Then, he turned and looked at me sharply and when he spoke his voice was not soft now, but hard and possessive.

'I want you to be happy. I'll give you everything you ask for. There's no need for you to go back to England. You can be better off and happier here with me. You must stay.'

Now I knew exactly where I was – and what he was; not the altruistic friend but the watching, waiting, pouncing Machiavel that I had seen at the beginning. But we still had nowhere else to go for the Nawab didn't write. I had to go on using him – but I didn't mean to pay.

It would be a hard evasive game, a game of nights, each night a trick to be cunningly taken and secretly counted, trick after trick until I could go. I knew I could play it – and win.

I smiled at him gratefully and told him how happy I should be to stay and make my home with him. I kept him talking half that night about the way we should live, the things we would do, the rich future that was ours. And he never touched me. He lay beside me but never even kissed me, never even took my hand. That first night was easily won. When I left he took me to the door.

'Tomorrow night you will come to me naked, in your dressing-gown.'

I lay upon the soft hairy skin and he pulled the black fleece over us because the night was cold. I told him that we must not hurry that we had many years before us and love, real love, needed time, patience and consideration for its full development. If we rushed violently into it, I said, we should expend it without ever having fully known it whereas, if we could wait, have patience with each other now, its consummation in the end would be so much sweeter and more enduring. I was always slow to awake, I told him, but passionate and constant when finally aroused and I begged him to give me time to accustom myself to the rich changes in my life and to all that he was offering me. Like this, I again kept him talking, only kissed him once and promised more tomorrow. That second night was easily won.

'I have a fine piece of jewellery in my bank,' he told me the next morning. 'I'm going to get it out and give it you. It's a bracelet of amethysts and pearls and it dates back to the Mogul empire and has been in my family for centuries. It's beautiful. You'll enjoy wearing it.'

'How good you are to me. But I shall only wear it on special occasions. I'm longing to see it.'

'I'll be going to the bank tomorrow.'

Jewellery was easy to carry and easy to sell. That night I charmed him all I could. I had lots of pleasing things to talk about and attractive ways of wasting time and I kissed him now and then and caressed him a little and promising more tomorrow, left him happy and content. The third night was won as easily as the others. But he did not go to the bank the next day. He found he was too busy.

As talk lost its power, I thought up new tricks and diversions; I made excuses, feigned indisposition and made endless promises but still I kept him satisfied for each night I gave a little more – more kisses and caresses. I gave and gave but I never gave myself. And so the nights passed and the days but still we did not hear from the Nawab.

We began to wonder if Ali was intercepting our letters, a very common practice in India and one in which he would, no doubt, have had experience. With a bribe, even at Maidens, he might have done this.

He never went to the bank. It was too unsafe, he decided, to keep the bracelet in the house. But it was mine, all the same, he assured me and when the occasion arose, I could have it out and wear it. And then he gave me the car.

'I don't need it,' he said, 'and you do. You'd enjoy running about in it. It is yours now and you must treat it as your own.'

But without the documents I knew it wasn't mine and I didn't believe in his gifts any more. The *syce* had told me that the horses were hired and as for the bracelet – I was sure it had never existed.

A month passed. My mother was very unhappy and the strain of that detestable game was growing unbearable. I wasn't sure how much longer I could play it and I felt that I'd pushed it far enough. We decided to go to Bhopal – welcome or not. And we packed rapidly and secretly. I even toyed with the idea of stealing Ali's car, loading it up at night, driving off and then selling it in Bombay. But without the documents I dare not risk it. I had won so much and he would be so angry when we left that he would never let me win the car.

Only at the last moment did I tell him that we were going. If he had intercepted the Nawab's letters he must have believed that he had stopped us and he would never expect us to go, uninvited. His expression did not change and he said nothing but I knew what he was thinking and I knew that we must get away quickly. I had the luggage loaded onto the car and with him beside me, still silent, I drove it to the station. We thanked him for his hospitality and then turned away and left him. I hated him and wished I had been clever enough to give him less – to cheat him more.

From the station, we sent a telegram to Bhopal saying that we were on our way. Unless they refused to receive us they would have to put us in a guest-house. When we arrived, everything went just as we had hoped. A car met us and took us to a bungalow, beautiful enough to be the home of a cultured English family. From the moment that we left the train we were aware that this state was different. The jungle was all round it, just the same, but not *in* it. The streets were broad and clean, the houses well built and well kept and the people all looked prosperous and proud. There was civilisation here, advanced and purposeful, keeping the jungle in its place.

What joy it was to be there! No more the prisoner of that man; no more detested nights upon those planks between those skins; no more humiliating days in that black crowded hell; and no more of that awful selling. Joy! Oh, what joy!

Nobody came near us. We were not sure if this was a sign of their displeasure or just their way – the abstracted, timeless way of India. But we didn't mind for we felt so peaceful and happy and for company, we had a *box-wallah* from England, a high-class salesman doing business in the state and living in the guest-house with us. He was very friendly and quite interesting to talk to and it wasn't long before my mother marked him down. For all the selling and free living, we still needed £20 to get us home and he was just the man, she thought, to beg from.

But when he realised what we were really like and how he had misjudged us, he changed at once. After listening to her hard-up story, his face gone white, his lips compressed and his eyes like little beads, he didn't refuse to help – but he wouldn't *give.* He agreed to lend the money in exchange for a post-dated cheque and for as many fool-proof guarantees as we could give him.

As I listened while my mother struggled and watched his face, watched him examine the credentials which I brought and then watched him write his cheque out with a fine gold-banded pen, then watched her borrow it and write out hers and then the covering letters he demanded – I hated him. Even then, he was suspicious and unhappy and when he rose from his chair and turned his back, his stiff cold back, and walked out of the room I wished that she'd never asked for money from that mean compassionless man – and that we'd not received it. But my mother was pleased. She was so conscious of her uselessness, the burden that she felt she had become. Now, she had helped, she had raised the money that we needed and she didn't much care how.

Suddenly, I noticed that on the low brass table on which all the writing had been done, he had left that beautiful gold-band fountain pen. I looked quickly round at the windows and then picked it up and slipped it in my pocket. Another act of punishment and pure criminality. I had not moved – I was at the bottom still.

The house was full of servants and no one in particular would take the blame, but when the search began it was not the servants that he suspected and we were happier when he left, a few days later. We could have gone ourselves now. But I did not want to. I knew I had to stay.

It was nearly a week before our presence was acknowledged. The Nawab was away we were then told, but the Begum would be pleased if we would go to tea with her. We drove to the long low unpretentious bungalow in which the ruler and his family lived and were shown into a room which could have been a London drawing-room. A moment later, Her Highness, a charming, dignified, sophisticated woman came in. We sat down and were soon talking as easily and naturally as if we had known each other all our lives. Later, the door flew open and the children all came tumbling in, like happy children anywhere, home from school. By the time we left, we felt we had come home ourselves.

The next day, we were moved to the old palace which stood alone on the top of a bare hill with the lake below and the city, spreading white and new and modern, on the other side. This palace was only used now for special guests and we felt honoured and happier still.

Before breakfast, the next morning, two superb horses were waiting at the bottom of the steps and a magnificent grey-bearded *havildar-major* salaamed and helped me mount. Before I rode with him I thought I was quite good but he showed me, in his stern yet gentle way, that I could not ride at all. He made me start from the beginning – without stirrups, without saddle and then he taught me to jump. I loved that old cavalry-man and, in the early mornings, could have ridden the jungle paths with him forever.

We went from bungalow to bungalow taking tea with all the women of the family. The old ones were still in *purdah* but even they were well-educated and interested in the affairs of the world. And the children – they were lovely. I played bicycle polo with them and we careered round a *maidan* slashing at the ball with polo sticks and crashing into each other, with laughter and happy shrieks. And the others, the girls and the young men of my own age – they were the best of all.

They came every evening in a crowd after their work or studies and we chose our teams and put on roller skates and played wild games of hockey in the marble hall, weaving round the pillars. Often, they took me into the jungle and we spent the nights crawling through the undergrowth and creeping over rocks and lying for hours, silently, in 'hides', watching countless animals pass below while we waited for the tiger to return to the kill. I learnt how much better it was to listen, to watch and be aware, to experience oneness with the jungle than to coerce it, shatter it with diabolic noise and introduce unnecessary death.

The weeks slipped timelessly by in this good place, this little oasis in the middle of so much barbarity, uniting what was good in east and west. I had not been so happy since I was a child and I became a child again, recovering something of my innocence and simplicity, playing with the friends which, after so much searching, I had found at last in this sweet land – this veritable Garden of Eden.

Then, one night, after they had gone, I went to bed but instead of falling asleep I became even more awake, growing big and powerful as I did long ago when, as a child, I had that vision. I waited. A moving screen then appeared at the foot of my bed and I saw myself upon it, living out again each act and episode of the long blind search for my purpose. I saw the moment of my first mistake when my eyes were dazzled and I chose a vulgar, senseless goal and slipped onto the wild, rough, painful road which led me up and down the world fighting for vain, useless things that I didn't really want; my desires and ambitions, my pleasures, satisfactions and my triumphs. I saw them all, standing out so clearly, all so insufficient and so foolish; I saw my failures and my falls, my guilt and all my pain; I saw my lovely youth corrupted and the genius of my family squandered once again in a sordid sea of ignorance and tragical futility. I watched the horror that had been my life, watched the actress play her sad repulsive part, through scene after scene, right up to the awesome moment of awakening.

Then, just before she faded from the screen, I saw my golden thread again, bright and broad and unbroken, a line of fulfilment joined to the All and to Eternity, running through my centres. And I knew that I would never again lose it and have to be pulled back and back, for I had found my road, which was – my Self.

Gigantic, in a field of glory, I danced for the remainder of the night and in the morning someone else rose from my bed, someone newly made and – different.

I spent the day out on the hill above the lake not knowing how to use the tumbling words and flaming force of my writing. I worshipped what I did but still without acknowledging my passion. In the evening I said good-bye to all my friends, for now I had to go, and from the sea, a few days later, looked back a second time, at India.

I had seen and known so little of the achievements of my own people and seen and understood so little of India herself, yet what they did and what she was, were the two conjugal sides of the one thing. Their action impregnated her dark ground, while her wisdom and sublimity moved everywhere, were the breath of everything, however barbarous. One did not need to see and understand – one knew. And one knew as well, that the hand which held the ends and energised the centres of the golden thread would reach down and divinise it all.

We travelled 3rd Class in an unventilated cabin where the air was so foul that one slept as if drugged yet, for me, the air was sweet, every moment was bliss, every grain of life was a feast.

In the ship's library, I found a book of essays by Maurice Baring and one of them was on the drama. I had scarcely ever been to the theatre and I had read no plays, except at school but suddenly, I was flung into another ecstasy when I saw that my task was to write – and write plays. I went forward laughing and leaping and loving.

My mother saw the change and triumphantly proclaimed the assertion of my genius. She had waited so long. From the moment I was desired she had sacrificed her talent and now, bound by the persisting forces of the family dream, she devoted the remainder of her life to the furtherance of mine. Of all the characters who moved through that dream she was the finest, her love the greatest — she was the genius.

I was 24 when we returned once more to England. My relationship with her, my country, had been so stormy, so filled with misdirections and estrangements but in this final landing, there was reconciliation. It was once again the coming home of a lover.

INDEX TO "THE GOLDEN THREAD"